READING
POPULAR ROMANCE
IN EARLY MODERN
ENGLAND

READING
POPULAR ROMANCE
in
Early Modern England

Lori Humphrey Newcomb

COLUMBIA UNIVERSITY PRESS

New York

Columbia University Press
Publishers Since 1893
New York   Chichester, West Sussex

Copyright © 2002 Columbia University Press
All rights reserved

Library of Congress Cataloging-in-Publication Data
Newcomb, Lori Humphrey.
Reading popular romance in early modern England / Lori Humphrey Newcomb.
p. cm.
Includes bibliographical references and index.
ISBN 0-231-12378-7 (cloth : alk. paper)
ISBN 0-231-12379-5 (pbk. : alk. paper)
1. Greene, Robert, 1558?–1592. Pandosto. 2. Books and reading—England—History—16th century.
3. Books and reading—England—History—17th century. 4. Popular literature—England—History and
criticism. 5. Shakespeare, William, 1564–1616. Winter's tale. 6. Romances—Appreciation—England—
History. 7. Greene, Robert, 1558?–1592—Influence. 8. Popular culture—England—History.
9. Servants in literature. I. Title.
PR2544.P33 N49 2001
820.9'003—dc21   2001017188

Columbia University Press books are
printed on permanent and durable acid-free paper.
Printed in the United States of America
c 10 9 8 7 6 5 4 3 2 1
p 10 9 8 7 6 5 4 3 2 1

CONTENTS

ACKNOWLEDGMENTS

This book is about a much-revised, much-read text, and my friends and colleagues know why. First thanks go to Dale Randall, who offered a graduate seminar on Renaissance fiction and indulged my fascination with the legend of *Pandosto*. Annabel Patterson let me convince her that *Pandosto* merited a dissertation, and rightly held it to the highest standard she could. The convictions underlying the project were forged in Duke's canon wars, especially by Barbara Herrnstein Smith. Also aiding my progress at Duke were Carl Anderson, Stanley Fish, Robert Gleckner, Michael Moon, James Rolleston, and Jennifer Thorne. Naomi Wood, Doug Lanier, Sue Walsh, Glenn Wallach, Margaret Corvini, Margaret Rose Jaster, Jane Jeffrey, and Ruth Porritt were friends and readers. I thank John Gaunt and Michael Peich at West Chester University; Jim Butler, Justin Cronin, Kevin Harty, and Linda Merians at La Salle University; and Jane Donawerth, Judy Hallett, and Adele Seeff at the University of Maryland, College Park. My work was greatly encouraged by early believers in the project, including Peter Blayney, Cedric Brown, Jonathan Goldberg, Gabriela Jackson, Peter Lindenbaum, Marianne Novy, Lois Potter, and Constance Relihan. Much earlier, Susan Casteras, Jonathan Lear, Conrad Russell, Greg Thalmann, James Winn, and above all Alan Liu provided models of the scholarly life.

No young scholar could have more generous colleagues than the senior Renaissance faculty at the University of Illinois at Urbana-Champaign. For their kindness and discretion I thank Richard Wheeler, Jan Hinely, David

Kay, Joan Klein, Ania Loomba, and Michael Shapiro. Time and time again, Achsah Guibbory has demonstrated scholarly judgment and intellectual independence, and Carol Neely has given trenchant readings and inexhaustible support. Without their faith in the project, I might never have finished the book; now that it's done, I look forward to years of work and play with them. Cathy Prendergast has been a perceptive reader and ally, and my new colleague Zack Lesser has already shared bibliographic expertise. For thoughtful readings of parts of the manuscript by departmental colleagues Leon Chai, Phil Graham, Jed Esty, Suvir Kaul, Lisa Lampert, Julia Walker, and Gillen Wood, I'm grateful. In a supportive department and university, I particularly appreciate the advocacy of Dennis Baron, Jesse Delia, Alma Gottlieb, Bruce Michelson, Cary Nelson, Paula Treichler, and Rene Wahlfeldt. For Friday-evening cheer, thanks to all at the Bread Company, especially Dara Goldman, Trish Loughran, Bill Maxwell, and Adam Sutcliffe. Past undergraduates Joanna Barch, Zachary Fisher, Kath Klimas, Tiffany Meier, Alison McDowell, and Amanda Sonneborn have become unaccountably devoted to Robert Greene; and graduate students in three seminars, especially Abram Steen, Charles Conaway, and Jen Munroe, have investigated audiences, artifacts, and authors, popular and elite. Thanks to Bill Regier, Christina Walter, and Patricia Hollahan of the University of Illinois Press. Marsha Clinard spoke up for readers, and Cathy Moore restored order. Kim Woosley has been a superlative research assistant and acute interlocutor.

For opportunities to present my work I thank Peter Garrett of the Unit for Criticism and Interpretive Theory at UIUC, Mara Wade of the Renaissance Seminar at UIUC, Don Beecher, Betty Hageman, David Loewenstein, the Evening Colloquium of the Folger Institute, and the Literature and History Conference at the University of Reading. At these and other presentations I have enjoyed conversations with Pamela Brown, Michael Dobson, Fran Dolan, Stacey Jocoy, James Knapp, Joyce MacDonald, Andrew Murphy, Sasha Roberts, Laura Rosenthal, Scott Shershow, and Mihoko Suzuki. I hope that Goran Stanivukovic and Chris Warley benefit from our collaborations as I have. The irrepressible Ann Christensen and Barb Sebek have shared hotel bills, survival skills, and magpie scholarship. I have been fortunate in two extraordinary friends—neighbors, confidantes, intellectual collaborators, and women of taste—Lynette McGrath and Ann Abbott Barbieri.

Various stages of the project have been aided by a James B. Duke Fellowship from Duke University and by funds from the Bibliographical Society of America, the National Endowment for the Humanities, the UIUC Research Board (special thanks to Janet Glaser), the Lilly Library, and the Newberry Library. For opportunities given by the Folger Institute I thank Lena Cowen Orlin, Kathleen Lynch, and Carol Brobeck. Countless librarians have helped me track down and reproduce copies of *Pandosto*; especially helpful were Georgianna Ziegler at the Folger Shakespeare Library, John Morris at the National Library of Scotland, and Emily Walhout at the Houghton Library at Harvard. In UIUC's wonderful libraries, Barbara Jones, Nancy Romero, Jane Somera, and Bill Ogg have helped me find books, and Bill Brockman, Diana King, Kathleen Kluegel, Laura Neumann, and Carole Palmer have helped me unlock the databases.

Working with Columbia University Press has been all that I could wish. With Jennifer Crewe's quiet professionalism came assurance that this manuscript could materialize into a book. Jennifer Barager provided timely rescues. Leslie Kriesel has worked thoroughly, thoughtfully, and patiently to refine the manuscript, teaching me a great deal along the way. Thanks to Susan Brady, Gillian Forester, and Celina Fox for help in locating the painting for the cover. I am enormously indebted to Bill Sherman and an anonymous reader for their enthusiastic and wise responses to the book manuscript. The remaining faults are of course my own.

Portions of chapter 2 were previously published in "'Social Things': The Production of Popular Culture in the Reception of Robert Greene's *Pandosto*" (in *ELH* 61 [1994]); and of chapter 4 in "The Romance of Service: The Simple History of *Pandosto*'s Servant Readers" (in *Framing Elizabethan Fictions: Contemporary Approaches to Early Modern Prose Narrative*, ed. Constance C. Relihan [Kent, OH: Kent State University Press, 1997]); and "The Triumph of Time: The Fortunate Readers of Robert Greene's *Pandosto*" (in *Texts and Cultural Change, 1520–1700*, ed. Cedric C. Brown and Arthur F. Marotti [New York: St. Martin's, 1997]).

In this book, I've tried to capture some things I've learned from my family, especially my mother, Lois Humphrey, a bookworm; my father, Dick Humphrey, a bookkeeper; my brother, Gary Humphrey, a craftsman; my sister, AJ Humphrey, an educator; and my mother-in-law, Jane Newcomb, a storyteller. Tim Newcomb has waited longer, worked harder, and sacrificed more than we ever anticipated. This book about separations and reunions, quiet ambitions and shared pleasures, is dedicated to him with gratitude and love.

The following standard reference works are cited in-text with familiar abbreviations:

Dictionary of National Biography, ed. Sidney Lee, 63 vols. (London: Smith, Elder & Co., 1885–1900) (DNB)

Oxford English Dictionary, 2nd ed., prepared by J. A. Simpson and E.S.C. Weiner; repr. with corrections (Oxford: Oxford University Press, 1991) (OED)

Short-Title Catalog of Books Printed in England . . . , 1475–1640, rev. ed., ed. Katharine F. Pantzer et al., 3 vols. (London: Bibliographical Society, 1976–91) (STC)

Short-Title Catalogue of Books Printed in England . . . , 1641–1700, 2nd ed., rev., ed. Donald Wing (New York: Modern Language Association, 1994–98) (Wing)

Information on publishers and printers is drawn from:

Dictionary of the Printers and Booksellers . . . , 1557–1640, ed. R. B. McKerrow et al. (London: Bibliographical Society, 1910) (McKerrow, *Dictionary*)

Dictionary of the Printers and Booksellers . . . , 1641 to 1667, ed. Henry R. Plomer (London: Bibliographical Society, 1907) (Plomer 1)

Dictionary of the Printers and Booksellers . . . , 1641 to 1667, ed. Henry R. Plomer et al. (London: Bibliographical Society, 1922) (Plomer 2)

Ian Maxted, *The London Book Trade, 1775–1800* (Folkestone, Eng.: Dawson, 1977) (Maxted)

Information on early editions often draws on the CD-ROM *English Short-Title Catalog* (London: British Library Board, 1998), *Nineteenth-Century Short-Title Catalogue* ([London]: Avero Publications, Ltd., 1996), and *Early English Books On-line* (Ann Arbor, MI: Bell & Howell Information and Learning, n.d.). Acknowledgment is hereby made for materials reproduced from two CD-ROM databases, *Editions and Adaptations of Shakespeare* Copyright © [1995] Chadwyck-Healey Ltd. and *Early English Prose Fiction* Copyright © [1997] Chadwyck-Healey Ltd.

Because the changing textures of the printed book are essential to my subject, I have quoted original or old-spelling editions whenever possible. However, certain quotations from Robert Greene's *Pandosto* that do not reflect a specific edition have been taken from Paul Salzman's *An Anthology of Elizabethan Prose Fiction* (New York: Oxford University Press, 1987). In old-spelling quotations, the letters i, j, and v are silently modernized, as are years in old-style dating. I have supplied foliation where possible for unpaginated books.

FIGURES

differences between two closely related works. By the nineteenth century, scholars had constructed *Pandosto* as a quintessential work of English popular literature, born high, fallen low, but present as an alter ego to a work by the national poet. Yet through the early modern period, large numbers of readers encountered *Pandosto* in one form or another without any awareness of its relationship to Shakespeare. *Pandosto* enjoyed a long life as a classic of popular literature on its own terms, as new audiences continued to find it a "pleasant history."

First extant in a 1588 edition, *Pandosto* was steadily republished, translated, versified, dramatized, pirated, adapted, and abridged, last appearing in cheap print in 1843. I have identified sixty-odd extant versions of the tale, some forty-five in prose and fifteen in verse (see appendices A and B). For over two and a half centuries, then, an edition of *Pandosto* was published, on average, once every four years. Given print runs of 1,250 copies per edition, we can estimate that at least 75,000 copies of the text found buyers; given early modern reading practices, we can imagine that a typical copy was read not just by its first buyer but also by the buyer's friends and, as long as it lasted, descendants.[4] The work's continued popularity far exceeds what past bibliographers have estimated, particularly for the latest, most-overlooked era of its popular life. In 1953, Charles Mish placed it near the top of his list of "Best Sellers in Seventeenth-Century Fiction," noting "some eighteen editions during the century" and "a few further editions" in the eighteenth century.[5] My research, in libraries, microfilms, and new electronic databases, has confirmed Mish's eighteen editions and one more before 1700; setting aside versifications, which Mish does not count, I have found not "a few" but some two dozen popular reprints after 1700. The surviving copies indicate that the publication history of this short work of vernacular fiction was impressive in both frequency and duration, and anecdotal evidence suggests that many more editions were lost.[6]

Every literary history before this one has seen *Pandosto*'s remarkable trajectory as a downward plummet, since an eighty-page fiction in courtly prose was reduced, by the eighteenth century, to an authorless tale of twenty-four pages, with a few small woodcuts and a catchy title. These brief, relatively cheap "chapbooks" were sold throughout the early modern period by traveling peddlers, or chapmen. The last editions of *Pandosto* were printed on inexpensive paper in small formats, in such provincial backwaters as Darlington, Tewkesbury, Stirling, Dublin, and Boston, Massachusetts. The shrinking of the volume has been taken to figure the decreasing status of its presumed readership—and, it generally follows, their intellectual capacities.[7] The implication has been that the chapbook editions of *Pandosto* trickled down to audiences content with cultural runoff.

Ironically, for evidence about chapbook distribution and audiences, much modern scholarship relies on *The Winter's Tale*, into which Shakespeare inserted a distributor of popular print, the rogue ballad seller, Autolycus. One early twentieth-century edition of *Pandosto* wrote that Greene's romance was "turned into a chap-book, to be hawked about by the Autolycuses of the period." Such invocations of *The Winter's Tale* are commonplace in more recent accounts of the trade in cheap print.[8] Chapbooks are referred to as "unconsidered trifles" because Shakespeare's roguish chapman uses that phrase to describe some of his wares. Their readers are said to be credulous because the shepherdess Mopsa remarks, "I love a ballad in print, a life, for then we are sure they are true."[9] That a chapman sells ballads in *The Winter's Tale* and later generations of chapmen sold prose condensations of *Pandosto* seems proleptic, as though Autolycus's pack of dubious goods were *Pandosto*'s inevitable home. Instead of reading the romance's conversion to chapbook form as a downward slide, I explore how material changes enabled the *Pandosto* story to move outward, reaching new readers and offering new interpretations. When condensed as a chapbook or adapted as verse, the story repeatedly met the needs and desires of new audiences.

The changing fortunes of *Pandosto. The Triumph of Time* resemble the sprawling story told on its pages, a tale of dramatic reversals, of gender distrust and class conflict, and of the faults of one generation redeemed by the next. In the language of the 1588 title page, Greene's romance is "a pleasant Historie" that shows how "Truth" is "concealed" by "sinister fortune," and then "most manifestly revealed" when "Time," Truth's daughter, finally triumphs over Fortune. Pandosto, the King of Bohemia, is happily married to Bellaria, and they have a young heir. Suddenly, Fortune frowns, and Pandosto is seized by unfounded suspicions about his wife and his visiting friend Egistus, the King of Sicilia. He orders his cupbearer, Franion, to kill Egistus, but Franion instead leads Egistus out of the country. Pandosto publicly charges Bellaria with adultery and treason, and condemns a newborn second child, a girl, as a bastard. On Bellaria's pleading, the child is not killed but exposed in a small boat on the sea; Bellaria provides her with an identifying chain and a purse of gold in case she is found. On trial before the king, Bellaria defends herself staunchly and asks that Pandosto consult the oracle. The oracle's message confirms the innocence of all but the tyrant king, and promises that he will "live without an heir, if that which is lost be not found."[10]

As if to punish Pandosto, both the young prince and the long-suffering Bellaria suddenly die. A repentant Pandosto provides a magnificent tomb with
a verse epitaph.

Meanwhile, the babe floats to the shores of Sicilia. Porrus, a poor shepherd, mistakes her cry for that of a lost lamb, picks her up, and marvels at
her godlike beauty, her jeweled chain, and the gold wrapped up in her
mantle. He and his wife, Mopsa, adopt the child as their own, naming her
Fawnia for her wild origins. Grown to girlhood, Fawnia dutifully tends the
flock that Porrus purchased with the gold. Her beauty and demeanor, far
above her station, enchant Dorastus, crown prince of Sicilia. He courts her,
first in all the glory of his position and then in the guise of a shepherd, and
the two vow their love across their wide social gap. Not daring to confront
Egistus, they elope, bringing Franion and Porrus along. A storm carries
them all, despite multiple improbabilities, to the shore of Bohemia. There,
Pandosto questions their aliases. He assaults Fawnia with sexual offers and
threats, but she defends her virtue. When the irate Pandosto threatens to
kill the whole party, Porrus brings out the mantle and chain to prove that
Fawnia is not his child. Pandosto knights Porrus and embraces his daughter, recognizing that the lost has been found. But Fortune chooses "to close
up the comedy with a tragical stratagem": Pandosto, ashamed of the incestuous desire that caps his previous violence against friend and family, com-
mits suicide, leaving the lovers to marry and rule in Bohemia ever after
(Salzman, *Elizabethan*, 204). The younger generation fulfills the oracle,
redeems Pandosto's faults, and restores the class order.[11]

Thus, Fawnia was high-born, rejected out of unreasoning jealousy, sent
to the country, forgotten by some, adopted and loved by others, renamed,
attacked, and eventually recovered—much like *Pandosto* itself. While
Greene's title page claimed that "truth is the daughter of Time," and Fawnia is saved by being the daughter of Pandosto, *Pandosto*'s problems of lineage are not so easily resolved. The work can claim high origins: Greene's
use of Greek romance in this piece of vernacular fiction was innovative and
influential. However, it is far better known as the ignoble ancestor of *The
Winter's Tale*. Today, the connection keeps Greene's romance in print, and
Shakespearean scholarship accepts *Pandosto* as a sort of poor relation, but
earlier generations of Shakespeareans saw the legitimacy of *The Winter's
Tale* as threatened by the faultiness of its parent *Pandosto*.

This reading of *Pandosto* as an allegory of its own reception is meant to
point out the deep but troubled bond between the stories loved by past
readers and the stories critics tell about them. Literary history, founded on

the discourse of cultural stratification that I trace in this book, has turned the popularity of *Pandosto* into a legend of degeneration that pervades Shakespeare scholarship. One prominent example is in a 1995 biography of Shakespeare, written for a general audience:

> *Pandosto* . . . , in spite of its crude construction and often slack prose, was popular for a phenomenally long time. It had been reprinted four times by the time Shakespeare came to write his play, . . . and went on being read and printed for at least 150 years. It seems to have appealed to a not very highly educated class of reader. In Shakespeare's lifetime it was said that a typical chambermaid "reads Greene's works over and over," and the same kind of girl is shown reading it in Samuel Richardson's novel *Clarissa*, published in 1747–8. It was about this time that scholars took over from the chambermaids and started reading and reprinting the book as a Shakespearian source.[12]

This account underestimates *Pandosto*'s many reinventions and long success with a wide variety of readers, but it does touch on the circumstances that make the romance a fascinating case in the study of popular literature. It begins by implying that crudity and slackness fit a work for popularity.[13] It then characterizes the "class" of *Pandosto*'s readers, gendering and generalizing the conditions of nonelite readers on the basis of two anecdotes a century apart. Its closing picture of chambermaids dutifully handing Shakespeare's source back to the scholars masks a full century in which *Pandosto* was, in fact, known to both chambermaids and scholars. The continued popularity of *Pandosto* explains why early scholarship on *The Winter's Tale* so nervously reiterates the play's superiority to its source.

My interest in *Pandosto* began with that arresting but improbable legend about its being the perennial reading of maidservants. It seemed to me that the story of the work's changing readership would have all the adventure and human interest of *Pandosto* itself, and that its persistence had to evince its appeal to a wide range of readers. I set out to reconstruct the inventive ways that the romance was published and read throughout the early modern period. By weaving together the material evidence of the work's successive editions and anecdotal evidence of its readers left by elite contemporaries, I uncover the dynamics of cultural distinction that shaped this persistent legend. In Gerard Genette's terms, I am reconstructing all of the romance's successive "paratexts," or "productions" that "ensure the text's presence in the world."[14] Genette's paratext includes both peritextual elements located in

tingent grouping, socially inclusive yet formed by acts of exclusion. By attributing such social dynamism to popular literature, I hope to strengthen the sense of continuity between elite and popular "cultural uses of print" that is now emerging in book history.[27] The common theme of Roger Chartier's influential work has been to define popular literature as a set of reading practices rather than as an objectively separate body of texts. That project answers earlier historical work that treated popular culture as the autonomous territory of a separate class and therefore regarded print as an intrusion. Increasingly, Chartier's project of redefinition has entailed recognizing that popular reading practices are themselves constructed. His evolving position merits tracing in detail, especially as it bears on my claim that popular and elite reading practices continually constitute each other.

In a 1995 essay, "Popular Appropriation: The Readers and Their Books," Chartier proposed deciphering "literate representations of the popular," which constructed popular practices through "the specific modes of their production, the interests and intentions that produced them, the genres in which they were inscribed, and the audiences at which they were aimed."[28] While this method was intended to deconstruct elite perceptions of popular reading practices, it still treated the latter as derivative, defining them as "constructed by way of mediations and dependencies that tie[d] them to dominant models and norms" ("Popular," 95). Rather than viewing only popular reading practices as mediated and dependent, I assume that all literary practices, elite and popular, are tied to the material conditions of book production, and that the meaning of those conditions is variable and contingent. Extending Chartier's assertion that the "forms" in which texts are read shape the "meanings" their readers may construct, this book explores how the meanings of forms were themselves continually reconstructed in response to the changing products of the print trade.[29]

In "Reading Matter and 'Popular' Reading" (first published in France in 1997), Chartier has more strongly asserted the constructedness of popular reading practices, as signaled in his title's single quotation marks around "popular."[30] He notes that elite descriptions of popular reading practices magnified small differences and suppressed the threat implicit in the spread of literacy. Scholars of the book should be wary and not "take representations for actual practices" or "restrict the category of the 'popular' to an overly narrow social sense" ("Reading," 283). Drawing on the work of literary scholars, he proposes that the history of reading might extend to interpreting texts that themselves portray and shape reading practices.[31] That is what this book aims to do. To rephrase one of Chartier's most important formulations, this study goes beyond examining how "common cultural sets are appropriated differently" ("Popular" 89) to examining how common cultural sets are appropriated *differentially*, so that elite representations of popular reading practices work to characterize elite practices as well. My interest is in the social dynamics revealed when works derived from a "common cultural set"—the story shared between *Pandosto* and *The Winter's Tale*—are appropriated not only differently by different groups of readers but also *in order to differentiate* among those groups so that the commonality among their tastes and practices is denied.

Like many historians of the book, I now define my object of study as "popular literature," rather than "popular culture." The latter term can suggest an organic and independent popular culture existing outside of elite influence; in contrast, "popular literature" is by definition a product of literate practices, no matter how socially diverse, remote from elite norms, or collective they may be. This terminological difference is not meant to operate as a litmus test, however, since much current work on "popular culture" analyzes the presence of popular literary material and queries old assumptions about the organicism of "folk" or "popular" culture. I have chosen an unusually "literary" object of study: *Pandosto* was authored by an Elizabethan "University wit," trained in an emphatically literate tradition. Once, those origins would have disqualified this work from recognition as authentic popular culture. My conception of "popular literature" challenges its traditional separation from elite literature, to discharge any lingering sense that a text that starts out high and ends low is inauthentic or exhausted.

Claims that popular literature was a separate realm have deep roots, as I will show. Modern historians' questioning of that separation can be traced to Peter Burke's landmark study, *Popular Culture in Early Modern Europe* (1978).[32] Although Burke's study set terms for the modern scholarly quest for an independent popular culture, it also forthrightly confronted the difficulty of reconstructing it from the material records of a literate culture. At several key points, Burke turns away from defining popular culture as organically opposed to literate culture. The book begins with a brilliant survey of "The Discovery of the People," the efforts of eighteenth- and nineteenth-century folklorists and collectors that defined the "popular" as other even as they preserved it. Toward the end of the book, Burke holds that this "discovery" evinces upper-class "withdrawal" from participation in popular culture (270). At the same time, however, he begins to question the orthodox view that print stamped out traditional popular practices such as ballad singing: "One begins to wonder," he muses, "whether print did not preserve and even diffuse traditional popular culture rather than destroy it. How many ballads would there have been for collectors to record from 'oral tradition' in the nineteenth century, had it not been for the existence of broadsides?" (257). The argument that I present here closes the circle between Burke's two points. Early modern collectors could preserve "popular culture" (starting in the late eighteenth century) precisely because so much of it was already in print, and thus accessible to all its potential audiences. No matter how much collectors purchasing popular literature might employ discourses of distinction to separate themselves from nonelite readers, they were still effectively part of its audience.

Less tolerant elite attitudes toward popular literature were recorded in anecdotes about *Pandosto*'s nonelite readership that writers embedded in literary works for elite audiences. As I show in chapters 2 and 4, these claims took the form of "scenes of consumption"—vignettes of nonelite readers involved in the physical acts of buying or reading books. These scenes, portraying *Pandosto* as the popular opposite of elite genres, are the basis for the legend of the work's fall into popularity. But they were also foundational in establishing the credibility of the literary genres in which they appeared, from the short-lived prose character to the enduring eighteenth-century novel, deflecting anxieties about the frivolity or commerciality of printed entertainments. Beneath their claims for cultural distinction, these scenes of consumption are always legible as acknowledging the continuity between popular and elite literary forms. The complex ties between *Pandosto* and those who alluded to it allow me to strengthen the connections between Elizabethan fiction and two other major genres: Shakespearean romance and the eighteenth-century novel. Scholars working in these genres have become very interested in their respective material conditions of production; my study demonstrates how close those conditions were to those for popular romance. By reforging these links between *Pandosto* and its canonical intertexts, my analysis challenges the division of popular and elite literatures and recovers some of the dynamism of early modern cultural exchange.

First, by reconstructing period uses of both *Pandosto* and *The Winter's Tale*, I hope to undo critical axiologies that raise Shakespeare's plays above their sources.[33] When early Shakespearean scholars identified prose romance precursors for many of Shakespeare's plays, they originated arguments for treating the romances as dated hack works and the plays as ageless literature. However, this distinction was problematic in the case of *Pandosto* and *The Winter's Tale*. From 1640 to 1740, *Pandosto* was in constant publication, but *The Winter's Tale* remained unperformed and little read.[34] Shakespearean criticism of the eighteenth and nineteenth centuries eventually asserted the play's superiority to its source, a process I treat in chapter 3. A further critical reclamation of *The Winter's Tale* occurred in the twentieth century, with the reclassification of Shakespeare's late plays as "romances." The uniquely Shakespearean genre of dramatic "romance," for which there is no period authority, affiliates the late plays with an international and intergeneric tradition, giving little credit to the native prose romances that were so familiar to Shakespeare and his audiences.[35] The category of "romance" is particularly ironic when applied to *The Winter's Tale*, the late play that most relies on an English prose romance source, despite the gentle mockery in its title. This book helps to resituate Shakespeare's late plays in the context of English enthusiasm for romance inventions in many genres.[36] Moving beyond Shakespeare's career, it also traces the lively diversity of such works in later centuries, treating both plays and "pleasant histories" as members of "common cultural sets" appropriated in many forms and to many ends.

I thus demonstrate a dynamic and ongoing interchange between romance "sources" and Shakespeare's plays, analogous to the interchange that critics now propose between Shakespeare's plays and their later appropriations. Studies including Gary Taylor's *Reinventing Shakespeare*, Margreta de Grazia's *Shakespeare Verbatim*, and Jonathan Bate's *The Genius of Shakespeare* have shown that editions and stage adaptations once seen as violating the works in fact continually transformed and renewed their cultural importance.[37] Such studies celebrate the energies of a host of appropriators but ultimately tend to reproduce Shakespeare's cultural centrality by portraying the plays as founts of appropriative invention. If we want to see how differences among cognate works are culturally constructed, we need to imagine as complex a relationship between Shakespeare and his precursors as between Shakespeare and his appropriators.

Indeed, the surprising convergences in the histories of *Pandosto* and *The Winter's Tale* suggest to me that cultural appropriation should always be read as a reciprocal process, driven by social forces larger than the building of Shakespeare's reputation. Chapter 3 analyzes the ongoing material dissemination of cultural artifacts as "re-commodification," a term that emphasizes the circulation of texts in tangible, exchangeable, alterable forms. Unlike the term "appropriation" invoked in past studies of Shakespearean authority, it imagines negotiations over cultural material that pertain to issues other than authorial ownership. This reading supplements three

ature remained in productive interchange with elite literature. Such interaction is not peculiar to modern culture but is the condition of any high/
low split, always historically contingent, always being renegotiated. The
ingenuity of elite writers in ridiculing popular romances may attest to the
constant urge for distinction, but the interpretive energy of the romances'
many publishers and readers reveals their endless capacity to reshape their
preferred texts and to revitalize a shared culture.

The long, rich life of Elizabethan popular romances prefigures the success of later pulp fictions, but that is not the full extent of their contemporary relevance. Thinking about how those romances were constructed as
popular advances some of the most urgent projects of cultural studies:
imagining pleasure reading as more than a cloak of false consciousness;
seeking more diversified models for the cultural uses of reading; re-viewing
the negotiation between low and high cultural forms as fully dynamic;
resolving ambivalence about the materiality of print culture. By tracing
how social meaning was attached to *Pandosto*'s many material appearances,
I demystify the process that distinguished romance from novel, hack from
Shakespeare—and that continues to distinguish cultural material today.
Above all, I show that although social discrimination may masquerade as
cultural distinction, it never succeeds in drawing an uncrossable line.

CHAPTER ONE

"Growne so ordinarie"
Producing Robert Greene's *Pandosto* and Sir Philip Sidney's *Arcadia*,
1585–92

> *I became an Author of Playes, and a penner of Love Pamphlets, so that I soone grew famous in that qualitie, that who for that trade growne so ordinary about London as Robin Greene.*
> —Robert Greene, *Repentance*[1]

> *To understand the practices of writers and artists, and not least their products, entails understanding that they are the result of the meeting of two histories: the history of the positions they occupy and the history of their dispositions.*
> —Pierre Bourdieu, "The Field of Cultural Production"[2]

The endurance of *Pandosto* has been a puzzle for literary history at least since 1912, when Arundell Esdaile's *List of English Tales and Prose Romances Before 1740* showed it to be the only Elizabethan prose romance, other than Sir Philip Sidney's *Arcadia*, that had survived the Civil War in continuous publication.[3] Esdaile noted—without comment—that *Pandosto* had seen at least twenty-four editions by 1740. Literary historians, baffled that earlier readers' enthusiasm for this romance so far exceeded their own tepid responses, attributed *Pandosto*'s survival to Greene's own self-produced popularity. A 1915 biographer wrote that "it was one of Greene's most deep-rooted characteristics to write what he thought he would have a market for."[4] A 1985

survey of Renaissance fiction remarked on "Greene's adept use of the prevailing fashions which would ensure the popularity of his fiction."[5] Greene
has been seen as a "provider" of slight but pleasurable reading material, and
the later success of *Pandosto* as confirmation of his canny aim at a degraded
popular taste.[6] Thus, calculating author, undemanding text, and unselec-
tive audience are locked into an unchanging relationship of popularity.[7]
Only recently have scholars questioned this portrayal of Greene as the "quintessential hack writer for the Elizabethan period and beyond."[8]

In this chapter, I reject stereotypical conceptions of the popular work
and the popular author, which fail to identify the uniqueness of *Pandosto*
among Greene's works, or of Greene among other writers. *Pandosto* did not
just attain popularity but, more unusually, held it; somehow, as Esdaile
noted, "this one tale alone" among all Greene's works "had been found to
suit the taste of different generations" (xix). Popular tastes are not rigid,
predictable, and unchanging; few works popular in one generation remain
so for generations afterward. More specifically, I reject overly simple conceptions of the relationship between any book and its author that grant
credit for a text's long-term survival solely to the latter. I maintain that no
text or author, and certainly not *Pandosto* or Greene, is inherently popular,
and therefore that *Pandosto*'s popularity and longevity cannot simply be
attributed to calculation on Greene's part. *Pandosto* was not written once by
Greene but repeatedly *produced*, shaped first by him and then by the publishers and printers who assembled its various editions. The "popular" reputation of *Pandosto* was also produced, growing from the "popular" authorship that was improvised over the years through the joint efforts of Greene,
the stationers who presented his works, and the preface-writers and commentators who reacted to them. Greene's status as "popular" author arose
from a unique convergence of texts, events, and responses, as various agents
sought to locate his works on a very new spectrum of authorial production
in which literary authority stood close to notoriety, and schemes to circulate texts actively fought with impulses to circumscribe them.

The "popularity" of *Pandosto* was constructed much more gradually than
that of Greene; most of that story lies in further chapters. *Pandosto*'s pre-
eminence among Greene's works was not apparent until well after his
death, and even then it was hardly accounted a work likely to busy publishers for two more centuries. In Greene's lifetime, it was simply one
among some twenty-five titles, in subgenres ranging from courtly or pastoral romance to frame tale to crime exposé (the "coney-catching" pamphlets) to deathbed confession.[9] Walter Davis has divided Greene's many

works into four stages: "experiments in the euphuistic mode (1580–84); [framed] collections of short tales (1585–88); pastoral romances strongly influenced by Greek romance (1588–89); and pamphlets of repentance and roguery, in the main non-fictional (1590–92)."[10] Collectively, these works "dominated" the market for English fiction in the 1580s (Salzman, *English Prose Fiction*, 59) and made Greene's name a household word. But the meaning of that name changed irrevocably in 1592, when Greene died in "extreamest want," victim of a grotesque "surfett of pickle herringe and rhenish wine."[11] These and other undignified details were bandied about in a series of pamphlets about and (ostensibly) by him, a posthumous free-for-all that, more than anything else, reveals his authorial fame to have been collaboratively produced. In all this furor, *Pandosto* was not even mentioned. That it was reissued after his death, would become his most reprinted work by 1640, and would still be in wide circulation two centuries later are obviously circumstances beyond Greene's control, and other chapters will credit them to other producers over the years.

Here, I lay the groundwork for *Pandosto*'s later survival by placing its first appearances in the context of Greene's "popularity," as it was produced from the start of his career through the years immediately after his death. I situate the romance's initial trajectory within the collaborative production of Greene as a popular print author, a signal event in the emergence of "the popular" as a cultural category. To isolate what was unique in Greene's case, I compare it to the simultaneous production of Sidney as literary author. These close contemporaries, both working in prose romance, were not as separate in their aims as we now think; the contrast between their larger-than-life reputations was heightened by the agency of others writing about them before and after their early deaths. The publishers, relatives, vilifiers, and imitators who generated texts marked as by, like, or about Greene or Sidney were integrally involved in producing the two authors' reputations, and their activities and attitudes are essential to my argument.[12]

Although this chapter loosely follows the sequence of Greene's and Sidney's publications, it treats the making of *Pandosto* and *Arcadia* less than the making of their makers. In Greene's case, early editions of *Pandosto* drew meaning from his authorial persona as it had been produced through the end of his life. I survey Greene's works and *Pandosto*'s editions, Sidney's works and *Arcadia*'s editions, through 1592, the year of Greene's death, recognizing that afterward, experiences of *Pandosto* were refracted through posthumous appropriations of his name, just as experiences of *Arcadia* were refracted through changes in Sidney's reputation after *his* death in 1586. The reputations of the two near-contemporaries enacted the volatility of Elizabethan authorship while creating models for future authors. If Sidney's was one of the most spectacular instances of posthumous canonization as literary author in English literary history, Greene's was a formative instance of posthumous canonization as popular author.

Greene's career allows me to posit an emerging category of popular print authorship, a phrase that coordinates three approaches to early modern culture—studies of popular culture, of print culture, and of the author-function. By looking closely at the construction of Greene's works as popular print literature, I hope to avoid essentializing the text and the impact of print on popular culture. If the spread of print sharpened the need for cultural distinctions, it also gave popular culture a fuller history than it had had before; some of its makers could now be identified and remembered as authors. I also hope to supplement work by historians of print culture, such as Margaret Spufford and Tessa Watt, which has recovered the roles of publishers and readers in circulating cheap print while treating it as characteristically authorless. Instead, I assert that named authorship was crucial to the development of popular print, but that authors alone could not make themselves popular.

Finally, I demonstrate that attending to popular as well as literary print authorship can defamiliarize both, revealing their common conditions of possibility. Studies drawing on the theories of Roland Barthes and Michel Foucault have reconstructed the fascinating, volatile emergence of English vernacular authorship. Most have addressed major literary figures, such as Sidney, Edmund Spenser, Ben Jonson, the once-lionized Beaumont and Fletcher, and William Shakespeare; or pioneering women writers, such as Aemilia Lanyer, Elizabeth Cary, and Margaret Cavendish.[13] They have shown that publication does not in itself confer authority on a writer. Still, these studies tend to assume that authorship first emerged as *literary*, originating in writers' appropriation of authorizing strategies from the classics in order to justify their involvement in commercial publication alongside mercenary writers. But what was the status of those writers against whom the new literary authors defined themselves: in any sense, was *their* commercial publication in their own names authorial? J. W. Saunders's 1951 article, "The Stigma of Print," demonstrated the reluctance of gentle writers to enter print but, too early to question authorial status, implied that it was anonymity that made print authorship demeaning.[14] Today, Saunders's generalization about the stigma of print has yielded to what Alexandra Halasz calls "a highly nuanced understanding of various opportunities and strategies" for publication and self-authorization.[15] If the disincentives to publication drew on a belief that gentle authors should not act like writers known to be commercial, then some incipient notion of authorial popularity was in place. Not accepting that this notion simply projected the literal "popularity" of this first mass medium, I postulate that there was a category of popular authorship, perhaps not preceding literary authorship, but growing up side by side with it.

In sum, rather than assuming that the sixteenth century offered a fully developed popular culture industry complete with a role for popular authors, I ask how that role was invented. Greene and Sidney have been categorized as popular and literary, respectively, because Greene always wrote for publication (or the stage) and Sidney apparently wrote only for manuscript circulation. The opposition of print and manuscript generates a series of antinomies: common/exclusive, commercial/coterie, calculated/disinterested, commodified/unique, derivative/original. However, recent studies on authorship have deconstructed many of these oppositions, or historicized their origins. For instance, H. R. Woudhuysen has argued that "Sidney's role in the process of changing manuscript culture can be related to his self-consciousness as an author."[16] His view of Sidney as developing an authorial self-consciousness apart from print valuably counterpoints my analysis of Greene's print-based authorial self-consciousness. My study also demonstrates how many figures other than the writer were involved in shaping his authorial role. In manuscript and in print, Sidney and Greene (and their coproducers) faced the same problem: in an era suspicious of widespread publication, how could a writer produce and disseminate an image of himself as author without making himself notorious? Both authors struggled, with and against other producers, to control their personae within what Halasz identifies as the constitutive paradox in the construction of early modern authorship: its "apparently contradictory demands" for "free circulation on the one hand, and socially recognized forms of exclusivity on the other" (64).

Of course, Sidney's texts, which obscured their implication in manuscript circulation by claiming their exclusivity, quickly accrued and continue to accrue greater value than Greene's published texts, which more frankly embraced circulation and sacrificed exclusivity. Canonized authors are said to be self-conscious and in control of their personae; other writers are portrayed as calculating and exploitative. Sidney falls in the first category, while Greene came to stand for the second in the last years of his life, and still does. I believe, however, that there was (and is) no absolute line between self-authorization and calculation; in the early modern period, when authorial roles were volatile and controversial, writers found it extremely difficult to predict how effectively they could define or control their reputations. Indeed, in early modern texts, gestures toward textual control and calculations of commercial strategy were strongly implicated in one another. Greene's publications often transparently appropriated coterie gestures, while Sidney would be constructed as exclusive by the very coproducers who dragged his work posthumously into the marketplace.

WHO SO ORDINARY?

The writings from Greene's last year of life treat authorial notoriety with rare frankness, even though (or because) they cannot be authorially attributed. Consider the extraordinary claims of my first epigraph, from *The Repentance of Robert Greene*, entered in the Stationers' Register a month after his death in September 1592. One section narrates, in the first person, "the life and death of Robert Greene Maister of Arts." From the deathbed, the speaker (is he Greene or "Greene"?) styles himself "an Author of Playes, and a penner of Love Pamphlets." Sarcastically, the honorific title of "Author" is assigned to the dramatic writing that Greene elsewhere claimed to despise most. For both kinds of work he has grown so "famous" that no writer in the city is more "ordinarie" than the nicknamed "*Robin Greene.*" "Ordinarie" wittily suggests not only its modern sense of everyday familiarity but also the official role of someone who holds a post "in ordinary" and the boozy intimacy of the "ordinary" inn and gambling house. Greene's name is as famous on title pages and playbills as his person is in theaters and taverns, although the fame is in his "trade," a degrading term. What Greene boasts of here is a reputation for his writings as a group that makes his name a household word and singles him out, even among writers, for special attention. His celebrity is specifically authorial, too, unlike that of Richard Tarlton, the clown, who gave his name to jestbooks and whose picture appeared on ordinary signs.[17] The claim that "Greene" is a brand-name author worked because in the last years of his career, Greene began to use the possessive form of his own name in his titles, a relatively new strategy that I will discuss below.[18] Whether this celebration of ordinariness is by Greene or by a ghostwriter, its appearance in print claims Greene's authorial name as public knowledge—and, more riskily, as public property. The pun on "ordinarie" opens up the dangers of being public: to be ordinary as an author is to be, at some level, notorious.

Greene and his fellow producers gradually invented an authorial role that risked that notoriety, a process that can be traced through the entire sequence of his publications. The story implied in the peritexts and plots of Greene's work is that he fell morally, intellectually, and socially when he became an "ordinarie" author; he claimed this so early—and so often—that he almost seems to have willed it. Richard Helgerson notes that like many other university-trained humanists of his generation who wrote for publication, Greene was fascinated by the narrative of the prodigal son.[19] Helgerson reads Greene's use of that narrative as allegorizing his own repentance for his dissolute career, but admits that although Greene created many repentant heroes and heroines, he himself was slow to follow suit. The question is not just whether Greene foreswore his ordinariness, but more fundamentally, whether he regarded it as his own accomplishment. If notorious authorship constituted a fall, did he jump or was he pushed—or both? How willing was Greene to become a notorious author?

It is tempting to read the allegory of the prodigal son as autobiographical because it pervades the otherwise disparate subject matter of Greene's works. This narrative may even have been the theme of Greene's first publication, if the ballad promising the repentance of a youth, entered in the Stationers' Register for 1581 as "by Greene," was his (Arber 2:391). Greene's first known romances replicate the prodigal course of John Lyly's titular protagonist in *Euphues. The Anatomy of Wit* (1578); Greene sometimes even names this hero in his own titles (e.g., *Euphues his Censure* [1587]). But Lyly had left fiction writing after giving Euphues a successful repentance in *Euphues and his England* (1580). As Greene reiterated and diversified the prodigal convention over the next decade, his titles replaced Lyly's signature character, Euphues, with the brand of his own name—implying that this commonplace of Elizabethan fiction had become Greene's narration of himself *as* fiction writer.

Although Greene insisted that this role of notorious author, prodigal penner, was beneath him, he increasingly seemed to embrace and exploit it, mingling confession and ploy. Sometimes he embedded clues that he, like his protagonist, was wallowing in prodigality: in two of Greene's tales, the prodigal's nadir is conspicuously transposed from swineherding to playwriting (Crupi 20). But more frequently, one authorial voice after another claimed a long-overdue reform, then apologized for being sinful again. If publishing "pamphlets" was Greene's defining sin, the appearance of each account of repentance proved that repentance to be false. Critics puzzled by this phenomenon have tried to pinpoint whether Greene sincerely repented in 1590, when the promises came thickest, or on his deathbed in 1592, as in the (dubiously authored) *Repentance*.[20] But Greene's recidividism, like the theme of prodigality itself, pervades his works from the start.

Critics have repeatedly charged Greene with deliberately adopting this habit in order to spark interest in his works. They assume that just as Greene wrote what would sell, he performed the sins that would sell. To say that Greene avoided repentance for literary profit is to ignore his final poverty and isolation and to assume that he could have predicted, from the start, the market appeal of his decline. Accounts of Greene and the other university wits often describe them as the first to risk the notoriety of Grub Street, but if they were the first, those risks were incalculable.[21] It is a mistake, then, to take this darker interpretation of the prodigal son narrative, with Greene as the willful founder of Grub Street, as the key to his career, or to identify his early, Lylyesque works with his later, more desperate prodigal tales. Whatever popular notoriety Greene reached by 1592, it had little to do with the writing of *Pandosto* in the 1580s: that romance is not part of some devious long-term plan for popularity.

A more plausible reading of Greene's postponed repentance and movement toward more sensational genres is that he could see no way to reform the career that he eventually improvised for himself. The seminotorious authorship he had developed over the course of his career was so unprecedented, and so different from his earlier courtly orientation, that his ambivalence about repenting seems fully understandable. His strategies for self-promotion, improvised or borrowed from less famous precursors, combined with the efforts of producers and fellow authors to yield results that went beyond his control. His calculations were not a lifelong habit; nor can a single sharp turn toward calculation be pinpointed. There is no telling when his usual title-page billing, "Robert Greene, Master of Arts in both Universities," ceased to claim courtly status and began to flaunt his dramatic fall.

Nor could Greene have anticipated that his sordid and premature death would be so profitably exploited in print by his publishers, printers, and contemporaries, including Gabriel Harvey, Henry Chettle, and Thomas Nashe. That posthumous intensification of interest in him demonstrated just how boldly an authorial persona could be reshaped by other producers, friendly and hostile. Harvey's much-quoted invective, registered two months after *The Repentance*, echoes that text's celebration of Greene's authorial name but resignifies his notorious writing career as calculated coney-catching:

> He, they say, was the Monarch of Crosbiters, and the very Emperour of shifters. I was altogether unacquainted with the man, & never once saluted him by *name*: but *who in London* hath not heard of his dissolute, and licentious living; his fonde disguising of a Master of Arte with ruffianly haire, unseemely apparrell, and more unseemelye Company . . . his piperly Extemporizing, and Tarletonizing . . . his impudent pamphletting, phantasticall interluding, and desperate libelling.[22]

Greene, although a "Master of Arte," has fallen to "pamphletting" and "Tarletonizing"; he has joined the "unseemelye Company" of popular print authors, and worse, expanded its social reach. Greene's alleged popularity, then, emerged from the stance he improvised at the vulnerable leading edge of notions of authorship, the efforts of his coproducers, and the harsher responses of other producers after his death. With generic pioneering, collaborative development, and posthumous embellishment, Greene's authorship was produced much as Sidney's was, though the two authors are now seen as worlds apart.

POSITIONS

My second epigraph, from Bourdieu, suggests that the production of authorship may be seen as a complex negotiation, a historically specific process, and even as a collective activity. For Bourdieu, understanding the practice of a writer requires reconstructing two different histories. One is the "position" of the writer in his society, and specifically within a certain genre or mode: the "cluster of representations" and "mechanisms" that support his work and define his place in a "hierarchy of literary crafts" (342). The other is the "disposition" of the writer, meaning his "habitus," the personality traits shaped by his "social trajectory," which includes his social capital (family origins), economic capital (wealth), and cultural capital (education) (311, 341). The meshing of position and disposition produces the writer's *"prise de position,"* his habitual assumption of an authorial stance.[23] These are apt terms for my comparison of Greene and Sidney. Although the two obviously differed in disposition, as contemporaries and writers of prose romances they occupied much the same position, a simi-

larity recognized in coproducers' reactions to *Pandosto* and *Arcadia*. Therefore their *prises de position*, their authorial stances, offer a telling comparison
(even though Greene's has left a thinner record than Sidney's, the latter a
byproduct of his privileged disposition).

Bourdieu intends his analysis to yield a portrait of the literary field by
generating a pattern of *prises de position*, a range of authorial stances, sur-
mising that when writers' dispositions and positions strongly correspond,
the literary field must have developed its own powerful self-regulatory
forces (342). That understanding must be reversed for the early modern
period: that writers as noncorrespondent in disposition as Greene and Sidney could occupy almost the same position indicates the volatility of the
field. Such volatility also demanded that the writers accommodate their
personal dispositions to a position without clear models or institutional
controls, working out unique authorial stances that would reconcile the
tensions between textual circulation and exclusivity.

Bourdieu's model explains why Greene and Sidney, occupying the same
ill-defined position of Elizabethan romance writer, have far more in common than has been admitted by literary history. If the model tends toward
determinism, it can be complicated by considering how quickly their
posthumous reputations were pushed apart—which requires admitting the
agency of coproducers. After Sidney's death in 1586 and Greene's in 1592,
their coproducers' insistence on the two writers' respective dispositions
prevailed over their common position. The retroactive constructions of
their authorial stances became, with each passing year, more strongly differentiated in class-specific terms, pushing Greene's reputation toward the
popular and Sidney's toward the literary.

We now know that Sidney circulated his works more eagerly than we
once thought but was only defined as a literary author posthumously and
unevenly; similarly, I propose, Greene circulated his works more anxiously
than we thought and was categorized as popular much more gradually.[24]
Although we should have moved beyond seeing Sidney as a golden poet-
prince and Greene as the envious mocker of Shakespeare, Sidney scholarship
still tends to isolate the *Arcadia* from other works of vernacular prose
romance. In fact, the position shared by Greene and Sidney was quite specific: not only were *Pandosto* and the *Arcadia* written contemporaneously,
but they are the period's two strongest integrations of a common set of influ-
ences, all imported via Continental writers and translators: chivalric
romance, pastoral romance, and the Greek romance of Heliodorus. The two
works' similar intellectual roots and generic markers place their authors in

comparable positions within the cultural field.[25] Although it has been commonplace to treat Greene as an imitator or popularizer of Sidney, the truth is that when Greene's *Pandosto* was published, the circulation of Sidney's romance still was closely circumscribed. Greene apparently came to these similar materials on his own and worked with them on his own terms. Once both works were available in print, in the 1590s, they reached overlapping audiences and passed through the hands of many of the same publishers.[26] For readers who insisted on enforcing class separation between two writers whose dispositions now seemed so opposed, their work in the same genre was too close for comfort. Even Harvey, well known for hanging on Sidney's literary coattails, implicitly classed him with Greene among "luxurious and riotous Pamphlets" in a 1592 invective: "the Countesse of Pembrokes Arcadia is not greene enough for queasie stomackes, but they must have *Greenes* Arcadia: and I beleeve, most eagerlie longed for *Greenes* Faerie Queene: o straunge fancies: o monstrous newfanglednesse."[27]

In their afterlives, the two romances would overlap again and again, as though the works themselves continued to share positions. The chapbooks based on *Pandosto*, generally known as *Dorastus and Fawnia*, were matched by a chapbook love story excerpted from the *Arcadia* by way of Francis Quarles's 1629 versification, *Argalus and Parthenia*. That mirroring continued in the eighteenth century, when *Argalus and Parthenia* was rewritten as *The Unfortunate Lovers*, and *Dorastus and Fawnia* was published with the story of Hero and Leander as *The Fortunate and Unfortunate Lovers*.[28] The two stories appeared side by side in advertisements by major chapbook printers throughout the century. *Argalus and Parthenia* copies are rarer in the nineteenth century than *Dorastus and Fawnia* copies, but the story from Sidney actually may have outlasted the story from Greene. In an 1862 biography of Sidney, Julius Lloyd reported that the "pleasing" story of *Argalus and Parthenia* had "been more than once published separately" and was "still sold in a cheap form by hawkers."[29] As chapbooks sharing the position of perennially reprinted love stories, these works differed in one key circumstance: *Dorastus and Fawnia* was no longer identified as authored by Robert Greene, while *Argalus and Parthenia* was always identified as a story taken from Sir Philip Sidney. The asymmetry is characteristic of the divergence I trace here—Sidney's name was held to confer value to chapbook customers, while Greene's was not.

Even the vast differences in these writers' dispositions consisted more of social and economic capital than of cultural capital. Greene, apparently the son of a Norfolk saddler, attended St. John's College, Cambridge as a sizar.

Although not a distinguished undergraduate student, he went on to earn a master's degree at Clare Hall, Cambridge (fifth out of a class of twelve) after he began publishing. His works evince an inexhaustible and rapid facility, grounded in wide (if not painstaking) reading in the classics and extracurricular reading in modern Continental languages. His social contacts were unstable; he was championed by some university classmates when his first romance debuted, by Nashe a while later, and by the bookseller Chettle after that, but never found a steady patron. Sidney's immediate family, not aristocrats themselves, stretched their social and financial resources to give their promising son princely training; he excelled at the Shrewsbury School and at Oxford, impressed the humanists of the Continent on his European tour, and was matched to the daughter of the Secretary of State. Despite his dazzling charisma (well beyond even Bourdieu's theorizing), Sidney did not gain the court preferment he sought and turned instead to an abortive career as a Protestant knight.[30] None of his works was printed in his lifetime, but those that circulated in manuscript were highly praised and treasured. In Bourdieu's terms, Sidney aspired to the dominant fraction of the dominant class, the elite group whose cultural dabbling was supposed merely to ornament substantial socioeconomic responsibility, while Greene, educated beyond his economic position, at best occupied the dominated fraction of the dominant class, the Bohemian group whose economic vulnerability Greene confirmed by his allegedly willful poverty. The circumstances of the two writers' deaths reinforce the contrast in their positions and were exaggerated by biographers to make it even starker. Sidney's place in the dominant fraction, however tenuous in life, was clinched when he succumbed to a foolishly earned battle wound, gaining the status of a romantic military hero; Greene died in a shoemaker's garret after his infamous "fatall banquet" of pickled herrings and Rhenish wine, with his pathetic final requests for money detailed in the deathbed pamphlets and exaggerated in responses by Harvey, Nashe, and Chettle.[31] Through all these events, Sidney apparently never sought the name of an author as an end in itself, while Greene's authorial stance became ever more "ordinary."

The comparison between Sidney and Greene is most interesting and surprising during the years immediately after their deaths, in 1586 and 1592 respectively, when both their authorial personae were dramatically reshaped by coproducers. The living Sidney's disposition enabled him to be far more resistant than Greene to print publication, and indeed to avoid presenting himself as an author. The living Greene preserved as long as he could the myth that his name circulated only as he wished. Their deaths detached Sidney's unpublished works and Greene's valuable brand name from the two writers' efforts at control. Sidney, who before his death had been known as an author only within certain coterie cultures, quickly became England's literary star, his works printed and pirated; Greene, known to some as courtly romancer, to others as sensation pamphleteer, became the center of disputes over the social value of print entertainments, while new works were falsely attributed to him. For a few years, the print marketplace conspired to push Sidney and Greene closer together in authorial reputation, to make their deaths and their works alike *causes célèbres*. Then, after 1593, Sidney's friends employed strategies of social distinction, attempting to protect his prestige in print as he had protected it in manuscript. The events that led these two writers' reputations to converge and then diverge suggest how collectively authorial reputations were made and how contingent was the divide between literary and popular print.

The following more or less chronological account pairs the publications and events that made up Greene's reputation as a romance writer with events in Sidney's career as precedents or contrasts, as the production of the two writers first moved them into common positions, then insistently differentiated their dispositions and thus their authorial stances. That movement is replicated within each of five sections that explore the conditions shaping authorship in print and separating popular from elite authorship. The section headings invoke terms used by Greene, Sidney, and their coproducers to describe the work of textual production; most are derived from authorial dedicatory epistles, prime sites for *prises de position*, where an author's disposition intersects visibly with his historical position. The claims made by epistles are so conventionalized and so ingeniously deprecatory of the works that they are seldom accepted as evidence of authorial intentions. But a whole set of epistles by an author can begin to suggest an idiolect of self-production in which he or she variously accepts conventional forms for self-representation, marks out a more idiosyncratic set of concerns, and responds to the pressures of others' perceptions.[32]

The epistle dedicatory published with sixteenth-century editions of *Pandosto. The Triumph of Time* introduces three of Greene's favorite tropes for his authorial stance, as it negotiated between circulation and exclusion (figures 1.1 and 1.2). The epistle suggests that "the mind is sometimes delighted as much with small *trifles* as with sumptuous triumphs" before introducing the romance as "the triumph of time, so rudelie finished." Likewise, Greene tells his dedicatee, "I seek to *shrowd* this imperfect *Pamphlet* under your honours patronage," for protection against slanderers and

TO THE RIGHT HO.

norable George Clifford Earle of Cumber-
land, Robert Greene wisheth increase
of honour and vertue.

H E Rascians (right honorable) when by
long gazing against the Sunne, they become halfe blinde, recouer their sightes
by looking on the blacke Loade-stone. V-
nicornes being glutted with brousing on
roots of Licqnoris, sharpé their stomacks
with crushing bitter grasse.

Alexander vouchsafed as well to smile at the croked picture of Vulcan, as to wonder at the curious counterfeite of
Venus. The minde is sometimes delighted as much with
small trifles as with sumptuous triumphs, and as wel pleased
with hearing of Pans homely fancies, as of Hercules renowmed laboures.

Syllie Baucis coulde not serue Iupiter in a siluer plate, but
in a woodden dish, Al that honour Esculapius, decke not his
shrine with Iewels, Apollo giues Oracles as wel to the poore
man for his mite, as to the rich mã for his treasure. The stone
Echites is not so much liked for the colour, as for vertue,
and giftes are not to be measured by the worth, but by the
will. *Mison* that vnskilfull Painter of Greece, aduentured to
giue vnto *Darius* the shielde of Pallas, so roughlie shadowed,
as he smiled more at the follie of the man, then at the im-
perfection of his arte. So I present vnto your honour the triumph of time, so rudelie finished, as I feare your honour wil
rather frowne at my impudencie, then laugh at my ignoran-
cie: But I hope my willing minde shal excuse my slender skill,
and your honours curtesie shadowe my rashnes.

A 2

They

FIGURES I.I AND I.2
Epistle dedicatory, Robert Greene, *Pandosto* (London, 1588; shelfmark 95.b.18/4).
BY PERMISSION OF THE BRITISH LIBRARY

They which feare the biting of vipers doe carie in their hands the plumes of a Phœnix. Phydias drewe Vulcan sitting in a chaire of Iuory. Cæsars Crow durst neuer cry, *Aue*, but whē she was pearked on the Capitoll. And I seeke to shroude this imperfect Pamphlet vnder your honours patronage, doubting the dint of such inuenomed vipers, as seeke with their slaunderours reproches to carpe at al, being oftentims, most vnlearned of all : and assure my selfe, that your honours renowmed valure, and vertuous disposition shall be a sufficient defence to protect me from the Poysoned tongues of such scorning Sycophants, hoping that as Iupiter vouchsafed to lodge in Philemons thatched Cotage : and Phillip of Macedon, to take a bunche of grapes of a country pesant : so I hope your honour, measuring my worke by my will, and wayghing more the mind than the matter, will when you haue cast a glaunce at this toy, with Minerua, vnder your golden Target couer a deformed Owle. And in this hope I rest, wishing vnto you, and the vertuous Countesse your wife : such happy successe as your honours can desire, or I imagine.

Your Lordships most duetifully to com-
maunde: Robert Greene.

"sycophants." He concludes with the hope that "your honour, measuring my worke by my will, and wayghing more the mind than the matter, will when you have cast a glaunce at this *toy*, with Minerva, under your golden Target cover a deformed Owle."[33] The emphasized terms are conventional, but as they imply the value of the work they pretend to belittle, they also betray conflicting pressures toward circulation and exclusivity. "Trifles" and "toys," more or less synonyms, speak to the alleged triviality, childishness, and femininity of fiction writing, even as Greene predicts that the dedicatee will be "delighted" by indulgence in reading. "Shroud" summons up both the vulnerability of the published author and the possibility of protection offered by the names of patrons, prior authors, family, or, more boldly, the author's own name. Both terms are, then, strategies of authorial control over the text, known not only to Greene but also to Sidney. The third term, "pamphlet," opens up the tension between authorial control over the text and the agency of other producers. Although the offhand word reduces Greene's commitment to his work and to the print industry, it admits anxieties about both the imperfections of printing and the uncontrolled circulation of print works.

Joining with Greene's three tropes for authorial production, my last two section headings emphasize the agency of other producers who made claims on the authorship of Greene and Sidney: "copies" refers to the legal status of early modern printed texts as the property of publishers, not authors; "ghosts," in this chapter, refers not to bibliographic phantasms but to texts that are published and extant but falsely attributed to a dead author. Under these five terms, the respective rights of authors, their contemporaries and editors, their publishers and printers and readers, were negotiated; each stands out in writing of the period as a way of talking about conflicting impulses to contain or expand the dissemination of texts. All of the terms were used widely by those who produced Greene and Sidney as authors: their occurrences at first draw together the two writers' positions, then, increasingly, distinguish between their dispositions. They point up the collective processes that formed both Greene's authorship and Sidney's, culminating in the years immediately after each writer's death. Below, "Toys and Trifles" describes how both writers sought men's attention through ostensible address to women readers; "Shrouds," how both offered semiautobiographical texts while using their own names and those of others for protection; "Copies," how the works of both were recorded as the property of eager printers; "Pamphlets," how both carefully manipulated forms of publication, though Sidney's was manuscript; and "Ghosts," how the writers' premature deaths allowed their public and textual refiguration. These are the key words that made the makers of *Pandosto* and the *Arcadia*.

TOYS AND TRIFLES

"Toys" and "trifles" are coded terms, both licensing the circulation of texts and limiting authorial claims for them. These terms participate in the complex gender dynamic of what Juliet Fleming calls the "ladies' text."[34] When a male writer designated his work as a "toy" or "trifle," he framed it as a sweet for women, thereby detaching himself from responsibility for its potential triviality. He also claimed his virility by implying contempt for women's tastes, and signaled his "deliberate and spectacular waste of talent" (Fleming 168). I see these terms as also using gender to displace nervousness about the commerciality of authorship, since "toys" and "trifles" were often purchased goods, including gifts for women and children. When Greene and Sidney dismissed their works as "toys" and "trifles," they actually recommended them for circulation among valued coterie members or customers, under cover of keeping them exclusive to a circle of female intimates.

"Toy" was the word that Philip Sidney used to characterize all of his completed literary works. His sonnet persona, Astrophil, complains that "My youth doth waste, my knowledge brings forth toyes"; *The Defence of Poetry* is "this ink-wasting toy of mine." Sidney refers to the composition of the *Arcadia* in a letter to his brother dated October 1580, and promises a February delivery of the completed "toyfull book."[35] Sidney's most famous dismissal of his work is the letter dedicating the work to his sister, Mary Sidney Herbert, Countess of Pembroke. The language of this letter again mingles dismissal and pride:

> Here now have you (most deare, and most worthy to be most deare Lady) this idle work of mine. . . . For my part, in very trueth . . . I could well find in my harte, to cast out in some desert of forgetfulness this child, which I am loath to father. . . . If you keep it to your selfe, or to such friendes, who will weigh errors in the ballaunce of good will, I hope, for the fathers sake, it will be pardoned. . . . For indeede, for severer eyes it is not, being but a *trifle*, and that *triflinglie* handled. . . . Read it then at your idle tymes. . . . And so, looking for no better stuff then, as in an Haberdashers shoppe, glasses, or feathers, you will continue to love the writer. . . .   (Garrett 89–90, emphasis added)

The bulky manuscript is a trifle, a tiny imported luxury, like beads or feathers; it is both a sweet for a baby and a bastard infant that Sidney is "loath to father." The offspring of the writer's own infancy, as the sibling intimacy of the letter makes clear, it is also, at a metaphoric level, the offspring of the writer and his (pregnant) baby sister, since "it is done onelie for you, onely to you."[36] The letter shows Sidney's class disposition in its easy wit but reflects common anxieties of Elizabethan writers about broad circulation and textual misinterpretation.

The appearance of this letter in all published editions of the *Arcadia* links it to the many other Elizabethan romances that were marked as "ladies' texts": romances, published by men, that rhetorically seduced female readers and thus offset the degradation of print in other men's eyes. But there is a complication in extending that label to the *Arcadia*, for this epistle, with its definitive ladies' text tropes, was written while Sidney was still circulating the romance in manuscript. Although published with the book, it was not written with publication in mind. It therefore indicates that the rhetorical strategy of dismissing a work as a "toy" was not peculiar to print circulation but reflects broader dynamics of gender and class inflecting romances and other entertainments in any medium of circulation that permitted access to female or socially diverse readers. That context of social intercourse links Sidney's invocation of the trope in reference to his romance, and Greene's invocation of it in the published *Pandosto*.

Sidney's references to "toys" have left critics struggling to explain his gross underestimation of his literary accomplishments. One possibility is that the modesty is false. Fulke Greville, Sidney's best friend, recognized the formula as protecting the writer's prestige, noting "that hypocritical figure called Ironia wherein men commonly (to keep above their works) seem to make toys of the utmost they can do."[37] Katherine Duncan-Jones, in "Philip Sidney's Toys," argues that "toy" should not be read merely as conventionalized *sprezzatura* or false modesty. She wants to prove that Sidney's secular writings might have seemed to him the works of youth, to be left behind when he took up his brief career as Christian soldier. The difficulty is that these dismissals as "toys" are embedded in works drafted in Sidney's early twenties, not confined to a reflection from the end of his life.

For instance, the crucial reference to *Arcadia* as a "trifle" in the letter dedicating it to the Countess of Pembroke is much earlier than its publication date would suggest. The letter seems to have been delivered to her with the *Old Arcadia*, completed in 1581–82. It was then published as an epistle dedicatory with the 1590 *Countesse of Pembrokes Arcadia* (consisting only of three books of the revision begun in 1584), and with the 1593 and 1598 composite editions that folded in material from the first version. Apparently, Sidney's self-assessment was not a view from later years but a fresh reaction to a just-completed work, coding his position through his disposition as pet brother of a Countess. The publication of the letter seems to represent the stance of an author in print, but what Sidney had taken was a stance as manuscript romance writer. The *Countesse of Pembrokes Arcadia*, old, new, or composite, was dedicated to a lady and referred to as a "trifle," but the anxiety that guided that self-deprecation pertained to authorship, not to print alone.

Words like "toy" and "trifle" imply that authorship is a threat not only to masculinity but also to the economic and moral health of the nation. That concern lurks in Sidney's association of his manuscript with imported luxuries such as beads and feathers. George Pettie's *Allarme to England* (1578) voiced a common concern about the importation of sweets and fashions as the "conveying away commodities, and returning of incommodities, vaine trifles, which are not necessary for humane life, but only to maintaine women and children in pride, pomp, and vainglory" (quoted in Fleming 169). A 1580 Act of Parliament, vying unsuccessfully to control the print market, extended the charge to printed toys, complaining of "sundrie bookes, pamfletes, Poesies, ditties, songes and other woorkes, and wrytinges, of many sortes and names serving (for a great parte of them) to none other ende (what titles soever they bear) but only to . . . set up an arte of making lascivious ungodly love." For Parliament, the bottom line seemed to be economic rather than moral: these trifles were printed on imported stock, so that the "treasure of this Realme . . . is thearby consumed and spent in paper, being of it selfe a forrein and chargeable comoditie" (Arber 2:751). Such anxieties may have informed Sidney's remarks about an "ink-wasting toy." But unlike Parliament, Sidney extended his worries to a manuscript copy, whose reproduction would waste paper and ink at a much slower rate.

Sidney's anxiety makes more sense if we think of him as making his romance "public" at the writing of that letter, albeit in manuscript rather than in print. Because all the *Old Arcadia* manuscripts bore the title *The Countesse of Pembrokes Arcadia*, they all qualify as "ladies' texts." As a printed work's claim to be a "toy" or trifle for women could help to disguise the writer's reliance on commercial circulation, so the same claim, attached to Sidney's manuscript work, must have protected him from embarrassment in circulating his witty "toy" to a number of male readers. Even granting

Sidney's claim that the romance was written for the Countess first and foremost, its confinement to an all-female coterie must have been brief indeed. The original was drafted, Sidney's letter said, "most of it in your presence, the rest, by sheetes, sent unto you, as fast as they were done" (Garrett 89). The romance's first-person narration and many references to "fair ladies" imply that Sidney may have read it aloud to a primarily female audience. But from that time on, those recorded with private access to the *Old Arcadia* are men. Sidney was traveling with the Earl of Angus when he was "in travail, or had brought forth rather" the *Old Arcadia*, and "he delighted much to impart it to Angus, and Angus took as much pleasure to be partaker thereof" (quoted in Woudhuysen 301).

Much more significant, according to Woudhuysen, was the scale of the *Old Arcadia*'s manuscript circulation: ten manuscript copies are extant, and eight more copies may once have existed, all made during the two years between the completion of the *Old Arcadia* and the start of Sidney's never-completed revisions (310). Sidney's active role in allowing copying on this scale, Woudhuysen argues, "may have changed the private character of manuscript production, altering and reviving it while at the same time seeking to preserve its origins, which [Sidney] saw as primarily literary" (8). Sidney, then, took an authorial lead in circulation even while he maintained an extremely exclusive text. Crucially, all of the individuals whom Woudhuysen documents as passing on the text or commissioning scribal copies are male, and early critical reactions not only claimed the *Arcadia*'s place in male literary culture but also largely glossed over any female audience. Sidney's secretary Edmund Molyneux, publishing the accomplishments of his late master in 1587, gave this account of the work's circulation:

> Before his further imploiment by her majestie, at his vacant and spare times of leisure (for he could indure at no time to be idle and void of action) he made his booke which he named *Arcadia*, a worke (though a mere fansie, toie and fiction) . . . as few works of like subject hath beene either of some more earnestlie sought, choiselie kept, nor placed in better place, and amongst better jewels than that was; so that a speciall deere freend he should be that could have a sight, but much more deere that could once obteine a copie.[38]

For Molyneux, the romance transcends its objective status as "toy" not because of the work its author has put into it but because of the value its coproducers have invested in it. The coproduction of Sidney's sister has vanished: the time Sidney spent with her is now a "void" of inaction averted by his solitary effort. Sir John Harington similarly asserts the text's social value in the heading he wrote on his copy: "A *treatis* by Sir Philip Sidney *of certeyn accidents in Arcadia . . . made in the yeer 1580 and emparted to some few of his frends in his lyfe tyme and to more sence his unfortunate deceasse.*" These "frends" are presumably male. Harington's own use of the manuscript pressed the masculine sexual agenda of the ladies' text: as he read the work aloud to his scribe, he sometimes dictated "prurient" remarks to be interpolated where Sidney had merely teased.[39]

The inclusion of the letter to the Countess with the 1590 *New Arcadia* therefore was a belated reassertion of the romance as a ladies' text, well after Sidney had devised homosocial strategies for its manuscript circulation. The letter appeared to insert his work posthumously into the kind of eroticized position that Greene's early works had occupied from the start. Ironically, while the letter's presentation of the text as a trifle for ladies might have been consistent with the intimately narrated, earthy, and sexually frank *Old Arcadia* to which it referred, it was at odds with the more high-minded *New Arcadia* drafted by Sidney and prepared for publication by his sister, his friend Greville, and the rest of their editorial team. In providing the letter, which does not appear in any extant manuscript of the *Old* or *New Arcadia*, the Countess must have been actively involved. Rather than publishing Sidney's more intimate first version of the text, she helped to produce the revision's family-style peritext, perhaps because the letter explained the invocation of her own name in the title, making the romance a virtuous sibling version of a ladies' text. In other words, the presentation of *Arcadia* as a ladies' text may be a rare instance where that trope worked to protect the name of the woman. The particularities of this decision demonstrate just how integral the interests and agencies of coproducers were to the creation of the Sidney myth.

In Greene's case, too, the trope of toys and trifles was deployed in deliberate interchange with the ladies' text tradition and in cooperation with coproducers. When *Pandosto. The Triumph of Time* was first published, Robert Greene was known as a writer of fashionable romances, unlike the unpublished Sidney. Neither a courtier nor (apparently) gentle-born, Greene drew on his Cambridge training to write the euphuistic fiction that was the height of literary fashion. Within a year of taking his B.A. (22 January 1580), he conceived a courtly romance in imitation of Lyly's *Euphues*, which had been a sensation at court, in the city, and in the universities since its publication in 1578. While *Euphues* brought Lyly little political success, it proved hugely successful for Thomas Cawood, who published three editions and entered a sequel by the end of 1579. This precedent must have encouraged Thomas Woodcocke to enter Greene's title, *Mamillia*, promptly in 1580. The first dated edition of *Mamillia* is from 1583, although an alternate setting survives that may date to 1580 or 1581.[40] If the first part was reissued within two or three years, Greene's debut had been highly successful.

The genre of euphuistic fiction allowed direct cultivation of the market for sequels. *Euphues* had promised that Euphues and Philautus would retain "the conjunction of their minds" though "they went their separate ways," and Lyly quickly issued a sequel to confirm that promise. After that, the phenomenon of *Euphues* did not seem to need more stimulation: by 1583 it had gone through four additional editions and *Euphues and his England* had seen five editions of its own.[41] Following Lyly's example, Greene had fanned expectations of a sequel at the end of *Mamillia*, promising that "as Soone as I shal either hear, or learn of [Pharicles'] abroad, looke for newes by a speedy Post. *Robert Greene*" (Grosart 2:135). No imitator could match Lyly's phenomenal hit, but Greene was hot on his heels, immediately seizing on the potential of his own first romance to offer publicity for his next.[42] The crucial point in these proceedings is that Lyly also preserved his claim to gentility: what both writers were creating was a fashionable sensation rather than an openly commercial line of goods.

Although the parts of *Mamillia* were reaching a large audience for the period (five editions would total 6,000 to 7,500 copies), their peritextual trappings emphasized social and intellectual exclusivity. The elaborately bordered title page of the 1583 edition attributes *Mamillia* to "Robert Greene Graduate in Cambridge." There is a signed epistle dedicatory to Lord Darcy, another signed letter "to the Gentlemen readers," and commendatory verse by "Roger Portington Esquier" (Grosart 2:3–12). Those markers and the first part's quick sales might explain the interest of the ambitious young publisher William Ponsonby, who entered Greene's sequel, *Mamillia. The Triumph of Pallas* (*Mamillia* Part 2) in September 1583. McKerrow cites this acquisition as launching Ponsonby's career as "the most important publisher of the Elizabethan period" (*Dictionary* 217–18): at this stage, Greene was fashionable enough to make a young publisher important. The sequel's second edition, printed by Thomas Creede for Ponsonby in 1593, notes that Greene is "Master of Arts in Cambridge." The front matter of *Mamillia* Part 2 is, if less socially ambitious than the first part, more intellectually ambitious. None of its three dedicatory letters and two verse epistles dares to reach as high as a lord; instead, they aim to reinforce university connections. The first dedication is to Robert Lee and Roger Portington, both "Esquires" and hence probably recent graduates at the Inns of Court (Grosart 2:141). It is signed "From my Studie in Clarehall the vij. Of Iulie. Robert Greene" (2:143), the very date when Greene received his M.A. from Clare Hall, Cambridge. The date was retained in the printed work because it was important to both Greene and Ponsonby: like the degrees mentioned on the title page, it secured a gentle affiliation for a writer who, upon graduation, had little else in the way of social capital. The verses in Part 2 signed "G.B." were probably by William Boston, who took his M.A. from St. John's shortly after Greene arrived there. Euphuism was a Cambridge phenomenon as well as a court phenomenon, and the *Mamillia* sequel emphasizes university ties to authorize Greene's publication.[43]

Authorship is also constructed in both parts of Greene's first romance by a strong revision of Lyly's ladies' text trope. Lyly himself had followed the precedent set in the 1570s by Barnabe Riche and George Pettie, both of whom offered their translated fictions "onely" to women.[44] The formulation that opens "A Petite Palace of Pettie his Pleasure" (1576) is indicative of the tone: "Gentle Readers, who by my will I would have onely Gentlewomen"; "will" captures the courtly ambition, forcefully displaced onto women readers, that Fleming has identified as the agenda of the ladies' text (161). Lyly was relatively cautious in picking up this trope, mentioning female readers only in his continuation, and then only in a dedicatory letter "To the Ladies and Gentlewoemen of England," safely disposed between letters to a nobleman and "To the Gentleman Readers."

In claiming a female audience, Greene was much more direct than Lyly but less suggestive than Pettie. The first part of *Mamillia* was subtitled "A Mirrour or looking-glasse for the Ladies of Englande. Wherein is deciphered, howe Gentlemen under the perfect substaunce of pure love, are oft inveigled with the *shadowe of lewde lust*," until, the subtitle continues, they reform (Grosart 2:3). As Suzanne Hull points out, *Mamillia* is the first English romance with only a woman's name in its title (78). Greene couples the alleged moralism of euphuistic fiction to the patriarchal didacticism of the mirror (first turned to women readers in Thomas Salter's *Mirrhor of Modestie* [1579]), but the frankness of the subtitle is all his own. The second part, *Mamillia The Triumph of Pallas* (another woman) has an even more contentious subtitle: "Wherein with perpetual fame the constancie of Gentlewomen is canonised, and the unjust blasphemies of womens supposed fickleness (breathed out by diverse injurious persons) by manifest examples clearly infringed" (Grosart 2:139). Greene again positions himself as defender of women's virtue, by implication against attacks made by Lyly. But in his own way he, too, is exploiting women's virtue for a male audience, turning from Lyly's general male prodigality to specifically heterosexual misconduct, to be detailed in "manifest examples."

In varying Lyly's ladies' text trope, Greene acted not in isolation but in interchange with his coproducers. This second part of *Mamillia*, for instance, was dedicated to "his especiall friends" Lee and Portington but included (after a letter "to the Gentlemen Readers") a very interesting verse epistle "to the Curteous and Courtly Ladies of England," written by minor poet Richard Stapleton. Stapleton's letter exemplifies "that interpellation of the female reader on which the ladies' text . . . depend[s]" (Fleming 163). He reports that Greene defends "peerelesse Brittaine Dames" against the misogyny of classical "Authors"; then he asks the ladies to "shrowde Mamillia safe, / tis that the Author crave" (Grosart 2:141–48). It is quite explicitly the protective shrouding of the ladies that renders Greene an "Author" rather than simply a romance writer (although elsewhere, Greene asks the gentlemen readers, too, to "shrowd" Mamillia, and by extension, *Mamillia* Part 2, "my toy" [Grosart 2:145]).

Even more unusually, Greene ends the sequel with an embedded miniature that is multiply marked as female. A letter from Mamillia, warning another female character about the things men learn from Ovid, it is preceded by verses from "G.B." that delicately suggest that *Mamillia* Part 2 might "not displease her noble Majestie," and then by a letter wishing health to "the vertuous Gentlewoman Mary Rogers" (Portington's married sister). Greene explains "why in dedicating my Booke to others" he has "inserted your worshippes name": because her "constant, vertuous and godly disposition caused me . . . to ingrave your name in a worke where Gentlewomens constancie is so stifly defended" (Grosart 2:251–52, 335). Mary Rogers occupies, for just a few pages, the position that Mary Herbert occupied in the print *Arcadia*: that of "ingrave[d]" guarantor of a toy. Yet the epistle also contrasts with Sidney's letter to his sister in that Rogers is not named as a member of Greene's coterie or as already knowing the work. It would seem that any "ladies" in Greene's audience only read the printed version.

G.B.'s hopeful mention of "her noble Majestie" is the closest Greene ever got to court service, but the invocation of the Queen here, alongside the obscure Mary Rogers, valuably fills out the social class dynamics of this ladies' text. The Queen, representing the top of the social scale, may have had a symbolic force in shaping the Elizabethan romance as ladies' text, but most of the members of its audience who counted were male (in contrast to the stronger subcultures fostered by the Stuart queens).[45] The text's appeal can be transferred not only from the "gentlewoman reader" to the gentleman-courtier, but also from the eroticized, mixed-gender world of the court to the aspirant, again mixed-gender, world of the fashionable and would-be fashionable, including university students, members of the Inns of Court, provincial gentry, and merchants. These audiences were in tension, which the ladies' text placed under the sign of women, figures of the open circulation of print.

Tensions about print circulation are feminized in Lyly's irresistibly quotable lines in the preface to *Euphues and his England*:

> I am content that your Dogges lye in your laps, so *Euphues* may be in your hands, that when you shall be wearie in reading of the one, you may be ready to sport with the other; or handle him as you doe your Junkets, that when you can eate no more, you tye some in your napkin for children, for if you be filled with the first part, put the second in your pocket for your wayting Maydes: *Euphues* had rather lye shut in a Ladyes casket, then open in a Schollers studie.   (Salzman, *English*, 41)

As is often remarked, Lyly's flight of fancy plays a knowing gender game: it encourages women readers to think of the book as a sweet toy, while "Schollers" in their "studies" are invited to pocket a different reading. The less-recognized turn of the argument—that female tastes for "toys" slide down the social register—would reappear, to insidious effect, throughout the later history of romances. Lyly knowingly predicts that although gentlewomen are entitled to their enjoyment of sensual indulgences, they will pass their pocketed sweets (and other secrets) on to the "Maydes" who wait upon them and for such pleasures. Thus he offered privileged male readers both the comfort of essentializing female foolishness and the *frisson* of contemplating cultural exchanges across class lines. Chapter 4 explores how this motif would become a cliché in commentary on the romance and the novel in the next two centuries, a scene of consumption that united gender and class anxieties to support the rhetoric of distinction that grew up around fiction.[46] Lyly's scene seems to prefigure—more directly than anything Greene himself wrote—the later social descent of romances like *Pandosto* to cheap reading material for lower-class women. Lyly is shaping a tradition that fuses emerging concerns about women's vulnerability to romance and the printed book's circulation, vividly portraying the printed romance as transferring erotic knowledge across class lines. His cross-class erotic transfer stands in for anxiety about the cross-class transfer of cultural goods permitted by print itself. As the fad for Lyly was forgotten, such figurations of the book as empty, erotic, and socially degraded would become attached to Greene.[47] For instance, even Nashe, in defending Greene against Harvey, suggested an incipient class slide in which Greene's quickly penned works made a treat for the pockets of servingmen.[48]

The next few works that Greene published after *Mamillia* continued in courtly forms: single romances, which in Greene's hands became less euphuistic and more pastoral; and framed collections of tales, often with themes of masculine prodigality and feminine chastity. Greene's offerings referred to female readers with a regularity beyond convention, but, as Hull notes, "none of his books has a direct dedication to women" as a group (81). Instead, many works included a "feminine" subtitle, a dedication to a prospective patroness, or a verse addressed to "ladies"—always counterpoised by a letter "to the gentlemen readers" or "to the gentle readers" (addressed as males). Even the frame-tales that took female virtues as their primary topics—the *Myrrour of Modestie* (1584) and *Penelopes Web . . . a christall myrror of faeminine perfection* (1587)—maintained the usual addresses to gentlemen readers. In this putative double audience, the rhetorical advantage was given to males, as in the letter to them accompanying *Penelopes Web*:

> I adventure to present what I write to your judgementes, hoping as my intent is to please all . . . I was determined at the first to have made no appeale to your favorable opinions, for that the matter is womens prattle, about the untwisting of Penelopes Web. But . . . *Mars* will sometime bee prying into *Venus* papers, and gentlemen desirous to hear the parlie of Ladies. (Grosart 5:144–45)

As Lyly did in his earlier letter, Greene differentiates between an audience of ladies who are easily pleased and a jury of gentlemen who exercise sterner "judgementes" over material in which they claim to take only vicarious interest; this differentiation sets up another voyeuristic scene in which godlike men "pry into" women's written secrets. The implication is that Penelope's web, too, is a secret that men can "pry into" by "untwisting." Although Greene claims "to please all," it is men's opinions that matter: as Fleming points out, "the female audience to which [the ladies' text] is often addressed" is "invited to assist at the spectacle of its own discountenancing" (168). So, in the *Myrrour of Modestie*, Greene reports the request "of a certaine Gentlewoman whose sute I durst not denie to pen out this storie of Susanna" (Grosart 3:5). Her "sute" undermines her "modestie," her anonymity allows any "Gentlewoman" to be suspected, and the address of the book to gentlemen gives away the game. As Derek Alwes suggests, the "invidiousness of Greene's dual addresses" is inescapable (376).

When Greene began to turn away from love stories, whether out of repentance or not, around 1590, he became even franker about this ladies' text game. He speaks of his "trifles" and his "toys" as simply erotic, although even that denies the pleasure that he must have taken in framing their presentation. *Greenes Never Too Late* (1590) promises "I have done with frivolous toyes"; *Greenes Mourning Garment* (1590) claims to be "the last of my trifling Pamphlets" (Grosart 8:8; 9:222). And the posthumously published *Greenes Vision*, also conceivably written around 1590, stages a debate between Chaucer and Gower about whether Greene had "doone well or ill, in setting foorth such amorous trifles" (12:213–14). Submitting himself to their judgment, its "Greene" worries that he has produced exactly the kind of sexual propaganda against which Parliament had inveighed in 1580: "I cald to minde, how many idle fancies I had made to passe the Presse, how I had pestred Gentlemens eyes and mindes, with the infection of many fond passions" (Grosart 12:203). Sincere or not, autobiographical or not, these comments reveal Greene's consciousness of the complex social dynamics of the ladies' text. They contradict the claim made, as late as *Greenes Orpharion* (entered 1590), that Greene's goal is the "praise of women-kind" (1599 title page) and bring out the irony in Nashe's acerbic comment in 1588, perhaps in reference to *Penelopes Web*, that Greene was "the *Homer* of women" (McKerrow, *Nashe*, 1:12). Whatever calculation might have gone into his early defenses of women and his ongoing double-addressing of his texts, it seems that by 1590, Greene regarded his reputation as a woman's writer as a liability—moral, commercial, or both. The trope that had secured Lyly's glory had become more demeaning, and therefore less exclusive, in Greene's hands. The cause is not, I think, that Greene pressed those claims too hard, but that elite culture had turned away from them. Unbeknownst to Greene, Sidney was also turning away from the ladies' text as he revised the *New Arcadia*. Only the intercession of the Countess of Pembroke and Greville imprinted his romance as a high-toned ladies' text, an unwilling exploiter of the theme Greene had explored in so many works.

SHROUDS

Greene's earliest works, so conspicuously centered on women, and the pamphlets of 1590, so adamantly antiwoman, make especially obvious use of gender dynamics to simultaneously license and dismiss his authorial efforts. But in the interim, Greene experimented with other forms of authorial self-validation that alternately spotlighted his name and shrouded it in the names of others. The titles alone of the works published between 1584 and 1589—that is, in the period of *Pandosto*'s publication—suggest his sequential testing of strategies of self-presentation. After the *Myrrour of Modestie*, all of the fiction titles of 1584 and 1585 revert to a formula that neatly follows the title of *Euphues. The Anatomy of Wit*—a protagonist's name and a fanciful genre name exploring a broad theme: *Gwydonius. The Carde of Fancie* (entered April 1584), *Arbasto. The Anatomie of Fortune* (entered August 1584); *Morando. The Tritameron of Love* (first edition 1584, expanded edition entered August 1586). This quick sequence indicates success as well as efficiency; Greene was placing one book after another with publishers of note, including Edward White and Hugh Jackson as well as Ponsonby. And their investment in his titles was also successful, since all three proceeded to a second edition in three to five years. The title patterns suggest that *Pandosto. The Triumph of Time* comes from this series, although its first extant edition dates from 1588; there is further evidence for a mid-1580s debut detailed below. Certainly well before 1588, Greene had abandoned this formula, which implicitly followed Lyly, and turned to a new strategy of self-authorization: the use of his own name in his titles.

Although apparently more confident, this strategy, too, originated in imitation, and perhaps hesitantly. The title "Grene his Farewell to Folly" was registered by stationer Edward Aggas in June 1587. Especially with the subtitle that appeared on the printed book—*Sent to courtiers and Schollers*—it deliberately echoes *Riche His Farewell to the Military Profession*. Greene's title promises change in a direction opposite Riche's, away from love themes rather than toward them, but both titles privilege male social worlds over the feminized world of love. Despite this landmark entrance in 1587, the earliest extant edition of 1591 appears to be the first, since its epistle mentions the recent publication of *Greenes Mourning Garment* (entered and published 1590). In any case, beginning in December 1588, five fiction titles incorporated Greene's authorial name. This new formula made Greene's name into a brand endorsing his innovation in genre-naming: *Alcida. Greenes Metamorphosis* (1588), *Greenes Orpharion* (1590), *Greenes Never Too Late*

(1590), *Greenes Farewell to Folly*, and *Greenes Mourning Garment*. *Greenes Metamorphosis* thematizes the author as innovator: the title and the epistle remind readers that they know Greene to be not only Ovidian but also metamorphic. The next genre names bear out that claim, alternating between fashionable classicism (*Metamorphosis*) and vernacular repentance (*Never Too Late*, *Farewell to Folly*). *Greenes Mourning Garment* underlines the series' ambitions and reversals: it is "the reformation of a second *Ovid*," but this time, Greene insists, he is not just "changing the titles of my Pamphlets" but showing the genuine "inward metamorphosis of my minde" (Grosart 9:121, 122).

When Greene began publishing his coney-catching pamphlets in 1591, his name disappeared from his titles and became more understated on his title pages. *The Blacke Bookes Messenger*, billed as "naming names" in the crime world, is signed only with the initials "R.G." after the preface to the reader. The *Disputation Betweene a Hee Conny-catcher, and a Shee Conny-catcher* (1592) also has only his initials. Like the other coney-catching pamphlets, it has the innovative, eye-catching element of a custom woodcut. It shows not coney-catchers but coneys, one female and one male, fashionably dressed and vigorously disputing (see figure 1.3).[49] Publishers who went to the expense of commissioning an illustration certainly were counting on the title going into multiple editions: the illustrations indicate market success, if not "popularity." Greene, having associated his name with changeability, could rely on even the near-anonymity of his initials on a coney-catching pamphlet to mark his fame. His name was an effective brand when coupled with his speedy composition and his relentless self-advertising: he continued to embed references to his upcoming works and to deliver on those promises with constant innovation. Modern marketing strategy says that brands need recognizability, continuity, and novelty; Greene somehow coordinated all three. The preconditions for his aggressive use of his authorial name bear emphasis: a disposition we might call "nothing to lose," and a position in a rapidly expanding vernacular marketplace with apparently endless demand from audiences and publishers.

To say that Greene had nothing to lose is not to say he was without anxiety. The turn to his own name as authorization, indeed the energy that went into experimentation in marketing his books, can be set against his evident failure to secure regular patronage. There was a gradual decline, too, in the number of other writers willing to praise Greene's name in prose and verse contributions to his volume, although 1589 saw something of a rally (see below). Greene's reliance on his own name to shroud his efforts

A DISPVTATION,

Betweene a Hee Conny-catcher, and a

Shee Conny-catcher, whether a Theefe or a Whoore, is
moſt hurtfull in Couſonage, to the Com-
mon-wealth.

DISCOVERING THE SECRET VILLA-
nies of alluring Strumpets.

Wich the Conuerſion of an Engliſh Courtizen, reformed
this preſent yeare, 1592.

Reade, laugh, and learne.

Naſcimur pro patria.

R. G.

Imprinted at London, by A. I. for T. G. and are to be ſolde at
the Weſt ende of Paules. 1592.

FIGURE 1.3
Title page, R.G., *Disputation Between a Hee Conny-catcher,
and a Shee Conny-Catcher* (London, 1592).

admits the lack of another's. As he became more ingenious in identifying his books with his own name, his dedicatees became less distinguished, and a certain desperation creeps into the conventional topoi of self-debasement. In 1590, dedicating *Greenes Mourning Garment* to George Clifford, Earl of Cumberland, also the dedicatee of *Pandosto*, Greene repeated the figure of the patron as shroud, now given a darker emphasis by the title of the work. He claims that this garment signifies his regret for his "sundry wanton Pamphlets"; he has "turned my wanton workes to effectuall labours, and pull[ed] off their vain-glorious titles." He can explain his title's allusion to sin, but not why he has "attempted to shrowd it under your Lordships patronage, as if . . . it were a perswasive Pamphlet to a Patron toucht with the like passion." The claim for Clifford's sinlessness that should follow is not there, perhaps because he already had a wild reputation.[50] Instead, Greene lamely promises him credit for any young readers of his "garment" who "looke on it, and handle it," and find their vices "shaken from under the vayle of pretended vertue"(Grosart 9:119–21). Still unprotected by a patron, Greene faces being "handled" by readers of dubious merit.

The epistle to *Greenes Vision* (1592) invokes the shroud topos even more pathetically, expressing faint hope that the winding sheet, or at least the grave, can hide the damage that self-publication has done to his name:

> Gentlemen, in a vision before my death, I foresee that I am like to sus-taine the shame of many follies of my youth, when I am *shrowded* in my winding sheete. . . . I crave pardon of you all, if I have offended any of you with *lacivious Pamphleting*. Many things I have wrote to get money, which I could otherwise wish to be supprest. . . . In seeking to salve pri-vate wantes, I have made my selfe a publique laughing stock. Hee that commeth in Print, setteth himselfe vp as a common marke for every one to shoote at. . . . This booke hath many things, which I would not have written on my Tombe. (Grosart 12:195–96, emphasis added)

The writer of this passage, Greene or not, has penetrated to the real reason that Greene's reform has been so endlessly deferred: it is not the amorous contents of the pamphlets but the conditions of their publication that are wanton. These conditions have affected his disposition irreversibly: having published under his own name, he has "made [him]selfe . . . publique." By "com[ing] in Print," Greene has become "common," his work, name, self "marke[d]" as wanton, mercenary, vulnerable, and shameful. He hopes that his tomb will not be marked as his books are, but it is clear that the real threat is his internalized "shame," which no shroud can exclude. These circumstances can be contrasted to *Pandosto*'s epistle dedicatory and epistle to gentlemen readers, where the "shrowd" of Clifford's "patronage," or the gentlemen's "curtesie," need only protect the author against external attacks as "unlearned" or "imperfect" (Salzman, *Elizabethan*, 153–54). In retrospect, it is clear that these adjectives studiously avoid naming the printed format of his work. Greene's last textual shroud in *Greenes Vision* announces, in print, in the year that he filled the stationers' shops, his failure to negotiate a successful authorial relationship with print.

During his own lifetime, Sidney, too, felt irreconcilable pressures to imprint authorial fame and to avoid undue exposure by shrouding himself in others' names. Sidney seems to have eschewed print on principle, since no work certainly attributed to him was published during his lifetime; but he could not hide his work altogether. Publication was for the hopeful authors whose work he critiqued in his (manuscript) *Defence of Poetry*; it was not for someone like him who had "slipped into the title of a poet," "(I know not by what mischance) in these my not old years and idlest times."[51] The elaborate modesty of that remark is the most direct statement we have of Sidney's awareness that others saw him as a poet, and its denial of the title is almost persuasive. At the same time, he used manuscript publication boldly as early as 1578–89 (with his famous letter of advice to Queen Elizabeth). The earliest published references to the *Arcadia* worry the question of its circulation. In 1581, Thomas Howell, his sister's most humble household poet, published lines "Written to a most excellent Booke, full of rare invention"—the unpublished (probably still unfinished) *Old Arcadia*. Faithfully echoing the pastoral theory that Sidney developed in the *Defence of Poetry* (written between 1581 and 1583), Howell reports that this book contains "Discourse of Lovers, and such as folde sheepe, / Whose sawes well mixed, shrowds misteries deepe." Given Sidney's shrewd shrouding (or veiling) of his political content, Howell argues, he need not "hidste so perfit worke." Instead, he should "shewe they selfe and seeme no more unkinde," which might mean circulate, print, or merely complete the book. Then Howell advises:

Goe yet with speede I say thy charge delyver,
Thou needst not blushe, nor feare the foyle of blame:

The worthy Countesse see thou follow ever,
Till Fates doe fayle, maintaine her Noble name.

Attend her wyll, if she vouchsafe to call,
Stoope to her state, downe flat before her fall.[52]

Sidney should not only "delyver" his "charge" (presumably the finished book), but also abase himself to his sister in service to her "Noble," which is to say titled, name.

Howell's reference to Sidney's "Booke" as maintaining the Countess's name may allude to the book's title or coincidentally anticipate a later choice. When Sidney did name *The Countesse of Pembrokes Arcadia*, he both protected himself with "her Noble name," and offered his "toyfull booke" as a "stoop[ing]" to her in service. Thus Sidney shrouded his authorship under the name of his patron, and their family relationship shrouded her patronage. The title was a canny gesture for a young man whose proper aspiration would have been to be a patron like his well-placed sister, rather than an author.[53] It was apparently original: no earlier English book title follows the model of announcing itself as a woman patron's property. The first imitations naturally appeared in the Countess's own circle—Abraham Fraunce's *Countesse of Pembrokes Emanuel* (1591) and *Countesse of Pembrokes Ivychurch* (multiple parts in 1592).

Not surprisingly, this title pattern was appropriated by Greene himself for his last published romance.[54] The epistle to Greene's *Philomela. The Lady Fitzwaters Nightingale* (entered 1 July 1592) explains that his title is a compliment to Lady Fitzwater's husband but directed to her since everything else he had handy was "worthlesse of his Lordshipe." More tactfully, Greene says his title links the "far-spred" reputation of his dedicatee to that of Philomela. He is "imitating heerein Maister *Abraham France*, who titled the Lamentations of *Aminta* under the name of the Countesse of Pembrookes *Ivie Church*" (Grosart 11:109–10). For all of Greene's anxious comparisons in this dedication, the most obvious—of his own fiction to Sidney's—is never named. Matching the compliment with an insult in the tradition of the ladies' text, the letter to gentlemen readers justifies publishing a love pamphlet from his bottom drawer despite his vow "never to busie my selfe about any wanton pamphlets again"; this was "writ afore my vow, and published uppon duty to so honourable and bewtifull a Lady." Still, to protect his vow to male readers, he would have published the pamphlet "as an orphant without any name to father it" if not for the "earnest entreatie" of the printer for him to sign it (Grosart 11:113–14). The juxtaposed epistles slyly imply that only the printer's recognition of Greene's valuable name protected the chaste Lady Fitzwater from giving *her* name to a fatherless wanton pamphlet. The "orphant" also echoes Sidney's "child" in the epistle to his sister, which prefaced the 1590 *Countess of Pembrokes Arcadia*. Sidney agrees to "father" his romance on his sister's "desire," giving the child his authorial paternity, but her name; Greene affixes his authorial paternity only on the urging of the "printer." Sidney's name is buttressed by his sister's; Greene claims his is constructed by publishers. But it is also constructed via Greene's indirect appropriation of Sidney's appropriation of his sister's name to shroud his own romance. Sidney may have issued his title in manuscript, Greene in print, but both were remarkably subtle in their use of titling to devise new routes to self-authorization.

COPIES

Clearly, the other major circumstance encouraging Greene to find new ways to use his authorial name was booksellers' demand for print fiction. Greene's writings were some of their publishers' most valuable copies, according to his own boast. A number of sources confirm this, although all of them are also interested in producing his authorship in their own ways. The most famous evidence is posthumous, as in Harvey's attacks about Greene's endless shifting in the marketplace. Then there is Nashe's qualified defense in *Strange News* (1592): "in a night & a day would he have yarkt up a Pamphlet as well as in seaven yeare, and glad was that Printer that might bee so blest to pay him deare for the very dregs of his wit" (McKerrow, *Nashe*, 1:287). The remark is probably most reliable because it places Greene in a stronger position than Nashe himself, who in 1592 was living with his publisher, John Danter, probably taking room and board in lieu of cash payment. Nashe pointed out, meanwhile, that the penniless scholar Harvey was living with Wolfe, who was "keeping him . . . at livery" in repayment for the costs of publishing Harvey's unmarketable works (McKerrow, *Nashe*, 3:90, 1:258).[55] If Greene's publishers, conscious of a very close bottom line, were willing to pay more than the going rate in cash for his pamphlets, they must have been confident that his name could sell anything. The publisher Cuthbert Burby said so in the epistle he provided to *The Repentance of Robert Greene*: Greene's "pen in his lifetime pleased you as well on the Stage, as in the Stationers Shops" (Grosart 12:155). Of course, Burby's epistle was a sales pitch itself, and a strong one, since the *Repentance* was of dubious origins, having been entered by John Danter a month after Greene's death. The year 1594 brought nettled testimony from Thomas

Bowes, who had graduated with Greene from St. John's: "This fellow in his life time and in the middest of his greatest ruffe, had the Presse at commaundement to publish his lasciusous (sic) Pamphlets."[56] Greene really was widely recognized as a trade phenomenon, and that recognition was obviously self-perpetuating.

More objectively, during Greene's own lifetime, the sheer number of titles he succeeded in publishing, and of publishers involved in producing his fame, suggest that "Printers" were indeed "glad" of his works, and perhaps even competed for forthcoming material. The value Greene's works held for members of the Stationers' Company is underlined by the value the Register recorded in his name. The scribes were faithful in documenting the use of Greene's name in titles (starting, of course, with *Greenes Farewell to Folly*), and occasionally attributed other works to him, extra effort conferring some honor. Works listed as "by Greene" range from the lost ballad of 1581 to the political pamphlet *The Spanish Masquerado* (1589) and *Philomela* (1592). The problem of notoriety was that Greene could claim no monopoly on his name, so it also appears in works that contend with his, such as *The Defence of Conye Catchinge: or a confutacon of those ii Injurious pamphletes published by R. G. againste the pratisioners of many nymble witted and mistical sciences* (1592; authorship sometimes attributed to Greene), and, after his death, "Doctor Harvies *Letters and certen Sonnettes touchinge Roberte Greene and Thomas Nashe*" (Arber 2:609, 623). In the Stationers' Register, an environment concerned with securing property value to publishers (and only peripherally with reflecting authorial prestige), Greene's name is itself a valuable property, transferring easily to titles (advantageously for him and publishers alike) and to other, hostile authors (to his disadvantage). Its appropriation by other authors and by the publishers is one sign, even before his death, of the collaborative production of his fame. All of the appearances of Greene's name in the company's records would have redounded to his long-term reputation, since when copies were assigned to new owners, the Register was searched for old entries and their wording repeated in the new ones. But did this prominence confirm his authorial status or reduce him to a hack? The phenomenon of the "ordinary" author is too new, I would argue, for Greene's publishers to have been any more certain where his reputation would end up than he was himself.

Pandosto, as it happens, was not initially entered in the Stationers' Register, so bibliographers once assumed that it was first published for Thomas Cadman in 1588, the date of the first extant edition.[57] A recent study of a stationer's stock records offers evidence for an earlier edition, not to mention a reminder that books are shaped by their sellers as well as their writers. In 1958, Alexander Rodger published an analysis of a 1585 stationers' shop inventory, and identified a listing for "Triumphe of Time" as "an unrecorded first edition of *Pandosto*."[58] The 1585 record, itself a triumph of time, gives vivid clues to this lost edition's production. The shop had an astonishing nineteen copies in stock, compared to only a couple of copies of each part of *Euphues*. Two other Greene titles made a smaller presence: "7 mirror of modestie" and "i Antomy of fortune" (*sic*; both published in 1584; Rodger 252–53, 257). The latter is *Arbasto*; as with *Pandosto*, the scribe ignored the title's initial proper names for their descriptive phrases, perhaps seeing them as fuller records, or perhaps finding them easier to spell. The note of seven copies of Greene's *Myrrour* is important, because its only surviving edition was printed and published by none other than Roger Ward, who owned this shop. Ward's retention of so many copies of "Triumphe of Time" likely meant that he had an interest in it, too, as publisher or at least as printer.[59]

From this slim record, two scenarios for *Pandosto*'s unentered first publication may be spun out, giving slightly different pictures of the value of the manuscript in the publishers' marketplace. Ward could have printed the book for Thomas Cadman, who published the 1588 edition; Cadman had hired Ward for other projects, including two editions of Greene's *Spanish Masquerado* in 1589. Cadman entered that topical work in the Stationers' Register (as "by Greene"), but he did not enter *Planetomachia*, which he published in 1585. Or Ward could have published the book as his own acquisition, like *Myrrour*, and omitted the small expense of having it entered in the Register. He then might have sold the copy to Cadman, perhaps when he was clapped into jail for the debts that occasioned this inventory in the first place. It is more flattering to imagine Greene selling his *Pandosto* to Cadman than to a near-bankrupt Ward. But if Ward was the Stationers' angriest member, repeatedly harassed for setting up illegal suburban presses to publish catechisms pirated from the monopolist stationers, Cadman was almost as angry, and also sold Ward's pirated catechisms. The uncertain attribution of *Pandosto*'s first edition makes a fitting debut for a work whose place in the social register would be debated for so long.

Another indication of the breadth of *Pandosto*'s potential audience is that the shop being inventoried was neither Ward's legitimate print shop in London nor one of his surreptitious presses, but what appears to be a retail outlet in Shrewsbury. Ward's deep stock in the classics and textbooks identifies this shop's primary market as boys and masters from Shrewsbury School (Sidney's alma mater). If Ward printed *Pandosto*, he did so in London, but he clearly anticipated solid sales of the work in Shrewsbury as well. No fiction title is stocked in a larger quantity. Forty copies of *The Nine Worthies of London*, nonfiction citizen portraits by romance writer Richard Johnson, which Ward is known to have printed in 1584, are listed just above "Triumphe of Time" (Rodger 252). *Pandosto*, like *The Nine Worthies*, must have been printed in London, but the quantities available here suggests that Ward saw both titles as interesting to his Shrewsbury clientele. If Shrewsbury schoolboys (many of them upper class) were buying *Pandosto* from the start, they initiated an enduring tradition: chapbook versions of the romance would sell well to Rugby schoolboys two hundred years later (see chapter 4). On the other hand, *Pandosto* was a new book, and more sophisticated in title, style, and subject matter than *The Nine Worthies*, so it also would have made fashionable light reading for the boys' masters and tutors. To appeal to all ages, Ward's title page probably included the formula seen in every later edition of *Pandosto* (up to 1660): "Pleasant for age to avoid drowsy thoughts, profitable for youth to eschew other wanton pastimes, and bringing to both a desired content." Ward's inventory offers, however inconclusively, a picture of Greene's romance circulating from the start to readers well beyond London, appealing to a range of ages, and reaching male readers attached at some level to one of the nation's best schools—not just the degraded or even "middle-class" audience sometimes imagined for Greene.

Of Greene's romances, *Pandosto*, apparently introduced by the opportunists Ward and Cadman, would outlast those offered by the serious-minded Ponsonby. The importance of the difference in printers should not be exaggerated, however, especially since the second and third extant editions of *Pandosto* clearly show that it was in the mainstream of Elizabethan publishing and regarded as prestigious and profitable. The 1588 edition, now extant in a single imperfect copy, was printed for Cadman by Thomas Orwin (who also printed a good bit of Sidney and Shakespeare) (figure 1.4). It has a peritext elegant enough for its time, if not as elaborately bordered as *Mamillia* or as multiply verse-epistled as Ponsonby's *Arbasto* and *Gwydonius*. This copy presents *Pandosto* as a novelty, but a courtly one. Cadman certainly knew that courtly works were good opportunities: he had had a great success in 1584 with two comedies by Lyly, "played beefore the queenes majestie by her majesties children": *Campaspe* (three editions) and *Sapho and Phao* (two editions in 1584). Cadman stopped publishing in 1589, and the Lyly plays passed on to William Brome, who promptly reprinted them in 1591. A year later, Brome died. His widow, Joan Brome, not only retained those copies but also secured a virtual monopoly on Lyly's

PANDOSTO.

¶ The Triumph
of Time.

VVHEREIN IS DISCOVERED
by a pleasant Historie, that although by the meanes
of sinister fortune Truth may be concealed, yet by Time in spight of fortune it
is most manifestly reuealed.

Pleasant for age to auoyde drowsie thoughtes,
profitable for youth to eschue other wanton
pastimes, and bringing to both a de-
sired content.

Temporis filia veritas.

¶ *By Robert Greene* Maister of Artes
in *Cambridge.*

Omne tulit punctum qui miscuit vtile dulci.

Imprinted at London by *Thomas Orwin* for *Thomas*
Cadman, dwelling at the Signe of the *Bible,* neere
vnto the North doore of Paules,
1588.

FIGURE 1.4
Title page, Robert Greene's *Pandosto* (London, 1588; shelfmark 95.b.18/4).

plays.[60] Some assignments to Stationers' widows were short-term acts of charity, but Brome ran this large, well-established shop for ten years, leaving it to her apprentice on her death. Whether or not Brome read Lyly and Greene herself, she knew the value of these copies, and her later reissues were astute. For out of the several Greene titles that Cadman owned at his death and passed on to Brome, it was *Pandosto* that she republished in 1592—a well-timed choice, as I will show, and one that may have helped *Pandosto* to rise among Greene's works.

Three years later, Brome published *Pandosto* again, proving that the 1592 edition had sold steadily. Five years later, in 1597, she paid the Stationers' entrance fee to record, retroactively, her ownership of the copy to four books: *Pandosto*, *Campaspe*, *Sapho and Phao*, and one more serious title, Du Plessis de Mornay's *Trueness of Christian Religion*. This belated record of transfer is multiply interesting. It is the first appearance of *Pandosto* in the Register. Its wording tells something of Brome's position: the copies, "which were Thomas Cadmans" (William Brome is not mentioned), are hers "to enjoy Duringe her widowe[hood] or that she shalbe a free Stationers wife of this companye" (Arber 3:82). Above all, Brome's retroactive entering of these copies records her increasing awareness of their long-term value—or rather, her success in helping to produce that value. Reissuing these works on quick cycles, she was grooming the first three as leisure-reading classics; the last was already a theological classic. Further proof is that she issued *Pandosto* in 1600.[61]

Brome's nomination of *Pandosto* as an enduring title was seconded in 1601, upon her death, when her heir and former apprentice George Potter recorded the transfer of these four valuable titles (Arber 3:191). Potter apparently never published Lyly's plays, and he only published de Mornay once more, but he too found success with *Pandosto*, publishing it four times within twelve years—in 1607, 1609, 1614, and 1619. In the temporary joining of *Pandosto* and de Mornay in publishers' hands, the publishing histories of Greene and Sidney almost brush. As I will show, this translation of de Mornay, falsely attributed to Sidney at its 1587 debut, was the first instance of the frenzied trading in Sidney's name—and copies—that would begin at his death.

PAMPHLETS

The quiet disappearance of *Pandosto*'s first edition and the work's low-key survival into the next century must be contrasted with the much more aggressive collaborations between author and publisher that produced most of Greene's works from 1590 on. In the 1580s, Greene had apologized for publishing *Pandosto* as an "imperfect pamphlet"; in later titles, he and his publishers fully exploited the pamphlet qualities of brevity, imitativeness, and feigned carelessness. Sidney's works, meanwhile, although held apart from such imperfect forms of publication, could not withstand the demand for new material that characterized the late Elizabethan book market.

Greene's stationers did not merely publish him to meet demand but worked with him to heighten it. One of these joint strategies was the issuing of sequels. Greene's use of sequels had improved on Lyly, but with the coney-catching pamphlets it became an elaborate dodge. *A Notable Discovery of Cosenage* and *The Second Parte of Connye Katchinge* were entered in the register on 13 December 1591, the first to Edward White and Thomas Nelson, the second to William Wright, "to be printed always for him by John Wolf," a peculiar stipulation that suggests Wolfe had disputed Wright's ownership of the title. In any case, the first extant editions of both were printed by Wolfe. The same year, Wolfe and Wright reissued the second part as "The Second and Last Part," while a "Thirde and Last Part" was entered to Thomas Scarlet, who had meanwhile picked up the job of printing the first part. The apparent battle for the "last part" suggests just how desirable a commodity Greene's series had become. The always aggressive Wolfe would go on to publish the most sensational success of 1592, Greene's *Quip for an Upstart Courtier*, and to print the runner-up, *Greenes Groatsworth of Wit*. Edwin Haviland Miller points out that with six impressions of 1,500 copies selling at sixpence apiece, Wolfe probably netted £100.[62] The simultaneous registration of the first two parts suggests that stationers and author were conspiring to their mutual benefit (or that Greene was making the stationers "pay dear" and they were trying to make the best of it). The publishers apparently cooperated in commissioning the custom woodcuts of skinny rabbits dressed as would-be urbanites. The investment certainly suggests they were all counting on multiple editions.

The advantages of publishing a work in parts bear analysis, since they confirm the historical conditions that enabled Greene to turn from composition for patronage to composition for paid publication. For the publisher, dividing one pamphlet into two would not greatly increase the profit, since price was determined by the number of signatures. However, division certainly allowed for more padding. Meanwhile, for the author, contemporary references suggest that one pamphlet might earn a nominal gift of £2 from a patron, while, if the author were a known seller, a publisher might pay him £2 for the manuscript.[63] An author unsure of regular patronage could send out dedications blindly and gamble on getting the £2 gift on his luckier guesses, but an author of assured marketability could bring in a certain £2 payment for each title. Exploiting his marketability, Greene adapted the stationers' economy of the pamphlet to named authorship. Frequent, short titles with quick sales would be more profitable than widely spaced, ambitious, or enduring works. Publishers were precocious among the early modern crafts in mass-producing consumer goods speculatively (that is, in advance of demand), and "pamphlets" began to denote that speculative quality. Greene was precocious among early modern authors in experimenting with his own place in that economy, and more or less gave up his tenuously gentle status by doing so.

Gradually, Greene does seem to have increased his profits within his position as romance writer, by recirculating material already published in his work or others' (a common Elizabethan practice), publishing his romances in quick sequence, and moving to shorter fictional forms. These early concessions to the market (if they were not his preferred practice) apparently did him little harm in the eyes of his targeted readers, scholars and courtiers. The coney-catching pamphlets represented a more radical departure that might have killed his reputation as a romance writer had poverty not killed him first. This about-face, which has always been seen as the inevitable outcome of Greene's calculated popularity, suggests to me that Greene's earlier calculations were imperfect; his alleged "success" as a writer apparently left him in a position he could not afford to maintain. The logic of the marketplace explains why his authorial fame backfired: selling titles was better than finding patrons in the short run, but as works went into multiple editions, Greene may have had trouble selling new works in the old genres, having saturated the market. The old titles, buoyed by his fame, went into repeat impressions that benefited only the publishers, who held sole right to the copies. Only the first sale would generate income for the author. It was to Greene's advantage to write highly ephemeral material that publishers would buy once—and only print once—but his very fame made it impossible that the appeal of his titles would expire so quickly. Greene never entirely held "the Presse at commaundement," as Bowes complained; if he had, he would not have died in abject poverty, no matter how dissolute his personal habits.

This irony was not understood by his contemporaries. Nashe suggested that Greene's carelessness was attributable to lack of authorial foresight: "Hee made no account of winning credite by his workes, as thou [Harvey] dost . . . his only care was to have a spel in his purse to conjure up a good cuppe of wine with at all times" (McKerrow, *Nashe*, 1:287). That theory of Greene as a poor controller of authorial "credite" is inadequate to explain the bind in which Greene found himself (as are the prevailing explanations of his calculated "popularity"). The works of his last years should be thought of not as simply popular but as strongly topical, for topicality brought cash, while broad-based, sustained popularity would bring only "credit," of which Greene had more than he needed. Thus, his most calculated works were *not* those that would survive the longest as popular bestsellers; Greene made no special claims for *Pandosto*, which became a bestseller in the hands of future generations of coproducers.

There was no single turning point in Greene's life from self-authorization to calculation, or from the pose of exclusivity to the embrace of circulation. Even after Greene began to put his authorial name in his titles, he returned periodically to shroud himself in associations with university culture or with other authors. The last romances he published, interspersed among the repetitive autobiographical and coney-catching pamphlets, vigorously assert his appeal to an exclusive audience. *Philomela. The Lady Fitzwaters Nightingale* is most obvious. Two romances of 1589 have more scholarly peritexts than Greene's other works: Greek and Latin verses accompany *Ciceronis Amor*, a love story starring the hero of rhetoric; the young Thomas Nashe's cocky "Preface to the Gentlemen Students of both Universities" appears in Greene's full-length pastoral, *Menaphon. Camillas alarum to Slumbering Euphues*. These late-career courtly romances were the Greene titles that went into multiple editions in the Jacobean period, retaining favor with male and female readers. They have also been favored by modern critics for their relatively uneuphuistic style and their generic innovations. The title of *Pandosto* may fit the pattern of Greene's earlier romances, but its reception has coincided most closely with the 1589 romances, *Menaphon* and *Ciceronis Amor*.

Of Greene's late romances, *Menaphon* is the most valuable in understanding both *Pandosto*'s emergence as a favorite Greene title and the common conditions of publication that produced both *Pandosto* and *Arcadia*. *Menaphon*, appearing in 1589, and *Pandosto*, appearing in 1585, may now be recognized as works of strong originality, coinciding with developments in the *Arcadia* rather than dependent on it. Today, these are Greene's most-read romance titles, often linked as pastoral romances (and as "imitations" of Sidney). Indeed, the main critical resistance to moving the publication date of *Pandosto* to 1585 is that doing so separates it from *Menaphon*. But an earlier

date for *Pandosto* can sharpen our awareness of Greene's generic innovation—in the peculiarly Renaissance sense of finding new Continental and
classical models to adapt. The presence of an extensive pastoral episode in
Pandosto does not hinder redating it from 1588 to 1585, since Greene had
explored pastoral in earlier romances, had mixed pastoral prose and verse in
several works, and had developed a distinctive note of native earthiness in
assimilating the Continental models.[64] The same claim can be made about
the influence of Heliodorus in *Pandosto*: Greene knew the work before 1585,
because he mentions the famous lovers Theagenes and Chariclea in *Mamillia*, as casually as Sidney mentions them in his contemporary, but closely
guarded, manuscript *Defence* (Grosart 2:67). Heliodorus was, after all, readily available in Thomas Underdowne's translation (1577 and reprints). Still,
Pandosto was the fullest response to the *Aethiopica* yet published in Elizabethan fiction, whether in 1585 or 1588, picking up its plot of a lost princess
restored, its shipwrecks and oracles, and even its theatricality.

"Published," of course, is the key term, for literary historians measure
Greene's innovations in the 1580s against Sidney's work on the *Old Arcadia* and its revision in the first half of the decade. The generic innovations
of *Pandosto*, Heliodoran and a little pastoral, and *Menaphon*, full-scale pastoral, have often been read as imitative of Sidney, as though it would not
have occurred to Greene to explore these resources independently. But
Greene's earlier works show that as he turned away from Lyly, he did pull
ideas from the same models that gave Sidney his "webb"—"*Heliodorus* in
greeke, Sanazarus *Arcadia* in Italian, and *Diana de montemaior* in Spanish"—
or at least from their English translations.[65] *Menaphon* has stimulated argument about Greene's access to the *Old Arcadia*. Long ago, Wolff pointed out
that not just certain plot elements but also the key characters' names
seemed to be variants on Sidney's (443). But the styles and tone differ
vastly; Thomas Lodge's *Rosalynde* (1590) seems to more closely approximate the texture of Sidney's first version. Other critics have been skeptical
about other writers' access to the *Arcadia*, basing their objections on the
social distance between Sidney and the likes of Greene and Lodge. For
Woudhuysen, the possibility that Lodge saw a manuscript (perhaps sharing it with Greene) is tantalizing, because if the socially marginalized
Lodge (a suspected recusant) had access to a manuscript, it was circulating
far beyond Sidney circles (302–3).[66]

The resemblances between *Menaphon* (1589) and the *Old Arcadia* are primarily names, former character names, which can be explained if Greene
had access not to a manuscript but only to a grapevine. In 1589, *Menaphon*

had a Lylyesque subtitle, "Camillas alarum to slumbering Euphues." In 1599, it gained a Sidneyesque half title, "Greenes Arcadia." Euphues, Greene, Arcadia: the series compactly names the three successive leaders in Elizabethan fiction. The half title seems to be only a half reference to Sidney's unpublished manuscript, unlike the unmistakable and unabashed borrowing from the printed book that would appear three years later in *Philomela. The Lady Fitzwaters Nightingale.* By 1592, even Harvey was forced to read Greene's titles as advertising a resemblance to his adored Sidney, when he said that "the Countesse of Pembrokes Arcadia is not greene enough for queasie stomackes, but they must have *Greenes* Arcadia." His prediction was accurate: eventually, the first title was dropped, and the work was republished as *Greenes Arcadia* in 1610, 1616, and 1657 (presumably intervening editions have been lost).

A more intriguing possibility is that *Menaphon* borrowed the names of Sidney's characters not from a manuscript or oral source but from a printed version. In fact, Sidney's containment of *Arcadia* in manuscript had began to leak as early as 1588. Abraham Fraunce's *Arcadian Rhetorike* was published in 1588 as a compliment to the Pembroke household, in which Fraunce served as tutor and poet. Fraunce illustrated the possibilities of rhetoric with examples from classical and modern literatures; his decision to give examples from the *Arcadia* constitutes the first certain appearance of Sidney's works in print, and his pointed placement of Arcadian examples under each heading has been heralded by modern scholars as an important landmark in the canonization of Sidney as a literary author. Yet the capacity of this work to disseminate Sidney's exclusive manuscript, to open up what had been sealed, has not been appreciated. The truth is that Fraunce, in praising Sidney, made him public. The speech tags that Fraunce provided for sterling rhetorical examples from the *Arcadia* would have given Greene enough information to work out the main characters in a manuscript to which he was denied access by his class disposition. All of the character and place names that Wolff notes as Greene's possible borrowings from the *Arcadia* appeared in Fraunce's *Arcadian Rhetorike*: Pamela (Samela in *Menaphon*), Pyrocles (Democles), Dorus (Doron), Arcadia, and Thessaly.[67] Writing *Menaphon* a year after Fraunce's work appeared, Greene could plug Sidney's names into his own expert knowledge of pastoral and Heliodoran conventions. This theory does not deny, of course, that Greene was imitating Sidney, but it refines that imitation and highlights Greene's resourcefulness and parallel literary interests. It also demonstrates that Greene did not violate manuscript secrecy to do his borrowing: bits of Sidney's work were brought forth into the world of print, and Greene met them there. As creative writers and as entrants in print, Sidney and Greene converged.

Greene knew of Sidney's *Arcadia* secondhand in 1589, then, but could not follow it extensively until 1592, after its publication. Those facts serve to credit Greene with originality in devising the pastoral *Menaphon*; they also mark the successive stages that brought Sidney's work into the realm of publication Greene had occupied for so long. Greene's partial knowledge of the *Arcadia* in 1589 did not require access to a manuscript through what Molyneux had called a "special deere freend" of Sidney's family, for that exclusivity was eroding rapidly. Molyneux's own comment was published in 1587, for one thing; and if Greene wanted to know more about this "booke . . . named *Arcadia*," he could have drawn on his innumerable publisher contacts, since its copy was already the subject of contention. In 1587, no publisher would have known more about the potential publication of *Arcadia* than William Ponsonby, who in that year issued the second edition of Greene's *Gwydonius* (it had sold out in just three years).

It might have been Ponsonby's success in selling Greene's prose romance—as well as some higher principles—that led him to take an extraordinary interest in Sidney's romance in November 1586. Stepping out of the normal role of a stationer on motivations that can only be inferred, the young publisher effectively appointed himself as negotiator between the forces of print circulation and authorially sanctioned control.[68] Ponsonby approached Sidney's friend Fulke Greville to tell him that "ther was one in hand to print, sr philip sydneys old arcadia"; indeed, that the manuscript had already been forwarded to the ecclesiastical censors. Having guessed that the unidentified stationer had gotten the manuscript by unauthorized means, Ponsonby asked Greville whether this publication scheme had the consent of Sidney's "frends." Greville, a statesman who had never published anything in his life, and who displayed his ignorance of the print trade by identifying his visitor as "one ponsonby a bookebynder in poles church yard," immediately recognized the urgency of the problem, and wrote the frantic letter to Sir Francis Walsingham from which I am quoting (Woudhuysen 416). The letter urged Walsingham to action to protect the reputation of his late son-in-law, but Greville's plan was not simply to withhold the work from publication. Rather, he wanted to publish the revised version that Sidney had left to him in a unique copy, "fitter to be printed then that first which is so common." Evidently, manuscript circulation was out of control even before the stationers got involved. Greville's letter also suggested that Sidney's reputation could be protected by publishing his translations of devotional works. Sadly, one of these, "du plessis book agains atheisme," was "since donn by an other"; but out of respect for Sidney's "Judgement, I think fit ther be made a stey of that mercenary book to." It required the "care of his frends . . . to see to the paper & other common errors of mercenary printing"; any "Gayn" could be "disposed" to "the poorest of his servants" (Woudhuysen 416). Greville's repetition of "mercenary" and his apologies to Walsingham for troubling him with the matter convey a sense of shock: Sidney's friends and family were unprepared to see him thrust this quickly into the print marketplace and realized they had to cooperate in the business of publication. Keeping the works exclusively in manuscript was no longer possible, now that Sidney was not alive to defend his name.

In the case of the translation from Du Plessis de Mornay, it was probably already too late. The title had been assigned in the Stationers' Register to Cadman on 7 November, a date suspiciously just two days after Sidney's body arrived in London. Cadman published it in 1587 with this embarrassing title page: "*A Woorke Concerning the Trewnesse of the Christian Religion*. Begun to be translated by Sir P. Sidney and finished by A. Golding." Little or none of this translation was Sidney's. The family probably regretted the false publicity, but at least the work was virtuous. This dubious attribution marked the first appearance of Sidney's name as author of a printed book, and it announced the beginning of the print market's relentless push to appropriate that name. This work would later travel with *Pandosto* through the Stationers' Register, transferred from Cadman to Brome and then Potter. The connection is less an accident of the marketplace than a confirmation of the value of both authors' names, however spuriously assigned.

Meanwhile, for his tact (and ingenuity), Ponsonby was rewarded with the privilege of publishing an *Arcadia* approved by Sidney's self-appointed literary executors. The entry in the Register, dated 23 August 1588, privileges the author's name: "a booke of Sir Philip Sidneys makinge intitled Arcadia" and "a translation of *Salust de Bartas*. Done by the same Sir P. in the English" (the latter, which looks like Greville's brainchild, never appeared) (Arber). This *Arcadia*'s appearance, if not its text, should be thought of as a collaborative product: the decision to publish was negotiated between November 1586 and this entrance, among Ponsonby, Walsingham, Greville, and the Countess. It may be that at the time Greene published *Menaphon*, Ponsonby was still waiting for a final manuscript from the editorial team put together by Greville and the Countess. Scholarship on the editing of the 1590 *Arcadia* has identified a power struggle among those attempting to generate a text. Greville's letter mentions righteously that Sidney had left him the new *Arcadia*, and "a direction . . . undre his own hand how & why" it was to be further "amended," but it also admitted that he had sent the revised manuscript to the Countess on her request. The Countess, by virtue of the book's name and its letter of dedication, had her own proprietary interest.

The prospect of publication invited each coproducer to develop his or her own vision of Sidney's authorship, and the negotiation among those visions continued through the 1590 edition (three books of the revised version, in quarto); the 1593 edition (the "combined" edition in five books, in folio) and the 1598 edition (in folio, with Sidney's other secular writings). Woudhuysen seems to favor Greville's vision of a "Protestant knight" over the Countess's view of her brother as "a secular writer of erotic works," which prevailed in the 1598 volume (235). Michael Brennan, on the other hand, discounts Greville's efforts, crediting the rise in Sidney's reputation to "the combined efforts of the Countess of Pembroke and William Ponsonby in ensuring the transmission of his compositions through print."[69] The larger point is, of course, how fully the family circle became involved in the process of shaping an authorial reputation, and how strongly that process was stimulated by the efforts of stationers, more and less benign. As Victor Skretkowicz puts it, describing the 1593 composite text, Sidney "was being *marketed* now as the creator of a massive and complex work embracing both the heroic and romance traditions."[70] Ponsonby's trustworthiness became an important stimulant to authorizing not only Sidney's publications but also those from living members of the circle: as unofficial house publisher he brought out Fraunce's various offerings to the Countess, and her own volume of translations.

The family was overconfident, however, in their capacity to control the circulation of Sidney's "toys" now that he was dead. In 1591, the unauthorized publication of *Astrophil and Stella* provoked another crisis, harder to reconstruct. This quarto invited trouble: it had an appendix of poems misattributed to other authors and two very knowing epistles. All of these elements were dropped from a second quarto published in the same year. One epistle was from the publisher, Thomas Newman, claiming that the sequence had "spred abroad in written Coppies"; he had gotten help in correcting this "corruption" and "restoring it to his first dignitie" (Garrett 118–19). The other was by Thomas Nashe, fulsomely claiming the Countess had authorized the surely shocking publication, while inscribing it as a stolen ladies' text. Poetic fame, Nashe crowed, may "be oftentimes imprisoned in Ladyes casks . . . , yet at length it breakes foorth in spight of his keepers, and useth some private penne (in steed of a picklock) to procure his violent enlargement" (McKerrow, *Nashe*, 3:330). Nashe's epistle justifies book piracy as the liberation of poetry from the privileged confinements of ladies' caskets and gentlemen's manuscript caches. Tellingly, however, no one involved in this first quarto dared to put Sidney's full name (just "Sir P. S.") on the title page, an evasion that neutralized Nashe's praise of "So excellent a Poet, (the least sillable of whose name, sounded in the eares of judgement, is able to give the meanest line he writes a dowry of immortality)" (McKerrow, *Nashe*, 3:329). Sidney's name might immortalize whatever he wrote, but it could not be imprinted with the lines stolen away from his family's control.

Perhaps the rather squalid circumstances of the sonnets' publication led the Countess to hire Hugh Sanford, a sometime family secretary, to help her re-dress the *Arcadia*'s second edition in more dignity than the first. Part of Sanford's work was an epistle explaining away the "disfigured face" of the 1590 version. Borrowing Sidney's language from the letter to his sister, Sanford called it a "childe" misdelivered on the "fathers untimely death." The Countess's textual revisions, including grafting on the last two books from the *Old Arcadia*, made the work "as it was, for her: as it is, by her" (Garrett 134–35). The social stature of the book was also raised by peritextual changes: a new folio format, an elaborate title page drawing on heraldic and classical elements, the omission of the florid chapter titles (too reminiscent of chivalric romances?). But the entrance of a printed book into public comment could not be forestalled, and the differences between the editions provoked more squabbling. John Florio, who had provided the chapter titles for the 1590 edition, said in print that the 1593 version was not just a hybrid but incompetent. History repeated itself in 1595, when Ponsonby had to fight to protect his rights to the *Defence of Poetrie*, entered in November 1594; in April 1595, Henry Olney managed to enter "An apologie for poetrie," suspiciously without an author's name. When Olney began printing the essay, Ponsonby complained, got the duplicate entry canceled, and apparently negotiated the right to sell Olney's copies with his own title page. Ponsonby and the Countess of Pembroke solved the problem of these challengers the only possible way: in 1598, they published the *Arcadia* with *Astrophil and Stella*, the *Defence*, and *The Lady of May*, in a volume dedicated to the Queen herself. The volume was not presented as Sidney's "works"—it would be another generation before Samuel Daniel took vernacular writing that seriously—but it had a solidly pre-emptive effect on spurious publication. The publisher and the family had built a monopoly in Sidney, an edifice of authorial respectability that left no room for any other stationer to profit.

The struggles over publishing Sidney's works reveal the confrontation between a social circle that had assumed its exclusivity and a profession newly bold in circulating anything it could acquire. As Molyneux implied and Woudhuysen has theorized, Sidney's careful adjudication of the circulation of his poetry and of the *Old Arcadia*, together with their inherent merits, led owners of his works in manuscript to value them highly as *authorial* productions. The high value of Sidney's name made these works, while in manuscript, difficult to keep out of print, and, once in print, difficult to protect from reappropriation. The early manuscript controls only heightened later demands for print. In sum, the pressure to circulate his works demanded constant vigilance from those who favored control and led to the production of new forms of distinction.

If cultural aristocrats could not maintain a barrier between manuscript and print, they had to draw lines within the field of print. (The Jacobean revival of manuscript culture would try to solve the problem another way.) The title of Sidney's work had been a successful signal of exclusivity, and the protective quality of the Countess's patronage was developed and emphasized. The engraved title page of the 1593 edition was an extravagance not granted to Greene's romances; the 1598 folio definitively separated Sidney, master of multiple genres, from writers like Greene whose every work—romance, tract, drama—appeared in quarto, which is to say, as a pamphlet. Still, much later, Greville would express his regrets about the publication of the *Arcadia*, "as much inferior to that unbounded spirit of his as . . . other men's works are many times raised above the writers' capacities." He claimed that Sidney had condemned "this unpolished embryo" to the fire (countering the letter to his sister that rescued the child from desertion). Sidney's youthful works, Greville insisted, "were scribbled rather as pamphlets for entertainment of time and friends than any account of himself to the world."[71] "Pamphlets" is a revealing revision of the previous letter's reference to writing in "loose sheets": both terms connote ephemerality and underdevelopment, but as Halasz has shown, the pamphlet's peculiar associations in this period are with the speculative quality of print. Greville admitted in this retrospective passage that Sidney's works were difficult to protect once they came to print because the problems of manuscript and print circulation were not so different in the first place.

GHOSTS

Greene understood the print world better than Sidney or his circle, but even he could not control it: his authorial name was developed more publicly and deliberately than Sidney's but proved even less effectual in protecting the boundaries of his work. After Sidney's death, his authorial name was raised to pre-eminence by his loving survivors; after Greene's death, his name was appropriated as an authorial ghost by a host of speculators. As evidence of the market's voracity, the flood of Ponsonby Pembrokiana in 1592 complemented the rash of pamphlets offered by and about the dying Greene. As evidence of the market's ruthlessness, the letters in the first quarto of *Astrophil and Stella* can be compared to the most shameless posthumous appropriations of Greene's name. Some, like Danter's preface to *Greenes Funeralls* (1594), reveled in violating privacy: these slight verses on Greene were written by "R.B." as "his private study at idle times," but Danter was publishing them "contrarie to the Authors expectation," in order to give readers "one daies pleasure in reading this Pamphlet."[72] In Greene's case as in Sidney's, Nashe could be relied on to both give the name-stealing game away and start playing a tougher one. When he heard of Greene's death in September 1592, he added a new feature to *Pierce Penniless*, which had gone to a second edition within months: the facetiously titled "private Epistle of the Author to *the Printer*." Its conceit was to list other items that Nashe could have attached to his "meer toy" in its second edition: "Had you not beene so forward in the republishing of it, you shold have had certayne Epistles to Orators and Poets, to insert . . . ; As namely, to the Ghost of *Machevill*, of *Tully*, of *Ovid* . . . ; and lastly, to the Ghost of *Robert Greene*, telling him, what a coyle there is with pamphleting on him after his death" (McKerrow, *Nashe*, 1:153). Had this epistle existed, it would have recorded Greene's ghost's report about which of the pamphlets of 1592 were *by* Greene, and which *on* him: but Nashe's text is itself a ghost.

Plenty of other authors were willing to write about Greene's ghost, picking up on the game that had started with Greene's own alleged glimpses of ghosts of Gower and Chaucer in *Greenes Vision*. The most developed conjuring was stationer Henry Chettle's *Kind-Hartes Dream, Contein-*

ing five Apparitions with their Invectives against abuses raigning, which brought out the ghost of Greene along with those of Tarlton, the comic player; Anthony Now Now, a ballad singer; William Cuckoe, a juggler; and Master Doctor Burcot, for what Halasz has analyzed as a debate on "the production and circulation of discourse" (48). One irony was that all this material followed Chettle's preface, which justified his role in circulating *Greenes Groatsworth of Wit.* Greene, Chettle calmly explains, had died "leaving many papers in sundry Booke sellers hands." All Chettle had done was "writ it over, and as neare as I could" for "Greenes hand was none of the best, [but] licensd it must be."[73] Chettle's preface denied having interpolated *Groatsworth*'s offensive passage insulting the players (or, for that matter, having written the whole pamphlet); it implied that unauthorized posthumous publication was business as usual. But while Chettle claimed in his epistle that he was a mere stationer and no ghostwriter, the rest of *Kind-Hartes Dream* amply proved his facility in writing ghosts—so much that it may have undercut the denial for knowing readers.

Ghostwriting Greene had become almost honest work, and others were inspired to follow. B. R. (Barnabe Rich) brought out *Greenes Newes both from Heaven and Hell* (1593), of which the best part was the rest of the title: "Prohibited the first for writing of Bookes, and banished out of the last for displaying of *Conny-catchers*." The title's failure to specify that it was Greene's *wanton* books that kept him out of heaven—generalizing his sin to all his writing (except his crime exposés)—confirmed the discovery that Greene had made in *Greenes Vision*. Rich's pamphlet goes on to create an early canon of Greene's topical and autobiographical works, with nary a mention of the romances that Greene would once have considered the worst offenders. Rich mounts a disquisition between the much-missed writer and characters from the sensation of summer 1592, *A Quip for an Upstart Courtier.* Ghost-Greene explains to Cloth breeches and Velvet breeches, as they all travel reluctantly toward St. Peter, that they should all have reviewed his books in time to learn their errors: "if you had but seene *Greenes farewell to folly*, me thinkes the bare tytle, without turning over leafe to looke further into the matter, might have moved you" (B2). *Greene's Ghost Haunting Conie-catchers*, published by Samuel Rowlands in 1602, is the tail end of the sequence, but more interesting is John Dickenson's *Greene in Conceipt* (1598). Dickenson's central story is a tale of domestic virtue tested, told in a mixture of euphuistic and earthy styles, not a particularly slavish imitation of Greene. But the frame presents the tale as having been dictated to Dickenson by Greene's ghost (his preface, meanwhile, dismisses that frame as a "humor" [A2v]). Delightfully, the title page's woodcut illustrates the ghost, "suted in deaths livery," writing the tale out for himself (figure 1.5). The pictured writer does not particularly fit Nashe's memorable description of Greene—his hair is disappointingly short and hidden under the folds of the shroud;[74] it is an apparition without authority, suitably enough. Instead of a miserable garret, he enjoys a capacious chair and a well-equipped writing table, and he appears to be writing boustrophedon, as though in Greek. The details of the image thus memorialize Greene the scholar, reflecting the taste of Dickenson, who would write his remaining works in Latin. But this conjuring of Greene's ghost so as to appropriate his name makes sense only through the events of the preceding years and in an emphatically vernacular and topical frame.[75]

In the years after his death, then, Greene the author had a double image: the scandalous pamphleteer had not entirely displaced the scholarly romance writer. But that double image did not mean a divided audience, for many were familiar with Greene in both guises. Nor had Greene's courtly efforts been rendered obsolete by the *Arcadia*'s appearance in the market for print fiction, the way Lyly's romances had been disappearing in the face of Greene's metamorphic competition. Nor did Greene's sordid final year, the media event that he apparently rigged up around his illness, repentance, and death, and the exploitation of that event by Nashe, Harvey, and Chettle drag Greene's name down far enough to discredit his romances. The continued life of Greene's works, particularly his most sophisticated titles, depended upon two stationers who were unfazed by his seamier developments. One is Ponsonby, who despite his busy schedule publishing Pembrokiana took the opportunity to reissue *Gwydonius* when it sold out again in 1593, and *Mamillia* Part 2 the same year. These titles were printed by Thomas Creede, who also printed Ponsonby's 1595 issue of Sidney's *Defence*. The other is Joan Brome, the only publisher known to have reissued one of Greene's elegant romances during 1592: *Pandosto*. Their reprintings of these works, along with regular reprints of *Ciceronis Amor* and *Arbasto*, guaranteed that Greene's name would continue to be associated with artful, full-length fictions as well as short, sensational pamphlets. Brome and Ponsonby would not have reissued these lengthier titles without substantial confidence that they would sell. As the most successful woman publisher and the most careful literary publisher of the 1590s, Brome and Ponsonby also signal that Greene's appeal to readers of both genders was not a sign of social degradation.

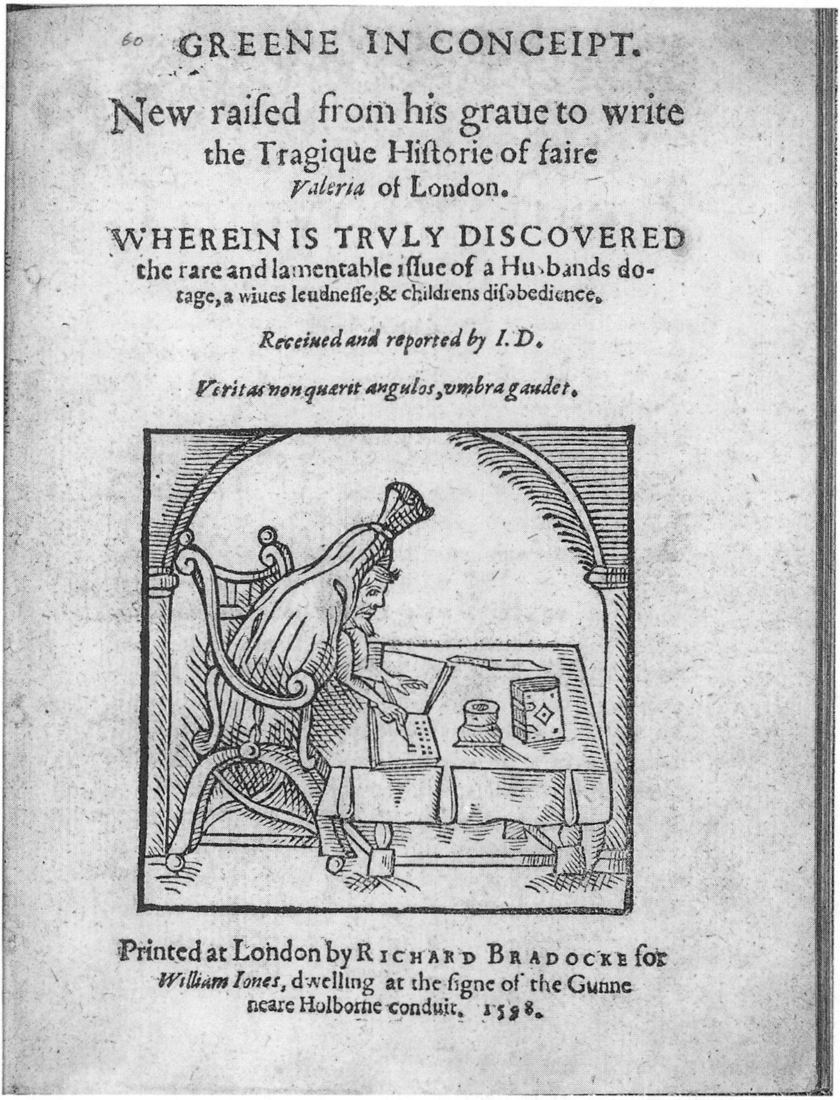

60 GREENE IN CONCEIPT.

New raiſed from his graue to write the Tragique Hiſtorie of faire *Valeria* of London.

WHEREIN IS TRVLY DISCOVERED the rare and lamentable iſſue of a Husbands dotage, a wiues lewdneſſe, & childrens diſobedience.

Receiued and reported by I. D.

Veritas non quærit angulos, vmbra gaudet.

Printed at London by RICHARD BRADOCKE for *William Iones*, dwelling at the ſigne of the Gunne neare Holborne conduit. 1598.

FIGURE 1.5
Title page, John Dickenson, *Greene in Conceipt* (London, 1598), representing Greene in his shroud.

The limited evidence about the audience for Greene in the first decade after his death suggests that the works that now seem popular—ephemeral pamphlets, overbilled crime sheets—and those that now seem more elite—the full-length romances—were equally well known. So were the dramas, which came into print only after 1592. Greene's fame in each genre of writing probably added excitement to readers' experience of his work in the others. That is the implication of Francis Meres's anthology of 1598, *Palladis Tamia, Wits Treasury*. This volume is a famous landmark in Sidney's reception because in his "comparative discourse of our English poets with the Greeke, Latine, and Italian poets," Meres consistently puts Sidney at the head of several lists of generic "bests." Greene is listed here among the "best Poets for Comedy" (quoted in Smith 2:320). But in the final pages of the section, Meres's similes become more jocular, and Greene makes a more prominent showing: "As *Achilles* tortured the dead body of *Hector* . . . : so *Gabriell Harvey* hath shewed the same inhumanitie to *Greene* that lies full low in his grave"; as "*Archesilaus Prytanoeus* perished by wine at a drunken feast . . . so *Robert Greene* died of a surfet taken at pickeld herrings and Rhenish wine, as witnesseth *Thomas Nashe*, who was at the fatall banquet" (quoted in Smith 2:323, 324). The posthumous invectives of 1592 have dragged Greene's name through the mud, which Meres is happy to sling again. Sadly, Meres does not address prose romances; it would be interesting to see how he would fit Greene's courtly titles into his pioneering taxonomy of English authors.

Greene had become memorable not just for these colorful events or for the variety of his works but for their sheer number. *Greenes Funeralls* helpfully provided readers with a verse "Catalogue of certaine of his Bookes":

Camilla *for the first and second part.*
The Card of Fancie, *and his* Tullies love.
His Nunquam Sera, *and his* Nightingale.
His Spanish Masquerado, *and his* Change.
His Menaphon, *and* Metamorphosis.
His Orpharion, *and the* Denmarke King.
His Censure, *and his* Loves Tritameron.
His Disputation, *and the* Death of him,
That makes all England shed so many teares:
And many more that I have never seene
   May witnes well unto the world his wit,
   Had he so well, as well applied it. (McKerrow, *Greenes Newes*, 83)

The list is heavily weighted toward the courtly romances, *Mamillia*, *Gwydonius*, *Ciceronis Amor*, *Philomela*, and *Arbasto* (the "Denmarke King"). That and the "tears" probably reflect the tastes of Richard Barnfielde, the likeliest author of the volume. But the set is rounded out with the most topical pamphlets, including those on the Spanish, the Royal Exchange, and the disputation of coney-catchers, and even with the most sensational autobiographical items, *Never Too Late* and the *Repentance* ("Death of him"). Sixteen works, half of Greene's nondramatic output, are listed; but amazingly, *Pandosto*, the work that would last the longest, is not mentioned.

If R.B. is representative of Greene's readers, the literature of courtship could coexist with the literature of sensation. Between them was no gulf, but a certain tension. Only writers as well-placed and high-minded as Greville and the Countess of Pembroke could try to participate in the former field without contacting the latter; and they were not entirely successful. Still, their early efforts to barricade the most elite printed productions prefigure the next century's more widespread and obvious raising of gentle authorship. The prestige accorded to "Sir Philip Sidney," posthumously created an author, would set examples for constructing the privilege of Jacobean literary gentlemen. The beginnings of that differentiation in poetic culture are present in Meres's ratings and the canonizing effects of the other printed anthologies of 1598–1600. A need to similarly differentiate fiction is forecast in Meres's chapter listing books "to be censured of" as "hurtfull to youth," a futile condemnation of all the chivalric romances, most of which would be reprinted through the following century and made into chapbooks.[76] The project of social distinction among print fictions would progressively narrow Greene's canon throughout the seventeenth century. Yet by a series of contingencies that the next chapters will detail, *Pandosto. The Triumph of Time*, a mere ghost in Ward's catalogue in 1585, absent from R.B.'s catalogue in 1594, would be the last of Greene's romances to survive, well into the nineteenth century.

For an author, the first triumph of time is staying in print. As no less popular an author than John Taylor the Water-Poet explained later, "In paper many a Poet now survives / Or else their lines had perish'd with their lives" (*The Praise of Hemp-seed* [1620]). Taylor went on to list a poetic canon in which Greene remains, now clearly subordinated to Sidney:

Old *Chaucer*, *Gower*, and Sir *Thomas More*,
Sir *Philip Sidney*, who the Lawrell wore,

Spenser and *Shakespeare* did in Art excelle
Sir Edward *Dyer*, *Greene*, *Nash*, *Daniell*,
Silvester, *Beumont*, Sir *John Harrington*,
Forgetfulnesse their workes would overrun
But that in paper they immortally
Do live in spight of death, and cannot die.[77]

"Forgetfulnesse" might "overrun" the reputation of an untitled, unlaureled author. But Greene could live "immortally"—or at least in modest persistence—in paper and print, as long as his name appeared on editions of *Pandosto*. That the materiality of print allowed an ordinariness more resilient than personal notoriety was clearly understood by Riche, who ghostwrote this line for Greene:

> I am the spirite of Robert Greene, not unknowne unto thee (I am sure) by name, when my writings lately priviledged on every post, hath given notice of my name unto infinite numbers of people that never knewe me by the view of my person.
>
> (McKerrow, *Greenes News*, 4)

What Greene, Riche, and Taylor did not predict was that *Pandosto* would remain a writing "privileged" even in authorless adaptation, known to "infinite numbers" of readers who never knew Greene's name.

CHAPTER TWO

Social Things

Commodifying *Pandosto*, 1592–1640

> *A commodity is therefore a mysterious thing, simply because in it the social character of men's labour appears to them as an objective character stamped upon the product of that labour. . . . This is the reason why the products of labour become commodities, social things whose qualities are at the same time perceptible and imperceptible by the senses. To the {producers} . . . the relations connecting the labour of one individual with that of the rest appear, not as direct social relations between individuals at work, but as what they really are, material relations between persons and social relations between things.*
>
> —Karl Marx, *Capital*[1]

After 1592, Greene's personal fame lessened while his novelties became steady sellers; his name survived as a label for a large, diverse, entertaining, and highly vendible set of books. "Robin Greene" had been the most colorful figure in print authorship in the 1590s; "Greene's works" became a synecdoche of the book market in the next generation. The continued success of his romances in the Jacobean period exemplified two phenomena that obsessed elite observers: the capacity of the book market to produce commodities of little apparent value, and the extension of pleasure reading to nonelite readers. The rise of ephemeral books and nonelite readers was uneven during most of the early modern period, but Tessa Watt suggests that both proliferated rapidly in "the late Jacobean and early Carolinian period."[2] The case of *Pandosto* shows that as early as 1615, writers for the elite experienced that proliferation of books and readers, or at least imagined it, especially acutely, worrying that if worthless books were profitably sold and eagerly read by the humble, their own writings would be corrupted. To defend their exclusivity, they studded their new works with harsh portrayals of older pleasure-reading texts as degraded by market conditions or a too-broad audience. These Jacobean claims for distinction divided the field of cultural production along a line that would later come to define the opposition between literary and popular print cultures. Prose romances, much reprinted and widely read, were seized upon as quintessential entertainment commodities; and *Pandosto* was singled out from among Greene's works as a defining text of a nascent popular literature.

The fashion of attacking the romance proved broadly influential, particularly on later attitudes toward popular culture, but it emerged in the early seventeenth century as a historically specific consequence of the maturation of the English book industry. Against the backdrop of that industry's growth, the Stuart devaluation of popular print can be seen as the successor to the Elizabethan elevation of vernacular authorship discussed in the last chapter. In 1592, when the concept of authorship was by no means finally established, Thomas Nashe was already crying out for a corrective to its alleged overextension: even "poore latinlesse Authors" themselves could not "spy a new Ballad, and his name to it that compilde it: but they put him in for one of the learned men of our time" (McKerrow, *Nashe*, 1:194). Nashe chose a distinct print form, the broadside ballad, for his *reductio ad absurdum*, as though authors had multiplied so quickly that only the most obvious physical differences could ground distinctions among their works. Nashe was just one of many sixteenth-century writers who mocked the broadside as a printed commodity from the vantage of that other notorious commodity, the pamphlet.[3] In the seventeenth century, the attack on ephemeral print turned from the broadside to the romance; now, unable to simply demonize an entire printed form, writers had to subdivide the quarto format and attack certain titles.[4] The project of ostracizing romances, or rather certain romances, was difficult without firm generic categories: romances were not sharply distinguished from histories, nor was there a classical generic theory for them. The obvious step taken by writers for the elite was to mock older, more familiar print romances. Certain groups were easy to identify: Continental chivalric romances, best-selling Elizabethan romances. The second group, unlike the first, could be conjured up by a single name: Robert Greene.

The elite writers' attacks on chivalric and Elizabethan romances were launched in genres that were not prose fiction but were nonetheless entertainment commodities: the prose character, which succeeded verse satire as the vehicle of coterie skepticism; and the stage comedy, which in quarto form began to rival the sales record of print fiction.[5] Class consciousness was integral to both genres, within which writers currying elite favor devised what I call "scenes of consumption," stereotypical vignettes of nonelite readers buying and enjoying their books. These scenes placed print romances in the hands of women, servants, upstarts, and country folk, readers apparently so distant from the writer and his privileged audience that the social threat of shared reading material was defused. The low status of the nouveau literate was confirmed by the alleged poverty of their cultural choices. That ritual damning of texts and (other) readers by mutual association exhibits the circularity that Bourdieu finds integral to the process of distinction. Discourses of distinction posit hierarchies of taste in cultural goods in order to buttress threatened social hierarchies among consumers, even though those hierarchies of taste ultimately refer to nothing more than the insecure social hierarchies. At the same time, as I will show, the social dynamics of these scenes of consumption fulfill Marx's famous characterization of a commodity, quoted in my epigraph: they show books to be "things" powerfully invested with "social" meaning.

Between 1592 and 1640, scenes of romance consumption appeared in a number of prose characters and stage comedies. Their cumulative effect was to reshape the status of romance in the public literary marketplace by attributing the broad and lasting success of chivalric and Elizabethan romances to the backward taste of the unfashionable.[6] These scenes appear to be the documentary records of a popular canon (and so most literary historians have taken them), but they are better read as interested constructions of the popular as a degraded cultural category.[7] Stuart writers tacitly admitted that Greene's works had been fashionable enough for their circles a generation or two ago, while asserting their own absolute separation from his current readers. They imply, then, that popularity means dropping to a new, unfashionable audience.

But none of the surviving material evidence confirms that *Pandosto* took so sharp a drop. Rather, its readership continued to diversify. Even if these Stuart commentators succeeded in tearing a few elite readers away from Greene, and even if the lower-class readership was growing, Greene's audience still ranged across the social spectrum. As Diana Henderson and James Siemon have recently claimed for ballads, "it was their very mingling of popular and elite audiences, undermining social distinctions, that may have made such forms worth denouncing."[8] So, too, it was the social diversity of the audience for pleasure reading that drove elite efforts to marginalize certain authors and titles as "popular."

Ironically, such denunciations of popular literature testify to elite acquaintance with the texts in question: scenes of consumption are effective only if elite writers and readers can and do recognize the texts that they claim to eschew. As a group, these scenes prove that texts as appealing as Greene's could startle, threaten, and even fascinate the elite; they reflect the challenge that the spread of literacy, and of entertainment commodities, posed to those near the top of the social hierarchy. A further element made romances prime territory in the battle for sociocultural distinction: their narratives of fortunes reversed, identities lost and regained, and social differences transcended. These narratives corresponded all too closely to ideologies of aspiration, both sexual (as writers of the period insisted) and socioeconomic (as twentieth-century scholars claim). Works such as *Pandosto* motivated elite writers to build walls of distinction because pleasure reading itself threatened to break down gender and class barriers.

This chapter surveys scenes of consumption that construct romances by Greene and other authors as popular, demonstrating that the two faults with which romances were repeatedly charged—overproduction as objects for sale, and excess stimulation of pleasure—were projections of the newly obvious condition of commodification that implicated all printed books. It also shows that the discursive work of projecting these faults onto certain romances shaped existing gender and class prejudices into a more sharply articulated model of cultural distinction, inventing a literary print culture exempt from commodification and a popular print culture that embodied it. Beginning with a detailed analysis of the most obvious use of Greene's romances in a scene of consumption, a prose character from 1615, I draw on Marx's account of the commodity to penetrate the character's masking of gender and class relationships. I then analyze a number of other scenes that enact the dynamics of the commodity: they grant social meaning to "things" by carefully specifying romance titles, but they objectify human relationships by stereotyping romance consumers. These scenes link entertainment commodities either to consumers in nonelite occupations or to female consumers. In the first type of scene, writers object to the presence of men of low cultural capital, country folk or craftsmen, who buy books in a bookstall, hypocritically charging that public consumers of entertainment commodities are vulgar and their manual labor turns their reading into a crude manipulation of objects. In the second type, writers depict women readers, including ladies and their servants, enjoying the peculiar intimacy of print and the warm pleasures of romance; these scenes voyeuristically condemn the private, sensual enjoyment of entertainment commodities as proof of feminine credulity. Of course, these two allegations support each other: if the private experience of pleasure reading is feminizing and corrupting, so is the public spread of the printed commodity that makes that experience available to any man. Printed romance was criticized as "bothe commune and pryvate," as Juan Luis Vives put it—a paradoxical but enduring complaint that still haunts our thinking about popular cultural commodities.[9]

The chapter ends by revealing this double complaint at work in a famous portrayal of humble readers buying the humblest of print commodities: the ballad-selling scene in Shakespeare's *The Winter's Tale* (performed 1610–11). I argue that the play's unique attention to the public and private effects of the commodification of print was driven by its indebtedness to Greene's *Pandosto*. By fusing the double complaint against printed entertainment commodities with older prejudices against mimetic entertainments, this scene trivializes not only Greene's works but also early modern popular literature more broadly. At the same time, the scene pays tribute to the appeal of mimetic entertainments, printed or not; through it, Shakespeare's play admits its continuity with Autolycus's "unconsidered trifles" and Greene's romances.[10] *The Winter's Tale*, today dignified as a *Shakespearean* romance, betrays a very complex attitude toward prose romance, simultaneously mocking its conventions and appropriating its power. Shakespeare's play can draw on Greene's romance in this way because by 1610, *Pandosto* had stood at the meeting point of circulation and exclusivity long enough to stand for that very struggle over cultural dissemination.

Throughout this chapter, as I trace the discursive construction of the audience for Greene's romances by seventeenth-century writers, I question their distinction-driven claims that patterns of readership neatly matched existing hierarchies of social rank. These writers have long been taken as reliable witnesses to reading patterns, but their repeated and self-contradictory assertions all too plainly reveal deep discomfort. These anxious claims must be set against another kind of evidence: the material record of the romances as they were published. Throughout this period, Greene's romances maintained their original format with remarkable fidelity. The Stuart scenes of consumption detailed in this chapter construct them as degraded books for social inferiors, but the texts were materially the same as they had been in Greene's lifetime. Greene's works are mentioned as though they have been cheapened by the marketplace, but the price of a given Greene text, based on its unchanged length, also would have remained the same from 1588 to 1615.[11] Greene's romances were constructed as popular commodities in a discursive reaction to the state of all books as commodities, not in recognition of any significant reduction in their format. Previous historians' accounts of *Pandosto* have conflated the unfounded scorn of Jacobean writers with *Pandosto*'s later life as a chapbook, yielding the assumption that this text was already discounted or degraded by the Stuart period. That can be disproved by briefly reviewing *Pandosto*'s circulation in the early seventeenth century, in imitations, translations, and accurate reissues, and in records of readership.

In the Stuart period, for the first time, *Pandosto* was singled out from among Greene's other works, becoming identifiable as a favorite title for some readers and an apt one for some adapters. One early hint at its specific appeal is given by the presence of two bold-faced imitations. John Hind's 1604 romance, *The Most Excellent Historie of Lysimachus and Varrona, Daughter to Syllanus Duke of Hypata in Thessalia*, has a pastoral plot borrowed from romances of the 1580s and entire sentences taken from *Pandosto*; William Bettie's *Titana and Theseus* (1608) lifts its plot, much of its narration, and even its title-page motto directly from *Pandosto*.[12] These imitations prove that Greene's works remained influential among the educated; as Mish put it, such "tales of sentiment" show "where the action is" in early seventeenth-century fiction.[13] Their reliance on *Pandosto* confirms what the reprint record was beginning to show: that this work in particular had especially strong appeal (and commercial potential). A more creditable two-part verse adaptation by Francis Sabie, *The Fissher-mans Tale* and *Flora's Fortune*, appeared in 1595.[14] The most famous confirmation of Jacobean interest in *Pandosto* is Shakespeare's stage adaptation in *The Winter's Tale*, to be discussed below.

More remarkably, *Pandosto* was the first English prose romance that the French deemed worthy of translation, preceding the *Arcadia* by a decade.[15] The first translation, by Louis Regnault (1615), was dedicated to the king's sister, and the second was by le Sr du Bail, "gentilhomme" (1626). There were stage adaptations for the Commédiens du Roy as well, by Alexandre Hardy (lost) and by Olivier Puget de la Serre (printed Paris, 1631; Lyons, 1632). Regnault called his prose translation an "Histoire tragique," and Puget de la Serre called his play *Pandoste ou la Princesse malheureuse, Tragédie en Prose.*[16] Retaining a sense of Greene's romance as tragic, the French adapters granted it the seriousness that Stuart commentators denied—a seriousness not indebted to Shakespeare's play. They all, like Shakespeare, embraced the wide sweep of Greene's story without worries about the unities. Extant sketches of scenery from the Hôtel de Bourgogne show that simultaneous staging was used for *Pandoste.*[17] Du Bail's story was published with two elegant engravings of ingeniously created composite scenes. The first depicted mostly Bohemian events, except for the finding of the babe on the Sicilian coastline; the second fit together the Sicilian wooing with the Bohemian denouement (figures 2.1 and 2.2). The figures were heroic and classically dressed; the prince is a mounted knight, not a shepherd.[18] The two illustrations thus emphasize the work's Heliodoran precedent, and, in their symmetry, its claim to classical form. In the text, too, the application of French polish removed some of the distinctiveness of Greene's style, as La Serre noticeably sentimentalized the pastoral presentation of "Favvye," "déguisée en bergère," and her virtuous adoptive parents, called only "paysan" and "paysanne" (Thomas 107).

The translations and adaptations also removed traces of Greene's authorship: Regnault's title page claimed only that the work had been translated first "en Anglois, de la langue Bohême, et de nouveau mis en François" (Jusserand, *Introduction,* xxix). Less surprisingly, the theatrical adaptations replaced Greene's name with that of the playwright. The same thing happened with a play published in Amsterdam in 1637 in Dutch as *M.P. Voskuyl's Dorastus and Fauniaas,* subtitled "a tragicomic play."[19] If *Pandosto* moved into two Continental languages in the Stuart period, it still must have been circulating in the purview of the educated, and indeed those with international connections. *Pandosto* was precocious as an English text appealing to Continental tastes. Judging from the illustrations and titles, its appeal rested in its Greek-romance lineage and its tragicomic plot. Still, none of these appropriations, dignified as they are, balked at erasing Greene's authorship; his reputation was not translatable.

Back in Stuart England, while anecdotes assigned romances to progressively less prestigious readers, the text of *Pandosto* remained remarkably stable. In one edition after another, the identical wording of the front matter shows that Greene's name and his self-advertising formulae still attracted buyers. The body of the text, too, was reproduced page for page, virtually type for type. In the context of seventeenth-century freedom in textual reproduction, characterized by D. F. McKenzie as "the normality of nonuniformity," this respectful duplication is meaningful.[20] Although compos-

Porte qui
trouue Faunie

Faunie
exposée
à la mer

Fandosie

Bellaire

Le Preuost

Bellaire

FIGURE 2.1
Illustration from Du Bail's *Pandoste ou la Princesse Malheureuse* (Paris, 1626),
representing early events in the story.

BIBLIOTHÈQUE NATIONALE DE FRANCE

Pandoste
Faunie
Canope
Canope
Doraste
Faunie

FIGURE 2.2
Illustration from Du Bail's *Pandoste ou la Princesse Malheureuse* (Paris, 1626), representing later events in the story.
BIBLIOTHÈQUE NATIONALE DE FRANCE

itors certainly found it more efficient to reproduce a text page-for-page than to change formats needlessly, reissues prepared with a high standard of accuracy reflect their producers' high valuation.[21] Greene's texts were too well known to be printed negligently. One small textual change of 1607 suggests that someone—the publisher or printer, a proofreader, or a compositor—bothered to read the text attentively upon reprinting it. That producer altered Greene's wording of the oracle—"the king shall live without an heir if that which is lost be not found"—to the more idiomatic and precise, "die without an heir." Of course, the lost heir (albeit a daughter) *is* found, making the correction immaterial to the story. Still, this change has interested Shakespeare scholars, because when the oracle appears almost verbatim in *The Winter's Tale* (act 3, scene 2), the older "live" is preserved. It would seem that Shakespeare consulted a pre-1607 edition of *Pandosto* in writing a play that debuted in 1610–11.[22] Thus, one of the few substantive variants in the Jacobean text of *Pandosto* is also one of the few instances when Shakespeare's reading can be tied closely to the particularity of print.

Pandosto's state of relative textual stability was matched by geographical stability: every edition from 1588 up through 1619 was issued from the same bookseller's shop, occupied successively by Thomas Cadman and Joan Brome. Their careful transfers of the romance (detailed in chapter 1) and their frequent and accurate reissues demonstrate *Pandosto*'s valued place in their stock-in-trade. The shop, known by the sign of the Great Bible, stood near the North Door of St. Paul's; Paul's Churchyard had long been the center of the City's book trade.[23] Despite claims from the start of the seventeenth century that Greene's romances had fallen to the cultural margins, the first publisher of *Pandosto* located outside the City, Francis Faulkner of Southwark, did not acquire the romance until 1629, a period when many other stationers also moved into larger suburban premises.

Finally, readership and ownership records for pre-1640 editions of *Pandosto* do not support claims that it was being consigned to a socially inferior audience.[24] In 1606, the twenty-one-year-old William Drummond, long before he became a poet and conversed with Ben Jonson, read quite a bit of Greene in a crash course in courtly vernacular literature. En route from taking his M.A. at the University of Edinburgh to studying law on the Continent, Drummond visited his father, gentleman-usher to King James, attended tourneys for the visiting King Christian of Denmark like those that Pandosto staged for his royal guest, and wrote to a friend about the witty love debates of the court. But mostly he read, listing his readings in a memorandum book: works of divinity and politics; Guazzo and Castiglione;

Ovid's *Metamorphoses*; *The Rape of Lucrece*, naturally; and plays by Shakespeare and Greene, including "Loves Labours Lost, comedie," "Romeo and Julieta, tragedie," "A Midsommer Nights Dreame, comedie," "Orlando Furioso, comedie," and "Alphonsus historie, comed." Above all, he read romances, from pastoral to chivalric: *Euphues*, *Galatea*, "S.P.S. Arcadia," "The 4 part" and "the 8 book of the Miror of Knighthead," "Three volumes of Diana, in English," "The 2 volume of Amadis de Gaule, English," "Eurialus and Lucrece, English"—and "Dorastus and Faunia." Clearly, Greene's notoriety was no handicap to Drummond's interest in *Pandosto*, since he also listed (Harvey's) "Certaine Letters concerning Greene."[25] Like most later readers, Drummond referred to the romance by the running title that featured the young lovers. Of all Greene's romances, it was *Pandosto* that belonged, by 1606, on the reading list of a young scholar-poet.

The records of a mid-seventeenth-century library prove that at least one socially privileged, if provincial, reader owned a Greene romance. Fraunces Wolfreston, the matron of a Midlands family of minor country gentry, lived from 1607 to 1677; her large collection of useful, godly, and light reading included an early edition of *Mamillia*.[26] Wolfreston's holdings confirm the ongoing association between women and Greene's romances, but the details of her life are far from the eroticized leisure of the ladies' text trope: she managed her household for decades, since her husband and youngest son were apparently in poor health, and she purchased many of her books used. Nor should we assume that the readership for Greene was exclusively or increasingly female. There are no dated signatures in editions of *Pandosto* to 1640, but Harvard's copy of the 1607 edition has doodling in Greek in an early hand. That educated but careless owner was probably male. The Bodleian copy of the 1611 edition of *Ciceronis Amor* is emphatically inscribed on the final leaf, "Zachariah Spence his Book now and as Long as he Lives 1699." The Bodleian's 1628 edition of the same title bears two copies of the ornate signature of one "Thos. Smith." This Greene romance, at least, was still read proudly by men well into the century.

Another survival pattern links Greene's romances to well-heeled buyers: a significant percentage of Greene titles published between 1600 and 1610 are collected in Central European libraries. A sole copy of the 1600 edition of *Pandosto*, bound with the 1599 edition of *Menaphon* and several other works by Greene and others, has recently turned up in Gdansk; the 1605 and 1616 editions of *Menaphon* are known only from copies in Wroclaw and Vienna, respectively.[27] One of two extant copies of the Dutch tragicomedy *Dorastus and Fauniaas* is in a library in Linkoping, Sweden. Although the exact provenance of these copies is unrecoverable, some may have been exported during the seventeenth century, when English trade was expanding into the Baltic and German regions; copies could have been carried as souvenirs by returning diplomats or brought by English merchants as gifts. There is ample evidence of the reciprocal phenomenon in English library catalogues of the seventeenth century. T. A. Birrell has noted that until the eighteenth century set new standards of taste for the gentleman's library, English gentry were perfectly happy to collect vernacular light reading, not just in English but in foreign languages as well.[28] Birrell's library analysis shows that those who collected printed English drama tended to prefer chivalric romances in English and Continental languages as well as newer, more exclusive genres like the prose character.[29] Many gentleman book buyers of the Stuart period collected and read these "light" genres avidly, immune to others' desires to distinguish among them.

Did the Stuart project of articulating cultural distinctions respond to some sudden leap in nonelite literacy? Early modern literacy is notoriously hard to quantify, but it appears that the reading population of London was increasingly diverse in its socioeconomic makeup; David Cressy has argued that by this time, the most accurate predictors of literacy were not social class but specific occupation and proximity to the city.[30] What is clear is that the elite *perceived* that new groups of nonelite men and a noticeable number of women were reading for pleasure in the late Elizabethan and Jacobean eras, especially in London. Urban craftsmen and servants, male and female, acquired literacy disproportionally because it was occupationally useful. They were probably also featured in scenes of consumption because their work made their presence—and their social ambitions—particularly visible to the urban elite.[31] Because social mobility was so often coded through fashion in Jacobean culture, it is likely that when elite writers mocked others' romance reading as the following of an outdated fashion, they were deflating and trivializing the threat of more substantial social aspiration. But the reverse could also be true: in acquiring once-exclusive reading tastes, some craftsmen and servants were acquiring cultural tastes to match their socioeconomic gains.

THE WORK OF DISTINCTION IN THE AGE
OF MECHANICAL REPRODUCTION

My first scene of consumption clearly demonstrates how mentions of Greene's romances aimed to restore class boundaries around stereotyped readers. In 1615, a prose character typified "A Chamber-maide" by the fact that "Shee reads *Greenes* workes over and over."[32] This economical statement manages to characterize Greene's works at least as vividly as the chambermaid: she is defined by her taste for romance reading, and Greene's texts are marked as proper to chambermaids. The reference to "*Greenes* workes" *en masse* reduces them to interchangeable commodities, which must be consumed "over and over." Rather than giving the chambermaid substantial pleasure, they are repetitive, vacuous, even addictive. The word "workes," pretentious in reference to a vernacular author in 1615, is undercut by the implication that they fail to satisfy.[33] Above all, the romances bear the weight of sexual insinuation that is the constant theme of this character. It associates her reading of Greene with the "*Greene-sicknes*" (aching virginity) she could cure by lying in her master's chamber. Now, having read both "*Greenes* workes" and "the *Myrrour of Knighthood*," the maid is "so carried away" that she is "many times resolv'd to run out of her selfe, and become a Ladie Errant" (Paylor 43). Greene's works join this most maligned chivalric romance in tempting the chambermaid, taking the blame for her errors even as the description portrays her as innately unchaste. The comparison of these selections is unflattering to both Elizabethan and chivalric romance: Greene's unindividuated works are diffusely corruptive, leading the maid astray by sheer repetition, while the *Myrrour of Knighthood* poses a direct ideological threat in the person of its errant heroine, Clarinda. As print made it easier for readers to reproduce their entertainment experiences by reading "over and over," it also, allegedly, encouraged them to reproduce those experiences in their own lives, to become "carried away" by ideologically dangerous examples.

Of course, print spread the stereotyping character as effectively as it did the supposedly corrupting romance. The volume in which "A Chamber-maide" appeared, the sixth edition of Sir Thomas Overbury's *A Wife*, was by 1615 already a phenomenon of fashionable and successful publishing. *A Wife* (1611) was published only once before Overbury's death by poisoning in 1613; in 1614, it was reprinted with the addition of twenty-two characters that the title page attributed to Overbury and "other learned Gentlemen" (Paylor 1). Three more editions appeared in 1614, and a competing set in 1615. Further interest was piqued when Overbury's murderers were identified as Robert Carr (King James's favorite, to whom Overbury had been secretary) and his new wife, Frances Howard. The two were tried in 1615 and convicted in 1616. Meanwhile, the sixth edition, of 1615, added "A Chamber-maide" and some forty other characters to the collection, and the ninth edition, in 1616, added even more (Paylor xxxii–xxxiii).

"Overbury's" characters thus combined the glamour of the elite, the tinge of sexual and criminal scandal, and the momentum of a media sensation.[34] The characterization of the chambermaid exploits these appeals: despite her low rank, she is "her Mistresses shee Secretarie," keeping her secrets "very private"; and she is blackmailing her master and other sexual partners. She is even compared to a "starcher," perhaps a link to Anne Turner, the laundrywoman who was a key accomplice in the murder (Paylor 43). The character retails scandal as it condemns the maid's scandalous tales.

As an account of the demographics of reading, "A Chamber-maide" is of doubtful value. Far from being typical of Greene's readership, this female domestic servant probably represents the lower limit of its spread. The existence of a romance-reading chambermaid is plausible enough, since in the early modern period, unmarried women of almost any class background might go temporarily into domestic service, and even lower-born women could gain literacy in service. However, a chambermaid would probably have borrowed her Greene from her employers (as Lyly imagined for a waiting maid), since a full-length romance in quarto would have taken much of her cash income.[35] The character implies that Greene's romances, having become popular with servants, garner only mockery from the educated; but readers well above the servant class were still happily reading Greene "over and over." The Overburian character came too late to prevent the spread of Greene's romance to nonelite readers, but too early to witness a real falling off from its centrality in print culture. Rather, its 1615 appearance points to a quick drop in elite tolerance of the social diversity of romance readership.

In claiming that the Overburian scene of consumption and others like it reveal more about elite ideological production than popular cultural consumption, I am guided by Marx's warning that commodities misrepresent the social relations among their producers and consumers. In *Capital*'s discussion of the "Fetishism of commodities," a crucial passage for theories of ideology, Marx marvels that under capitalism, the products of human labor become commodities with the "grotesque," "wonderful," and "mysterious" quality of being "social things." Apparently inanimate objects begin to develop their own hierarchies and symbolisms, replacing social relations as mass production abstracts human labor from its products, and the marketplace alienates producers from consumers. In Marx's words, commodities are not just puppets enacting social relations but also texts recording them: "the social character of men's labour appears to them as an objective character stamped upon the product of their own labour" (320). That textual image has invited scholars of the early modern period to recognize the printed book as an early, definitive instance of the alienated commodity.[36]

If this recognition is correct, it is no wonder that print became the subject as well as the vehicle of socioeconomic anxieties. As material objects reifying the words of absent authors, signal early modern examples of interchangeable mass production, and highly speculative and sometimes ephemeral goods, books confounded valuation. Certainly books' exchange value was fixed, set by the company of stationers on the basis of format or length; but its correspondence to use value was notoriously unstable. In sum, the relationships between books as commodities and their producers and purchasers enacted, with extraordinary self-reflexivity, the confusion and alienation that Marx would later diagnose. A book's scene of consumption could assert its social distance from other books, describing "social relations among things": thus elite writers inserted Greene's works in a grotesquely imaginative, often sexualized mythology. And these scenes reduced social relations to impersonal economic judgments, describing "material relations among persons": they slotted the multiplicity of readers into stereotypes of gender, class, and occupation.

Indeed, that experience of alienation in the print marketplace seems to be the wellspring of the prose character, the ultimate "social thing." Each character isolates one social type, usually by profession, and renders it impersonal by the indefinite article: "A Servingman," "An Ostler," "A very Whore." Collectively, the characters are vignettes of social life without interaction. The members of these professions are granted no productive value by the writer, although the gentle depended on their goods and services; the portrayals suggest that theirs is essentially demeaning work, further lowered by characteristic corruptions. Even the form of the genre is alienated: the series of individual characterizations adds up to no narrative, but has the randomness of an urban crowd. Within an individual character, the subject is frozen in his or her faults, manipulated through the verbal conceits that Overbury made fashionable. Isolated and lifeless, the subject is less socially embedded than are his or her defining fashions, belongings, and cultural preferences. This isolation is balanced by the rich social meaningfulness of the textual commodity, in which is imprinted ("stamped") a lesson for readers about the social relations they apparently lack in real life. As Richard Brathwait wrote in his 1631 volume of characters, "What else are *Characters* but *stampes* or *impressures*, noting such an especiall place, person, or office."[37] The genre is named for the act of printing that replaces human relations. It fulfills or perhaps exceeds Marx's definition of the commodity, showing that the "social character of men's labour" is not even "stamped upon the product of [their] labour" but indirectly stamped upon the product of the labour of printers.

"A Chamber-maide" follows this pattern by reducing social relations to rituals of objectification or consumption. She reverses ideologies of domestic service: instead of advancing the household economy, she advances her self-interest against her master. Her sexual self-indulgence replaces any sense of earning her keep: "Her Mistris & she helpe to make away *Time*, to the idlest purpose that can be" (Paylor 44). The only real work represented in the character is ideological: her reading material makes this servant "long" to "run out of her selfe" into the inappropriate role of a "lady." This generalized maid is never named, but "Greenes works" are, implying that their status is more stable than her own, and perhaps more dangerous. As Helen Hackett points out, the character denies that the servant might really rebel against her place, instead "pre-emptively" labeling her book the only culprit, guilty of the trivial crime of fantasy.[38]

Within the character, Greene's works also become "social things" because their relationship to this volume is more complex and vital than the relationship of the writer to the putative chambermaid. The character's author is utterly detached from his lower-class subject, writing from an all-knowing perspective and in elaborately manipulated language. Amused contempt is the only emotion projected by the narrative voice. In general, the character asks its readers to share this detachment from lesser social beings, but this particular mockery of other texts creates more immediate and substantial social dynamics. It invites readers to congratulate themselves on having chosen this fashionable book rather than a dated romance; it validates their choice as more inherently valuable than the merely commodified works of Greene, and as more licit than a tempting romance.

Above all, the character writer uses the embedded reference to romances to allay the anxieties of his own position. In guaranteeing his elite readers' tastes, he displaces his own social alienation and cloaks his own ambition or need for money; in deflecting the stigma of print onto the printed popular romance, he dissociates himself from the labour of writing, whose "objective character" should be "stamped" on his printed work. However, the writer himself was undoubtedly an alienated producer of commodities on Marx's model. Character writers may have been gentlemen by birth, but in terms of social capital they were more aspirant than established, and by definition they were engaged with the print marketplace. After the notoriously ambitious Overbury set the fashion, character writing quickly became alienated labour, the production of a highly reproducible commodity, as demonstrated by the repeated but uncredited expansions of the volume after Overbury's death. From the second edition (1614) onward, a letter from "The Printer to the Reader" (the bookseller was Laurence Lisle) promised that the provided additions were by "Gentlemen of the same qualitie" as Overbury; similar claims were added to the title pages of some later editions (Paylor 2). But no edition ever distinguishes a particular added character as being by anyone but Overbury: the productive work of other contributors is completely invisible. The author of "A Chambermaide" has never been identified, although another new block of characters in the same edition has been attributed to John Webster (son of a tradesman). It appears that Lisle hired a professional writer to expand the volume—as the gentleman John Stephens insinuated in his competing set of characters published in 1615 (Paylor xvii–xxiv). From Stephens's viewpoint, the recruitment of Webster violated the amateur rules by which the game of character writing was played. Meanwhile, Lisle lacked writers who could supply the desired commodities: his third edition advertised additions, but none appeared until the next (Paylor xviii, xxxii).

Stephens's complaint, published but ineffectual, demonstrates how essential social exclusion was to the genre—and how unattainable it was in practice. As Bourdieu would insist, Jacobean writers' efforts at distinction were always unsuccessful, the cultural and social boundaries constantly broken. When an elite writer figured other texts as mere commodities for lesser readers, he and his own audience could deny their own engagements with the commodified system of publication. But only those denials figured the writer as elite; he was still socially or economically dependent on that system, and his readers were still consumers of print commodities on an increasingly impersonal market. Sharon Achinstein points out the irony that the character writers found their "unlikely expression in the press, against whose debasing influence the writers rail" (325n43). Unlike poets in the coterie circles, the character writers apparently could not afford not to publish. Their scenes of consumption might deny that their output shared its means of production with romances, but that continuity could be read from the books' imprints. Indeed, Thomas Creede, who printed this sixth edition of Overbury's collection, had himself printed *Pandosto* in 1614, just one year earlier.[39]

As an emergent form of cultural criticism, the character formulated what we can now recognize as an opposition between literary and popular cultures. Its agenda of social discrimination, implied in the scenes of con-

sumption, appears more frankly in its apparatus. Lisle's 1614 letter from
"The Printer to the Reader" regretted that few could appreciate "the deepe
Arte of Poetry," especially since they had been misled too often by "a col-
lusive flourish onely fronted with the name of excellent." Never having
learned to recognize true artistry, readers "overlook" most efforts at poetry
as "frivolous, and fantasticke labours, putting no difference betwixt the
horse pictured on a signe-post, and the curious limbd *Pegasus*." Still, even
such undiscriminating readers would have to recognize that Overbury's
works were not the ordinary stuff of inn signs, but the mythic stuff of a true
poet, "such an Author" as "the ancient Romanes" would have memorialized
in statuary. The early modern alternative for preserving this author was
"our easie conversations of wit, by printing" (Paylor 2). These were pretentious claims for a genre that was slight in texture and thinner in classical
references than Greene's romances, but mocking them helped to represent
the collection as the work of "learned Gentlemen."

The character did not survive to enter the modern canon of genres,
but its strategies of distinction were echoed and developed over the next
centuries in sophisticated stage comedy, in the critical essay, and in the
novel, examples of which will appear in my remaining chapters. Moreover,
these strategies survive today in critical views of early modern prose
romance, its current neglect reflecting the long tradition of class-driven
devaluation that I trace here. The distinctions posited by Stuart writers
have been cited at face value for far too long. The Overburian scene has
been claimed repeatedly as documentary evidence of Greene's readership;
others like it have enabled the general claim that chivalric and Elizabethan romances appealed to a lower-class readership, particularly a female
one. In fiction criticism of this century, the chain of references to that readership runs from Henry Thomas's *Spanish and Portuguese Romances of
Chivalry* (1920) through Wright's *Middle-class Culture in Elizabethan
England* (1935) to Caroline Lucas's *Writing for Women* (1989) and beyond.[40]
From ideologically driven early distinctions among prose romances, scholars have projected a division between exclusive courtly romances (meaning
Arcadia) and others "churned out" for popular audiences by hack writers or
translators. Such attempts at classification should have foundered long
ago—after all, as I will show, evidence from the period often condemns
Arcadia with the allegedly lesser romances.

A crucial step in undoing this division has been feminist critics' analysis
of the ladies' text trope as a gendered construction. Helen Hackett pinpoints
its hypocrisy: "Male readers could enjoy romance as a lightweight entertain-

ment, while simultaneously enjoying a sense of intellectual superiority, knowing that they were distinguished by gender from the kind of foolish creatures who took this nonsense seriously." Her new *Women and Romance Fiction in the English Renaissance* (2000) is a landmark study, systematically reconsidering the identification of romance with women readers.[41] Much rarer is critical questioning of romance denigration as class-driven. One instance is Trevor Ross's suggestive discussion of the humanists' "blacklisting" of the romance as a "negative form of canon-making . . . that emanated from a fear of plurality, of the heresy of allowing everyone to choose what to read" (79). The Stuart denigration of romance had enduring effects because it worked through both class and gender. Indeed, when the attack on romance aligned class distinction with gender hierarchy, the discourse defining popular culture took its characteristic form. As nonelite readers became a significant part of the pleasure-reading audience, old prejudices against their illiteracy were rewritten as new prejudices discounting their appetite for reading matter; as women joined that audience, prejudices against their ignorance were rewritten as gendered prejudices against their credibility. To call a text feminine became yet another way to identify it as lower-class; specifying its readership as both female and lower-class was uniquely effective in marking a work as merely "popular."

The case of *Pandosto* demonstrates just how powerful and enduring this dual identification could be. Early descriptions of its audience, despite their patently ideological motivation, continue to be repeated at face value, as in Stanley Wells's 1995 comment (quoted in my introduction) that *Pandosto* "seems to have appealed especially to a not very highly educated class of reader"—unlike, it is implied, *The Winter's Tale* (*Shakespeare* 338). This characterization not only cites the Overburian character as evidence but also reproduces its attitudes: the literary taste of the "Chamber-maide" is discounted as a lack of education, although this literate chambermaid is quite well educated for a woman of her time. Shakespeare's work, the fare of the modern, educated, and presumably male reader, is safeguarded from mere popularity and again confirmed as universal, thanks to romance, its opposite, which is once more constructed as popular material for the nonelite and female reader.[42] Recently, Henderson and Siemon have proposed reintegrating prose romance with the now more canonical drama and verse romances into a broader romance mode that "defied the boundaries between court and popular culture, respected literature and suspect entertainment" (216). They remind us that the subgeneric hierarchies within romance always were permeable as well as constructed. To deconstruct them, however, may also require recognizing how central the denigration of romance was to defining literary and popular realms.

Ultimately, the value of decoding this pernicious dual identification extends far beyond rescuing the reputation of *Pandosto*, or even that of prose romance. The dual identification has shaped long-standing assumptions about popular culture: that, unlike those of the elite, its texts are commodified and vulgar and its pleasures illicit and effeminate. Despite all that has been done to deconstruct the myths of literature's disinterestedness and transcendence, reciprocal myths linger, portraying popular literature as excessively material and pleasurable. Modern views of popular culture as economically and morally wasteful are continuous with early modern scenes of consumption that placed romances in the hands of nonelite buyers, whose touch could turn cultural objects into worthless commodities; and in the laps of pleasure-loving women readers, whose desires led them from ostensible preprint purity to sexual temptation. The next two sections reconstruct the seventeenth century's two characteristic elaborations of these scenes: versions set in bookshops, in which the (elite) public space of the "gentleman reader" is marred by the insulting presence of craftsmen as book buyers; and versions set in women's chambers, in which the private space of the ladies' text is parodied as the yielding of credulous female servants to books' intimate pleasures. These scenes attest that discounting Greene's works as fit for craftsmen and servant women seemed urgently necessary to the Jacobean elite; my readings identify deep historical roots for those prejudices.

THE GENTLEMAN IN THE BOOKSHOP

In the Harvey-Nashe debates of 1592, described in chapter 1, access to printed cultural commodities emerged as a highly visible marker safeguarding social difference; the writers impugned each other's works as mere commodities fit for lower-class male readers. Writers gratified themselves and their gentle readers with the pretense of exemption from trade by implying that it was other, lesser groups of customers—servants, craftsmen, farmers—whose acts of buying turned books into commodities. In elite depictions of the commodified marketplace, these customers are anonymous and stereotypical, reduced to their status labels; energies are focused on the fetishized objects and spatial settings of cultural consumption. The bookshop itself symbolizes the alienated class encounters that the exchange of printed commodities permitted, while scenes set in it work to distinguish among both kinds of buyers and kinds of books.

Supposedly defending Greene against Harvey, Nashe joined in the game of protecting his class status while denigrating romance readers. He wrote in *Strange News* (1592): "Of force I must graunt that *Greene* came oftner in print than men of judgment allowed off, but neverthelesse he was a daintie slave to content the taile of a Tearme, and stuffe Serving mens pockets" (McKerrow, *Nashe*, 1:329). Nashe's comments are accurate to a point: Greene did publish frequently rather than carefully, and some of his last works are ephemeral pastimes. But Nashe places Greene's works in a more damaging social context by representing their proper audience as "Serving men" who stuff trifling stories into their pockets. His image parodies the descent of Lyly's ladies' text from the fashionable lady's "lap" or "pocket" to her "Wayting Maydes"; now it is a nonelite man who stows these sexual fantasies in his most private place. Lyly had described his work as a toy for women; Nashe imagines the author of such toys as a "daintie slave," both less masculine and less free than the servant reader who uses his "stuffe" so intimately. For Nashe, publication transforms an author's work first into sexualized chattel, then into the most grossly material of objects. In an earlier variant on this remark, Nashe had identified the lowly servant with cheap print's final destination as waste, mocking that so-called wit "which walkes abroad for wast paper in each serving-man's pocket" (McKerrow, *Nashe*, 3:314).[43] The context of that remark, in the preface of Greene's *Menaphon*, had of course been to praise Greene as a true wit; but two years later, Nashe dismissed Greene's works as mere stuff.

Nashe probably concocted that reversal. His similar reference to passing "the taile of a Tearme" by reading Greene seems to pertain to the experiences of Nashe's own social class as much as those of servants. Men most needing pastimes in term were the young hangers-on about the Inns of Court, or more broadly, the social class whose legal and financial business brought them to London during the season—the kind of audience that Nashe presumably sought most eagerly. If reading Greene was a pastime that was not quite novel, it was nonetheless strongly associated with the minglings of cosmopolitan life, which in 1592 were socially promiscuous enough to induce the anxiety that Nashe projected onto imagined reading servants.

This slip from cosmopolitan mingling to social promiscuity troubled Nashe's opponent even more—and indeed helps to account for Harvey's obsession with Greene. In his attacks, Harvey ruefully admitted that many of his well-educated acquaintance would share a taste for Greene's works.

He blamed this preference among "yoong Gentlemen" on the physical
ubiquity of the books: "their mindes were no lesse possessed with the toyes
of his irreligious braine, then their chambers and studies were pestered
with his lewde and wanton bookes" (cited in Pruvost 536). But it was Harvey himself who felt most "pestered." In a paraleptic attack on the late
Greene in the third of *Four Letters* of 1592, he wrote:

> I will not condemne, or censure his workes, which I never did so much
> as superficially overrunne, but as some fewe of them occursively pre-
> sented themselves in Stationers shops, and some other houses of my
> acquaintaunce.[44]

Harvey claims that he could not avoid happening on works that struck his
eyes as a curse, that inscribed Greene's publication across his path. He
implies that Greene's "workes"—that mocking word—appear without
qualification in sites that should be reserved for men of learning like himself. Harvey's physical disgust extends from Greene's books to the "Stationers shops" where readers of various levels of cultural privilege could
peruse and select from books for many tastes.[45] Of course the shops of his
"acquaintaunce" included John Wolfe's printing shop, where Harvey was
then living as an economic dependent: his horror at Greene's commerciality, then, involves self-hatred or at least regret at his own position.

Again denying his own role as a producer of ephemera, Harvey repeatedly objected to the taste for print as a taste for mere novelty. Reflecting on
Greene's prolific issue of "new, newer, & newest books," Harvey wrote, "I
would, some Buyers had either more Reason to discerne, or lesse Appetite
to desire such Novels" (Grosart 1:190–91). Such obvious denials of the
writer's role as commodity producer would become even more common a
generation later. Webster, the dramatist and character writer, expressed
similar disgust at novelty seekers in bookstores, "those ignorant asses (who
visiting Stationers shoppes their use is not to inquire for good books, but
new bookes)" (Miller 28). Harvey's obsession with novelty and the marketplace, his bibliagoraphobia, if you will, reflects mixed loathing for and
dependence on print, the training of a humanist struggling against the
impulses of a prolific controversialist. Harvey's rhetoric, but not his practice, remained loyal to preprint culture. Yet his complaints also looked
ahead, registering (though unenthusiastically) the potential of the printed
book and the bookstore as democratizing forces.

In the Jacobean era, it became even more clear that the bookshop was a space for public consumption of once-exclusive goods. Its environs temporarily brought together those normally separated by rank: leisured gentlemen and barely schooled artisans. Elite commentators reacted to the anomalous experience of entering a bookshop where men in crafts or service "occursively presented themselves" buying and reading books for pleasure. These elite reactions characteristically designated the new readers only by the trade they were trained to perform, following a traditional pattern of defining a nonelite man's status by his craft.[46] Henry Parrot, in a 1615 verse satire, lists the motley patrons of a bookstall by profession. "Your Countrey-Farmer" prefers a chivalric romance, like "Sir *Guye*." "My Serving-man" is given the ladies' text trope, telling the stationer's apprentice that no "new Bookes" will "please our Maides" except "bookes of Ladies or some valiant Knight." Having paraded his knowledge of women as his betters would, "Those wittie workes buys hee."[47] Elite identification of book buyers by occupation may be developed humorously but carries reminders that most of these jobs would once have been incommensurate with literacy, and that any labor was incompatible with leisure reading. In fact, as Cressy points out, the varied usefulness of reading and writing skills in different trades helps to explain literacy's "enormous variation from trade to trade" (124, 130). The discursive identification of workers as leisure readers implied that the spread of literacy was disrupting labor, but what was really being disrupted was the exclusivity of leisure reading.

These scenes of craftsmen with money and time to buy books, along with related images of servant women with time to read, register elite concern with the permeability of social boundaries. The new diversity of the leisure-reading audience raises the problem of status inconsistency, the discordance between culturally embedded expectations (of privilege, of firm hierarchy) and lived experience (of open access, of violated boundaries). This problem is doubly present when the offensive leisure reading is fiction, for the driving concern of so many early modern mimetic narratives is to explore status inconsistency. Michael McKeon minimizes the threat posed by this subject matter in sixteenth- and seventeenth-century fiction, alleging that romance resolved it until the novel opened it up.[48] I will question that distinction more fully in chapter 4; for now, I assert that the deep-rooted hostility to nonelite romance reading suggests that elite readers saw these works as capable of questioning the status quo. It is no accident that the maligned romance readers represent the status groups most often seen as aspirant in both economic life and fictional representations. For example, scenes of distinction often centered on reading servants because the presence of servants within the household brought social differences to the surface, and because the social mobility of servants was so often a concern in Elizabethan romance narrative. Artisans were also featured, perhaps as coarse reductions of that category—the citizens/craftsmen/tradesmen—that now, anomalously, included the extraordinarily wealthy freemen of the City. In fiction, too, artisans turned plutocrats, such as Thomas Deloney's famous weavers, had become mythic figures of mobility. Lingering around the denigration of romances as reading for these aspirant groups is the unspoken charge that romances are themselves commodified aspiration.

Mockery of artisans as the poorest of readers may also address anxiety about those commodities speculatively produced by two particularly problematic kinds of artisans: the printer/bookseller and the author. Certainly scenes of reading artisans insist on the materiality of reader and book alike, even as the authors forswear their own commodification. In another of his 1615 poems, Parrot shudders that his book's title page might be hung "on Posts . . . / For every dull-Mechanicke to beholde."[49] In a 1617 satire, Henry Fitzgeffrey enumerates all the pamphlets he scorns, blacklisting that "number numberlesse that march (untolde) / Mongst *Almanacks* and *Pippins*, to be solde." He begs that his book will not be bought by "each Pesant, each Mecannick Asse, / That neer knew further then his *Horn-booke* crosse."[50] In defining minimal literacy, Fitzgeffrey associates the "Mecannick Asse," the Bottom of the social ladder, with the cheapest primer, consisting of a single page printed with the cross and the alphabet, mounted under a sheet of horn on a wooden paddle. For other writers, any book was, in its commodified materiality, so available to a vulgar audience that print must be rejected altogether; among them were the Jacobean writers who revived coterie manuscript circulation. In *The Furies* (1614), Richard Niccols ridicules this elitist fear of contamination in the bookshop:

> Many idle humorists whose singularity allowes nothing good, that is common, in this frantik age, esteeme of verses upon which the vulgar in a Stationers Shop, hath once breathed as of a peece of infection.[51]

But he is clearly familiar with the pose. Ben Jonson mocked both the vulgar and the poseur. His epigram "To My Bookseller" grudgingly concedes that his book can "lye upon thy stall" but should not be "offer'd," by posting its title page, to "some clarke-like serving-man, / Who scarse can spell th'hard names: whose knight lesse can." Parrot's imitative *Ad Bibliopolam* asks that his book be segregated in the bookstore, "not with your Ballads mixt" (quoted in Wright 95).

The reaction against cross-class encounters in the bookshop, then, was virulent by the 1610s; but a decade earlier, the longest of Jacobean bookstore scenes portrayed the social dynamics of book buying more subtly, perhaps because its author's own readership was far from exclusive. Samuel Rowlands's *Tis Merrie When Gossips Meete* (1602) brings together Nashe's image of the pocket and Harvey's nightmare of bookstore novelties but seems to welcome the social instability of these spaces for consuming pleasures. Rowlands was a professional writer, probably not university educated, who wrote brief, humorous works in many subgenres. His first title, *Tis Merry When Knaves Meet*, was censored in 1600, as were satires by many elite writers. The rest of Rowlands's undemanding titles could be considered joco-seria, but to the most fashionable, they were merely popular: Fitzgeffrey disdainfully refers to "*Rowland* with his *Knaves* a murnivall; Non worth the calling for, a fire burne em all" (Wright 97). *Tis Merrie When Gossips Meete* is a pamphlet that purports to tell in rhyme what women talk about over beer.[52] Its readers are led into the alehouse through an elaborate framework. After the Chaucerian prefatory verse epistle, readers are thrust unexpectedly into a Monty Pythonesque "Conference" between a bookseller's "Prentice" and a country "Gentleman" (Rowlands 5). Gradually, the purpose of the "Conference" is revealed to be the Prentice's overcoming the Gentleman's objections to purchasing this very pamphlet. Thus the discourse is at once a clever embedded advertisement, a rare and ideologically complex depiction of class interaction in the book market, and a self-reflexive meditation on the relationship between Rowlands's novel entertainment commodity and more established commodities, such as Greene's.

As the dialogue begins, the gentleman customer is resisting the apprentice's urging of a "new Booke new come foorth." Such works are not to his "humours liking"; rather, "there are some old Bookes that I have more delight in then your new, if thou couldst helpe me to them." In particular, he requests "all *Greenes* Bookes in one Volume." The apprentice, experienced in handling customers who seek familiarity before novelty, answers that of Greene's titles he lacks "*Conny-catching*, and some halfe dozen more," quickly adding that he can procure the missing books from another dealer in town.[53] The customer insists that he wants to own *all* of Greene: "But I will have them every one, not any wanting" (5).[54] This fan takes his mirth seriously; compelled to possess every available pleasurable commodity, he is the inverse of a Gabriel Harvey obsessed by the profligacy of commodification. The apprentice tries to satisfy his customer's compulsion, offering "all the Parts of *Pasquill*"; the customer is surprised to learn there are more than two such jestbooks. This gentle taste for Pasquill's jests, lowbrow as it seems, was shared by the letter writer John Chamberlain, a dilettantish son of a merchant.[55] Rowlands's fictional gentleman, like Chamberlain and Nashe, knows that to read fiction for pleasure is to possess a form of currency in urban life—even if one's chosen reading is not the *dernier cri*.[56] But the dialogue skirts the possibility that the ambitious young apprentice may be more fashionable than this fuddy-duddy gent, whose taste for the familiar is not just belated but also a little obsessive.

From the booksellers' viewpoint, of course, too much loyalty to old books had the commercial disadvantage of limiting customers' willingness to buy new titles. The clever apprentice therefore builds from his customer's request for the familiar toward an endorsement of the new, Rowlands's own book, which he associates with the proven records of Greene, Breton, Chaucer, and Nashe. Once more the gentleman tries to resist. Pretending he already knows *Tis Merrie When Gossips Meete*, he cries, "why, that Title is stale," and reels off a list of other "merry meetings" in book, ballad, and proverb—including previous works by Rowlands (6). The gentleman's misguided pedantry provides a further opportunity for Rowlands to drop familiar titles as endorsements to the reader, even as it demonstrates that novelty is a relative claim. Rowlands here inserts himself into an entertainment-reading canon that can be called popular literature—yet claims that the category's appeal extends to gentleman readers.

The apprentice, frustrated by the gentleman's ambivalence, turns to another kind of narrative pleasure. He describes the textual meeting of the wife, the maid, and the widow as a form of forbidden sexual intimacy. Usually, jests the apprentice, a man may not "deal with" a wife because she is "another mans commoditie." The book, on the other hand, can be any man's commodity; owning it, the gentleman may commodiously "carry *Wife*, *Mayde*, and *Widdow* in [his] pocket." The gentleman catches on: "be-like thy Booke is a conjuring kinde of Booke for the Femenine Spirits, when a man may rayse three at once out of his pocket" (7). To close the sale, the apprentice appeals to barely moralized voyeurism: if you "sit alone privately in your Chamber reading of it, . . . peradventure the time you bestow in viewing it, will keepe you from . . . [the] Bawdy-house." The owner of fiction can have a privileged "viewing" of women's secrets in the privacy of his own home. Eagerly, the gentleman concludes "wee must needes have some Traffique together," confirms the price, and hands over his sixpence (8). Now the book, like the imagined wife, has become "another mans commoditie," and the trafficking between tastes and classes so feared by Harvey has become, for this imagined moment, a traffic in women. Rowlands resolves class tensions in the cultural marketplace by transforming the alienable material commodity to an intimately possessed sexual commodity.

Having completed his transaction, the gentleman revives the verbal exchange, asking the apprentice, "What is this an Epistle to it?" The apprentice replies, "Yes, ti's Dedicated: To all the pleasant conceited London *Gentlewomen*"; this title, set in large type, ends the page and then appears again as the title of the epistle dedicatory on the next leaf, moving from the fictive dialogue into the typographic frame (8–9). Rowlands's pamphlet thus invites every reader to join in an inspection of the materiality of the book and the gendering of its audience. More specifically, it invites its implied readers—men—to imagine themselves transformed into ladies.[57] Those who imitate the gentleman and read the dialogue in the bookshop not only use the built-in endorsements the way a modern browser uses book-jacket blurbs but also are literally and pleasurably written into the book. Much as the depicted common currency of fiction titles violates the barrier between apprentice and gentleman, the preface's self-reflection blurs the boundary between text and reader. No one can escape reading Rowlands's book, a cultural commodity that virtually creates its own consumers.

Rowlands's dialogue names a group of authors as central to the pleasure reader's marketplace; the pride of place given to Greene recognizes Rowlands's own debt to him. *Tis Merrie* was a success, with the canny inset references to Greene no doubt playing their part; it survives in four editions issued over the Stuart period, as well as two editions of a sequel. Rowlands borrowed from Greene more thoroughly in his other 1602 publication, an imitation of Greene's coney-catching pamphlets. *Greenes Ghost Haunting Conie-catchers* (also discussed in chapter 1) effectively replaces Greene's *Conny-catching*, so pointedly lacking from the *Tis Merrie* apprentice's stock. Using one of his titles to help create demand for another, Rowlands here engages in cross-marketing of a type in which Greene had specialized. The choice of criminal subject matter also shows that like Greene, Rowlands was willing to fictionalize lower-class life for an audience mostly in the middle of the social range, from aspirants in service and trade to established gentlefolk. His bookshop dialogue shows that while popular books might feature characters who were socially distant from many of their buyers, an important part of their appeal was their claim to span lesser social distances among their readers. Rowlands's strategic reference to Greene worked because a range of Jacobean readers were still enjoying Greene's characters; perhaps much as Rowlands's customer thrilled with voyeurism in the bookshop, they were excited by class intercourse in their reading choices. Rowlands's dialogue reveals that in the nested spaces of the pamphlet, the bookshop, and the book market, social mingling was an experience that was discursively rejected but in practice clearly embraced.

THE MAID IN HER CHAMBER

Over the course of the seventeenth century, rewritings of the private scene of consumption discounted the ladies' text trope, revising downward the social rank of female pleasure readers. The trope was also contentiously redirected: Lyly used it to toss off his work as a mere trifle, but seventeenth-century writers invoked it to mark other texts, not their own, as trifling. The Overburian character is one of a number of satirical Stuart texts that expand scenes of maids' expertise in romance to make the social class sub-text of the ladies' text trope increasingly explicit, demeaning, and unreliable. I do not deny that many of England's literate women, including those in service positions, must have read romances with pleasure. But it is clear that these scenes statistically over-represented the presence of women among that readership. Women, particularly servant women, were seen as taking over the genre because their literacy produced particular anxiety. In terms of gender as well as class, claims that the romance was dropping in social prestige actually registered concern about those with the potential to move up.

The dominant rhetorical strategy of these scenes—projection—is extended from gender to class. As a mixed-gender audience was imagined as female, so a mixed-status audience could be imagined as déclassé. This strategy is developed strikingly in Lyly's preface to *Euphues and his England* (1580), quoted in chapter 1, which sets up a ladder of descending social worth, from male scholars to lady readers to female servant readers. Ladies enact downward cultural circulation when they lend one volume of *Euphues* to their "wayting Maydes"; they maintain distinctions by making the maids "wayt" for the other part. Thirty-five years later, the Overburian "Chamber-maide" who reads romances as Lyly predicted does not vindicate his demographics; rather, the later character simply varies his strategy of distinction, pushing the romance further down that ladder. Where Lyly showed reading material being shared across class lines, the Overburian piece omits any elite women's interest in the romance—precisely to fore-stall such sharing. The implication is that "ladies" (not to mention gentle-men) have passed to their inferiors not just an extra volume but the whole genre of romance. Lyly's partial displacement has become an absolute denial, a more rigid social boundary.

The Overburian revision of Lyly claims the irrelevance of romance to elite men, but intervening scenes of consumption hint otherwise. Even when a scene assigns romances to women readers, its details inscribe the concerns of male writers, revealing those allegedly worthless romances to be invested in struggles for textual and authorial control. The scenes deny the value of romance to male readers, perhaps because womens' comfort with the genre was threatening: a surprising number of anecdotes depict men undone by women with superior knowledge of romance. Another sign that men are reluctant to cede the romance entirely to women is the occa-sional effort to exempt certain titles from condemnation, as Cervantes's curate salvaged the least offensive romances when burning Don Quixote's library (book I, chapter 6). Much as the curate and the barber do, many scenes of consumption compare particular romances: typically two titles are mentioned, one chivalric, the other more recent, native, and authorial, and possibly less corrupt. Whether the scenes compare the expertise of various readerships or the dignity of various titles, they modulate what might have been a uniform attack on the romance into a more complex discourse that gradually asserted class distinctions among seventeenth-century women readers of these sixteenth-century romances. Chivalric romances, Greene's romances, and the *Arcadia* were imagined as appealing to different ranks of women readers and even as inviting different kinds of reading; but these boundaries were continually under construction.

Once Stuart writers had begun to distinguish romance readers not only by gender and class position but also by reading practices, they began to for-mulate a theory of popular print culture in everything but name. Ross holds that seventeenth-century depictions of female readers figure "the autono-mous, unguarded consumer of print, the non-productive 'common reader' " of any sex, "as opposed to the authoritative 'learned reader' " (83). However, I see Stuart writers dividing that "common" readership already. They pred-icate popular reading practices as unforgivably nonproductive, indeed coun-terproductive, while gesturing toward elite women's reading practices as nonproductive yet literary (a move that Ross dates to the eighteenth cen-tury). By mid-century, Stuart imaginings of women's romance reading identified two very different kinds of pleasure, one old-fashioned and gullible, the other fashionable and knowing. The downmarket practice was identified with chivalric romances, and, as the Overburian character shows, with Greene's works, however prematurely. The latter reading practice was newly invented and pertained to the *Arcadia* alone of the romances left from the last century. That was no accident: by inventing literary leisure for reading ladies, writers rescued Sidney's text to support the court's "royal romance," as Annabel Patterson has termed the Caroline habit of self-understanding through the myths of English and French romance.[58]

If the *Arcadia*'s rescue has not been noticed before, it may be because critics have been unwilling to face how close that work came to sharing the ignominious fate of Greene's romances. The scramble for the *Arcadia* indicates the scope of the Stuart denigration of romance—and the limits of its efficacy. The attack actually allowed Greene's romances and the *Arcadia*, coupled in a reference of 1599, to be assigned to separate realms a few decades later. As chapter 4 will show, the language invented to rescue Sidney's romance would be echoed and developed in the novel and ultimately used to attack *Pandosto*: the first drawing of a shaky and contentious line between the two Elizabethan authors was in the Jacobean period.

The seventeenth-century English denigration of romance as women's reading had sixteenth-century origins: even as the first Continental romances were translated, treatises by Vives and Ascham warned youths of both sexes against romance reading (Wright 110). As Helgerson points out, each generation that repeated those judgments against romance increased their satiric violence and social condescension, and their specific aim against women.[59] As the warnings were elaborated into full-blown scenes of consumption, any moral force they possessed yielded to voyeuristic energies. "A Chamber-maide" is too alluring to constitute a serious condemnation of romance, but that tradition is legible in its contrast to "A Faire and Happy Milkmaid," another character added in 1615. The milkmaid is free of romantic notions: "She makes her hand hard with labour, and her heart soft with pittie: and when winter evenings fall early (sitting at her merry wheele) she sings a defiance to the giddy *Wheele of Fortune*" (Paylor 56). While the chambermaid is passive in the hands of her printed romance and corrupt in her household relations, the milkmaid actively generates oral entertainments and works productively at her duties. The literacy of the chambermaid aligns with her dissolution; the illiteracy of the milkmaid confirms her innocence. The pointed pairing singles out low-status women as peculiarly subject to romance temptations of sexual and class aspiration. This discourse was a far cry from the humanists' concern for the best young minds.

One influential intermediary between the humanist antiromance tradition and the Stuart character writers was Jonson, who worked his contempt for chivalric or Elizabethan romances into several of his stage comedies. In *Every Man Out of his Humour* (1599), a rather obscure conversation marks a very thin line separating Sidney's quality from Greene's. The infatuated Fastidious Brisk marvels that the pretentious court lady, Saviolina, "does observe as pure a phrase, and use as choise figures in her ordinary conferences, as any be i' the Arcadia." Responds the cynical Carlo Buffone, "Or rather in *Greenes* works, whence she may steale with more security."[60] Both authors' romances are guilty of licensing her affectation, but only Greene's are disreputable, clichéd, or prolix enough to be plagiarized without risk. Jonson still associates reading Greene with pretense to fashion, placing Saviolina a notch above the citizens he portrays reading chivalric romances and *Euphues*.[61] This strategy of satiric characterization through cultural tastes prefigures the Overburian scene of consumption; more broadly, this play is often cited as an influence on the prose character because it was published with Jonson's capsule descriptions of the dramatis personae, or, as the title pages of the 1600 editions put it, "With the severall Character [sic] of every Person."[62]

If the Overburian characters were broadly modeled on Jonson's play, their respective views of romance readership are at odds. It seems unlikely that the romances Jonson associated with a lady of cultural pretension and her social circle in 1599 could become, by 1615, the exclusive property of serving maids. Equating Greene's works with the chivalric romances, "A Chamber-maide" implies that the distinction Jonson noted had collapsed after only fifteen years. Publishing history supports Jonson's audience analysis, not the character's; his own publishers were actively reissuing Greene's steady-selling romances.[63]

From the publishers' viewpoint, Greene's works merited securing. But respect for the publishers' copies did not prevent very direct borrowing. Hind and Bettie, mentioned above, stole "with security" from Greene's work, even though it remained in frequent republication during the same period. Thomas Creede, publisher of Hind's romance and printer of Bettie's, himself printed *Pandosto* a few years later. These facts confirm that the kind of borrowing Jonson condemned in a lady's conversation was tolerated among authors and publishers (though not by Jonson). Yet Jonson's and later scenes repeatedly project the problem of textual imitation from the book market onto female readership, as though appropriation by women readers was the most important violation of textual property. Stephens, in the same volume that exposed the professional authorship of the Overburian characters of 1615, matched Jonson with another anecdote about women's authority in citing from Sidney. A lawyer's clerk plans to woo "with bawdery in text; and with Jests, or speeches stolne from Playes, or the common-helping *Arcadia*" but is spurned "worthily" by a woman who can recognize his sources.[64] The joke here is the reversal of textual authority: women are preserving such property instead of signifying its openness, as they generally do. Stephens's startling description of the *Arcadia* as "common-helping" demonstrates that anxieties about the dispersal of romance across class lines were dogging even Sidney's work by 1615.

In other scenes, the alleged insecurity of romance was doubled, employing the semiotics of class as well as gender. In private-theater plays in particular, authority in romance became a basis for solidarity or competition between gentlewomen and their chambermaids. Their contact over their cultural objects rewrites Lyly, staging the ladies' text trope to dramatize the private promiscuity of the romance as entertainment commodity. Jacobean children's company plays are fascinated by mistresses and female servants who share romance reading and sexual secrets. In *Ram-Alley* (1608), Mistress Taffeta imagines her married life: she will "keep / My chamber by the month," and "have my maid read *Amadis de Gaul*, / Or *Donzel del Phoebo* to me." In *Eastward Hoe* (1605), a lady betrayed wails to her maid, "Would the Knight of the Sun, or Palmerin of England, have used their Ladies so?," appealing to chivalric norms learned from their shared reading.[65] Later scenes more pointedly developed tensions over rank, as mistress and maid began to rival each other in their knowledge of romance conventions. In William Browne's unpublished poem "Fido, an Epistle to Fidelia," Fidelia is imagined as an idle lady comparing her various love letters:

> Then meeting with another [letter] which she likes,
> Her chambermaid's great reading quickly strikes
> That good opinion dead, and swears that this
> Was stol'n from *Palmerin* or *Amadis*.[66]

Browne's lines rewrite the ladies' text trope as a scene of social rivalry; in the chamber, a maid's "great reading" in romance gives her the advantage of her mistress, herself quite worldly. The rest of the epistle reverts to the second person, as "Fido" desperately pleads with "Fidelia" to believe that he has not stolen his compliments to her but has talent enough to have written them himself. As Fido begs her to "allow" his "workmanship," this harrowing epistle hints that representations of struggle for textual authority between ladies and their chambermaids may deflect other struggles for authority between men and women.

Later Stuart drama moves from linking mistress and maid in their knowledge of romance to anxiously denigrating the maid's knowledge as mere credulity. Oriana, heroine of John Fletcher's *The Wild Goose Chase* (1621), mocks the populace to whom *Amadis* and *Palmerin* are "modest and true stories." Yet she herself is named after the heroine of the *Amadis*, and in her lovesick mad scene she calls her own brother Amadis. A confidante in Philip Massinger's *The Guardian* (1633) measures her mistress against the heroines of "all the books of *Amadis de Gaul*, / The *Palmerins*, and that true Spanish story / The *Mirror of Knighthood*, which I have read often, / Read feelingly, nay more."[67] Both of these plays pointedly assert that lower-class women readers take chivalric romances to be "true," but suggest that upper-class women are not sure what to believe. It is intriguing that both of these are King's Men plays, since the anxiety they betray about the "truth" of romance narrative strongly marks an earlier King's Men play, *The Winter's Tale*. As the last section of this chapter will show, that play, too, articulates class-specific relationships to the "truth" of mimetic narrative, with its primary referent not *Amadis* but *Pandosto*. Present in the repertory through this period—performances are recorded at the Globe in 1611 and at various royal banqueting houses in 1611, 1612–13, 1618, 1624, and 1634—*The Winter's Tale* contributed to the gradual segregation of reading practices.

The project of rescuing the *Arcadia* from its broadly devalued genre required a more direct reimagining of its problematic female readership. The "common-helping" *Arcadia* came very near to joining Greene's works and the chivalric romances in an emerging category of popular romance. That is most evident in Wye Saltonstall's 1631 character, imitating Thomas Overbury, of a "maid" who "would not willingly dye in Ignorance": "she reads now loves historyes as *Amadis de Gaule* and the *Arcadia*, & in them courts the shaddow of love till she know the substance."[68] The syntax equates the *Amadis* and the *Arcadia*, two steps apart in Jonson, as simulacra of immorality. To recode the *Arcadia*, then, elite writers needed to eliminate maids from its audience. The servant's presence had given Lyly an erotic stand-in for the male voyeur, but by the 1630s, only her absence could preserve the exclusivity of the *Arcadia*'s gentle readership. Other, more exclusive elements from Lyly's scene were picked up instead: the language of courtly love, the physical luxury in which gentlewomen read, and the intimacy between gentlewomen and their books as objects.[69] These features enrich mid-seventeenth-century portrayals of women reading the *Arcadia*, including poems by Francis Quarles, Richard Lovelace, and Charles Cotton, granting women readers a refined detachment sharply different from their coarse naiveté in the main stream of allusions to Greene and the chivalric romances.[70] These women readers were at least literary readers, a claim articulated in the language of class.

The discursive construction of this complex new reading practice, which both indulged and refused the sensuality of romance, paved the way for later claims that the reading of certain kinds of romances (and, later, novels) was an exclusive literary experience. For the purposes of this chapter, the important point is that this reading practice depended on the exclusion of nonelite women readers, and hence of older romance forms. But there are signs that these new refinements were within reach of the readers of *Pandosto* in the 1630s—not from elite writers, who do not mention *Pandosto*, but from the editions themselves. *Pandosto* enjoyed even more of a "little renaissance" than the *Arcadia*: editions survive from 1610, 1614, 1619, 1629, 1632, 1635?, 1636, and two from circa 1640. (It seems likely that a mid-1620s edition has been lost.) This sequence is impressive by any measure, but the acceleration after 1629 is striking. If *Pandosto*'s revival parallels that of the *Arcadia* (editions in 1627–29, 1633, and 1638), it was clearly not effected by or for the court circle; those who celebrate Sidney in the 1630s apparently assume that Greene is beyond the pale (this would change after 1640, as chapter 3 will show). The royal romance attempted to split the genre between courtly and popular modes; the contemporaneous revival of *Pandosto* may evince publishers' and readers' resistance to such splitting. Publishers, at least, understood that the *Arcadia* and *Pandosto* might appeal to many of the same tastes; but their championing of the latter by frequent, careful publication could make only partial headway against the silent but no doubt persistent scorn of the most fashionable. Once itself stylish, still broadly read, selling better than ever in its full-length form, *Pandosto* was too familiar for its reputation to be completely ruined or recouped. By 1640, it stood at the center of a range of printed entertainments that was being forcibly divided in two. There it might have been expected to symbolize the separateness of popular and literary print readerships, but instead it repeatedly symbolized their continuity.

Pandosto's ambivalent social position after 1630 is visible in small but significant textual changes. The most striking was a new title. In an edition of ca. 1635, what had been the half title and running title in all previous editions, "The Pleasant Historie of Dorastus and Fawnia," was raised to the status of main title (figure 2.3).[71] The romance would not be published again under the title of *Pandosto* until the nineteenth century, when Shakespearean criticism reestablished interest in the earliest editions of Greene (see chapter 3). This more or less new title constitutes a re-commodification, a reattribution of social value to the text, but its exact valence is hard to peg. It seems to minimize the plot strand that makes up the bulk of the text, the tragic jealousy of the King of Bohemia, in favor of the happier love story of his lost daughter and his rival's son. Because the new title replaces a singular patriarchal hero with a paired hero and heroine, it seems to seek or reflect increased female readership, and has sometimes been taken as implying that at this time, *Pandosto* fell to its proper place as *The Pleasant History of Dorastus and Fawnia*, cheap leftover and mere romantic fantasy. I question this entire sequence of deductions. In the narrowest sense, the change presents no *new* paratextual information: even in the earlier editions, that running title appeared on every page opening while the main title appeared only once per edition. The change is significant to book buyers browsing title pages, but less so to actual readers. The potential of *Pandosto* to be read as a love story had existed all along, not just in the free play of interpretation of the text but also in the paratextual signals. Nor was the change a strategy of desperate marketing: title changes were widely used in the early modern book market to introduce valued texts into new contexts.

In terms of the emerging hierarchy of genres, the new title sends complex messages rather than evincing a simple movement toward popularization. "Pleasant history," a formula applied to many of the older romances, strikes twentieth-century readers as quaint and spurious. But as Spufford points out, on the seventeenth-century book market, "history" had less to do with verity than with duration; it denoted a full-length narrative, as opposed to a chapbook. "History" was therefore not the downmarket signal it might seem. The title change can also be understood as an imitation of Quarles's *Argalus and Parthenia*, which similarly underscores the love plot of a long romance. Quarles, too, referred to his book as a "history," on the title page and in his preface; the word was not inconsistent with his ambitions to fashion. If the class orientation of *The Pleasant History of Doras-*

tus and Fawnia is complex, so is its gender orientation. The romance once titled for a male protagonist now divided the title roles between a man (mentioned first) and a woman, changing the target audience (perhaps) from male to mixed gender but certainly not orienting the book only to women readers, as commodity consumption scenes implied.

The most interesting changes in the editions of the 1630s appropriate features of Caroline royal romance to *Dorastus and Fawnia*, again suggesting that it remained current in the eyes of publishers and readers. Gradually, these editions introduce a new form for referring to Fawnia, the young heroine. In Greene's text, she, her lover Dorastus, and the narrator all comfortably identify her job title as "shepherd": the profession carries no gender markings. Just a few years later, the word "shepherdess" began to appear in English pastoral texts, most notably Lodge's *Rosalynde* (1590). *Pandosto*'s use of the unmarked job title was not revised until the 1632 edition, in which Dorastus praises Fawnia as "borne to be a Shepherdesse, but worthy to be a Goddesse" [D4], while a page later, Fawnia still tells herself, "thou art a Shepheard" [D4v]. The edition of 1635 adds the -ess suffix in several places, and in the 1636 edition, Fawnia is invariably a "shepherdess." Within three editions, Greene's romance has been shaped, retroactively, to the gender decorum of literary pastoral. The revisions also move Fawnia away from the realities of animal husbandry and toward decorative convention: already pastoralized, she is now pasteurized. In the characters, the use of workers' job titles had alienated them from social ties, but Fawnia's new title alienates her from even the status of worker.

The new title did sacrifice *Pandosto*'s links to Greene's other works with similar titles, which were now rapidly falling out of print. As the field of Greene's extant works narrowed, the titling conventions that had linked them lost meaning to readers. The title *Dorastus and Fawnia* connected with ongoing developments in the genre of romance rather than an authorial corpus or an era of original publication. Although Greene's name and motto continued to appear on the title page, the front matter had been dropped from the 1629 edition onward, effectively reducing the authorial context and freeing the romance to more current associations. This change, too, affected only the cultural positioning of the text, not its economic value; the quarto still ran to seven signatures and therefore still fetched the same price.

The change to "Shepherdesse" was thorough, but it was also isolated, not part of a general modernization of Greene's text. Thus it points to the

THE
PLEASANT
HISTORIE OF
Dorastus and *Fawnia*.

Wherein is difcovered, that although
by the meanes of finifter Fortune, Truth
may be concealed; yet by Time, in fpight
of Fortune, it is manifeftly revealed.

Pleafant for age to avoyd drowfie thoughts,
Profitable for Youth to avoyd other wanton
Paftimes : And bringing to both
a defired Content.

Temporis filia Veritas.
By ROBERT GREENE, Mafter of Arts in *Cambridge.*
Omne tulit punctum qui mifcuit utile dulci.

LONDON,
Printed for *Francis Faulkner*, and are to be fold at
his fhop in Southwarke, neere Saint
Margarets Hill, 1636.

FIGURE 2.3
Title page, Robert Greene, *The Pleasant Historie of Dorastus and Fawnia* (1636).

representation of women as an area of strong concern, conscious or not, among the producers of these editions in this period. It is unclear who took the trouble to make the change (and adding a syllable while resetting a densely packed page could initiate a domino-effect series of typographical adjustments). Conceivably the publisher (Francis Faulkner, who brought out every edition from 1629 to 1648) made or ordered some corrections. More likely the changes were introduced in the printing houses, where a series of compositors, over these three editions, looked at their copy text and were spontaneously moved to contribute their improvements. It is tempting to wonder about this process in the 1636 edition, which made the change uniform, because it was printed in the shop of a woman, the widow Elizabeth Purslowe (presumably she did not set type herself).

What cultural influence led compositors to squeeze in the feminine suffix? The introduction of this change in the 1630s—not back when Greene's contemporaries first began to use the term—points to the romance sensibility of Caroline court literature.[72] In a letter of 1625, John Donne commented on the arrival of Henrietta Maria, urging another courtier to come "see this, the Queen a Shepperdesse" (quoted in Patterson 170). Since Greene's plot reveals Fawnia to be a lost princess, it is not surprising that her agricultural duties were renamed to match a title adopted by the Queen. A prompt response to specific literary and political forces, the revision demonstrates that although elite Stuart writers were unwilling to reclaim *Pandosto* as a version of the royal romance, Stuart publishers and readers recognized its continuities with the new styles (as did translators in France and the Netherlands). The royal romance defined itself as exclusive and romances like *Pandosto* as popular, but readers knew that queen and shepherdess could not be so readily separated.

That Dorastus and Fawnia could be identified with Charles I and Henrietta Maria would be confirmed, poignantly, in the edition of 1648, when Francis Faulkner filled the title page of his last edition of *Dorastus and Fawnia* with a large woodcut of a couple who look for all the world like the royal pair (figure 2.4).[73] Both are portrayed at full length: on the left is Prince Dorastus, in a full suit of armor, with flowing dark hair and a mustache; on the right is Fawnia, with Caroline sloped-shoulder dress, pearls, and side curls. She, looking toward the viewer, places her right hand in the hand of Dorastus, who gazes solemnly at her. The portrayals, arrangement, and courtly gesture closely echo the well-known double royal portraits of the 1630s, by Daniel Mytens and Sir Anthony van Dyck, in which Charles

The Pleafant

HISTORY

OF

DORASTUS and FAWNIA.

Pleafant for Age to avoid drowfie thoughts, profitable for Youth to avoid other wanton Paftimes : And bringing to both a defired Content.

By ROBERT GREENE, Mafter of Arts in *Cambridge.*

LONDON,
Printed for *Francis Faulkner,* and are to be fold at his fhop in *Southwark,* neare S. *Margarets* Hill, 1648.

FIGURE 2.4
Title page, Robert Greene, *The Pleasant Historie of Dorastus and Fawnia* (1648).

FIGURE 2.5

Robert van Voerst after Van Dyck, *Charles I and Henriette Maria* (1634).

BY PERMISSION OF THE BRITISH MUSEUM, DEPARTMENT OF PRINTS AND DRAWINGS

I and Henrietta Maria exchange a laurel wreath. The image circulated in a 1634 engraving (figure 2.5).[74] The two depicted on the *Dorastus and Fawnia* title page idealize both Greene's lovers and England's royal couple, playing out the neo-Platonic iconography of the "warrior knight laid low by the beauty of the queen," as Roy Strong puts it (74). But in 1648, Charles was being laid low by more deadly forces, and Henrietta Maria had long since fled to her homeland, inverting Fawnia's return from exile. Still, for all its royalist myth making, this woodcut was designed as an illustration specific to *Dorastus and Fawnia*: in the left background is a baby floating in a cock-boat, on the right an indeterminate shepherd/ess with crook and sheep. The first English illustration of the tale, humbler than its French precursors, this title-page woodcut nonetheless insists that both of its lovers are more noble than their surroundings. The fantasy was marked as royalist, but it was not class- or gender-specific. Long outliving both the royal couple and the publisher who commissioned it, the woodcut was reused on almost every *Dorastus and Fawnia* title page through 1688.

THE CARPENTER IN THE STREET

The story of *Pandosto*'s Stuart reception would not be complete without a consideration of the text that did most to construct the romance as a popular cultural commodity: *The Winter's Tale*. Even to think of the play as part of *Pandosto*'s reception is innovative: usually the relationship runs the other way, with the romance used simply to confirm the play's achievement as adaptation.[75] Treating the play as a reaction to Greene's romance, rather than the romance as Shakespeare's source, offers a new perspective on two striking features often observed by Shakespearean critics. First, the narratological self-consciousness of *The Winter's Tale* has been recognized as a meditation on the play's relationship to its prose source—an observation made as early as 1907 and refined by many critics.[76] More recently, critical interest has centered on Autolycus, the ballad seller with no equivalent in Greene's story, because he and his wares introduce the problem of the print commodity into the stage play.[77] I believe these two features are inextricably related: the printed commodity is brought to the stage in act 4 in response to the presence of the prose source in the play as a whole. In combination, these two features respond subtly to *Pandosto* and to its place as representative popular cultural commodity.

The Winter's Tale explores and shapes the status of early modern printed entertainments from the unique perspective of the stage (as recorded, of course, in the print of the First Folio). Certainly the play reflects philosophically on the differences between dramatic and prose romance in ways that critics have found stimulating. Stanley Cavell sets out a consensus: the play is "asserting the competition of poetic theater with nontheatrical romance as modes of narrative, and especially claiming the superiority of theater (over a work like [Shakespeare's] own 'source' *Pandosto*) in securing full faith and credit in fiction."[78] The play's evaluations of each genre's truth claims are not ideologically innocent, however, but encoded in the language of distinction, corresponding to the class-specific reading practices constructed in the period. The ballad-selling scene incorporates the Stuart attack on popular romance: it is a double scene of consumption that stages both the buying of popular print commodities by a newly literate "clown" and their eager consumption by an audience of female servants in husbandry. The play folds into its romance plot repeated representations of popular narrative as unsophisticated or foolish, as though denying its own reliance on such a tale. It presents mimetic narrative—in print but not on the stage—as feeding fantastic desires and threatening social hierarchies. These objections both echo classical hostility to mimetic narrative and anticipate the Marxian critique of the commodity fetish. Yet in the end, the play may ironize the distinctions it builds, confessing or even licensing theater's potential to be similarly disruptive and to appeal to diverse audiences.

All of the play's boldest plot changes may be seen as active responses to its origins in popular fiction—even the ending, which provides a tragicomic miracle where Greene concluded his "comedy with a tragical stratagem" (Salzman, *Elizabethan Prose Fiction*, 204). Greene offsets the discovery of Fawnia's identity with the suicide of Pandosto, but Shakespeare provides the extraordinary theatrical illusion of Hermione's statue, which, by deceptively seeming to revive, reveals the truth that the queen's death was a fiction. The improbabilities of Perdita's discovery and Hermione's return are explicitly celebrated for their resemblance to popular narrative. In the last act, three different characters note that the plot has been resolved like an "old tale," thus fulfilling the promise of Shakespeare's title and of Mamillius's unfinished "sad tale," "best for winter," from the first act. After the Third Gentleman recounts the offstage family reunion, the Second Gentleman marvels: "This news, which is called true, is so like an old tale that the verity of it is in strong suspicion" (5.2.27–29). Concurring, the Third Gentleman describes the next event in his narration as "Like an old tale still" (5.2.62). Later, the lady-in-waiting, Paulina, remarks of Leontes' reunion with his wife: "That she is living, were it but told you, should be hooted at like an old tale" (5.3.115–17).

These references, together with the play's title, apparently liken its miraculous endings to those of traditional, female-centered oral narratives, the "winter's tales" and "old wives' tales" told by the fireside on dark nights.[79] Crucially, however, the play's oral "old tale" slips into print in 5.2, when the Second Gentleman promises that "ballad-makers cannot be able to express" the events of the day (24–25).[80] The line forges a strong if paradoxical connection between the play's oral and print precursors: the play's events are so like an old tale that they become "news" (5.2.27). At that point where oral traditions meet cheap print stands the ballad maker, or at least ballad singer, Autolycus. The Autolycus plot is thus bound to the denouement, and cheap print to orality, identifying *Pandosto* as the kind of "old tale" that the play challenges.

Oral tales were already inserted into the matrix of literacy, portrayed as the particular province of the illiterate and as repositories of errors displaced from print sources. The *Triumph of Faith*, a devotional work from 1613, urged: "Let our mirth be . . . spirituall mirth . . . not winter tales, and foolish stories, the divels chronicles, which never need printing we can so well remember them."[81] Yet in *The Winter's Tale*, it is elite characters who invoke such tales: Mamillius's interrupted ghost story in 2.1, Paulina's image of the ghost of a jealous wife in 5.1. The setting of 2.1 among Hermione's maids implies that Mamillius has learned storytelling from his wet nurse or attendant.[82]

In fact, the most striking narrative techniques of *The Winter's Tale* were based on models known in this period primarily through the printed word. These conventions are the Greek romance features imported by Greene: ship journeys, exposed children, disguises, and oracles. Greene's *Pandosto*, then, is the old tale that *The Winter's Tale* follows and exceeds. A generation-old printed story, already discounted by Rowlands as reading for the countrified and by Jonson as reading for women, is labeled as an even less reliable oral tale, just one step away from an illiterate countrywoman, and transformed into an ephemeral ballad sold by a shape-shifting deceiver. The reduction of Greene's romance to both folk tale and ballad distances the play from its source, displacing the author's conditions of production down the social ladder yet again.

If a tale is so attractive that it can't be true, these courtiers know it should be "hooted at" or examined in "strong suspicion." It is crucial that these ridiculed mimetic narratives be popular and their detractors gentle: this dynamic identifies the courtiers as participants in a Platonic tradition that couples elite suspicions of mimetic narrative with elitist certainty that such lying stories will deceive only the masses.[83] This tradition is the intellectual bedrock of the attack on romance that I have traced throughout this chapter; I can now name it antimimeticism, by analogy to the more familiar antitheatricality.[84] The two prejudices share a pedigree, with roots in Plato's *Republic* and branches of humanist and theological attacks on certain forms of entertainment. The particular *locus classicus* of antimimeticism is Book 10, which holds that all literary forms participate in the dishonesty of mimesis. Socrates argues that the maker of fictions pretends to be a jack-of-all-trades but in fact is a maker only of lies. Unlike the carpenter who makes beds, the poet makes only imitations of beds, thrice removed from the Ideal form. As Jonas Barish argues in his famous study of antitheatricality, the poet, with no "true" trade, is unacceptable in a society where every man's craft is ordered, constant, and integral.[85] But the poet's worst fault is his potential to deceive others, described in a passage that reveals the project of distinction that lies at the heart of the antimimetic impulse:

> For example: a painter will paint a cobbler, carpenter, or any other artisan, though he knows nothing of their arts; and, if he is a good painter, he may deceive children and simple persons when he shows them his picture of a carpenter [displayed] from a distance, and they will fancy they are looking at a real carpenter. (Adams 35)

This primal scene of antimimeticism, itself a fantastic fiction, connects a deep suspicion of the epistemological status of mimesis with a smug assertion that those susceptible to it are the lower orders, the "children and simple persons."[86] If not for the governors who censor *in loco parentis*, one simple artisan could easily deceive another with a life-size cutout of a third.

The Platonic description of literary mimesis may be crude—Barish notes that "Plato's visual fixation seems to trivialize the whole argument" (7)—but its apparent illogic lays bare its social foundation. A fundamental instance of distinction, Plato's antimimeticism cloaks the arbitrariness of social differentiation as an absolute aesthetic or moral law. That law argues that mimetic narrative, like theater, should be condemned for its power to create make-believe that can pass for real. Underlying the argument are class-based fears: that those who yield to illusions are the lower classes, that those who manipulate illusions are also low-born, and that the representations they manipulate will portray the low-born—and even, unspeakably, the high-born. After all, if you can make yourself a carpenter, you can make yourself a king.

To fear that a medium of representation can alter the social relations it portrays is, as Marx shows, to see it as a fetish. That fetishization, far from perverse, can be explained by the principles of cultural capital. Mimetic narrative is dangerous because it offers the less educated and less privileged the opportunity to manipulate their self-representations for their own purposes. Such fiction could directly rival the larger fiction—the noble lie that sustains the Republic—or at the very least acquaint consumers with the nature of social fictions. Popular mimetic narrative, especially in print form, was a double threat to the early modern social order: as mimesis, it had the power to tell lies (or were they truths?) that countered dominant ideologies; as cheap print, it had the power to offer (indeed, to sell) those lies, mass-produced, to "simple persons." Much as antitheatricality is traceable to the power of performance to unsettle the foundations of gender identity, antimimeticism is identifiable as the fear that fictions, especially when circulated in print, could undermine the ostensible fixity of social hierarchy.

It is no accident that Plato and Marx converge in worrying about fetishes. Plato's deceptive "picture of a carpenter" lingers in Marx's commodity, which he exemplifies as a "form of wood" that "steps forth" and is misperceived in the eyes of men as a "social thing" (320–21). Marx disapproves of the Platonic hostility to the material, but his emphases on alienated occupations and the physicality of the fictive medium are indebted to Plato. Marx's concern with the alienated tradesman resonates with the Platonic image of the imaginative writer who furnishes a criminal but ambitious mockery of productive but humble craftsmen. His fascination with the mystery of the commodity revises the Platonic obsession with the representational medium that is grossly material, almost literally a stumbling block.[87] *Capital* follows *The Republic* in reporting horror at the capacity of things to enact social meaning; the difference is that *Capital* objects to treating lesser humans as mere counters. Nonetheless, because Marx's account remains haunted by antimimeticism, Plato's social prejudices reappear as the problem of false consciousness that makes workers vulnerable to ideology.

This Platonic scene is widely echoed in early modern commentary on the problem of mimesis, which continues to single out occupations and dwell on the materiality of fiction. It is repeated, for example, in the details of Ascham's objection to "fonde bookes, of late translated out of *Italian* into English, sold in every shop in London, commended by honest titles the soner to corrupt honest maners, dedicated over boldie to vertuous and honorable personages the easielier to begile simple and innocent wittes" (Smith 1:2). In a shop, every title page is as deceptive as the painter's painted carpenter. Henry Chettle, Greene's executor, cautions against the deceptive power of print over the "simple persons" "at a distance" from the city: "the sellers swear these are published by authority; and people far off think nothing is printed but what is lawfully tolerated" (Henderson and Siemon 213). In 1614, the publisher of the Overburian characters had commented that poetry readers had trouble distinguishing "betwixt the horse pictured on a signe-post, and the curious limbd *Pegasus*." Much later, but again in the context of the character (that genre whose very name is materially conscious),

Samuel Butler says that "A Romance Writer" "differs from a just Historian as a Joyner does from a Carpenter," focusing on surfaces rather than solid construction.[88] Only Sidney's *Defence of Poesie*, in rejecting the antimimetic critique of poetry, parodied its materialism and literal-mindedness. Children do not mistake the stage prop of an old door marked "Thebes" for Thebes, and even "a very partial champion of the truth" does not criticize a chess player "for giving a piece of wood the reverend title of a Bishop."[89] As Sidney demonstrated, it was the antimimeticists, not the simple people, who were fixating on material representations.

The features that have recurred throughout these scenes of consumption all reappear in *The Winter's Tale*. The antimimetic critique that the courtiers treat so lightly is developed at length in Shakespeare's other major addition to Greene's story: Autolycus. Rogue and ballad seller, he fulfills Socrates' prediction: here is a manipulator of narratives who has indeed seduced and deceived simple folk. From a distance, Autolycus can make himself look like a mugging victim, as a painter can make a carpenter: he is the ultimate craftsman-turned-criminal. A master of many imitative arts, he can sell ballads or sing them, serve nobles or impersonate them, sell notions or plant them in the "hearts of maids" (4.4.273). The repeated catalogues of the contents of his pack anchor him at the level of materiality that joins Plato's and Marx's accounts. His goods are fetishes, for he "sings 'em over as they were gods or goddesses" (4.4.209–10). Yet in his presence, humans are reduced to nothing but acquisitiveness and literally robbed of the profits of the labors that would fund their community feast. All of his wares are both "useless" and "noxious"; Socrates could take comfort only in the knowledge that Autolycus scorns his own craft as no craft.

Autolycus is also a demonized version of that unclassifiable, uncontainable craftsman, the early modern author. In Book 10 of the *Republic*, Socrates explains the hold of liars like Autolycus over people like Shakespeare's simple country folk:

> When anyone reports to us about someone, saying that he has encountered a human being who knows all the crafts and everything else that single men severally know . . . it would have to be replied to such a one that he is an innocent human being and that, as it seems, he has encountered some wizard and imitator and been deceived.   (Bloom 281)

To Socrates, such victimization by rogues is inevitable because undiscriminating simple folk lack the cultural literacy to "put knowledge and lack of knowledge and imitation to the test" (Bloom 281). The masses, seduced by Autolycus's craft of fiction, overlook his cunning craft of social self-transformation. Shakespeare seems to use Autolycus to embody Platonic fears that might well redound on the playwright.[90] He disempowers Autolycus later in act 4, so that he becomes a figure of stagecraft and narrative control gone wrong, the playwright as both criminal and ineffectual, a laughable evil twin to Prospero. He is absent from act 5, where Shakespeare redeems those transformative powers for himself. Autolycus's potentially dangerous role as "wizard" extends to chanting a "smock" into a "she-Angel" (4.4.211), but Shakespeare takes wizardry as far as the "lawful" "magic" that revives Hermione (5.2.111).

If Autolycus constitutes a demonized author of fictions who is exorcised to make Shakespeare's theatrical magic lawful, he is recognizable as that other infamous, shifting Bohemian, that yarker-out of unconsidered trifles, Robert Greene. Scholars have been reluctant to identify Autolycus with Greene, perhaps because the ballad seller has struck them as far more glamorous than *Pandosto*.[91] Yet Autolycus's tricks would have been widely recognized as derived from Greene's best-selling coney-catching pamphlets, a significant choice within this careful adaptation of Greene's romance. More broadly, the context of disreputable fiction lurking behind the acceptable old tale calls up Greene as Autolycus's precursor. Even Autolycus's tumble down the ladder fits: Greene, too, once "wore three-pile" and then scraped by in borrowed "lesser linen," could ooze "court-contempt" but then "compassed a motion of the Prodigal Son" and ran through "knavish professions" (4.3.14, 24, 93–94, 96). Greene, too, was anxious about whether his name would be inscribed in the role of rogues or the "book of virtue" (4.4.118). The parallel could be unconscious or Shakespeare's deliberate joke; if a joke, it could even be available to audience members, who, like Drummond, knew their Greene. The false "pedlar's excrement" that Autolycus doffs to become a courtier (4.4.713) could recall Greene's flamboyant beard, which Harvey described as a "fonde disguising of a Master of Arte with ruffianly haire." A long red stage beard would match Nashe's vivid description: "a jolly long red peake, like the spire of a steeple, which he cherisht continually without cutting, whereat a man might hange a Jewell."[92] Mamillius begins a story of a man who "dwellt by a church-yard," clearly a ghost story; Autolycus can be seen as the ghost of Greene, who lived by the produce of St. Paul's churchyard and was buried, Harvey said, "near Bedlam," in "the New-churchyard" (Crupi 28). Autolycus's ruses are drawn directly from Greene's *Second* and *Third Part of Conny-Catching*.[93] As

Rowlands had predicted in 1602 (see chapter 1), the play gives us "Greenes ghost," a haunting coney-catcher.

While Autolycus regards his wares as lightly as the loot he calls "unconsidered trifles," the ballads he sells can be recognized as stage representations of popular printed forms. Scholarly interest in Autolycus's ballads has centered on their truth claims, said to be typical in cheap print, or on their status as commodities alongside such items as wool and plays.[94] These readings underestimate the uniqueness of this scene, which speaks to a subject otherwise virtually taboo on the early modern English stage—the existence of the competing book market. While books and reading are symbolically important in many early modern plays, the acts of publishing or buying books are rarely mentioned or depicted.[95] Autolycus's ballads are the first printed commodities to be sold on the early modern stage in the first public staging of the book market. The scene sums up all the degrading sites that Parrot would list in 1615, asking his bookseller not to let his text be "with your Ballads mixt," or "at Play-houses, mongst Pippins solde," or "brought in Pedlers packs, To common Fayres" and "Solde at a Booth mongst Pinnes and Almanacks" (Wright 95–96).

Choosing ballads rather than plays in quarto (conceivably being sold at performances) or romances (perhaps too bookish), Shakespeare found a compact prop capable of invoking the complex status of the printed commodity. Of course the ballad is a diminutive and thus humorous synecdoche of the book market. But it is also theatrically effective, for the actual conditions in which ballads were sold and consumed answered the theatrical challenge of bringing print to life onstage.[96] As Natascha Wurzbach demonstrates, the distribution of ballads uniquely collapsed salesmanship and performance from the moment a ballad seller appeared and sang to customers a preliminary song advertising the wares (figure 2.6). The buying of the ballad and its performance were interwoven, since the negotiation of a purchase usually involved the singing of that ballad, sometimes by the seller and sometimes by buyer and seller together. So, too, Shakespeare's ballad-selling scene integrates buying and reading, the commercial world of the print market and the experiential world of readers' enjoyment.

The dynamics among Autolycus, the Clown, and Mopsa and Dorcas combine the portrayal of print-buying men by occupation with the portrayal of print-loving women in terms of class ambition and sexual desire. In this outdoor print marketplace, the Clown complains that the maids do not observe modest behavior, but make the private issue of their rivalry public. A rural counterpart to Niccols, the Clown objects to the breaths of

A Merry new Song
Les Chanteurs de Chansons
Cantarine di Strada

Mauron delin: P. Tempest exc:
                                 Cum privilegis

FIGURE 2.6
M. Laroon, *A Merry New Song* (depicting female ballad seller and male
customer), from *The Cries of London* (1711).

his fellow customers, until he is carried away by sharing pleasures with them. Mopsa and Dorcas are unsure about marrying a usurer or yielding their cold hearts, but they are eager to "bear" the burden of a suggestive song (4.4.293). The scene treats the dual problems of the printed commodity's "common-helping" availability and its power over the credulous. In a neat reversal, the traditional charges made by scenes of consumption against each sex here turn out to fit the opposite sex just as well or better. Although the women do not make any purchase, they want to buy everything, showing an eager aptitude for excessive consumption even if the man controls the purse strings. Meanwhile, the Clown is exposed as more gullible than the women; he will be fooled by Autolycus's pretenses again and again.

Much as later Stuart elevations of elite reading practices required the elimination of credulous maids, Shakespeare's version of antimimetic distinction requires that Perdita, the gentle shepherdess of his tale, take no interest in the commodities that fascinate the others. This romance heroine is not seeking self-transformation, although she has found it. Her famous argument against botanical cross-breeding (4.4.79ff) shows that she nurtures no desire to move beyond her position of birth (a point that Shakespeare makes much more unambiguously and insistently than does Greene); therefore, she is granted a transmigration to a noble place that is not a climb but a return to status. As she and her father enjoy their happy recoveries, however, Autolycus grovels before his new masters. Perdita's rube relations, his former victims, have now been rewarded with laughably inappropriate knighthoods: these shepherds profess themselves "gentlemen born," for a gentleman made is ideologically impossible (5.2.121ff). Thus the play's comic scapegoat for both narrative dissimulation and social aspiration bows before its comic tokens of improbability and mobility. The "news" of the family reunion may be more fabulous than Autolycus's ballads, but like the shepherds' promotions, it poses no social threat. By staging narrative's potential to disrupt the social order, *The Winter's Tale* differentiates its own dramatic restoration of that order.

But Shakespeare's use of the antimimetic tradition must also be evaluated as a tactic in his confrontations with antitheatricality. Both forms of prejudice would have contributed to his ambivalence about appropriating *Pandosto* and the many other popular fictions he adapted in his plays; the dramatist was even more vulnerable than the fiction writer to charges of misleading the public, offering to the gullible the noxious examples that threatened existing controls over social representation. *The Winter's Tale* does not, admittedly, put its representation of social questions foremost: the central role is reserved for the reestablishment of the patriarch's family. But the recurrent bucklings of social hierarchy form a powerful symbolic subtext that the play does not work to contain, any more than it succeeds in excusing its own implication in the dangers of popular narrative.

If Shakespeare's appropriation of *Pandosto* is double-voiced, his use of the antimimetic tradition is also ambivalent. Drawing on a romance by an author whose reputation is being reassigned from the fashionable to the popular, this socially aspirant playwright admits that such romances can speak to the needs and desires of a diverse audience and implicitly acknowledges the continuities between Greene's work and his own. *The Winter's Tale* picks up the thread of Platonic antimimeticism by putting fiction in the hands of stock characters from the laboring classes, and it certainly deflects the materiality of print far from the play itself. But it also uses the mythology of antimimeticism to expose the contradictions of antitheatricality to an audience well disposed toward narrative pleasures. The ballad scene, for all its mockery of the foolishness of ballads and buyers, reflects Shakespeare's investment in the performance of popular culture: the improvised concert by Autolycus and his customers inevitably mirrors the conditions of theatrical performance. The play prefers theater to other cultural forms, but it does not deny the links among them. More significantly, it does not fully endorse the emerging model of absolute separation between elite and popular print cultures. The ballad-selling scene cannot avoid betraying genuine affection for the popular practices that other writings of the period neglect or scorn.

The scene, especially in the context of the whole play, even suggests that popular print can be a "social thing" in a positive sense: it can do genuine social work. The ballad that Autolycus offers to the Clown, Mopsa, and Dorcas, to "the tune of 'Two maids wooing a man'," addresses the subject of jealousy in love (4.4.290). Not just a reminder of Leontes' jealousy, the song speaks to the dynamics the group has revealed elsewhere in the scene. Sings Dorcas: "Thou hast sworn my love to be," and Mopsa replies: "Though hast sworn it more to me." The Clown, resuming the lover's role briefly played by Autolycus, says "We'll have this song out"—and perhaps this argument (4.4.304–7). But regardless of this rivalry, the trio of lovers is in "three parts" of harmony about choosing this ballad (4.4.294). The ballad may achieve its success because Autolycus intuits his audience's needs, like a good salesman or an imaginative author. Or perhaps his audience guides him to those needs when they pick this ballad more eagerly than his first, less romantic offerings. The important point is that popular cultural goods, overproduced and excessively tempting as they are, still offer even the humblest readers something they can use.

This possibility is one that traditional literary criticism, founded on strategies of distinction, has been reluctant to consider. Mopsa waxes enthusiastic: "I love a ballad in print, a life, for then we are sure they are true" (4.4.255–56). Critics and historians have long quoted Mopsa's line in attributing a uniform degree of "ignorant credulity" to nonelite readers; in doing so, they read Shakespeare's play far too credulously.[97] At the least, this remark participates in the seventeenth-century topos of fatuous nonelite female readers (which recurred in later King's Men plays). Furthermore, the play is far too aware of competing media and competing truth claims to have offered Mopsa's words at face value. Fully appreciating their thematic importance requires crossing class lines. Mopsa, a shepherdess, echoes a queen, Hermione, who has struggled to articulate the truth of her innocence in the face of the preconceived "truth" set down in her indictment. Mopsa's words literalize and materialize the central question of textual truth posed by the oracle of Apollo in act 3.[98] More pointedly, they oppose the play's sharpest condemnation of mistaken attitudes toward textual authority. Leontes is brought the sealed scroll (from a distance). He avers that its contents will prove his suspicions even to those "Whose ignorant credulity will not / Come up to th' truth" (2.2.192–93). But when the scroll that contradicts him is publicly read, instead of believing it, he thunders, "There is no truth at all i' th'oracle . . . this is mere falsehood" (3.2.137–38). The immediate death of Mamillius proves his error, so that he sees the proverbial handwriting on the scroll.

Later, Leontes more deeply recognizes the relevance of seemingly fantastic texts to his life. He gradually accepts the viability of representations, in writing or, of course, in marble and paint. That openness to the "truth" of fictions contrasts with Polixenes, who in act 4 tolerates popular performance (the dances of satyrs and shepherdesses) but fails to see the humanity of the social class that entertains him. In 5.1, Leontes criticizes Polixenes for treating Perdita as a "trifle," a living, lying object, the social counterpart of Autolycus's degraded, lying ballads, his "unconsidered trifles" (223). Still, only in act 5 does Leontes realize that the "truth of [her] own seeming" surpasses any "old tale" (4.4.653). He has "come up to th' truth" as requiring a tolerance of illusion.

Even if Mopsa sounds like a mere commodity fetishist, she contributes to the ongoing conversation about alternate truth claims and competing media that is central to the play. Readers who laugh at her risk making the mistake of Leontes, assuming that the text will vindicate their values. This continued misreading of Mopsa's role in the scene of consumption is a definitive instance of the enduring critical pattern in which popular culture is blamed while literary culture is shielded. Shakespeare's version of the scene of consumption has been used as key evidence of the degradation of popular print culture, but if it is looked at not "from a distance" of critical superiority but in its full context of competing attitudes toward mimetic entertainments on page and stage, it tells another story. The claims that the newly literate were fooled by popular culture simply afford the well-educated the further privilege of fooling themselves.

CHAPTER THREE

Material Alteration

Re-commodifying *Dorastus and Fawnia* and *The Winter's Tale*, 1623–1843

> *We must be content to take Shakespeare as he is, "with all his imper-*
> *fections on his head," or not take him at all. . . . There is generally*
> *something so comprehensive and peculiar in his original design, that a*
> *material alteration of it is sure to be for the worse.*
> —Jean Genest, on David Garrick's stage adaptation of The
> Winter's Tale, in *Some Account of the English Stage* (1832)[1]

In claiming that *Pandosto*'s success provoked an ambivalent response in *The Winter's Tale*, I have diverged from a long critical tradition that has kept the two works on separate planes. For the last 150 years, the consensus has been that Shakespeare's stage adaptation of Greene's romance was not a mere change of genre but a metamorphosis. J. J. Jusserand, in 1890, made the point explicit: "Greene had, in truth, only modelled the clay; Shakespeare used it, adding the soul."[2] Although Jusserand briefly admits that Shakespeare "used" *Pandosto* extensively, his metaphor of vivification insists that the adaptation has risen entirely above the materiality in which *Pandosto* is mired.

This claim for vivification is still present, if implicit, in most modern evaluations of *The Winter's Tale*, underwritten by the play's transformative ending. *Pandosto* kills off its injured queen, but *The Winter's Tale* brings Hermione back to life in a spectacular *coup de théâtre*. It is a commonplace of *Winter's Tale* criticism to assert that the miracle of illusion that breathes life back into the never-dead Hermione is exceeded only by the miracle of authorship that breathes life into the moribund *Pandosto*.[3] Still, critics concur that the play's "resurrection" of Hermione works only through the performative material of theater, as the memorial "statue" erected in her honor is revealed to be a living actor's body. I argue that similarly, Shakespeare's work with his source does not transcend the materiality of text making but refits a narrative told in prose to the material conditions of the theater.

My greater concern with the myth of vivification is that it portrays *Pandosto* as lifeless, a judgment that is neither universal nor inevitable, but the product of centuries of distinction making. *Pandosto*'s supposed lifelessness in relation to *The Winter's Tale* was articulated during a long period, from the Jacobean era into the nineteenth century, when both works were successful as textual commodities. For most of this time, both were available in full-length textual reproductions as well as free adaptations; at various times, both appeared on stage as well as in print. In large part, they remained in circulation independently of each other. Unlike any other Shakespearean play and its source, *The Winter's Tale* and *Pandosto* had a shared history of endurance and variation in the entertainment marketplace.[4] Even more strikingly, their common history saw a reversal in their relative fortunes. For the first half of this period, *The Winter's Tale* remained near the bottom of the Shakespeare canon, while *Pandosto* was the more widely known of the two works. For over a century, from the 1630s to 1741, *The Winter's Tale* was absent from the stage; during the next thirty years, drastic adaptations attempted to correct its perceived faults of disunity and improbability. The last of these came in 1771, well after critical taste had turned against what Jean Marsden calls "radical adaptations" of Shakespeare.[5] Until 1741, *The Winter's Tale* was published only in collections of Shakespeare's plays. Meanwhile, *Pandosto* appeared at regular intervals, both in unadapted full-text editions through 1762 and in competing formats that met diversifying demands.

Once the two works were linked as play and source, *The Winter's Tale* gained credit and *Pandosto* lost it. The recognition came first, then the distinctions: in 1623, *The Winter's Tale* belatedly joined *Pandosto* as a print commodity, but no one linked the two; in 1688, Gerard Langbaine identified *Pandosto* as providing the plot of *The Winter's Tale*; in the 1750s, the relative merits of the two works became controversial; and in the 1840s, protocols of source study firmly justified the subservience of *Pandosto*. The distinction between them was complete in 1843, when Greene's text was reprinted as a curiosity for scholars in John Payne Collier's *Shakespeare's Library* while the last extant chapbook edition was printed at Belfast, its ongoing life unnoticed by the educated.

In the years following 1688, as knowledge of Shakespeare accumulated, critics realized that he had followed his source exceptionally closely in this play.[6] This closeness had to be acknowledged, but that other intimacy of play and source, the contemporaneity of their survival on the market, was repressed. The social threat presented by the two works' simultaneous lives in print is evident as writers' material distinctions increasingly attempted to segregate them as high and low; yet the ongoing uses of both works remained far too varied and inventive to allow such a division. To reconstruct this complex relationship, this chapter moves among three histories: the history that kept *Pandosto* alive in print and sometimes on stage; the history that kept *The Winter's Tale* alive, also in both print and performance; and the history of critical reception that first linked the two works, then gradually discounted *Pandosto* and elevated *The Winter's Tale*. My assertion is that these three histories are in fact only one, in which the two linked works' parallel lives on the marketplace were denied by an emergent critical practice founded on acts of material distinction.

The case of *Pandosto* and *The Winter's Tale* thus exemplifies how in Shakespearean source study, protecting Shakespeare's originality and isolating the plays from materiality go hand in hand. My epigraph shows how claims for Shakespeare's originality lead to claims for his immateriality: Jean Genest lauds Shakespeare's "original design," ignoring what is not original about the plays, as the reason his works resist "material alteration." Genest quickly glosses over the problem of source use in order to attack the problem of adaptations, but it is clear that both problems turn on the materiality of alteration: Shakespeare the alterer of sources differs from alterers of his plays in that only he can make works that unalterably transcend the material. In this chapter, questioning the "conventional pieties" about Shakespeare's use of sources, I treat both *Pandosto* and *The Winter's Tale* alike as "recyclable material."[7] I read the growing claims for the plays' superiority to earlier analogues and later adaptations as denials that Shakespeare participated, like Greene and later authors, in a continued process of re-commodification.

Re-commodification is the retelling and retailing of a textual commodity that already exists in some form. It markets the story to new audiences by more or less free deployment of highly visible features: in print, for instance, title, format, length, and signals of authorship and genre affiliate a text with other known print commodities. In 1623, the King's Men's stage play, based on Greene's prose romance in quarto, was printed as Shakespeare's in folio. By 1756, *Pandosto* could be purchased as an anonymous sixteen-page chapbook or in a multivolume octavo collection called *Shakespear Illustrated*, while *The Winter's Tale* circulated, on stage and in print, under various titles by various hands. Re-commodification asserts that comparable material work is done by Shakespeare's alterations of prose narratives for the stage, the once-notorious alterations of his plays for later stages, and the long-forgotten alterations of Greene's prose narratives for later readers. Yet the re-commodifications of *The Winter's Tale* have been forcibly separated from the other re-commodifications of *Pandosto* with which they share a history. This chapter traces that separation, showing how changing attitudes toward textual re-commodification repeatedly bound the works together but ultimately drove them apart. It shows that the tension between the persistence of *Pandosto*, so well suited to repeated re-commodification, and the canonization of *The Winter's Tale*, acceptable to later audiences only with textual and performance alterations, could be resolved only by denying the latter's adaptability.

Re-commodification allows Shakespeare's work with sources to be considered alongside the adaptations of Shakespeare that have been so productively reevaluated in recent appropriation studies. However, re-commodification is less concerned with the claims of ownership that are central to appropriation than with the remaking of existing cultural materials by new producers and sellers for new interests and audiences. Its key question is not who owns cultural material, but how and why a particular embodiment of that material can be claimed as a new work.[8] Because re-commodification takes as normative that cultural materials circulate to users across such contingent boundaries as authorship, it differs from appropriation studies, which, even in critiquing authorship as constructed, tend to reproduce the centrality of ownership in defining the uses of a text. The derivation of the word "appropriation" may foreground the effects of "making a text one's own," but studies of appropriation tend to focus on the negotiation for textual ownership and authority between the seizer and the prior possessor. Re-commodification sees authorial names as simply one feature in a wide array of changeable textual markers guiding audience use.

Re-commodification also insists that texts are embedded in circumstances of economic production and material form, which must be traced when one kind of material object is turned into another. Because any text that is published or produced is directed toward a market, a reshaping is not necessarily more commercial than the "original." Rather, the commerciality of a text is created discursively in portrayals of its material status: its existence as a physical object subject to editorial and typographic shaping; its production by authors and publishers seeking some sort of profit or result; its competition with other works that may use the same plot or a similar title; and the necessity of handling it physically in order to read it. I see this process of re-commodification as neutral, but from a viewpoint protective of elite exclusivity, it may be seen as invasive, reductive, or demeaning. If the print commodity reminded early modern elite readers that texts circulated publicly and materially, the re-commodified text reminded them just how arbitrarily and profitably texts could be embodied. Re-commodification, especially when it involved a reduction in the length of the work, was (and often still is) seen as a sloppy dispersal that both cheapened an "original" text and generated dubious knock-offs. The early modern commodified text in general was marked as female and nonexclusive; the re-commodified text was seen as even more degraded along lines of gender and class, as every shortening further reduced it to the capacity of the female, poor, and immature.

Elite onlookers saw re-commodification as a process that should be restricted to popular literature; but that could not be. Repackaging is necessary for any work, whether constructed as popular or elite, to endure and remain responsive to changing audiences. By taking "material alteration" as my chapter title, I assert the positive value of textual malleability, and its importance to both canonization and popularization. In *The Making of the National Poet: Shakespeare, Adaptation, and Authorship, 1660–1769,* Michael Dobson shows that "adaptation and canonization, so far from being contradictory processes, were often mutually reinforcing ones." If adaptation was a necessary precondition to Shakespeare's survival and hence to his canonization, it was also crucial to the popularization of non-Shakespearean works. Re-commodification delivered both Greene's romance and Shakespeare's play to further generations, although the process was increasingly evaluated along class lines. That constant re-commodification is needed to extend a textual tradition beyond merely antiquarian interests is a crucial point of continuity between elite and popular literatures, suppressed when literary works are held to be exempt from material alteration.[9]

While common economic conditions sent *Pandosto* and *The Winter's Tale* through parallel forms of re-commodification, the two works did not converge in the awareness of Shakespeareans until 1688, after which distinction rapidly effaced the similarity of their manifestations. I divide this complex history into five chronological periods from 1623 to 1843, identifying for each period the characteristic practices of re-commodification that shaped individual transformations of both works—and especially the attitudes toward re-commodification that shaped that most problematic act, Shakespeare's adaptation of Greene. In each of these sections I discuss prevailing economic conditions influencing re-commodification; focus on particular individuals who articulated new practices to advance various interests; analyze textual changes in *Pandosto* and *The Winter's Tale*; and characterize period understandings of their interrelationship. These sections are also framed by nineteenth-century scholarship, which I show to be riddled with misrecognitions that consolidate material distinctions between Greene's tale and Shakespeare's play and disguise the common conditions under which the two works were repeatedly remade.

During the Jacobean and Caroline periods, re-commodification is evident in fairly unself-conscious efforts to recirculate old tales in new forms, under the protocols of a small, self-governing publishing industry. Those who published *Pandosto* and *The Winter's Tale* made no connection between them but simply saved the works from obsolescence, which I argue threatened *The Winter's Tale* more directly than *Pandosto*. From 1640 to 1660, keeping pre-War literature in circulation required inventive conversions to small-scale, portable, topical forms that would sell quickly. Interregnum abridgments treated Greene's romance and Shakespeare's novel as virtually indistinguishable, in ways that would baffle later critics.

In the following generation, from 1660 to 1688, the all-too-material necessity of re-commodifying works was repressed as larger publishing and literary communities took shape. Booksellers and collectors effectively defined canons of pre-War literature through catalogues, collections, and illustrations; *Pandosto* was essential to popular romance, while *The Winter's Tale* was claimed for Shakespeare. After 1688, new standards were being articulated for both publishers' re-commodifications and authors' adaptations, and literary scholars constructed histories that for the first time linked *Pandosto* to *The Winter's Tale* and began to rank them. From this last decade of the seventeenth century, *Pandosto* was dismissed as a "delectable history" (in the title of a pamphlet version discussed later in this chapter) and blamed for the "palpable Absurdity" of the play's Bohemian seacoast setting. Finally, through the eighteenth and into the nineteenth century, a highly competitive market drove the distillation and shortening of both works, even as an emergent Shakespeare industry confronted the degradations of marketing the bard. From 1700 to 1843, both works were remade, indeed often reduced, into the forms of duodecimos, novels, drolls, garlands, and Arabian tales. Re-commodifications marked as Shakespearean were repeatedly vaunted while the rest were devalued, but *Pandosto* survived to be published by Charlotte Lennox in *Shakespear Illustrated* (1753– 54) and to influence David Garrick's reduction of *The Winter's Tale* to a brief dramatic pastoral (1756). The canonization of Shakespeare's oeuvre as transcendent was necessitated by its ongoing re-commodification in tandem with popular titles like *Pandosto*.

1623–40: OLD TALES

The story of the collective re-commodifications of *Pandosto* and *The Winter's Tale* must start in 1623, since the text of the play in the First Folio is the first that can be compared to *Pandosto*. Of course that play text is at two removes from Greene's romance: it re-commodifies *The Winter's Tale* as performed by the King's Men (debuting in 1610–11), which itself recommodified *Pandosto*. Like many stage productions, the pre-Folio performances of *The Winter's Tale* have left few textual traces. Many of these attest to performance as itself a commodity, since they are entries in one account book or another. A paper from the Office of the Revels documents a performance of "ye winters nightes Tayle" in 1612; the Lord Treasurer paid the King's Men for a performance at Princess Elizabeth's wedding festivities in early 1613; and Sir Henry Herbert's Office Book registers performances in 1623 and 1633.[10]

No trace of audience response to the staged *Winter's Tale* identifies it as a re-commodification of *Pandosto*. This omission is not surprising, since Shakespearean audiences (unlike Restoration audiences) generally paid little attention to questions of adaptation.[11] Yet *The Winter's Tale* is so self-reflexive that it seems to foreground that re-commodification. In particular, critics who have traced the theatricality of Hermione's transformation have concluded that Shakespeare's adaptation relied on audience members' familiarity with *Pandosto*. Inga-Stina Ewbank calls Hermione's vivification "the ultimate *coup de théâtre* for those who came to see the play, knowing *Pandosto*"; Dennis Bartholomeusz describes the play as "defying the expectations of those who had read the tale."[12] Unfortunately, the only seventeenth-century eyewitness of the play to have left a record, astrologer Simon Forman, failed to mention *Pandosto* or the statue scene in his notes for 15 May 1611.[13]

While there is no direct evidence that early audiences linked the two works, my reading of the play in chapter 2 could be taken as indirect proof: audience awareness of *Pandosto* is displaced onto references to "old tales." Except for the ballad-selling scene, which acknowledges the existence of printed prose texts, the play claims to turn oral narrative into theatrical experience, rather than a contemporary print commodity into a dramatic commodity. By treating its printed precursor as a preliterate text, the play has seemed to later critics to discount Greene's romance. But in later Jacobean and Caroline England, *The Winter's Tale* could not have positioned *Pandosto* as old, flawed, dated, lowbrow, obsolete, forgotten, lost, or dead—because increasingly many of these charges were leveled against the play as well. The current fashion, hard on *Pandosto*, threatened to be hard on *The Winter's Tale* as well, offering a salutary reminder that the elevation of Shakespeare's play was no more a foregone conclusion than the persistence of Greene's romance.

The play as published in 1623, joining *Pandosto* in print, is certainly more permanent than the version mounted theatrically, but the Folio text is troubled by its own discontinuities. In this it is not alone: in a series of accidents from 1623 up until the Civil War, either *Pandosto* or *The Winter's Tale* disappears just when its presence would seem most assured, as though enacting the oracle's warning about "that which is lost." For instance, at first glance, the Folio text projects a textual permanence that outweighs Greene's little romance in quarto. Within a volume that claims the plays as living monuments, *The Winter's Tale*, the last of the comedies in the Folio, has a prominent position. Yet an error momentarily makes the play disappear from the volume: consult the table of contents, turn to page 304 for *The Winter's Tale*, and find a blank page. Turn to page 277, and that which was lost shall be found. The error on the table of contents appears to have resulted from a gap between the printing of the previous comedies and that of *The Winter's Tale*. This delay is signaled by other breaks in the textual body of the Folio—an unprecedented blank verso page between *Twelfth Night* and this play, a tail-ornament that was dented by wear between its appearances in the two comedies.[14] These discontinuities reflect a brief time when no text at all occupied the place where *The Winter's Tale* now stands.[15]

Around the same time, a manuscript copy of *The Winter's Tale* also went missing. An August 1623 record (itself now lost) in the Revels office licensed "the king's players" to perform "an olde playe called *Winters Tale*, formerly allowed of by Sir George Bucke, and likewyse by mee on Mr. Hemmings his worde that there was nothing prophane added or reformed, thogh the allowed booke was missinge" (Pafford xvi). Textual scholars have speculated about the nature of this "allowed booke," with some hypothesizing that it was also the "fair copy" for the Folio text, but current analyses of the Folio's printing point to the two textual disruptions as unrelated.[16] Their causes are unrecoverable, but their eventual resolutions are strikingly different: the play reappeared in the Folio, carefully prepared by scrivener Ralph Crane; the show went on at court, without the allowed book. In contrast to the care Hemmings and Condell apparently took to secure *The Winter's Tale* for the Folio, the Revels office saw it as just "an olde playe."

There is no 1623 setting of *Pandosto* to compare with the First Folio; editions exist with publication dates of 1619 and 1629, but none in between. This gap is one of the longest in *Pandosto*'s publication history, and it is likely that an intervening edition did not survive.[17] In any case, *Pandosto* was so textually stable in this era that differences among the editions are not terribly consequential—except for the change in the oracle in the 1607 edition, in relation to *The Winter's Tale*. The First Folio oracle promises that Leontes will "live without an heir" as in early editions of *Pandosto*—not, as post-1607 editions have it, "die without an heir." Forman's paraphrase, "die without yssue," simply points up the Folio's dependence on Greene's wording (quoted in Pafford xxi). The textual variant among *Pandosto*'s editions shows not only that Shakespeare "had *Pandosto* at his elbow as he wrote" but also that his edition was printed in 1607 or earlier (Pafford xxxi). It was not brand new, but it could no more have been an old tale fifteen or sixteen years after its debut than *The Winter's Tale* could have become "an olde playe" to the Revels office after a dozen.

Ben Jonson, among all Shakespeare's contemporaries, had the most to say about Shakespeare's use of "old tales," although he never mentions *Pandosto* specifically. Two comments may reflect indirectly on source use in *The Winter's Tale*: the refusal to "Beget *Tales, Tempests*, and such like *Drolleries*" in the 1614 Induction to *Bartholomew Fair* (l. 130); and the vituperation against the stage, published with *The New Inn* in 1631, which calls *Pericles* a "mouldy Tale."[18] Jonson's immediate disdain for the late plays ran counter to contemporary taste, and it is likely that he was deliberately underestimating two of their charms: their typographically enhanced affectations of antiquity; and the sophistication of their reflections on the media of reproduction, including manuscript, print, and live performance. For example, one prose version of *Pericles* uses black-letter type, by then associated with older histories and chivalric romances, to give a fashionable new text an antique patina. This use contradicts Charles Mish's reading of black-letter type as a "class discriminant" between drama and fiction, discounting those romances (including *Pandosto*) that retained black letter into the seventeenth century, when drama was in roman type.[19] On the second point, although Shakespeare is generally seen as taking little interest in the publication of his company's plays, the late plays exhibit an especially strong interest in print, both bringing books on stage as props and evoking them metaphorically.[20] These references fit into a larger pattern of interest in modes of narrative transmission that has earned these plays, in the twentieth century, the revived label of "romances," all, in their own ways, at once theatrical, bookish, and tale-like. These works patently draw on "romance" stories widely available in print to convey an oral narrative experience in full stage dress.[21]

When Jonson sniped at Shakespeare's creaky romance conventions, he probably found the plays derivative, not of oral tales, as critics generally assume, but of written "tales" of little worth. He could have recognized that the "mouldy" conventions of Shakespearean romance found their precedent in Greek romance, having owned and marked a Latin copy of Heliodorus's *Aethiopian History*.[22] Like other Greek romances, the *Aethiopian History* makes self-reflexive jokes about the conventions of older genres, comparing its plot twists to the tragic *deus ex machina*, for instance. Greene, imitating Heliodorus, chose to "close up the comedy with a tragical stratagem."[23] Shakespeare's jokes about old tales turn the generic mockery back from drama to prose narrative, with additional reflections on print. Whether Jonson could fit Greene into a sequence of influence from Heliodorus to Shakespeare is uncertain; he never mentions Greene, and no work of Greene's survives from his library. Jonson may have implicated either *Pandosto* or Greek romances as Shakespeare's mouldy source; in any case, he faulted Shakespeare not for excessive imitation but for imitation of inferior works. This point would be lost as Jonson's more positive depiction of Shakespeare as poet of nature outweighed his criticism of Shakespeare's undereducation.

Another influential early commentator did even more to mask Shakespeare's use of sources. Leonard Digges's verses in the 1640 *Poems*, speaking of the plays, claim that "all that he doth write, / Is pure his owne, plot, language exquisite."[24] Since plenty of Shakespeare's "plots" must have been recognizable—those of the histories, at least—the only way to take Digges's claim at face value is to assume that he meant Shakespeare did not rely on the *drama* of others. By the Restoration, Paulina Kewes points out, there was strong consensus that to borrow or translate someone else's play was a less original and less demanding activity than to convert a prose source to a drama (89). What Kewes calls "appropriative license," then, was being negotiated by Digges as early as 1640, to Shakespeare's benefit.

After 1660, the myth of Shakespeare's natural originality, based on a partial reading of Jonson's reactions, took hold quickly. Margaret Cavendish, Duchess of Newcastle, was the first to offer a different view, characteristically unorthodox and prescient. In her *Sociable Letters* of 1664, she includes the first critical essay published on Shakespeare, which is also the first full acknowledgment of his reliance on sources. According to Cavendish, Shakespeare lacked

> Subjects for his Wit and Eloquence to Work on, for which he was Forced to take some of his Plots out of History, where he only took the Bare Designs, the Wit and Language being all his Own; and so much he had above others, that those, who Writ after him, were Forced to Borrow of him, or rather to Steal from him.[25]

Those who have "dispraised" him, she adds, do so "out of Envy." Cavendish's letter may follow the generic guidance of the folios in treating Shakespeare's histories as a group. Or, since "Plots out of History" could refer to prose fiction as histories, Cavendish could also be noting the use of romance plots in the comedies and tragedies. Given the period's ambivalence about romances, this broader implication could have been either accidental or deliberate.

Strikingly, Cavendish distinguishes between Shakespeare's adaptations and the work of his imitators, whom she charges with plagiarism. That distinction bears out Kewes's claim that Restoration culture perceived a difference in type between borrowings from fiction by drama and thefts from one drama by another. But Cavendish's passionate praise for Shakespeare seems to claim a difference in quality as well. Her response to the wave of Restoration adaptations of Shakespeare is doubly poignant, given her husband's long record of imitations of Jonson and her own insistence on devising original plots that were widely mocked.[26] Paradoxically, William Cavendish, an orthodox son of Ben, took the conventional view that Shakespeare devised his own plots; Margaret Cavendish, unabashed voice of originality, knew that he adapted them. The contrast between husband and wife prefigures rapid changes in the cultural attitude toward dramatic adaptation that would transform the reputation of *The Winter's Tale*. By 1688, like some other late plays of Shakespeare once regarded as faulty in uneducated creativity, *The Winter's Tale* would be recognized as an adaptation, faulty in its reliance on material that some found dubious.

1640–60: "ABBRIDGMENTS & ABBRIDGING"

The instability of the Interregnum allowed a temporary tolerance for practices of textual transmission that were less reverent than usual, less clearly marked by authorship, and more ephemeral. These abridgments would look to later Shakespearean critics like destruction, but they were actually means of preserving works like *Pandosto* and *The Winter's Tale*, carrying pre-War texts into suitable forms for hostile conditions. The changing tolerance is most striking in Royalist culture: aristocrats, who had defined their tastes by preferring folios with engraved title pages to cheaper forms, suddenly found their best weapon was the fugitive ballad: cheap, portable, easily produced on an unauthorized press and without license, and easily marketable even without an author's name. The history of the Royalist ballad demonstrates the failure of the Commonwealth to impose order on publishing at any time, and, of course, the lapse in the Stationers' economic control over book production. Under these circumstances, writers, printers, and booksellers could easily have produced romances and other entertainments with no attention to rights in copy. But in fact *Dorastus and Fawnia*—the title *Pandosto* never reappeared after the 1635 change discussed in chapter 2—enjoyed regular publication, through the Interregnum and beyond. It was published at full length by a series of printers who possessed legitimate claims to the copy—not to mention the woodcut that looked like Charles I and Henrietta Maria (see chapter 2).

Other uses of *Dorastus and Fawnia* during the Interregnum are remarkable for their ingenuity in turning an Elizabethan romance to new commercial and political ends. While Greene's text continued to be published unchanged, two new verse adaptations made the familiar story into a briefer but more politically pointed commodity. These re-commodifications demonstrate that the narrative was worth preserving but Greene's authorial claim was not. Like most other Interregnum appropriations of pre-War materials, they are much shorter than the work they replaced; unlike most, they respect the claims of the stationers holding the copy. But neither text acknowledges Greene as "original" author. Indeed, one draws indifferently on both *Dorastus and Fawnia* and *The Winter's Tale*, which became narratives of exile pressed indiscriminately into the service of populist royalism.[27]

These two Interregnum adaptations are so different from Greene's original that they probably could have been entered separately in the Stationers' Register in times of control. They are in verse and vary significantly in length and title from Greene's romance. While free and clear in legal terms, they present puzzles of chronology, authorship, and political motivation. Both are by prolific writers who supported themselves by publishing Royalist material, Thomas Jordan and Samuel Sheppard. Greene's *Pandosto* appealed to them as another Elizabethan romance that fed the taste for Royal(ist) romance; it also may have appealed to them as a Shakespearean analogue, since several of Shakespeare's plays were turned to the cause. The distinction is immaterial for Jordan, at least: his ballad adapts *Pandosto* and *The Winter's Tale* so freely that neither work can be claimed as its primary source. Jordan's fugitive working conditions encouraged such indiscriminate use of any cultural materials helpful to his cause and sustenance. His version exemplifies how the two works' shared plot could be employed when authorial name and stationers' copy were the last of concerns.

Jordan was one of a small handful of actor-writers who bridged the Caroline and Restoration stages. His Red Bull company, the King's Revels Men, fell somewhere between an adult troupe and a boy company; their repertoire was "popular," using Martin Butler's definition of the term in opposition to the exclusivity of the "elite" companies and stages.[28] During the war years, Jordan continued in surreptitious playing at the Red Bull; after the Restoration, he became an author of city pageants.[29] At the very start of the Restoration, desperate for a living, he turned a few verse compositions into a volume that he sold with an ingenuity far outstripping Greene's. He had *The Royal Arbor of Loyal Poesie* published in octavo by Elizabeth Andrews in about 1663, and later reissued various segments with different title pages.[30] Those who owned *The Royal Arbor* and then bought *Musick & Poetry, Mixed* or *A Rosary of Rarities* or *A Nursery of Novelties* would have found little in the way of novelty. Some of the extant title pages have dedications with blanks, in which dedicatees' names are printed in different ink: Jordan apparently inserted these on a nonce basis.[31] Clearly, he was selling his works himself, shamelessly pressuring a small and impoverished customer base. Even more than the ballad sellers immortalized in the Jacobean drama, he had vertically integrated all the components of popular publication.

Jordan's *Royal Arbor* included several "songs" of twelve to twenty-two stanzas that retell plots from pre-War drama in the compass of a ballad. In his second edition of Shakespeare's works (1858), Collier reprinted Jordan's "The jealous Duke, and the injured Dutchess: a story," explaining that its "foundation" was *The Winter's Tale*.[32] A century later, Stanley Wells identified the song as "evidently based on *Pandosto* rather than on *The Winter's Tale*."[33] Collier, claiming it as an "original publication [of the play] in the shape of a broadside," insists that "Jordan had in his mind not Greene's Novel of 'Pandosto,' but Shakespeare's play of 'The Winter's Tale,' " and marvels that "with such an exquisite original before him, a writer of admitted talents could make so little of his subject, and degrade it to so humble a level" (*Shakespeare's* 3:11). Clearly, he would have marveled less if "Greene's Novel" had been so degraded.

Wells, on the other hand, holds that Jordan's ballad corresponds to Greene's romance, since it begins with a generalization about jealousy, and ends without retrieving the Duchess from death. Like Collier, he does not imagine that Jordan did not choose one text or the other, but blended them. However, that is quite evidently the case: although Jordan wrote the first sentence with *Pandosto* at his elbow, the rest of the ballad shows he wrote with the play in mind as well. Jordan's injured Duchess dies as in *Pandosto*, but the jealous Duke lives to repent as in *The Winter's Tale*. The "bastard" child's abandonment follows *The Winter's Tale*, act 3: the baby is exposed in the homeland of the Duke's supposed rival, along with "a paper where was writ down the name."[34] These details, not in *Pandosto*, correspond to Antigonus's leaving Perdita and her "character" in Bohemia (3.3.47). Later, the lost daughter is described as "the prettiest Nimph / that trod on grass" (Collier, *Illustrations*, 125), echoing Shakespeare's description of Perdita as "the prettiest low-born lass that ever / Ran on the greensward" (4.4.156–57).

The fusing of sources in "The jealous Duke" demonstrates that as the Royalists worked to overcome cultural disruptions and recover the works of the pre-War era, authorial discriminations were less important than the preservation of pleasures nearly lost. Jordan selected elements from *Pandosto* and *The Winter's Tale* that best spoke to current traumas. When Greene's lovers arrive in Bohemia, Pandosto threatens them with death, a tragicomic crisis that Shakespeare's play omits. Jordan plays up that moment, and its resonance with the trials and dreams of the Royalists is all too plain:

> They were to suffer both alike
>> The Headsmans axe
> Was up to strike.
> Hold! quoth the shepherd: I bring strange news to town.
>> The Dukes were both amazed,
> And the axe was straight laid down.

(Collier, Illustrations, 3:127)

The moment of execution and its miraculous prevention are repeated widely in Royalist culture of the Interregnum and in the first years of the Restoration; this song, too, serves to help audiences "mourn the death of the 'holy martyr' while at the same time celebrating the restoration of his son."[35] The balance that Jordan works out is fair-minded: the death of the older generation (in this case, the Duchess of Parma) cannot be redeemed as it was in Shakespeare's version of the play: it is the next generation who defeat the "axe" and are restored. The end of the poem is a Restoration refrain: "Bonfires and Bells, the conduits all run with wine / By this we see there's nothing can / Prevent the Powers divine," which seemingly embrace both a providential God and a divine-right monarch. Lois Potter has acutely remarked that the tragicomic mode of Royalist culture, emphasizing the actions of Providence in protecting kings, licensed Royalists to "abdicate responsibility and leave matters in the hands of fate."[36] What Greene had attributed to arbitrary Fortune was for Jordan the effortless fulfillment of royal Providence. Jordan's adaptation thus transformed Greene's story of a unredeemable king and Shakespeare's story of a family reunited into a celebration of monarchy restored. The surprising thing is that even with the hints Jordan provided, no one revived *The Winter's Tale* for the London stage at the Restoration, as *Pericles* was revived.[37]

Jordan was not, however, the only Royalist writer to have adopted *Pandosto*. If *Fortunes Tennis-Ball: or, The most excellent History of DORASTUS and FAWNIA, Rendred in delightful English Verse; and worthy the perusal of all sorts of PEOPLE*, by "S. S., Gent." was indeed written by Samuel Sheppard, it probably appeared before Jordan's collection.[38] *Fortunes Tennis-Ball* is consistent with the work of this "particularly wide-ranging plagiarist" (Potter 123) in its expert suggestion of political allegory from behind a mask of indirection and changeability. Sheppard's title page puts only the thinnest of disguises on Greene's authorship, since after the first phrase (itself drawing on Sidney's glory), the title closely follows Greene's. The names "Dorastus and Fawnia" are the largest words on the 1672 title page. However, Greene's name and romance are never directly mentioned.

Fortunes Tennis-Ball draws on all the characteristic elements in Sheppard's unique intellectual mix to rework Greene's romance as Royalist allegory. No opportunity is wasted to score points for Royalism. Dorastus is the monarch who redeems the plot; that his right is divine is amply evident to Fawnia, who grovels before him far more than in Greene:

> Simple Shepherds never aim so hie
> As Princes Courts, the brow of Majestie
> Breaks their frail sences, Odours poyson them,
> They dare not gaze upon a Diadem.

(B2)

Fortunes Tennis-Ball further contributes to the re-commodification of *Pandosto* by adding a multiscene woodcut to the title page (figure 3.1). The first multiscene illustration in an English *Pandosto*, it selects three iconic moments also illustrated in the French translation of *Pandosto* (figures 2.1 and 2.2). The woodcut's spatial organization is more rigid than the fluid "simultaneous" organization in the French engravings, and better articulated than the casual insertion of baby Fawnia behind adult Fawnia in the 1648 woodcut. This picture looks like a comic strip, with three boxes to be read on two lines, although they are not in narrative order. The upper left quadrant depicts two figures, presumably Dorastus and Fawnia since they have shepherd's hooks; the upper right, the same two figures kneeling before a king while a turbaned guard interposes his blade between them; the bottom half, a baby in a cock-boat drifting up to a flock of sheep on a seacoast. Abridging the story to three pictures, the woodcut opens up alternative readings of the narrative's key moments. Its focus is not the Royalism Sheppard so insistently brings to the story, since it includes no positive representation of a monarch. Instead, the woodcut emphasizes the events of exposure, courtship, and monarchical misbehavior that befall Fawnia, which seem to invite less politicized or nonelite readers to identify with this story of courtship, danger, and displacement. Not just a crutch for those less literate, the woodcut invites readers to be coproducers with Sheppard, to add their own associations to the poem.

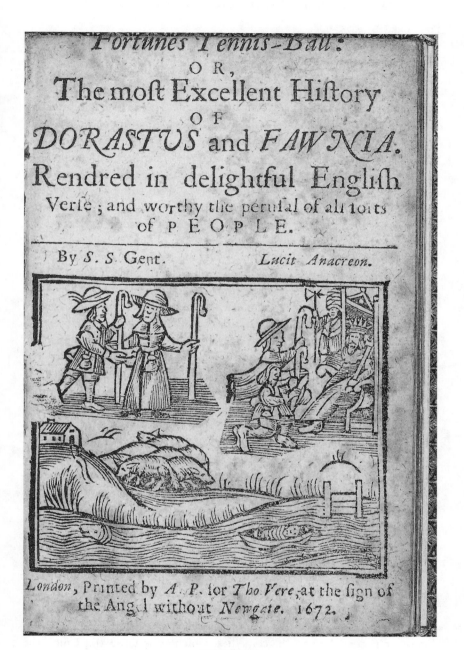

Fortunes Tennis-Ball:
OR,
The moſt Excellent Hiſtory
OF
DORASTVS and *FAWNIA.*
Rendred in delightful Engliſh
Verſe ; and worthy the peruſal of all ſorts
of PEOPLE.

By *S. S.* Gent.   *Lucit Anacreon.*

London, Printed by *A. P.* for *Tho Vere,* at the ſign of
the Angel without *Newgate.* 1672.

FIGURE 3.1
Title page, Samuel Sheppard, *Fortunes Tennis-Ball* (London: T. Vere, 1672).

Meanwhile, the woodcut of the elegant couple that had been preserved in one full-length version of *Dorastus and Fawnia* after another, from 1648 until 1700, also gained new meaning from its changing historical context. The 1688 edition of *Dorastus and Fawnia* repeats that image, which I have identified with Charles I and Henrietta Maria. The British Library copy bears (on a final leaf of advertising) the crooked signature of "Hennaratta Hobart her b[ook]." Hennaratta, conceivably named in remembrance of that ejected queen, is the first woman to have signed her name in an edition of *Dorastus and Fawnia*. But the date 1688 suggests another way of reading the couple in the woodcut: now they seem to represent William and Mary of Orange, who in fact correspond more closely to Greene's story than Charles II to Jordan's and Sheppard's Restoration versions. Here is the royal pair of a new generation, ruling by right of the "female heir." The reversals of royal fortune that continued throughout the seventeenth century put *Pandosto*'s meaning constantly in flux, both when it was radically re-commodified and when it was accurately reproduced.

The indiscriminate abridgment of *Pandosto* and *The Winter's Tale* is most fully enacted, however, in a manuscript commonplace book known as *Hesperides*, apparently written around 1660 but itself suffering an unusually cruel abridgment.[39] In 1973, Gunnar Sorelius detected a connection between two sets of manuscript fragments divided by an ocean. He linked the Shakespeare Birthplace Library's set of early manuscript extracts from Shakespeare's plays, little slips pasted into scrapbooks by James Orchard Halliwell-Phillips, to the Folger Shakespeare Library's handful of pages from the *Hesperides*. The first two pages of the latter have headings that start with the letter A; one of them is, appropriately, "Abbridgments & Abbridging." Since another surviving page was numbered 1028, Sorelius calculated that the original volume ran to at least 13,700 quotations (297). The Folger manuscript also includes "A Catalogue of the Bookes from whence these Collections were extracted" (Sorelius 296), listing a great deal of drama, especially from collected works that must have suited an operation on this scale; many English and Continental works of philosophy, politics, theology, and poetry; and several French heroic romances in English. Many titles are from the 1650s. The oldest work of fiction on the list, and the only Elizabethan romance other than Sidney's *Arcadia*, is "Dorastus & Faunia." As for the Shakespearean quotations in the Stratford scrapbooks, Sorelius reports, "Among the comedies, which are quoted 194 times, the compiler's favourite was *The winter's tale*, from which he quoted fifty times" (301). This anonymous compiler, like Drummond in the 1590s, found that

"Dorastus & Faunia" still belonged on a serious reading list. He also, like Jordan, found that both Greene's romance and Shakespeare's *Winter's Tale* were quotable around 1660 (although there is no way to know how often *Dorastus and Fawnia* was quoted).

The compiler's reading practices come to us in doubly fragmentary state: the commonplace book, *Hesperides*, fragmented its sources, and Halliwell-Phillips dismembered the commonplace book to make his scrapbook. Halliwell-Phillips's destruction of *Hesperides*, like Collier's fetishization of Jordan's ballad, was driven by the relentless reproduction of authorial boundaries; he took apart an anonymous collage of extracts from many authors in order to re-collect all the quotations from Shakespeare. Collier insisted on claiming as solely Shakespeare's a work that muddied the boundary between Greene and Shakespeare (he did, at least, reprint Jordan's *Royal Arbor* intact in his *Illustrations of Early English Literature*). Both ignored the nonauthorial purposes of "Abbridgers": the desire of the compiler to organize favorite topoi and the ingenuity of Jordan in turning old material to a new political agenda. Their high-handed recombinations dismantled the work of an educated but anonymous reader who digested printed books in private manuscript form; and of Greene and Jordan, like Greene a writer who learned to sell his works in fragments to maximize their profit. Like early modern readers, these Victorian collectors broke texts apart in order to preserve them. Assuming that their standards for fragmentation were superior to those of the past, they subordinated individuals' manuscripts and popular print to the interests of Shakespearean literature.

1660–88: CATALOGUES, COLLECTIONS, ILLUSTRATIONS

The Restoration made preserving pre-War works in abridgments and shards less necessary; instead, it invited large-scale recovery of texts in ways that fixed their literary status. Booksellers, collectors, and writers pulled together a canon of pre-War works, cataloguing them, collecting early printings, hastening to reissue them, and writing them into a literary history that imposed continuity over rupture. As the theaters reopened, Shakespeare's plays were spirited onto the stage in bold adaptations, and dubious attributions swelled his canon in the 1664 Third Folio. Full-length editions of Shakespeare were also much in demand, not yet as objects of scholarly study but as desirable commodities for leisure reading. This well-known rush to collect and catalogue early drama was matched by a quieter rush to collect and catalogue romances; this dual process further constructed drama as literature and romance as popular.

The first step in gathering a dramatic canon and a practice of literary history around Shakespeare was assembling and listing every known pre-War play in Restoration book catalogues (Kewes 99–105). Book dealer-collectors, before there were editor-collectors, made a point of amassing early dramatic editions and of cataloguing them for potential buyers and readers. Francis Kirkman, bookseller, publisher, and fiction writer, born in 1632, stands out among those who effected the literary restoration. In 1661, Kirkman reprinted an Elizabethan play, appending to it "an exact Catalogue of all the playes that were ever yet printed." In a preface to another of his 1661 dramatic titles, he explained that play collecting was both his love and his business:

> the pleasure I have taken in Books of this nature, (viz. *Plays*) hath bin so extraordinary, that it hath bin much to my cost; for I have been (as we term it) a Gatherer of *Plays* for some years, and I am confident I have more of several sorts than any man in England, Bookseller, or other: I can at any time shew 700 in number, which is within a small matter all that were ever printed. Many of these I have several times over, and intend as I sell, to purchase more; All, or any of which, I shall be ready either to sell or lend to you upon reasonable Considerations.[40]

Kirkman's readers thus could experience drama by reading his catalogue; by purchasing his editions of plays, some reprints and some from pre-War manuscripts; by bidding for his duplicate copies of older imprints; or by leasing books from his circulating library.[41] His willingness to lend out his early imprints, unimaginable today, reflects an experiential value that still outweighed their investment value.

Ten years later, in more settled times, Kirkman still maintained his circulating library, now with a new total of exactly 806 printed stage plays printed through 1671: "I really believe there are no more, for I have been these twenty years a Collector of them, and have conversed with, and enquired of those that have been Collecting these fifty years."[42] Kirkman's thoroughness has earned him a place in theater historiography. Less well known is his role in collecting and cataloguing romances. As he advertised in another 1661 dramatic reprint, "If any Gentleman please to repair to my House aforesaid, they may be furnished with all manner of English, or French Histories, Romances or Poetry; which are to be sold, or read for rea-

sonable Considerations" (Bald 23). More significantly, he published recommendations that shaped a canon of popular fiction. Through his varied
work as reader, collector, book dealer, librarian, publisher, bibliographer,
and romance writer, Kirkman promulgated parallel canons of romance and
pre-War drama. He assembled information that would aid later historical
consolidators in connecting the two canons, but differentiated their presentation, allowing future scholars to construct the dramatic adaptation of
romance as a literary elevation of popular materials.

Much of this work was done by the letter to readers in Kirkman's 1671
translation and expansion of a chivalric romance, *Don Bellianis of Greece*.
The letter is, in effect, a reading list for a self-taught course in popular fiction, based on Kirkman's personal experience: "I my self have been so great
a Lover of Books of this Nature, that I have long since read them all; and
therefore shall give thee some Account of my experience, that may be both
Pleasant and Profitable to thee" ([A4]). "Pleasant and profitable" is a familiar Horatian tag; *Pandosto* itself had been billed as "pleasant to age" and
"profitable to youth" from 1588 through the seventeenth century.[43] Can-
nily, however, Kirkman holds that chivalric romances are pleasant and
profitable to readers of *all* ages and *both* genders: "As first, I tell thee be thou
of what Age, or Sex soever, it is convenient for thee to read these sorts of
Historyes."

> If thou art Young, begin now, or else when thou comest to be Old and
> Hast any leisure, and if one of these Books chances into thy hand, thou
> wilt be so pleased with it, that read them thou must, and be in danger
> to be laughed at by those of the Younger sort, who having already read
> them, and being past that Knowledge, Laugh at thy Ignorance. For I
> have known several grave Citizens, who having formerly minded the
> many matters of the World, hath not only forborn reading themselves,
> but forbid their Children so to do, as being a vain and Idle matter, and
> loss of time; yet these very men in their latter dayes, having met with a
> Part of this History, or that of the Famous *Parismus*, have fallen so much
> in love with them, that they have become conceitedly Young and Am-
> orous, and so highly pleased that they have run through all the Books
> of this Nature and Quality. ([A4])

Kirkman's sophisticated understanding of popular romance reading has the
ironic generational awareness characteristic of contemporary popular culture: one must read the right books to keep up with one's generation, or

else one must catch up later. Above all, Kirkman captures a paradox that is central to this book: that those who disapprove of romances are neither ignorant of nor immune to their pleasures. Luckily, Kirkman implies, booksellers know "grave Citizens" long for forbidden texts that make readers "conceitedly Young" again. He plays on both emotional and frankly acquisitive impulses; helpful as it is, the preface is ultimately a sales pitch: "wherefore agen, recommending to you Historyes in general, and this of *Don Bellianis* in Particular. I rest your Friend, *FRANCIS KIRKMAN*."

Kirkman's pioneering survey of romances is arranged quite differently from his catalogue of plays, a bare listing arranged alphabetically, a format later revisers quickly replaced with authorial arrangements (Kewes 100–5). The survey of romances is itself a narrative: it sketches out a life in pleasure reading, grouping the titles into paragraphs like sets of graded readers. Each catalogue is systematic, but the differences in the systems reflect how the uses of drama and romance were already diverging and institutionalize that divergence for later booksellers. In popular fiction, this catalogue suggests, the experiences of readers are more important than the reputations of authors. England's readers have already developed the curriculum, Kirkman implies; he is merely its proud promulgator.

Starting with the youngest readers, Kirkman offers several endorsements for the familiar chivalric romances:

> *First*, I recommend to thee a Book called, *The Seven Wise Masters*; which is a very pleasant Collection of variety of that Witty History, and for the more Pleasure of the Young Reader, there is Pictures fitted to every particular History. This Book is of so great esteem in *Ireland*, that next to the *Horn-Book*, and Knowledge of Letters, Children are in general put to Read in this; and I know that only by this Book several have learned to Read well. ([A4])

Kirkman's suggestion that English readers might emulate the primary schooling of the Irish is, to say the least, startling. That romances were circulating in Ireland even at this early date, and serving educational functions, may be corroborated by another bit of contemporary evidence. A 1689 advertisement in a condensation of the *Seven Wise Masters* claims that "of all Histories of this nature, this exceeds, being held in such esteem in Ireland, that it is of the chiefest use in all the English Schools for introducing of Children to the understanding of good Letters" (quoted in Spufford, *Small Books*, 74). The advertiser could just be borrowing a page from Kirkman's book, of course; but my epilogue will explore evidence that chivalric romances were indeed widely used for centuries in Irish schools. Whatever the basis of Kirkman's claim, as a lover of romance, he urged young English readers to try illustrated romances, and as a bookseller and writer, he recognized Ireland as a potential market. To that end, he "purposely fitted" his *Don Bellianis* with episodes set in Ireland ([A4v]).

Kirkman's catalogue of romances is not only an unofficial curriculum but also a generic taxonomy and a pioneering literary history, identifying the major categories that still shape modern histories of early English fiction. His letter goes on to explain that all the romances he has listed so far are written in English, some even by a single author (Emanuel Forde, though Kirkman does not name him). The list is exhaustive, and *Dorastus and Fawnia* draws up the rear: "Thereare [sic] not many more Books of this nature Written originally [in] *English*, therefore you may for varietyes sake read them also, as . . . *Bevis of Southampton, Tom of Lincolne*, with the *Red Rose Knight, Dorastus and Fawnia*, and a few others" ([A4v]) Greene's romance, free of battles, seems out of place in this group, but by Kirkman's criteria of national and historical origin, its position makes sense. It certainly does not belong with the Continental works of the next paragraph, older chivalric romances "now grown so scarce that you can hardly purchase them"; these are "not worth the Printing agen, being now out of use and esteem by an other sort of Historyes, which are called *Romances*."[44] Some of these were "written originally in *English*, as namely, that Incomparable Book of its time called, *The Countess of Pembrokes Arcadia, Gods Revenge against Murther*"—John Reynolds and even Sidney go unnamed ([A4v]). However, Kirkman explains, most of the better romances of this new species are in French. The grand days of English chivalric romance, the core of his curriculum, are now well in the past.

The placement of *Dorastus and Fawnia* with the English chivalric "histories" and its contemporary and fellow pastoral, the *Arcadia*, with the French "romances" suggests another hidden criterion of importance to the bookseller-cataloguer: the chivalric histories were in cheaper quarto editions; the *romans de longue haleine* appeared in folios and multivolume octavos. Class distinctions, then, separate Kirkman's categories; this becomes plainer as he concludes that the romances, "not long since in great esteem with the *French* and *English* Nobility and Gentry . . . are also thrust out of use, by the present slighting and neglect of all Books in general, by the particular esteem of our late *English stage Plays*." With a condescending air, Kirkman then recommends *Don Bellianis* to his readers, who may be oblivious to fashion or "conceitedly Young and Amorous." He implies that the fashionable look down on popular romances, but his readers will surely look past social hierarchies to the pleasures he offers. His catalogue sets a canon in place but holds no one to it.

The other source of information about Kirkman's romance tastes is his *Unlucky Citizen* (1673), a picaresque tale generally taken as an autobiography. Like Greene, Kirkman expresses his own attitudes toward the romances he read within a mythologized autobiography that blends personal tastes and salesmanship; unlike Greene, Kirkman may be identified with his alter ego with little bibliographical or psychological complication.[45] The hero of *The Unlucky Citizen* must be Kirkman, since he is credited with translations of the sixth book of *Amadis* and of *The Loves and Adventures of Clerio and Lozia* (both 1652), and authorship of *Don Bellianis of Greece* (1671) and parts of *The English Rogue* (1668, 1671). *The Unlucky Citizen* gives much space to Kirkman's progress through the chivalric romance canon, which follows the list laid out in *Don Bellianis* two years earlier. His formative experience seems to have been purchasing a cheap book: as an apprentice he "happened upon" his first "Six Pence, and having lately read that famous Book, of the *Fryar and the Boy*, and being hugely pleased with that, as also the excellent History of the *Seven wise Masters of Room* [sic] . . . I laid out all my mony for [*Fortunatus*]" (28). He traded more penny books with his classmates at the St. Paul's School, who, as Margaret Spufford points out, clearly did not regard cheap books as beneath them (*Small Books* 73).

Young Kirkman was cash poor but comfortably born (his father was a member of the Blacksmiths' Company) and well educated. Yet he loved romances for conjuring dreams of greater socioeconomic glory:

> But when I came to Knight Errantry, and reading *Montelion Knight of the Oracle*, and *Ornatus* and *Artesia*, and the Famous *Parismus*; I . . . (believing all I read to be true) wished my self Squire to one of these Knights: I proceeded on to *Palmerin of England*, and *Amadis de Gaul*; and borrowing one Book of one person, when I had read it my self, I lent it to another, who lent me one of their Books; and thus *robbing* Peter *to pay* Paul, borrowing and lending from one to another, I in time had read most of these Histories . . . being wholy affected to them, and reading how that *Amadis* and other Knights not knowing their Parents, did in time prove to be Sons of Kings and great Personages; I had such a fond and idle Opinion, that I might in time prove to be some great Person.   (29–30)

Kirkman's youthful fantasy about his parentage provides the common denominator between *Dorastus and Fawnia* and the chivalric histories on his reading list. It led to real-life struggle, for our hero's father insisted on putting him to a trade, while young Kirkman "scorned to be any, hoping that I was not born to so mean a Quality" (30). He proposed becoming "a Bookseller, because, by that means I might read all sorts of history Books, and thereby please my self with reading, but I was mistaken therein, for . . . I, since I dealt in bookselling, have read fewer Books than formerly" (30–31). Apprenticed instead to the scrivener's trade, Kirkman took advantage of a master's lax business to begin uniting his vocation and his avocation. His collection of romances had "swelled . . . to such a number, that they looked like a Library, and my Master permitted me so to dispose them in his little Shop, that they were the best furniture therein" (173–74). The look of the shop may have given him the idea for his later lending libraries.

The *Unlucky Citizen* also tells how Kirkman, still an apprentice, launched a career as a self-published writer of romances. When his supplement to *Amadis* failed to sell, he realized that histories of "*Knight Errantry* were out of fashion" and so found a French romance "full of *Love-sick Expressions*" that he "let . . . pass as *English*" (Bald 20). At this point, Kirkman's autobiography and his recommendations dovetail again: the turn from histories to romances is a turn from the ambitious dream of a growing boy to the virile pretense of young manhood. But the dream of class mobility was only altered, not forgotten: when Kirkman's pseudo-French romance appeared, its title page declared him a gentleman.

Exposing the weakness of his gentle pretenses in *The Unlucky Citizen*, Kirkman could rest secure in his later success and his own membership in the Blacksmiths' Company. He was no gentleman, but he had made his errant way to fame and glory. Like a returning hero, he offered his reading experiences as a map for those seeking romance; as a businessman, he offered them as an advertisement for his own varied work. Together with the romances he wrote, his catalogues consolidated a reading list of the enduring works of fiction. His remarks about "grave Citizens" marked romances as universally popular (as opposed to narrowly vulgar), although he also implied a social gradation among the romances that he himself hoped to climb. Atop that ladder was, indubitably, the drama, which had "thrust [romance] out of use." In 1652, Kirkman had dedicated his prose romance *Clerio and Lozia* to William Beeston, leader of the evanescent pre-War troupe, Beeston's Boys (Bald 20–21). At the Restoration, Kirkman published his catalogues, lent his plays, and became known as a publisher of dramatic reprints. But he retained an attachment to popular fiction, authoring innovative criminal biographies—later parts of the randy *English Rogue*, and *The Counterfeit Lady Unveiled* (1673), an "autobiography" of the tinker's daughter who posed as a German princess.

As a boy, Kirkman vastly preferred his "popular" reading to his school-books, and saw the former as a tool of universal, not class-specific, value to the young. Decades later, he was willing to make that argument in the public venue of a preface that became the definitive statement of romance's popular status. His claims for *Dorastus and Fawnia* and other romances as developmentally useful may have been somewhat tongue-in-cheek, but they certainly counted on the romance enthusiasms of adults, who might either recall their past pleasures and share them with their children or snap up the romances for their own nostalgic enjoyment. The implied scene of multigenerational readers is more honest than the Jacobean scenes of woman and servant readers: it confirms that the young had reason to love romances and, for once, admits that adult males did as well.

KIRKMAN'S CATALOGUE WAS, for contemporary readers, probably the key articulation of prose romances as an emergent canon of popular fiction. But for historians' understanding of popular print, the canon-fixing collection has been that of Samuel Pepys, analyzed by Roger Thompson, Margaret Spufford (*Small Books and Pleasant Histories*), and Tessa Watt (*Cheap Print*). The chapbooks that Pepys acquired in the 1680s are, Spufford has determined, a very fair sampling of the offerings of chapbook publishers of the period. On the other hand, the chapbooks are constituted as a collection, a grouping most nonelite readers would not have experienced. Pepys, an apparently ordinary man of uncommon curiosity and good fortune, had the time to "quite systematically . . . buy from all the main publishers catering for the chapbook trade" (Spufford, *Small Books*, 135). He could afford to have his books bound in leather volumes, with the spines lettered "Penny Merriments," "Penny Witticisms," "Penny Compliments," "Penny Godlinesses," "Old Novels," and "Vulgaria." He carefully drew up tables of contents, such as the "Catalogue of the Several Tracts Contain'd in this 3 Volume of Vulgar Ware." He allocated space for them in his custom-made bookshelves, and even when he purged less desirable material and relegated licentious material to a drawer, he retained the chapbooks.[46]

Such deliberate consumption of downmarket commodities by the elite can be read, following Peter Burke, as evidence of an increasing sequestration of popular taste.[47] But the first great collections of English cheap publications were not retroactive reconstructions but immediate responses to new print forms. The promptness with which gentlemen registered and began collecting them suggests that cultural spheres were interconnected, not separated. Pepys's collection of broadside ballads built on those assembled earlier by his college acquaintance, the jurist and champion of "ancient rights" John Selden (1584–1654).[48] Selden's motivation to preserve the ballad in its heyday can be compared to the bookseller George Thomason's work in preserving the print ferment of the Interregnum: both reacted to contemporary publishing phenomena, not disappearing folk forms. Pepys captured the expanded scale of cheap-print operations in the 1680s as the well-established Ballad Partners were challenged by a new set of outsiders. On the other hand, his attraction to chapbooks was clearly personal rather than documentary. The successful bureaucrat, son of a former washmaid and a gentle-born younger son turned tailor, must have felt some mixture of guilty pleasure and pride when he had his bookbinder label these humble volumes "Vulgaria," or when he inserted his portrait bookplates. Vulgar works were held to define vulgar readers, but Pepys's chapbooks were vulgarity introduced systematically into genteel bureaucracy.

Pepys collected two versions of *Dorastus and Fawnia* that represent the growing diversity of form possible for cheaper titles within the well-established Restoration book market. One was a copy of the 1688 edition of Greene's full text, published by George Conyers, and extant in several different versions. The other survives only in Pepys's *Penny Merriments*: it is the first true chapbook of *Dorastus and Fawnia*, tentatively dated to 1680 (G1827bA). Its publisher, Charles Dennisson, was, like Conyers, part of the outsider set of chapbook publishers; a number of features suggest that he had no clear right to the copy. The title cleverly varies the one in all editions of the book since 1635, calling it a "delightful" rather than a "pleasant" history. Greene's name is omitted for the first time, a landmark in the adoption of this courtly romance as cheap print, now nearly a century old. The imprint protests legitimacy too much, beginning with a printed "license": "*This may be Printed*, R.P." and then reading "Printed for C. Dennisson, at the Stationers," with "Dennisson" and "Stationers" in black letter for extra authority. The title page also features an exciting plot summary and a different, comic-strip style, three-part woodcut (figure 3.2). This woodcut has more atmosphere than the Sheppard version, and its three parts are arranged in narrative order, better living up to the name of "story" that Tessa Watt says was given to such pictures (188). First is the façade of a palace, suggesting Pandosto's court, then a startled shepherd with dog

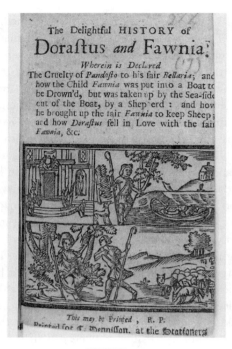

FIGURE 3.2
Title page, *The Delightful History of Dorastus and Fawnia* (London:
C. Dennisson, 1680?).

finding a baby in a boat, then below a dashing pastoral scene in which a majestically seated Fawnia receives a heroically gesturing Dorastus, chaperoned by an alert dog and a large flock.

Both this woodcut and the condensed text that accompanied it would still be in regular publication more than a century later. And no wonder, for within their economies, both are very effective. The Dennisson text of *Dorastus and Fawnia* is an exciting, forthright narrative, well adapted—bringing a fifty-six-page quarto text down to twenty duodecimo pages, and from sixpence down to tuppence. The text, in black letter in this first edition, is divided into seven chapters, preceded by plainly worded digests of the plot in roman type with names in black letter. The average sentence length is reduced from Greene's, although the vocabulary remains challenging.

This chapbook adaptation emphasizes, time after time, paradoxes and crises of class and gender privilege suffered by the characters. Bellaria, in prison, wishes "she had been born of mean Birth"—and at that very moment feels Fawnia stir (3). Greene's rhetorical set pieces are shortened in indirect discourse that heightens their social acuity. A "sighing" Fawnia tells her wooing prince that "Had he been a Shepherd she could have fancied him for a Husband, above all Men; but seeing he was a Prince, she durst not hope for such a happiness, therefore to respect him and admire his Generosity, was all she could do" (12). Although the Prince responds honorably, Fawnia's shepherd father has reason to fear "that the Prince should violate her Chastity, for that he would marry her, he could not hope" (12). The directness on social matters persists to the final episodes, when Fawnia is recognized and Pandosto apologizes profusely for having been a seducer, a "rough Man": " 'twas I thy unnatural Father that exposed you to that Hazard and Danger, for which (though unseemly for a King, *I* beg thy dear pardon a thousand times)" (19). This speech, set apart by roman type as the third display piece of the work, is a wholesale insertion; Greene's Pandosto felt guilt but never apologized.

The Dennisson adaptation consistently recasts Greene's complex tale as the triumph of virtuous young lovers over a corrupt authority. It ends with the young couple (Greene, oddly, had closed only with Dorastus): "so after the Funerals were over, Dorastus lived in peace with his fair Fawnia a long time after" (20). Its optimal audience, then, would seem to be young people—and its ending remembers young women better than Greene's. Pepys's library canonized both Greene's full text, much more centered on the flawed patriarch, and *The Delightful History of Dorastus and Fawnia*, which shifts sympathy to those victimized by his abuse of privilege. The Pandosto of the latter text resembles a royal version of Pepys, the ever-repentant but incorrigible sexual harasser. His desire to collect "Vulgaria," like his desire to fondle his housemaids, may have had psychological roots in uncertainty about his own social place, but that didn't prevent his acting on either impulse. Inconsistent attitudes toward seigneurial rights were also evident in the variant texts of *Dorastus and Fawnia* on the market in the late 1680s—and the cheaper version was much readier to object. Re-commodification had finally brought *Dorastus and Fawnia* within the economic reach of maidservants and given the story new potential to question their treatment.

THAT NOT ONE but two different English publishers had now invested in a custom woodcut for *Dorastus and Fawnia* indicates its reliability as a profit-turning entertainment, in either full-text or shortened form. As Kirkman

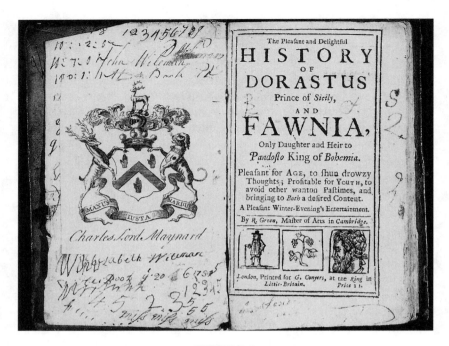

FIGURE 3.3
Title page, R. Green, *The Pleasant and Delightful History of Dorastus and Fawnia* (London: G. Conyers, 1696/1700?).
BY PERMISSION OF THE NEWBERRY LIBRARY, CHICAGO

claimed, the provision of an illustration widened access to the story and offered new kinds of aesthetic pleasure. That appeal was not limited to the linguistically incompetent, as the example of Pepys shows; but the title-page woodcut was becoming a strong marker of popular fiction, as important as the authorial name to elite literature. Indeed, in the case of the chapbook *Dorastus and Fawnia,* the illustration directly replaced that attribution.

Still, authorially marked texts of *Dorastus and Fawnia* also appeared steadily well into the eighteenth century, thanks to the continued efforts of bookseller George Conyers and printer William Onley. New editions came thick and fast, a clear indication that the work, which had already seen more than twenty prose editions, was still a steady seller. The 1700? edition by Conyers and Onley (G1832; the British Library copy is manually dated to 1696) seems to respond to the presence of a Dennisson competitor: Conyers's earliest editions had been of a "pleasant" history, but from now on, he published it as a "pleasant and delightful history," as though enfolding the experience that Dennisson had billed as an alternative. There would be a further step in that incorporation within a few years.

Significantly, this edition of the romance was the first in roman type. I have mentioned the tendency to fetishize or mock the persistence of black letter at a late date. Pepys himself comments on this in a manuscript title page in his first of five bound volumes of ballads:

> My Collection of Ballads Vol. I. Begun by Dr Selden; improved by ye addition of many Pieces elder thereto in Time; and the whole continued to the year 1700. When the Form, till then peculiar thereto, viz. of the Black Letter with Pictures, seems (for cheapness sake) wholly laid aside, for that of White Letter without Pictures.[49]

Presumably the economy to which Pepys is referring is the omission of the illustrations, but another kind of cheapness may have dictated the change to roman type. By this time, many publishers' sets of black-letter type must have been wearing out; most kept on hand only enough black letter for use as a display font. Still, many editions from the early eighteenth century used black letter for "Dorastus" and "Fawnia" on their title pages to confer the quality of history or even legend on those names. Educated onlookers, less interested in those connotations, drew the class conclusions about black letter that Mish later seized upon. Charles Gildon's pruned and sanitized version of Langbaine's *Lives and Characters of the English Dramatick Poets* (London, 1699), for instance, reported of "Robert Green" that "This Author has writ divers other Pieces, most of them Printed in an old Black Letter."[50] To Gildon, a black-letter edition is "old" in its own time.

The 1700? edition has on its title page only three small woodcuts: a male figure in modern dress, a floral branch, and a handsome Roman male's profile, as if to match the roman typeface (see figure 3.3). The title page also makes the first addition ever to Greene's original long title: the slogan, "A Pleasant Winter-Evening's Entertainment." This innovation probably refers to an immediate competitor on the book market. The *Term Catalogue* for Michaelmas 1686 advertised "Winter Evenings' Entertainments, in Two Parts," a miscellany of "Relations of many rare and notable Accidents" with "Fifty ingenious riddles."[51] "Winter-evening's Entertainment" recalls storytelling around the fire on dark winter nights, a practice that predates print; the phrase had been in the titles of many Elizabethan works, but never in *Pandosto*'s. It is probably only a coincidence that a few years earlier, Langbaine had first linked *Pandosto* to *The Winter's Tale*.

When Conyers advertised *Dorastus and Fawnia* in the *Term Catalogues* in 1704, he made the most of this new pitch: "The History of *Dorastus* and *Fawnia*, Daughter and Heir to the King of *Bohemia*; profitable to Youth, to avoid other wanton Pastimes. Being a pleasant Winter Evening's Entertainment. By R.G." Strikingly, Conyers omits Dorastus's royal title, emphasizing Fawnia, "Daughter and Heir," as the unifying character (which she is) but also, apparently, as the most appealing character to readers. In an ad read by both other book traders and the general public, Conyers touts this volume as reading for youths, and implicitly for women (Arber, *Term Catalogues*, 3:430).

Conyers's sense of his market also directed him to offer his readers a more miscellaneous text, for he added to *Dorastus and Fawnia* a very short tale called "Josephus, the Indian Prince." According to Arundell Esdaile, this text was ingeniously derived from the learned *Philosophus Autodidactus siue Epistola Abi Jaafar*, published in Arabic and Latin at Oxford in 1671. An English translation appeared without imprint in 1674, titled "An Account of the Oriental Philosophy, Shewing . . . The profound Wisdom of Hai Ebn Yokdan, both in Natural and Divine things; Which he attained without all Converse from Men (while he lived in an Island a solitary life . . .)." Other versions followed, under other serious-sounding titles, in 1686, 1708, and 1711.[52] In Conyers's much shortened version, this Indian prince has been renamed for Josephus, historian of the Jews (apparently conflating Arabic with Hebraic culture). A noble savage who arrives at Christian principles by independent reason, and a Crusoe-like self-sufficient autodidact, "Josephus" was clearly a hero for Conyers, the master of do-it-yourself books. Supplementing *Dorastus and Fawnia* with *Josephus*, Conyers balanced romance with practicality, and perhaps (stereotypically) a title appealing to young women with another aimed at young men.

My reading of Conyers's intentions is influenced by the condition of a copy in which every inch of blank space is filled with scrawls ranging from the experimental signatures of young writers to arithmetic calculations in more adult hands. Successive readers have signed over one another so often that it is hard to match dates with signatures, but the most mature signature, by John Wileman, appears to have been made in 1729. Richard Cooper signed the book in 1731, Elizabeth Wileman in 1734, and Ann Wileman in 1766.[53] The names of Dorastus, Fawnia, and Bellaria have also been scripted, suggesting that these readers may have identified with the characters even without illustrations. Two generations after this edition's publication, readers were using it much as Conyers had predicted: a multiple-page list of "*Books Sold at the* Ring *in* Little-Britain," unique to this copy of this edition, lists as its 46th item, "The pleasant and delightful History of *Dorastus* and *Fawnia*; a Book that not only diverts the Grownup, but allures Children to learn to Read. *Price 6d.*" The material state of this copy confirms the advertising claim. To the Coopers and the Wilemans, *Dorastus and Fawnia* was shared across genders and generations, retained not as a collectible but to be used actively and freely.

These marginalia can be contrasted to those of a collector named R. Farmer on another Conyers edition, that of 1703 (figure 3.4). On a flyleaf, Farmer signed his name and commented that the original piece was published as *Pandosto* in black letter in 1588. And he wrote all over the title page itself: adding information under the title "[hence ye Plot of ye Winter's Tale of Shakespeare.}," under Greene's name "[He died *about* 1592. See *Wood.*}," and around the woodcut "[He was buried ye 4th of Sept. 1592.}." Most interestingly, he inserted a "Re-" between "*London*" and "Printed by *W.O.* for G. *Conyers.*" In his scholarly way, R. Farmer interacts with his text as eagerly and freely as the Coopers and the Wilemans.

The rest of Conyers's editions of *Dorastus and Fawnia*, although they preserve the full text of the romance, move rapidly toward the appearance of the brief Dennisson duodecimo. Their changes demonstrate how competing formats of chapbooks evince not competitive piracy but a culture of interchange among an informal cartel of publishers. In fact, as Spufford has demonstrated, such sharing was commonplace among Jonah Deacon, Charles Dennisson, Josiah Blare, and George Conyers, who challenged the Ballad Partners' dominance of seventeenth-century cheap print. One of Conyers's editions, undated but apparently from about 1700, used on its title page the woodcut from Sheppard's *Fortunes Tennis-Ball*, last published by Deacon in 1688. On the upper left is the couple (of indeterminate gender) with giant hats and sheephooks, on the right the threatening court scene, and across the bottom the familiar floating baby in a pastoral landscape (G1838A). Deacon died in 1699; did he lend the block to his colleague or leave it to him? In either case, Conyers only used it once, and it never resurfaced. Instead, Conyers turned in a surprising direction.

At about the same time, Blare reprinted Dennisson's sixteen-page adaptation, but in roman type, in an edition dated to around 1700 (G1827A). As might be expected, Blare reused Dennisson's strip-style woodcut, more gracefully drawn than Sheppard's. In its next appearance, this woodcut

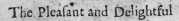

The Pleasant and Delightful

HISTORY

OF

Doraſtus and Fawnia.

Pleaſant for Age to ſhun drowſie Thoughts ; Profitable for Youth, to avoid other wanton Paſtimes, and bringing to Both a deſired Content.

[hence ẏ Plot of ẏ Winter's-Tale of Shakeſpeare]

By *ROBERT GREEN*, Maſter of Arts in *Cambridge*.

[He died before 1592. See Wood i [.137].]

London, Printed by *W. O.* for *G. Conyers*, at the Ring in *Little Britain*, 1703.
[Price 6 d.]

FIGURE 3.4

Title page, Robert Green, *The Pleasant and Delightful History of Dorastus and Fawnia* (London: G. Conyers, 1703).

has crossed over from the condensations to the full-length texts, appearing in yet another Conyers edition, this one clearly imprinted 1703. Although Blare remained alive and active through 1706, he apparently did not reissue the shorter version, although the extant editions must underrepresent its appearance in this period.[54] The sharing of the two woodcuts among the chapbook publishers indicates strong demand for all three re-commodifications of the *Dorastus and Fawnia* story: Sheppard's verse *Fortunes Tennis-Ball*, the sixteen-page condensation, and the full-length text.[55] As Spufford has shown, the field offered profits enough for all: at Blare's death in 1707, he had enough chapbooks in his warehouse to supply one for every forty-four families in the country, and investments that "put him decisively amongst the richest fifth of the inhabitants of London, and into the league of the merchants" (*Small Books* 87, 101, 89).

Two versions, full and shortened, of *Dorastus and Fawnia* came together in this last Conyers edition. The "story" woodcuts, usually read by historians as conveniences for the semiliterate, had migrated from the condensed version (and the verse version) to the full text, still substantial in price and verbiage and certainly not directed toward the barely literate.[56] The illustration was now an integral component of the popular fiction experience to which Greene's text had proved well suited. The cut originated by Dennisson was surprisingly enduring, later used by John White of Newcastle-on-Tyne in printing the sixteen-page adaptation.[57] As Newcastle's premier chapbook publisher, White was active from 1708 until 1769, printing a number of the familiar chapbook titles, often using custom blocks that he ordered or acquired used. In the hands of White's successor, George Angus, these old blocks began to attract the attention of collectors, as the chapbooks themselves had in an earlier century. A Victorian publisher at Newcastle, William Dodd, printed up the White/Angus collection as *Specimens of Early Wood Engraving* in 1862, and reproduced the *Dorastus and Fawnia* block (figure 3.5). In 1999, many of Dodd's specimens, including an altered and unlabeled, but unmistakable, version of the Dennisson/Blare/Conyers woodcut, were reissued by Dover Books in their clip-art series.[58] It seems only right that chapbook illustrations should find their final home in a copyright-free environment, for the whole trajectory of the chapbook *Dorastus and Fawnia* demonstrates that the canonization of popular classics ("popular" in the most inclusive sense) was confirmed, not challenged, by untrammeled re-commodification.

FIGURE 3.5
Woodcut illustration for *Dorastus and Fawnia*, from William Dodd, *Specimens of Early Wood Engraving* (1862; reprint, New York: Dover Books, 1999).

1688–1735: "DELECTABLE HISTORY" AND "PALPABLE ABSURDITY"

While the popularity of *Dorastus and Fawnia* was consolidated, a nascent critical practice had begun to define an exclusive canon of dramatic authors, Shakespeare increasingly prominent among them. The connection between *Dorastus and Fawnia* and *The Winter's Tale* was recognized in print and triggered early efforts to position the former as a lower-ranking work. Langbaine's 1688 catalogue, *Momus Triumphans: or, the Plagiaries of the English Stage; Expos'd in a Catalogue* . . . was less lurid than the title sounds (indeed, Langbaine claimed its publication under this title was spurious). It compiled source stories for most of those eight hundred plays noted by Kirkman, now arranged authorially. Under Shakespeare's name, the listing for *The Winter's Tale* is footnoted: "Plot from *Dorastus and Fawnia*, 4°."[59] The identification was amplified in Langbaine's 1691 *Account of the English Dramatick Poets*, which included longer comments. Its entry on *The Winter's Tale* notes that "the Plot of this Play may be read in a little Stitcht-pamphlet, which is call'd, as I remember, *The Delectable History of* Dorastus *and* Fawnia."[60] Neither reference identifies Robert Greene as the author.

Langbaine's observation is couched in terms that emphasize the distance between his scholarship and the romance (at this date, Shakespeare himself could still be treated rather patronizingly). His use of "Delectable" in the title, instead of the "delightful" seen in almost every edition of *Dorastus and Fawnia* to that date, bespeaks a certain carelessness about the attributes of popular fiction, or even a condescending attitude toward its consumers. However, the word was used in some chivalric romance titles, one of which is telling: Francis Kirkman's *Famous and Delectable History of Don Bellianis of Greece.* Langbaine's mistake ties his identification of *Dorastus and Fawnia* to the world of Francis Kirkman, whom he apparently knew. It even suggests that his work as cataloguer of "plagiaries" grew directly out of Kirkman's populist and commercial cataloguing.

Langbaine himself was no stranger to the world of popular-fiction publishing. As a younger son of a scholar, he was apprenticed to a bookseller (Nevill Simons) in St. Paul's Churchyard in 1672.[61] When his older brother died, he threw over this career for study at Oxford. According to Wood, the student Langbaine "wrote little things, without his name set to them, which he would never own." But he allegedly drew the line at a commission to assist Kirkman in writing a continuation of *The English Rogue.*[62] Apparently Langbaine did do hack writing for Kirkman, but its exact extent cannot be ascertained. Bald proposes that Langbaine "was doubtless indebted to Kirkman's collection for much of the reading on which his *Account . . .* was based" (32). If so, the possibility remains open that Langbaine's published information rested on Kirkman's unpublished observations. Kirkman could have linked, or helped Langbaine to link, *The Winter's Tale* to *Dorastus and Fawnia*, for his familiarity with Greene's romance is evident in the preface to *Don Bellianis*. Indeed, Langbaine almost appears to acknowledge Kirkman with his adjective "delectable," which points back to the 1673 text of *Don Bellianis*, where a single page spread juxtaposes the discussion of *Dorastus and Fawnia* with the half title for the *Famous and Delectable History of Don Bellianis of Greece.*

Elsewhere, Langbaine varies his epithet for this romance: "Honest *Shakespear* was . . . as much a Stranger to French as Latine . . . and yet an humble story of *Dorastus* and *Fawnia*, serv'd him for *A Winter's Tale*," he points out, in the context of his notorious attack on Dryden (*Account* 141–42). "Humble" asserts the virtue of this domestic source over the French romances Dryden used and exaggerates the plainness of both the romance and the "honest" playwright who adapted it. "Delectable," in the entry under Shakespeare, has no such polemical motivation, but it does seem to claim social distance from the romance, as does the mention of a "Stitcht-pamphlet." The 1688 *Momus Triumphans* lists a quarto; the later entry might mean that Langbaine had seen an early duodecimo edition (like Dennisson's) as well. Somehow, this pamphlet is worlds away from the quartos in which so many early dramas had been published. Langbaine does not insist on the materiality of plays, but in the case of the popular-fiction source, he refers to a physical object, implying minimal interest in its narrative contents or publication history.

Furthermore, though Langbaine had seen a quarto edition, which would have borne the name of Robert Greene on the title page, he did not portray the book as authored in this Shakespearean context. Ironically, he could have located this information within his own volume, where the entry for "Robert GREEN" as dramatist says of his nondramatic works: "I have never seen but two; *viz. Quip for an Upstart Courtier*; and *Dorastus and Fawnia*, tho' Mr. *Winstanley* reckons up several others" (*Account* 243). As defender of authorial rights, Langbaine serves Greene inconsistently.

Langbaine is cautious about relying on William Winstanley, "knowing how subject he is to take things upon report" (*Account* 241), but goes on to include his highly disapproving account of Greene's prodigality, which rested heavily on Harvey's "reports." Winstanley's *Lives of the Most Famous English Poets* (1687) had said: "*Robert Greene* (that great Friend to the *Printers* by his many Impressions of numerous Books) was by Birth a Gentleman . . . writing much against Viciousness, but too too vicious in his life" (74). To support his vices, "he made his Pen mercenary, making his Name very famous for several Books which he wrote, very much taking in his time, and in indifferent repute amongst the vulgar at this present, of which; those that I have seen, are as followeth" (75). Winstanley listed a dozen prose works, including "the *History of* Dorastus *and* Fawnia" (75), although he did not assess its popularity among the "vulgar" or report that it was the only Greene work still in "Impression." In Winstanley's view, Greene's "mercenary" writing had sunk to its naturally vulgar level.

Greene is described in similar but slightly more sympathetic terms in Anthony à Wood's *Athenae Oxonienses* (1691–92), as "author of several things which were pleasing to men and women of his time." The description of these "things" is mixed: "They made much sport, and were valued among scholars, but since they have been mostly sold on ballad-mongers stalls." Wood's list of Greene's romances, criminal pamphlets, "and other trifles" does not include *Pandosto* under any heading.[63] Wood, then, was willing to look out for Greene's works on ballad-mongers' stalls but had not yet found *Dorastus and Fawnia*, at least not in a full-length edition that included Greene's name. Meanwhile, Pepys was haunting the stalls gathering chapbooks for his collection, later to be enormously "valued among scholars." And Langbaine was proving that visiting ballad-mongers' stalls might bear scholarly fruit. The scene of consumption was becoming the site of scholarship.

ABOVE ALL, EARLY source study allowed critics to shift the blame for any perceived faults of *The Winter's Tale* to *Dorastus and Fawnia*. The most notorious was the geographical error of the seacoast of Bohemia. Strikingly, once this fault was blamed on *Dorastus and Fawnia*, it became evidence not of Greene's ignorance but of the material poverty of the romance itself, as though Shakespeare's text was something far more substantial. The earliest recorded objection to the Bohemian setting survives in Jonson's 1619 conversations with William Drummond of Hawthornden: "Sheakspear, in a play, brought in a number of men saying they had suffered ship-wrack in Bohemia, wher yr is no sea neer by some 100 miles." This record, however, comes from a manuscript not published until 1711.[64] It is impossible to know whether Jonson circulated this complaint widely. His reaction is to a detail from a staged play (although his memory does not correspond exactly to the act 4 shipwreck scene in the Folio text); there was little reason for Drummond to think of the same error occurring in the prose romance he had read in the 1590s.

Yet even before Drummond's manuscript was published, the problem of geographical accuracy arose in dueling editorial statements in the 1709–10 Tonson edition of Shakespeare. Its editor, Nicholas Rowe, in *Some Account of the Life, &c of Mr. William Shakespeare* (1709), commented that Shakespeare's

> Tales were seldom invented, but rather taken either from true History or Novels and Romances, and he commonly made use of 'em in that Order . . . in which he found 'em in the Authors from when he borrow'd them. So *The Winter's Tale*, which is taken from an old Book call'd *The Delectable History of Dorastus and Fawnia*, contains the space of sixteen or seventeen Years, and the Scene is sometimes laid in

> *Bohemia* and sometimes in *Sicily*, according to the original Order of the
> Story.   (Vickers 2:198)

Rowe's phrase "delectable history" shows that he relies on Langbaine. His claim that Shakespeare follows the "original Order" of Greene's geography overlooks the former's reversal of the two locales and atypically gives Greene's "Story" the status of an "original." But Rowe objects to the geographical disunity, not its inaccuracy. A year later, Charles Gildon raised the problem of the coast in his *Remarks on the Plays of Shakespeare*, the first critical essay to systematically survey *The Winter's Tale*, which appeared in Edmund Curll's spurious seventh volume to Rowe's edition (Vickers 2:216, 245). Gildon blames the prose romance: "This Tale is taken from an old story-Book of *Dorastus* and *Faunia*, whence I suppose the Absurdities are copyed and the making *Bohemia* of an Inland, a maritime Country" (Vickers 2:245). Gildon clearly assumes that the erroneous locale is familiar to Shakespeare's readers, but his is the first objection in print; the next year, a Scottish antiquarian magazine published excerpts from Drummond's manuscript, giving the problem of the maritime Bohemia the *imprimatur* of Jonson's still-formidable critical reputation.

In 1733, *Dorastus and Fawnia* regained its authorial name—but continued to serve as a provider of gross misinformation. In his 1733 edition of Shakespeare, Lewis Theobald assembled Langbaine's raw facts to conclude that: "The Groundwork and Incidents" of *The Winter's Tale* "are taken from an old Story call'd *The pleasant and delectable History of Dorastus and Fawnia*, written by Mr. *Robert Green*, a Master of Arts in *Cambridge*, in the Reign of Q. *Elizabeth*."[65] While the erroneous "delectable" points back to Langbaine, the addition of "pleasant" suggests that Theobald had seen an edition of the prose work. But Greene's authorial presence recedes when Theobald turns to the "palpable Absurdity" of the maritime Bohemia, which "our Author" (meaning Shakespeare) "copied from the same *Tale*" (Theobald 3:99). Theobald's edition also added a new detail under the play's dramatis personae: "The Plot taken from the old Story-book of Dorastus and Faunia" (unpaginated). That tag immediately became *de rigueur* in eighteenth- and nineteenth-century editions of Shakespeare; thenceforward, one piece of critical information that *every* reader of the play encountered was its derivation from an authorless "old Story-book."

Eleven years later, Sir Thomas Hanmer, former Speaker of the House of Commons, edited the play from Alexander Pope's text. His treatment of the Bohemian problem went straight to a bold emendation, which, like

Pope's earlier policy of free textual emendations, condemned the plebeian printers who had corrupted Shakespeare's noble text. He explained that the country

> here called *Bithynia*, hath in all former Editions been printed *Bohemia*. . . . This is a Blunder and an Absurdity, of which *Shakspear* in Justice ought not to be thought capable, and as he hath turned quite anew the Story contained in the old paltry Book of *Dorastus* and *Fawnia* . . . it is probable that he removed this Impropriety, and placed the Scene in *Bithynia*, which the Ignorance and Negligence of the first Transcribers, or Printers, might corrupt and bring back again to *Bohemia*, by a less Variation in the Letters than they have been guilty of in numberless other Places of this Work.[66]

Shakespeare, removing Greene's "Impropriety," is pictured as performing work exactly analogous to Hanmer's own textual emendation.

The urge to exonerate *The Winter's Tale* from error can be felt in the eagerness of eighteenth- and nineteenth-century critics and editors to adopt Hanmer's solution, or at least to cite *Dorastus and Fawnia* as the precursor that excuses the play's fault. David Garrick was briefly tempted in preparing his stage adaptation of *The Winter's Tale* in 1756; he adopted the locale of Bithynia in his first manuscript version of *Florizel and Perdita*, but returned to Bohemia in the printed text (Bartholomeusz 32). In the 1778 edition of Shakespeare's works by Samuel Johnson and George Steevens, a footnote to act 3 of *The Winter's Tale* delicately concedes that although Hanmer "would have us read Bythinia" (sic), "our author implicitly copied the novel before him" in selecting Bohemia. And so the opening page of the play indicates: "The story of this play is taken from the *Pleasant History of Dorastus and Fawnia*, written by Robert Greene." John Bell's 1774 "acting" edition of the play gave not Garrick's text but Shakespeare's, "studiously prun'd and regulated, by the ingenious Mr. Hull, of Covent-Garden, who has certainly made it more bearable than the author left it."[67] Hull was presumably responsible for setting the "SCENE, partly in Sicilia, and partly in Bithynia." Bell's edition may have challenged the Tonson monopoly in Shakespeare, but it followed Tonsonian tradition in specifying once more, "The plot taken from the old story-book of Dorastus and Faunia." The tag was clearly a guarantor of respectability to any version of the text. Even the hybrid acting edition published by Harrison & Co. in 1779–80, "The Winter's Tale, A Tragedy, As it is Acted at the Theatres-

Royal in Drury-Lane and Covent-Garden," which repeated the usual Tonson text but dubbed in Garrick's most untragic sentiments at the end, dutifully noted, "The plot taken from the old Story-book of DORASTUS and FAUNIA."[68]

Charles Kean most wholeheartedly accepted the Bithynian solution, making the cultural variations between Greece and Asia Minor central to his extravagantly researched production of the play in 1856. In a performance edition of that year, he tactfully explained that he had taken some liberties with the settings in Sicilia and Bohemia that Shakespeare shared with Greene. The *Illustrated London News* was less constrained by the facts, praising Sir Thomas Hanmer's suggestion of Bithynia "as the place intended by the poet and the novelist." The reviewer added that in characterizing Leontes, "Shakspear has been careful, by altering many of the details in Robert Greene's novel, to lend a dignity to the part which is not to be found in the 'Docastus [sic] and Fawnia,' and thus to preserve for [Leontes] a title to our respect."[69] The newspaper mistook Greene's title, although it cleared both him and Shakespeare of the Bohemian blunder.

By the mid-nineteenth century, the Bohemian seacoast was still the most-visited site in Shakespeare's play, and all that was left was to acknowledge that it had become laughable. So did William Brough's 1856 burlesque, *Perdita or the royal milkmaid*, an elaborate parody of Kean's production of *The Winter's Tale*, including the arbitrary rewriting of Bohemia as Bithynia. The opening list of settings, each one more preposterous than the last, includes a "DESERT SPOT, ON THE SHORES OF BOHEMIA, OR BITHYNIA, or wherever it is."[70] The burlesque begins with Time squarely confronting the problem: "I'm here as the Chorus. The fact is, this play, / As written by Shakspeare, won't do in our day." To a popular tune, he sings:

> Long time ago from Bohemia
> > Sailed the king—no, we're wrong about the quarter;
> For the king didn't come from Bohemia,
> > 'Cause he couldn't come thence by water.
> > > So we can't have that,
> > > But we'll place him at
> Bithynia—it's a name no shorter,
> > Nor longer than the other, so the lines come pat,
> And prevent the poor old dramatist's slaughter.

(Brough 4–5)

Best of all, the title page brings the joke home to the editorial tradition that had determined Kean's setting. For Brough billed his show as *Perdita or the royal milkmaid: being the legend upon which Shakespeare is supposed to have founded his Winter's Tale: a new and original burlesque*. In mock homage to the many editors who had presented *Dorastus and Fawnia* as the "foundation" of *The Winter's Tale*, Brough presents his "original" burlesque as a parallel re-commodification of *Dorastus and Fawnia* (never explicitly mentioned)— as, in other words, a text *prior* to Kean's as Greene's was to Shakespeare's. Brough's title calls Greene's romance a "legend," but the subtitle "The Royal Milkmaid" points intriguingly toward "The Royal Shepherdess," the title under which the story circulated in Scotland from the 1790s on. A link to such a chapbook form would be entirely in keeping with burlesque's cultural leveling.

By 1866, Collier almost audibly sighs as, in a bibliographical account, he mentions that Greene's romance solves a Shakespearean problem "so well known that it would be merely a waste of space to say anything of it here."[71] But after carefully establishing the antiquity of *Pandosto*—and the number of early editions "destroyed by the multiplicity and carelessness of readers"—he is drawn back to the wastes of Bohemia. He notes that *Pandosto* was made into "a prose chap-book in 1735, if not earlier, under the title of 'The Fortunate Lovers' "—and that the adapter, Hugh Stanhope, "adopted Greene's much ridiculed geographical blunder, which Shakspeare did not attempt to correct" (Collier, *Bibliographical*, 2:88). Earlier, in *Shakespeare's Library*, Collier had advanced a theory on why Shakespeare did not attempt the correction: Greene had put forward "over and over again" the idea of a maritime Bohemia, and Shakespeare, "supposing he knew better, did not think it worth while to disturb this popular notion" (4:15). In other words, Shakespeare allowed himself to be worn down by the repetitiveness of a popular misconception promulgated by Greene.

1700–1843: DUODECIMOS, NOVELS, DROLLS,
GARLANDS, ARABIAN TALES

Collier's reference to a 1735 "prose chapbook" was highly misleading. Far more substantial than chapbooks like Dennisson's, the 1735 text was an extensive retelling of Greene's romance, running to eighty close-set pages in the smaller duodecimo format. It was published under an omnibus title, *The Fortunate and Unfortunate Lovers*, which paired *Dorastus and Fawnia* with a prose version of *Hero and Leander* distantly derived from Christopher Marlowe's poem.[72] Neither Greene's name nor Marlowe's was on the title page; instead, a moralizing epistle was signed by Hugh Stanhope, the adapter. Stanhope (perhaps in concert with the volume's publisher), balanced two familiar love stories, more carefully than Conyers had padded a love story with the adventures of *Josephus*. Such combinations were characteristic of the period, not exclusive to popular literature: the pairing of a comic with a tragic story corresponds to the eighteenth-century theatrical practice of adding afterpiece to main piece. Like many of those mixed bills, *The Fortunate and Unfortunate Lovers* presented old pleasures in a form that reduced their moral problems and smoothed out their stylistic rough edges. However, the new title also affiliated the familiar stories with a nondramatic fashion, the sentimental fictional forms variously known as secret histories, romances, and novels.

This elegant duodecimo re-commodification had pretensions beyond those of brief chapbook redactions. The first edition of 1733 was produced by the very successful popular publisher Edward Midwinter. The 1735 imprint spotted by Collier was for "A. Bettesworth, C. Hitch, R. Ware, and J. Hodges."[73] Midwinter was a specialist in cheap print but was known for his disciplined and busy shop. Unfortunately, his extravagant standard of living left his fashionable daughter a pauper when he died; the fate of Miss Elizabeth Midwinter will be revealed in chapter 4.[74] Arthur Bettesworth was "chiefly a publisher of divinity, though he published many novels, &c., and like all the booksellers on the Bridge, dealt in some questionable literature."[75] Chapbook historian Pat Rogers argues that Midwinter and Bettesworth and partners, bringing out a substantial one-volume abridgment of *Robinson Crusoe* on the heels of the original, were well-established figures, far from "fly-by-night operators or fringe publishers."[76] Bettesworth had a long-standing partnership, specializing in novels, with Charles Hitch, who married his daughter. But of all the many highly visible, often literary, publishing jobs on which Bettesworth and Hitch collaborated, the most significant in this context must be the 1733 edition of Shakespeare's works (Theobald's edition), published by a syndicate of Bettesworth, Hitch, Tonson, and three others. Thus, in the early 1730s, Bettesworth and Hitch were publishing editions of both *Dorastus and Fawnia* and *The Winter's Tale*.

Like Theobald's edition of Shakespeare, Stanhope's *Fortunate and Unfortunate Lovers* purifies a familiar text and standardizes its irregularities; as Theobald's preface justifies his editorial practice, Stanhope's justifies his choice of a story with morally questionable incidents. Theobald manufactures a textual history to excuse Shakespeare's "absurd" geography; Stanhope manufactures a textual history in which Dorastus and Fawnia serve as moral exempla. His preface claims that the work is "Made *English* from the Originals, written in the *Bohemia* and *Grecian* Tongues, By a GENTLEMAN, who spent many years in travelling through most Parts of Germany, Greece, and Italy, where these Stories are in as much Credit and Repute, as any that are now Extant, or ever were Printed." The title page thus grants the text a spurious international authority—frankly spurious, since the full title names the familiar couple, "Dorastus and Fawnia." The preface goes on to explain that in Bohemia and Greece, both stories have "gained so much Applause" that parents give them to children to inculcate "excellent Rules of Morality." It is no accident that this modernization of *Dorastus and Fawnia* imposed a high moral tone reminiscent of the Augustan theater, for Hugh Stanhope was the pseudonym of William Bond, an unsuccessful tragedian and essayist.[77] Of course, Bond's use of a pseudonym signals that he estimated this work lower than his attempts at dramatic authorship. A nominal rewriting, no matter how morally sound, was Grub Street hackwork, not to mention a violation of a principle of authorial rights that was, by this time, the law of the land. Yet if the hackwork is characteristic of chapbooks, the authorial pretense of "translation" is also reminiscent of the transparently spurious documentary claims made in secret histories, romances, and novels of the day.[78]

In this version of the story, the center of interest is now Fawnia. The frontispiece illustration favors her tale over Pandosto's, omitting the court scene and retaining large images of Fawnia's waterborne discovery and sylvan courtship (figure 3.6). Even more than the Dennisson adaptation, *The Fortunate Lovers* expands the confrontation between Fawnia and the lecherous Pandosto in its final scenes, which I will analyze in chapter 4. Stanhope's insistence on Fawnia's imperiled virtue is characteristic of early eighteenth-century drama, and her many long speeches deploy the rhetoric of the so-called she-tragedy.[79]

Since the theme of imperiled virtue is heightened between the chapbook condensation of circa 1680 and this modernization of circa 1730, it is possible to argue that a popular favorite was hijacked to carry bourgeois values, losing much of its former autonomy. Keith Thomas, for instance, has argued that eighteenth-century literature was standardized by a tone of moral self-improvement (like that heard in Stanhope) that ultimately united metropolitan and provincial readers, from the upper through the middling classes, excluding only the lowest ranks:

Those who did not aspire to imitate their betters had to be content with an inferior brand of literature designed by commercial publishers for a

FIGURE 3.6
Title page, Hugh Stanhope, *The Fortunate and Unfortunate Lovers*
(London: E. Midwinter, 17–).
BY PERMISSION OF THE CLARK LIBRARY, UCLA

popular market. . . . The printed word thus either educated an imitative audience in accepted views or confirmed a passive one in a position of cultural inferiority.[80]

Thomas actually figures both parties as passive: those outside fashion are "content" with an "inferior" position, while those reading literature with greater pretenses are herded into an "imitative" one. But neither the Dennisson nor the Stanhope text limits its appeal to the wholly "popular" or the wholly aspirant; frank commerciality and social ambitions are inseparably bound in these repackagings. More important, neither version condemns its readers to the kind of class passivity imagined by Thomas. As I will argue when I return to *The Fortunate Lovers* in chapter 4, Stanhope's adaptation, modeling resistance to the abuse of power, may have encouraged rather than repressed readers' agency in negotiating class difference.

THE CRITICAL PROBLEM of the relationship between *Pandosto* and *The Winter's Tale*—including their respective histories of re-commodification— came to the forefront in Charlotte Lennox's *Shakespear Illustrated* (1753– 54), the first systematic gathering of Shakespearean source stories in print. Her evaluations adjudicate the relationships between Shakespeare's plays and the romances from which they derived—with unorthodox results, since her introductions to the prose generally assert their *superiority* to the plays. By republishing these stories, Lennox brought *Dorastus and Fawnia* to the attention of Shakespeare's readers to an unprecedented extent, allowing them to compare the two works in a context laden with scholarly significance.

The position Lennox takes on *The Winter's Tale* and *Dorastus and Fawnia* is complex: she cannot voice particular enthusiasm for an antiquated romance, but as Samuel Johnson's friend and protegée, she is no fan of Shakespeare either. This dilemma marks her entire project: her preface claims that plotting is the "highest" of "Powers" in a poet, then concludes that "a very small Part of the Reputation of this mighty Genius [Shakespeare] depends upon the naked Plot, or Story of his Plays" (Lennox, *Shakespear*, 1:iv–viii). Her skepticism about Shakespeare comes through even more strongly when she considers *The Winter's Tale*:

> It has been mentioned as a great Praise to *Shakespear* that the old paltry
> Story of *Dorastus* and *Fawnia* served him for a Winter's Tale, but if we
> compare the Conduct of the Incidents in the Play with the paltry Story
> on which it is founded, we shall find the Original much less absurd and
> ridiculous.   (2:75)

Lennox goes on to quote Hanmer (and indeed the phrase "old paltry Story" is his), but only in order to rebut his argument for Shakespeare's superiority. Language normally used to demean Greene at the expense of Shakespeare is turned around: now the story "served" to found Shakespeare's more "absurd and ridiculous" re-commodification.

Yet the comparison demonstrates that Lennox was not so much leveling what had already been ranked as asserting the continuity between "popular" and "canonical" forms that emergent criticism had begun to obscure.

The text of *Dorastus and Fawnia* that Lennox published was not Greene's, although his authorship had been established in Theobald's edition of Shakespeare in 1733. In 1961, Wells pointed out that what Lennox provided was "(as apparently has not been remarked) . . . not *Pandosto* but a paraphrase of it" (*"Perymedes"* xliii). As in the case of Jordan's poem, Wells only partially corrects a scholarly misrecognition, for Lennox paraphrases not Greene's original but Hugh Stanhope's moralizing adaptation, published twenty years before. Her free adaptation of Stanhope certainly violates the principle she had negotiated with the project's sponsor, Lord Orrery: "you are entirely right, Madam, to translate, and not to epitomize or imitate" (quoted in Kramnick 265).

Most of the time, Lennox did simply reprint Stanhope. For example, she reproduces a crucial speech in which Fawnia resists Dorastus's pretended threat to constrain her to love (a mild preview of her later resistance to Pandosto's incestuous love):

> I acknowledge your Power, Sir, said *Fawnia*, in all just and reasonable Things, but with Submission, I must say my Heart is only at my own Disposal; constrained Love is Force, and Force you have no Right to use over me: and believe me, it is not a vain Boast I make, when I tell you that poor as I am I set so great a Value upon my Chastity, that I would rather die than be the Mistress of the greatest King upon Earth, and my Birth is so mean and groveling that I am not fit to be a Farmer's Wife.[81]

Lennox borrows from Stanhope, word for word, a passage that negotiates courageously with the power of an aristocratic aggressor. Stanhope's language is more sharply politicized than Greene's, allowing Fawnia to deny Dorastus's "Right" to use "Force." Stanhope heightened the rhetoric to make the story more dramatic. Lennox repeats it to demonstrate that this romance is as decorous and rational as a novel. This scene would have edified rather than misled Arabella, the misguided romance reader from Lennox's *Female Quixote* (1752), which articulates new distinctions between romances and novels.

Elsewhere, Lennox paraphrases Stanhope more freely, adding material that develops Fawnia further as a novelistic heroine. Modernizing his modernization, she often breaks his long melodramatic speeches, which themselves recast euphuistic set pieces from Greene, into reflections punctuated by gesture and sensory experiences so that the characters' opposing impulses are seen as plausible responses to changing stimuli. These revisions were consistent with the purpose of *Shakespear Illustrated* as Jonathan Kramnick has reconstructed it: to show how "Shakespeare's 'romantic' antiquity declares his inferiority to the paradoxically modern form of the sources."[82] Lennox wanted to illustrate Shakespeare's mishandling of excellent source materials. His insistence on romantic improbability represents a step backward from the older tales that were sufficiently probable to merit Lennox's approbation as "novels."

According to Kramnick, Lennox's stance represents a chronology-breaking paradox, in which "Shakespeare antiquates the novel and makes it romance" (118). But the fact that Lennox turns to a recent "novelization" rather than to Greene's version lessens the paradox. Stanhope's adaptation had been shaped by more than a century of interchange among Greene's romance, its chapbook adaptations, Shakespeare's drama, and stage tragedy. Re-commodification had novelized it, effecting far more sweeping changes than the editorial improvement of Shakespeare's play. That she found this novelized romance more up to date than the play demonstrates how material alterations continually refitted a work to changing tastes. And of course Lennox altered it further to her own tastes, within the re-commodifying context of her anthology.

The anthology's critical reception was complicated by Johnson's letter of dedication to Orrery, which tried to defuse Lennox's heretical position and to reassert the literary excellence of Shakespeare. Johnson claims that the literariness of Shakespeare rests on the very romance qualities that Lennox rejects. But then, Johnson's own draw to romance is well known; he admitted his childhood addictions to chivalric romances and claimed a line from *Paradise Lost* as an allusion to, of all things, *Don Bellianis of Greece*.[83] The *Gentleman's Magazine* also worked to minimize Lennox's attack on Shakespeare. Its 1753 review of the anthology made her into a gentle Langbaine, stating that in her account of Shakespeare, "many beauties of which he was supposed to be the inventor [were] restored to those from whom they were borrowed." More tellingly, it listed her work not with the scholarly titles under "antiquities," but under "entertainment," with "true histories, novels, ballads, and the like." The point was that seekers of textual "beauties" might find Lennox's text entertaining, more so than Shakespeare. Kramnik concludes this was "certainly one of the last occasions when a publication could, without hesitation, pose the apparently popular form of the novel against the works of the nation's canonical author" (128). The magazine may have underestimated Lennox's project, which had the potential to deconstruct such cultural divisions by questioning the assumption of Shakespeare's superiority that was quickly becoming entrenched, and demonstrating that the sources abjured by elite readers could still satisfy their tastes.

THAT CONSONANCE BETWEEN allegedly separate cultural spheres is particularly evident when the history of re-commodifications of *Dorastus and Fawnia* is compared to the stage history of *The Winter's Tale*. Many of the strategies that publishers had used to re-commodify Greene's romance— padding, illustration, reformatting, sentimentalizing textual details— were paralleled in stage productions of Shakespeare's play, which focused on the same class and gender tensions that were concentrated in *Dorastus and Fawnia* adaptations. As the titles and illustrations of the chapbooks converged in making pastoral paradoxes the essence of the story, Shakespeare's complex romance was fitted to a revitalized taste for pastoral. It is even arguable that the popular uses of *Dorastus and Fawnia* opened the way for the belated revival of *The Winter's Tale*, for *Dorastus and Fawnia* was appearing as a droll during the long era in which *The Winter's Tale* was absent from the stage.

Scholars have had little to say about drolls, one-hour performances at summer fairs known only from rare playbill listings and advertisements. Drolls are seen as demeaned by their apparently minimal scripts and staging, and their parade of actors on an outdoor platform as a living advertisement. In fact, however, drolls gave summer work to many professionals from the major theaters, and both the "legitimate" stage and the drolls attracted mixed audiences. The free admittance of theatergoers' servants to the upper galleries was a fiercely defended privilege in the mid-eighteenth century (Hecht 136–39). Meanwhile, a 1739 visitor reported that "chambermaid and Countess sit / Alike admirers of the wit" at Bartholomew Fair in 1739 (Rosenfeld 46). In terms of class contact, the drolls differed from the London theaters primarily in that divisions were not architecturally reinforced; the fair's smaller facilities and relaxed conventions led to more intimate, even carnivalesque, mixing that put "Earl and footman *tête-à-tête*" (Rosenfeld 46). It was rumored that even royalty attended—incognito.[84]

The place of *Dorastus and Fawnia* in the droll tradition is yet another instance of re-commodification that has been seen as opposed to the cultural position of *The Winter's Tale* but can be productively read as continuous with it. *Dorastus and Fawnia* debuted at the 1703 Bartholomew Fair and is known to have been repeated in 1729 and 1749.[85] Making the most of its familiarity, one playbill called it "an historical Play."[86] Meanwhile,

Shakespeare's play was first revived briefly in the winter of 1741, as a great novelty: "a Play (not acted these Hundred Years) call'd *The Winter's Tale* Written by Shakespeare."[87] The Shakespeare Ladies Club is most directly responsible for bringing *The Winter's Tale* to the stage, along with a number of other revived Shakespearean comedies (the chill cast on new plays by the Licensing Act of 1737 was also a factor).[88] However, after a run of only eight nights at the nonpatent Goodman's Fields that season, and fewer nights at Covent Garden the next, *The Winter's Tale* was again set aside. Then, in the 1750s, adaptations of the play that reduced its length and complexity entered the repertoires of the legitimate houses. Thus, within two decades, London saw an hour-long staging of the prose romance in a booth at a fair, a full-length version of the play revived in an unauthorized playhouse, and several hour-long adaptations on the main stages.

What might appear to be separate phenomena—the fairground staging of a chapbook love story and the later revival of a forgotten Shakespeare play—are in fact linked. Wells discovered the startling evidence: the advertised cast list for the *Dorastus and Fawnia* droll of 1729 quite plainly draws on Shakespeare as well as Greene, referring to several characters by their *Winter's Tale* names. Wells concludes that the droll "was in fact a version of *The Winter's Tale*," but falls back on the two-class model to explain why the titular hero and heroine were named Dorastus and Fawnia. This "very astute move" reflects, Wells explains, "the continued popularity of Greene's pamphlet among the class of people likely to frequent theatres at the fairs; people who were not likely to be attracted by a title associated with a Shakesperian play unperformed in theatres of that period."[89] That analysis is unfair: no audiences of *any* class were drawn to *The Winter's Tale* in the 1720s. Wells treats the *Dorastus and Fawnia* drolls as a plagiarized adaptation of Shakespeare's play, a point that Michael Dobson reinterprets more flexibly:

> To the performers at Parker's Booth, apparently, *The Winter's Tale* remained part of the common stock of old stories and plays from which such entertainments might be generated; blissfully oblivious to the stirrings of Bardolatry, the bills name no author (the very idea of authorship being quite irrelevant to this genre), and the droll probably neither sought nor achieved the dignity of print. (106–7)

Dobson situates the droll in a "common stock of old stories and plays," outside of print and unacquainted with new authorial norms, from which

Shakespeare was being removed. Still, the kinds of authorial freedoms taken in this droll had long survived in print forms, first in the authorless publication of many early dramas and their novelizations and versifications, then in the easygoing form of chapbook adaptations. In a context unconcerned with authorship, the convergence of romance and play provoked no anxiety. For all we know, the freedom of the 1720s may have drawn on a century's casual recognition that the story took two forms.

The Dorastus and Fawnia drolls cannot be reduced to simple equation with a cut-down *Winter's Tale*. There is, for instance, no Autolycus in the cast list—although that role was seen as a crowd pleaser and expanded by those who adapted *The Winter's Tale* later in the century (and although it would perfectly figure the droll's spirit of unauthorized cultural circulation). The drolls were not cleaving to Shakespeare's text, but they were not isolated from the "stirrings of Bardolatry." One actor carried his experience from the fairground *Dorastus and Fawnia* to a *Winter's Tale* performed in a legitimate venue: the Chapman who played "Polixene" (father to Dorastus) in the 1729 droll is the Thomas Chapman who played Autolycus in the 1741 production at Covent Garden.[90] Autolycus's actor moves between venues as Autolycus moved among gentle service, ballad selling, crime, and puppetry; that Autolycus the chapman should be played by "Chapman" is nearly too good to be true.

Those long-lost Dorastus and Fawnia drolls seem to agree with the chapbooks in keeping their focus squarely on the young lovers, not on the king or Autolycus. Of the scraps of evidence we have for these drolls, the cast lists link them to a Shakespearean stage tradition, but the titles establish their continuity with the chapbook tradition. The 1703 droll was titled *The Famous History of Dorastus and Fawnia*, but the 1729 droll was called *Dorastus and Fawnia, or the Royal Shepherdess*, and the 1749 version, *The Royal Shepherd and Shepherdess*. The last title would survive in a distant and apparently unrelated context, Scottish chapbook adaptations of the romance extant from 1796 and the early nineteenth century.

In fact, that title did not originate with the 1729 droll but with a puppet play performed a year earlier, *Dorastus and Fawnia, or the Royal Shepherd and Shepherdess*,[91] and conceivably was inspired by Thomas Shadwell's tragicomedy, *The Royal Shepherdess*, performed and printed back in 1669. In the puppet play as in earlier Restoration tragicomedy, the titular juxtaposition of "royal" with "shepherdess" heightens social paradox and prettifies it. Whatever its origins, the title of *The Royal Shepherd and Shepherdess* follows a tendency already illustrated in chapbook editions of *Dorastus and*

Fawnia: describing the prince by his borrowed identity and the princess by her adopted one, it inserts the lovers into pastoral tradition, the taste for which was shared by elite and nonelite audiences. Nor was the puppet venue unknown to the gentle classes or too low for Shakespearean drama.[92] Pepys reluctantly admitted that anyone could enjoy a puppet play: "To Southwarke fair . . . and there saw the puppet-show of Whittington, which was pretty to see; and how that idle thing do work upon people that see it, and even myself too!"[93] Although not proud of it, Pepys enjoys the social bond that the experience creates; his comment identifies these informal theatricals as liminal, not marginal, events.

The appearance of drolls based on *Dorastus and Fawnia* on informal stages may have helped to pave the way for the revival of the Shakespearean *Winter's Tale* on a "legitimate" stage some dozen years later. But the real success of *The Winter's Tale* came not with this revival of 1741–42 but later, when its matter was reduced to the Bohemian action only. In 1754, Macnamara Morgan debuted a two-act afterpiece usually called *The Sheep-shearing*, which retained only the pastoral love story, dropping the Leontes/Hermione plot to textual background. The play had been reduced to an excuse for picturesque settings and song in keeping with the new taste for nature, according to Irene Dash.[94] Or, it could be argued, the play had been reduced to the essence of class encounter (however euphemized), to which the chapbook adaptations and drolls had also been tending. Certainly it cut out the more formal and verbose scenes of Shakespeare's play, much as chapbook adaptations and (presumably) drolls had cut out Greene's euphuistic figures and elaborate perorations. Of course elite play-goers' preferences for shortened dramas were not based on economic necessity, as were the choices of some chapbook buyers and droll attenders. But the simplifications of the text on page and stage responded to commonly felt commercial pressures and fed common, though contradictory, impulses toward sensation and moralism. Dobson, in fact, proposes that the Morgan version might have drawn on the fairground drolls, adapting them to "more up-market" fashion under the name of Shakespeare (106).

In 1756, David Garrick responded to Morgan with his own more ambitious production, *Florizel and Perdita*, a three-act main piece, or, as he called it, *A Dramatic Pastoral*. This was first performed with *Catharine and Petruchio*, his afterpiece based on *The Taming of the Shrew*, but later was reduced to an afterpiece itself. Thus, much as romance readers might have found *Dorastus and Fawnia* bound together with *Josephus* or *Hero and Leander*, auditors at theaters and fairs alike would have found performances of *The Winter's Tale* on a program mixing shortened play texts with ballads, ballets, and after-pieces. Garrick took it as a point of pride that he had retained more of Shake-speare's dialogue than had Morgan, but later critics have disagreed. Garrick cut out most of the first three acts, and the statue scene was apparently cut in later productions from his script.[95] He added bathetic lines to the final scene that made it, as Dobson mordantly comments, "in every sense, family enter-tainment for the 1750s" (190). The shared preference in both adaptations for the later, pastoral sections of the drama over the earlier tragic sections echoes the clear evidence from the chapbook's history that the second generation, not the first, captured the interest of readers. But Perdita's discussion of cross-breeding, Nature, and Art with Polixenes, which might seem an ideal pastoral set piece, is notably absent from both Morgan and Garrick. This excision seems to respond to *Dorastus and Fawnia*'s persistence, denying that Shakespeare, himself reconciling Nature and Art, had grafted his "bud of nobler race" on "a bark of baser kind" (4.4.94–95).

Garrick's version included perhaps the most characteristic statement of adaptation as canonization, the promise in the verse preface that he would "lose no drop of that Immortal Man," Shakespeare. The claim seems non-sensical in the context of an adaptation that cut the play in half, but the larger imagery makes Garrick's intention plain. With Shakespeare's cham-pagne he has mixed a bit of his own "perry" (cider), but what was less than vintage has been distilled away: the indignities other critics had noted, the printers' errors, disunities, coarse remarks, and unkingly Leontes of the first three acts. What has been added is musical effervescence. Adaptation by reduction had made Shakespeare a fortified spirit, a fine wine with a musi-cal kick.

Nevertheless, Garrick's image earned opprobrium from Theophilus Cibber in one of his *Two Dissertations on the Theatres* (London, 1756): "he does bottle him up with a Vengeance!—he throws away all the spirited Part of him, all that bears the highest Flavour; then as to some of the Dregs, adds a little flat Stuff of his own, and modestly palms it on his Customers" (37–38). Cibber's attack is remarkable for tracing a lineage between the ephemeral entertainments at the fairs and the airy adaptations of the legit-imate theaters. He observes that since "*Bartholomew Fair* has been some Years suppres'd," Garrick resourcefully "contriv'd to introduce Drolls on the Stage, at the Theatre Royal in *Drury-Lane*." *Florizel and Perdita* was quite literally a droll transposed: " 'Twas usual with the Masters of Droll Booths to get some Genius of a lower Class, to supply 'em with Scenes, detach'd from our Plays—altered and adapted to the Taste of the holiday

Audiences . . . and of this gallimaufry kind was the Pastoral . . . exhibited at *Drury's* Theatre" (32). Cibber contrasts Garrick's adaptation to Shakespeare's play, which

> tho' one of his most irregular Pieces, abounds with beautiful Strokes, and touching Circumstances; the very title (*A Winter's Tale*) seems fix'd on by the Author, as an Apology for, and a bespeaking of, a loose Plan. . . . The story affected his Mind, and afforded a large Field for his lively Imagination to wander in. (33)

Garrick had unfailing omitted these "most interesting Circumstances," leaving a "mixture of piecemeal, motley Patchwork" (33). *Florizel and Perdita* was, Cibber concludes, *The Winter's Tale* "mammoc'd into a Droll" (36). His polemic, although biased, evinces anxieties about re-commodification that few other writers were willing to acknowledge.

MID-CENTURY REDUCTIONS of the play, like the redactions of the chapbooks, fetishize the royal shepherdess, her pastoral beauty, and her reversals of fortune, provoking ambivalence among modern critics. Both Marsden and Dash point out that later in the century, a "penchant for Perdita" becomes a thinly veiled fascination with virtue imperiled. As Dash has shown, eighteenth-century adapters of the play were careful to reduce Perdita's assertiveness. Her observation that despite Polixenes's disapproval, "the self-same sun" shines on palace and cottage (4.4.445) does not appear in Morgan's version. Garrick recovers it, but cushions it with Perdita's speeches of apology and submission to her father, lover, and king. Her motives are thus rendered more feminine, in keeping with the greater emphasis on her beauty, her dress, and her floral garland. That the Perdita of the adaptations should be so constrained makes the firm self-assertion of Fawnia, particularly in Stanhope's version, all the more powerful. The world of the theater offered few such models of successful resistance. Mary Robinson, the young actress who played Perdita at Drury Lane in 1779, was immediately procured as a mistress to the Prince of Wales (later George IV), who sent backstage a letter signed "Florizel." Unable to appeal to honor like Perdita and Fawnia, Robinson did yield to the importunings of a prince, ending her acting career.[96]

Perdita's quiescence in the Morgan and Garrick adaptations tacitly endorses social inequities, even though audience sympathy with her so clearly feeds fantasies of class intermingling. Dobson argues that Garrick refitted Shakespeare's "thoroughly monarchist" play with "bourgeois values," to tell audiences that "rank does not necessarily equate with worth" (194). But that position had already been articulated by Shakespeare's Perdita and Greene's Fawnia; what Garrick did was remove the statement safely to the male characters (including the monarchs), leaving his Perdita devoid of economic sense or class complaint. The safe masculinization of bourgeois ideology depended on the denial of ambition to women and to the poor that is enacted in these adaptations, in explicit revision of both Shakespeare and Greene. Bourgeois pastoral insists, as the earlier writers could not, that the poor are *content* with their lot.

In Greene, that word occurs twice in the conversations between Dorastus and Fawnia. On their first meeting, Fawnia tells Dorastus that shepherds "are rich in that we are poor with content," to which Dorastus replies, "I see thou art content with country labours because thou knowest not courtly pleasures" (Salzman, *Elizabethan*, 184). When she challenges him on his intentions, he returns in shepherd dress, reminding her that "Thou wert content to love Dorastus when he ceased to be a prince and to become [sic] a shepherd." Contentment, she now stipulates, is not the issue; since Dorastus was not "born poor," his change of attire has not "made" him "a shepherd, but to seem like a shepherd" (Salzman, *Elizabethan*, 187). He concedes that he is indeed a prince and will marry her regardless: in other words, that he must accept her status, as he cannot change his own. Fawnia gently coaches Dorastus to an understanding of economic, mimetic, and social realities, and tests his final intentions. Although Shakespeare never echoes the debate over contentment and introduces the couple when their courtship is already completed, he preserves Perdita's realism about social difference: she knows that "a swain's wearing" does not change the prince within (4.4.9).

Morgan's version returns to the pastoral fantasy that Greene's Fawnia deflates. His Perdita tells Florizel, improbably:

> Oft, oft, I wish thou wert some peasant swain,
> Born lowly as myself; than should we live
> Unknown, unenvied in our humble state,
> *Content* with love beneath the cottage straw.[97]

and Florizel replies, "I wish I were just what you'd have me be, / Distinguish't only from the rest by love" (lines 142–43). The shepherdess who wishes away her prince's economic privilege is a far cry from Greene's Fawnia.

Such fantasies of willing cultural deprivation provoked ridicule even in their own time. In Garrick's version, Fawnia's fleeting claim of shepherd contentment returns as a song claiming that "*Content* and sweet chearful-ness open our door, they smile with the simple, and feed with the poor."[98] Boswell's *Life of Johnson* includes a memorable anecdote about those lines:

> Mrs. Thrale then praised Garrick's talent for light gay poetry; and as a specimen, repeated his song in 'Florizel and Perdita,' and dwelt with peculiar pleasure on this line: 'I'd smile with the simple, and feed with the poor.' JOHNSON. 'Nay, my dear Lady, this will never do. Poor David! Smile with the simple? What folly is that! And who would feed with the poor that can help it? No, no; let me smile with the wise and feed with the rich.' I repeated this sally to Garrick, and wondered to find his sensibility as a writer not a little irritated by it.[99]

Johnson, who knew poverty all his life, penetrated the pastoral convention; he also recognized it as Garrick's contribution, not Shakespeare's, and felt free to query it.

Ironically, the simplicity (or banality) of Garrick's song was probably meant to approximate the qualities of popular verse; the craze for ballad opera had sent mid-century dramatists to the sorts of materials that they had earlier purged from Shakespeare's works. Unconstrained by the histor-ical concerns of collectors, they made ballads instead of finding them. Mor-gan and Garrick invent cheerful new ballads for Autolycus, replacing his more salacious songs. Morgan expands Autolycus's part at the cost of his interlocutors' roles: they sing of pastoral delight, but not from ballads. Gar-rick keeps Shakespeare's scene of consumption but downplays it: the rus-tics sing their ballad, but their dialogue is sanitized. Dobson ingeniously observes that the energy of the excluded ballad-selling scene surfaces much later in Garrick's career, in the self-reflexive play on his Bardolatry, *The Jubilee* (1769). Sukey and Nancy, who are as coarse as Shakespeare's Mopsa and Dorcas, buy Shakespeare souvenirs they do not comprehend. These nonelite women carry the weight of Garrick's commercialism, exemplify-ing how "excluding vulgarity from Shakespeare's plays and excluding the vulgar from Shakespeare . . . go hand in hand" (Dobson 221*n*50).

The ballad itself had been re-commodified by this time. The publish-ers of cheap print began to replace the old, cumbersome broadside form with a more convenient format for chapmen, the garland. The typical gar-land was still a single sheet and held about as many verses of song as a broadside had. But it was folded in quarters, making eight pages that required no sewing; thus, it constituted the most minimal form of a chapbook. Unlike broadsides, garlands were often omnibuses, containing several varied songs—the name went back to Elizabethan song collections, including one by Thomas Deloney long reprinted as "The Royal Garland." They could embrace several popular subgenres, assuring a more diverse appeal than a typical broadside. Luckily, they were also more durable, and large numbers survive. They preserve the output of provincial presses, the characteristic concerns of their regions (many include dialect or local humor), and even the labor of their likeliest customers (many garlands tell the stories of shepherds, servants, sailors, and soldiers). These were the cheapest print entertainments in the kingdom in the late eighteenth and early nineteenth centuries, and their appeal ranges from urban to rural, from pastoral to bawdy.

The garland was a relatively novel form at the time of the Shakespeare Jubilee, and predictably enough, Shakespeare garlands were issued. Halliwell collected two of them: " 'Shakespeare's Garland, being a Collection of new Songs, Ballads, &c., performed at the Jubilee at Stratford-upon-Avon.' Composers listed. 8vo. London 1769"; and " 'The Warwickshire Lad's Garland, composed of several excellent new Songs.' 12 mo. Licens'd and enter'd according to Order."[100] Halliwell's collection also boasted another interesting item:

> "The Royal Courtly Garland, or Joy after Sorrow." 12mo. Tewkesbury,
> n.d. This garland was frequently reprinted during the last century, and
> its age should, if possible, be ascertained, for the title will at once
> exhibit its similarity to the *Winter's Tale*. It commences as follows:—"A
> tragical story I have to relate."   (Halliwell, *Notices*, 79)

Another edition of this ballad is now in the collection of the Folger Shakespeare Library, where it is catalogued under "Shakespeare—The Winter's Tale—Adaptations." It bears Halliwell's bookplate and a manuscript comment that it tells the story of *The Winter's Tale* (figure 3.7).

Needless to say, Collier, too, encountered the *Royal Courtly Garland* and identified it with *The Winter's Tale*. In an 1851 article, he comments on the white-letter broadside that he dates to 1690–1720 but believes is based on a "considerably older" original.[101] (With its Aldermary imprint, it must date to 1750 or so.) Comparing the text to Jordan's "jealous Duke," he marvels: "It is singular that two ballads, hitherto entirely unknown, should

THE
Royal Courtly GARLAND.
IN SIX PARTS.

PART I. How the King of *Bohemia* having married a most virtuous Queen, and being afterwards visited by a foreign Prince, of whom the King became jealous, and hired his Cup-bearer to poison him; the Prince being acquainted with it, went into his own Country, and was soon after crowned there.

PART II. How the King put his Wife in Prison, where she was deliver'd of a Daughter, who was by the King's Order put into a Boat, and left to the Mercy of the Sea.

PART III. How the King in a Vision being assured of his Wife's Innocency, released her who soon after died with Grief.

PART IV. How the Child was drove into that Country where the Prince reigned, taken up by a Shepherd, and kept as his own.

PART V. How the King's Son fell in Love with her, And embark'd with her and the old Shepherd for *Italy*.

PART VI. Being by a Storm drove into *Bohemia*, where confined; and how the King thereof knew she was his own Daughter.

Licensed and Entered according to Order.

FIGURE 3.7
Title page, *The Royal Courtly Garland, in six parts* (Newcastle?, 1770?).

have been written upon the same incidents of the same drama," by which he means *The Winter's Tale*. The pattern can be predicted: Collier is denying that his find could be a ballad of *Pandosto*. Since the garland has no character names, Bohemia, as ever, is the pivot: "in my *Royal Courtly Garland* . . . the places of action are reversed exactly in the same way as in Greene's novel of *Pandosto*. Moreover, the error of representing Bohemia as a maritime country belongs to my ballad, as well as to the novelist and the dramatist" (3). Ignoring the fact that the order of locales follows Greene, Collier seizes on the misrepresentation of Bohemia as connecting the *Royal Courtly Garland* to Shakespeare.

In fact, the *Royal Courtly Garland* lacks any direct Shakespearean link. It follows the familiar plot given in the various versions of *Pandosto*, its six parts not so different from the seven chapters of Dennisson's redaction, and ends with a providential message of a type that became commonplace in the chapbooks: "Now by what was acted we plainly may see, / How nothing can hinder what the heavens decree." The garland takes great care over its humblest characters. Franion, the cupbearer who disobeys Pandosto's treacherous commands, often makes a disproportionate showing in chapbook versions of the story. In the *Royal Courtly Garland*, the cupbearer's ethical resistance nets him fifty pieces of gold. And the last lines give a new and unique detail, that the "dancing" of "dame Mopsey" at the wedding of her adopted daughter "pleased the court to the life." The lowest-ranking woman in Greene's story, Mopsa does not even appear at the end of any other version, but is left in Sicilia. The garland's ending makes a modest claim on the grand fantasy promised in the title: those not fortunate enough to be recognized as royalty or courtly may at least earn courtly admiration for their energy in enjoying popular pleasures, whether dancing or garland reading.

The *Royal Courtly Garland* must have been ubiquitous, for it survives in at least ten different printings, from presses in London, Coventry, Newcastle, Tewkesbury, and Glasgow. The first broadside editions have no illustration, but later publishers furnished the garland with more or less alluring woodcuts on the title page. The undated Halliwell-Folger edition depicts an exotically dressed dark-skinned man smoking a pipe (figure 3.7). A 1792 edition has a more suitable woodcut of a king raising his huge scepter to a woman with a fine pompadour. The last extant version, from after 1800, seems to address an audience of rural women: its title-page woodcut may depict Fawnia at work, although she is milking her large cow in a similarly elegant dress and hairstyle (figure 3.8). Presumably read mainly by Britain's

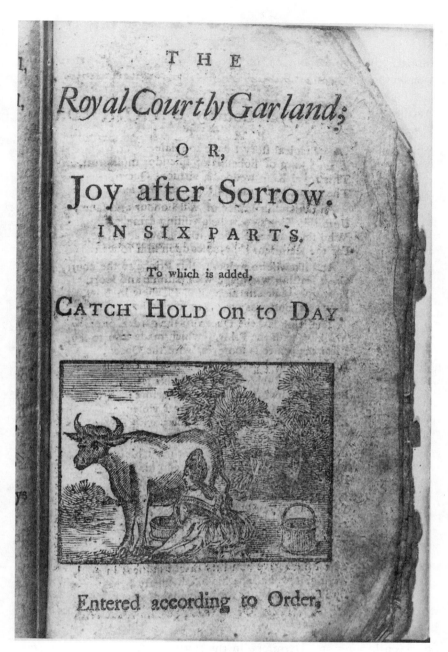

THE

Royal Courtly Garland;

OR,

Joy after Sorrow.

IN SIX PARTS.

To which is added,

CATCH HOLD on to DAY.

Entered according to Order.

FIGURE 3.8
Title page, *The Royal Courtly Garland or, Catch Hold on to Day*
(n.p., after 1800?).

Mopsas, the last editions of the "Royal Courtly Garland" offered rural women variant pleasures in small packages.

AROUND 1750, AS the penchant for Perdita developed on English stages, *Dorastus and Fawnia* resurfaced not in Stanhope's text but in Greene's full-text version, on regular offer from those quintessential chapbook publishers, Woodgate and Brookes. Picking up where Conyers left off, these were the last printings of Greene's full text for popular consumption. The team's dominance of the market for cheap pleasure reading was gradually ceded to a dynasty of Diceys, publishers from Northampton who moved to London to reach an enormous provincial market. At their press in Aldermary Churchyard, later Bow Churchyard, the Diceys produced up to "nine-tenths" of the chapbooks sold in Britain—some 150 titles, but "little or no original matter."[102] They worked their way through the canon of popular favorites, reducing nearly every title to a twenty-four-page chapbook. The Diceys' market extended to larger portions of Britain than chapbook publishers had ever served before; competitors imitated their format in more remote locations, such as Newcastle-on-Tyne (1775?) and Boston, Massachusetts (1795). Publishers always provided a title-page woodcut of the maiden or couple, and further generic illustrations in the text depending on their resources.

The Aldermary version of *Dorastus and Fawnia* may have been only twenty-four pages, but it had a newly expanded title. As rendered on a copy from about 1775, this read: "THE HISTORY OF *Dorastus* and *Faunia*. Setting forth their LOVES, MISFORTUNES, And HAPPY Enjoyment of each other at last." It featured the plentiful but noncommittal woodcuts typical of Aldermary products: an ambiguous indoor courtship scene on the title page, a generic ship, and a court feast at the end (figure 3.9). Like Dennisson's text, but newly prepared, this adaptation replaces Greene's dialogues with quick-moving narration. The text has been cleaned up in that complications and coarser details have been removed—Mopsa does not suspect her shepherd husband of adultery, and Pandosto, though as incestuous as ever, does not commit suicide. Above all, more sentimental material is added—much in the nature of the mid-century dramatic adaptations of *The Winter's Tale*. Just as Garrick had drawn out the marital reconciliation between Leontes and Hermione in the statue scene, the Aldermary text adds the detail that baby Fawnia's "gold glittering necklace made of oriental gems" (which Greene indicates is given to her by Bellaria) was originally "the same that Pandosta [sic] gave to Bellaria when he first courted her"

THE
HISTORY
OF
Dorastus and *Faunia.*

Setting forth their

LOVES, MISFORTUNES,

And HAPPY

Enjoyment of each other at laſt.

Printed anb Sold in Aldermary Church
Yard, Bow Lane, London.

FIGURE 3.9
Title page, *The History of Dorastus and Faunia*
(London: Aldermary Churchyard, 1775?).

(13). When Pandosto recognizes the grown Fawnia, he exclaims "this is the necklace I gave thy mother" (23). The necklace is simultaneously a narrative device with folk overtones, a material detail like those that give the eighteenth-century novel its texture of realism, and a touch of luxury and sentiment probably directed at young women.

The chapbooks popular in the provincial market have often been labeled as culturally belated, piratical, and impoverished. Admittedly, the only extant American popular edition of the romance, dated 1795, was published in obscure conditions. The publisher/printer of *The History of Dorastus and Faunia*, J. White, located "near Charles-river Bridge" in Boston (an area noted for production of early wallpaper more than books), appears to have borrowed the text of an Aldermary chapbook almost word for word.[103] There is only one very small woodcut on the title page, less illustration than would be seen in an English edition of the same type and date (figure 3.10). The text has charming traces of ownership: a signature on the flyleaf in a youthful hand ("Deborah Woods") and a homemade binding of early wallpaper backed with an old letter.[104] Although this is a shoestring production, the choice of *Dorastus and Fawnia* is not in itself belated—the Aldermary text was being printed simultaneously in England. That it was probably a piracy of an English title is simply typical of early American publishing. The first American edition of the works of Shakespeare appeared in the same year, and was creaky in its own way: as Gary Taylor points out, it was "simply a reincarnation of Johnson's edition, first published three decades earlier."[105] Taylor sees the turn-of-the-century production of "outdated editions" of Shakespeare as indicating that "oldness had become a relished attribute" (130–31)—a nostalgic attitude that united audiences for Shakespeare and *Dorastus and Fawnia*.

These were the first American printings of *Dorastus and Fawnia* and of Shakespeare's plays, but both were probably represented among the many cheap Irish editions imported to the United States during the eighteenth century. The 1792 Philadelphia edition of Shakespeare closely followed William Jones's 1791 "Royal Irish Edition," which sold for one third less than the English edition on which it was based (Andrew Murphy investigates such trade rivalries in his forthcoming *Shakespeare in Print: A History and Chronology of Shakespeare Publishing, 1590–2000*). In an article on "Chapbooks in America," Victor Neuberg reconstructs the scale on which Irish chapbooks were brought into the United States. An especially ambitious importer was the Irishman Andrew Steuart, who resided in Philadelphia and later in Wilmington, North Carolina, importing and perhaps

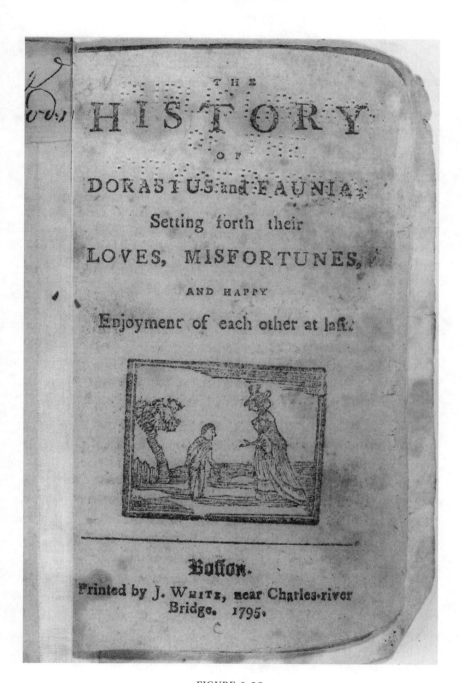

THE
HISTORY
OF
DORASTUS and FAUNIA;
Setting forth their
LOVES, MISFORTUNES,
AND HAPPY
Enjoyment of each other at last.

Boston.
Printed by J. WHITE, near Charles-river
Bridge. 1795.

FIGURE 3.10
Title page, *The History of Dorastus and Faunia* (Boston: J. White, 1795?).

reprinting cheap titles produced by his former master, James Magee of Belfast. American chapbooks with Steuart or Magee imprints are scarce, but Neuburg reports that an advertisement in a 1763 collection of Russell's sermons lists sixty-nine chapbook titles for sale in Philadelphia, including the sixteenth-century stalwarts, new classics like *Robinson Crusoe*—and *Dorastus and Fawnia*, with *Hero and Leander* on the next line.[106]

The last extant editions of *Dorastus and Fawnia* come from Ireland, where the story remained in print halfway through the nineteenth century, with imprints from Dublin (1793–94 and 1800?) and Belfast (1843).[107] The Dublin editions, running to about 144 duodecimo pages, fit a recognizable format for popular books in Ireland.[108] All three extant Irish editions retain Stanhope's preface, his name, and his title (figure 3.11).

The Irish editions added an intriguing subtitle from 1793, "The New Arabian Tales." Where did this come from? According to Robert Irwin's study of the dissemination of Arabian tales in the West, there was no translation of Antoine Galland's *Les Mille et une nuits* (Paris, 1704–17) until Jonathan Scott's *Arabian Nights Entertainments* in 1811. Only "cheap chapbooks" or "opportunistic translations by Grub Street hacks" were available in England.[109] This chapbook had an even more tenuous grasp on the title "Arabian," with nothing remotely Eastern in it; only the omnibus quality of *The Fortunate and Unfortunate Lovers* seems tale-like. Freedom with the name of an Arabian Tale is hardly a marker of low culture, however; plenty of fashionable novels were carrying orientalizing titles by the end of the eighteenth century. English "Oriental tales" of more literary ambition and influence included Samuel Johnson's *Rasselas: Prince of Abyssinia* (1759), John Hawkesworth's *Almoran and Hamet* (1761), Clara Reeve's *History of Charoba, Queen of Aegypt* (1785), and the Irishwoman Maria Edgeworth's "Murad the Unlucky" (1804). Irwin observes that "Most English oriental tales tended to be leadenly moral" (242), and so was the Irish "New Arabian Tale," which simply reprinted Stanhope's version, complete with preface and moralizing poem. Still, the use of the title in cheap print is precocious.

The taste for Arabian tales went hand in glove with the growing interest in folk culture that Peter Burke locates in late eighteenth-century culture, and led another generation of Britain's educated men to collect chapbooks. One of these was the insatiable young Scotsman James Boswell, who in 1763 took a nostalgic trip to the Dicey printing office in Bow Churchyard:

There are ushered into the world of literature *Jack and the Giants, The Seven Wise Men of Gotham* [i.e., *Seven Wise Masters*], and other story books

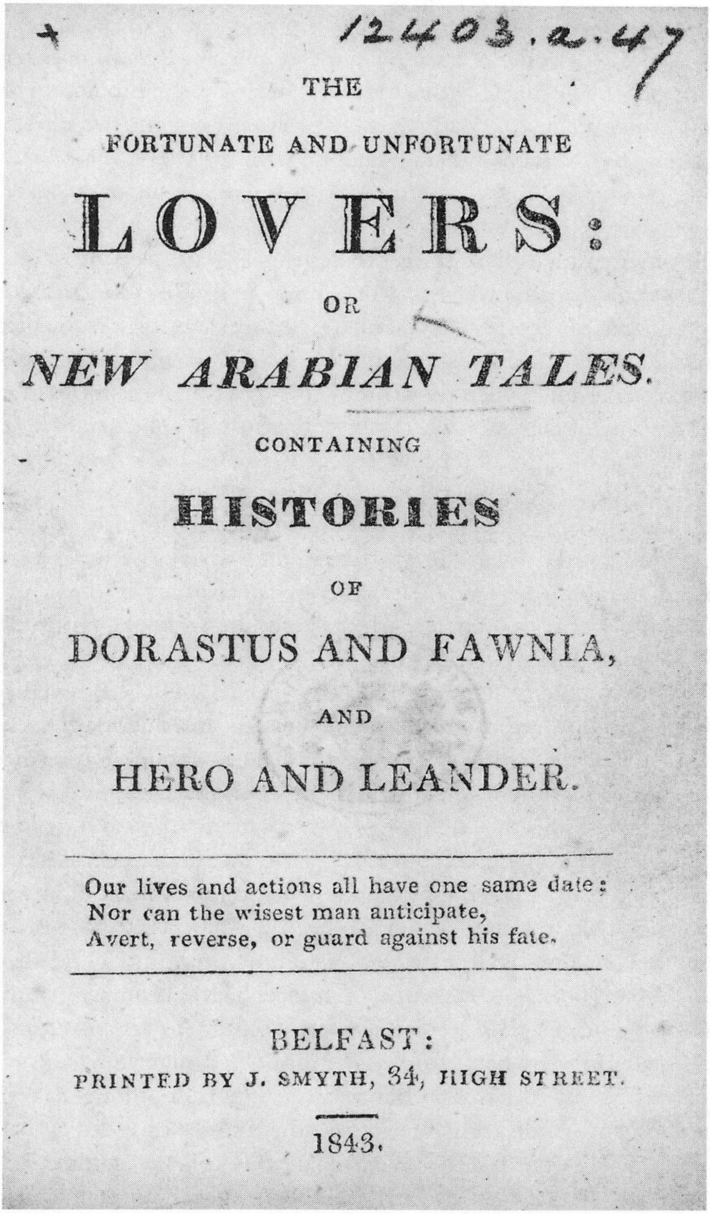

THE

FORTUNATE AND UNFORTUNATE

LOVERS:

OR

NEW ARABIAN TALES.

CONTAINING

HISTORIES

OF

DORASTUS AND FAWNIA,

AND

HERO AND LEANDER.

Our lives and actions all have one same date:
Nor can the wisest man anticipate,
Avert, reverse, or guard against his fate.

BELFAST:

PRINTED BY J. SMYTH, 34, HIGH STREET.

1843.

FIGURE 3.11
The Fortunate and Unfortunate Lovers: or, New Arabian Tales (Belfast: J. Smyth,
1843), shelfmark 12403.2.47.

which in my dawning years amused me as much as *Rasselas* does now.
I saw the whole scheme with a kind of romantic feeling to find myself
really where all my old darlings were printed. I bought two dozen of
the story-books and had them bound up with the title *Curious Productions.*   (quoted in Spufford, *Small Books*, 75)

Boswell unwittingly links a sixteenth-century English version of an "Arabian" tale to an eighteenth-century one. From *Seven Wise Masters* to *Rasselas*
is a great distance in intellectual maturity, he thinks. But his "romantic feeling" recalls both Kirkman's account of graver men grown "conceitedly
Young and Amorous" when they come across the romance stories of youth,
and the making of Pepys's *Vulgaria*: he collects those ephemeral stories and
gives them the binding of a grown-up gentleman's book; he adorns them
with a title confessing his pleasure while asserting his social distance.
Boswell adds to Pepys's response a touristic interest in the place where chapbooks are produced, so that the purchasing of the books becomes a trip not
to a factory but to Disneyland. The books are not so much "printed" as "ushered into the world" as "little darlings," children's books anthropomor-
phized as children themselves.

   Boswell's volume of "Curious Productions," now in the Boswell collection at the Houghton Library, does not include an Aldermary version of
Dorastus and Fawnia. However, the collection does contain a 1796 edition of
the story with a Stirling imprint, which must have been acquired by a relative after Boswell's death. *The Royal Shepherdess, or the Life and Adventures of a
German Princess* is a chapbook, but its text is unlike those debuted by Dennisson over a century earlier or by Stanhope in his modernization. It extends
the tendency toward detail begun in the Aldermary text; for instance, it
amplifies the report about Fawnia's earliest upbringing: "The shepherd
went to keep his flock, and his wife to look after her little nursery, but was so
wise as to wrap it in a plain woolen blanket, keeping it neat and clean" (15).
Mopsa's changing the baby from its embroidered mantle to an ordinary
blanket was not in Aldermary, but was restored from a longer version of
Greene's romance, indicating rare commitment to the full text.

   That detail also typifies the revision's newly explanatory tone. The narrator attempts to clarify the plot for readers, smoothing connections between events that most previous condensers had neglected. As never before,
this version makes the plot coherent by repeating the oracle on the last page
and explaining how Fawnia's return fulfills it. The changes suggest an
address to youth, but they set a high standard for vocabulary. For instance,

the floating Fawnia is referred to as a "precious depositum" (14). The story's setting is carefully explained: Bohemia is identified as "now subject to the German emperor" (2), which explains the subtitle, *The Life and Adventures of a German Princess*.[110] The title-page woodcut, a woman holding a scepter, also assigns Fawnia a political importance seen in no prior version (figure 3.12). Later in the text, Fawnia's pastoral labors are approximated by a woodcut of a young woman wielding a hay rake (14; figure 3.13).

Finally, the Stirling adaptation is remarkable for its full conversion to Calvinism. The end is sealed with a brief poetic moral that draws a Christian lesson from a pagan tale:

> Thus we see the providence of GOD
> Is great to them who never heard his word:
> And should not we, who see and hear it still,
> Depend with pleasure on his sacred will.
>
> (24)

The narration itself is not this morally reductive. There are warnings that virtuous actions may be misinterpreted and an extended consideration of Franion's moral dilemma. Together with the "woolen blanket," the rationalism and good-hearted Calvinism of this adaptation seem to reflect Scottish tastes. Indeed, this would become the version used for all later Scottish publications of *Dorastus and Fawnia*, from Glasgow in 1807 and Edinburgh from 1800–20, as well as one from northern England's Darlington. The woodcuts in these early nineteenth-century reprints are romantic and often artful, their gentle pastoral mood perhaps appealing to rural readers yet also suiting the turn toward nature seen in more elite forms of contemporary literature (figures 3.14 and 3.15; also compare figure 3.8).

A closely contemporary edition of Stanhope's text, *The Adventure* [sic] *of Dorastus and Fawnia* (London: J. Mackenzie, 1810) suggests a very different, possibly urban, orientation for its clientele. This, the last cheap edition of the text published in London, presents the story as a gothic or potboiling "Adventure." For just sixpence (the price stated on the title page), readers obtained Stanhope's full text, elegantly illustrated with copperplates on the title page and frontispiece. The title page has elaborate calligraphic ornament and an inset vignette of a shepherd attending a shipwreck in a sublime setting. The frontispiece depicts Bellaria throwing herself at the

THE

Royal Shepherdeſs:

OR, THE

LIFE AND ADVENTURES.

OF A

GERMAN PRINCESS.

STIRLING:

PRINTED AND SOLD BY C. RANDALL.

MDCCXCVI.

FIGURE 3.12
Title page, *The Royal Shepherdess, or the Life and Adventures of a German Princess*
(Stirling: C. Randall, 1796).

But it is high time to look after that precious
depofitum, that cruel Pandofta commanded to the
mercilefs waves, who, having been toffed, in her
little boat, for two days together, upon the tem-
peftuous ocean, was driven on the fhore of Sicily,
and taken up by a poor fhepherd, as he paffed by

to feek fome fheep that he was looking after, he
thought that the pretty infant's cry had been the
bleating of the ftarved fheep that he was looking
after, he efpied the boat, and faw a little child
ready to die with hunger, wrapped up in a crimfon
velvet mantle, embroidered round with gold, with
a necklace about its neck, which appeared as if it
had been made of ftars. This necklace, compofed
of divers forts of oriental gems, was that which
Pandofta gave to Bellaria when firft he courted her.
The fhepherd feeing her turn her head about, as if
to feek the pap and cry afrefh, he thought that it
was fome diftreffed infant, he took it in his arms,
and fpreading the mantle over it, out dropt a purfe
of gold : and, carrying the infant to his wife, fhe
imagined it to be his baftard, till he fhewed her the
pearl

FIGURE 3.13
Page 14, *The Royal Shepherdess, or the Life and Adventures of a German Princess*
(Stirling: C. Randall, 1796).

Dorastus and Fawnia:

OR, THE

Life and Adventures

OF A

German Princess

GLASGOW,
PRINTED BY J. and M. ROBERTSON,
[No. 18.] Saltmarket,
1807.

FIGURE 3.14
Title page, *Dorastus and Fawnia, or the Life and Adventures of a German Princess*
(Glasgow: J. and M. Robinson, 1807).

FIGURE 3.15
Title page, *Dorastus and Fawnia, or the Life and Adventures of a German Princess*
(Darlington: W. Appleton, 1812).

foot of the throne of an armored Pandosto with a twisted face; a fancy car-
touche gives the novelistic caption, "Then falling upon her knees she
implored the King P. 10."

Although Mackenzie's advertisement inside the back cover features
"Horn Books" and children's books at sixpence, including "Goody Two
Shoes" and "Reading Made Easy," this richly emotive work appeals to
adults or at least adolescents, particularly women. The plot summary on
the half-title page emphasizes seaborne adventure, but posits Fawnia as the
main point of identification by failing to mention Dorastus until the very
end:

> Giving an account of FAWNIA being found by a shepherd, in a boat,
> on the sea shore—likewise their being shipwrecked on their voyage to
> Italy on the Bohemian shore; made prisoners, as spies and condemned
> to death by her own father, the King of Bohemia: afterwards her mar-
> riage with Dorastus who became King of Sicilia.

This edition competed with new urban fiction forms by focusing on sensational events on the seas and in the throne room, and by adopting gothic
dress in the frontispiece, from its attenuated figures in contrasting white
dress and glossy armor to its arched brickwork frame (with flaming heart).
Mackenzie deemed the work worth the investment of two copperplates, but
it must not have been competitive in this new form; this was the last London adventure of *Dorastus and Fawnia*.

Thus, a late eighteenth-century chapbook adaptation of *Dorastus and
Fawnia*, with didactic overtones, became the last re-commodification of
that work to circulate in Scotland, while a longer novelization, with a
grander moralizing preface, lived in England till 1810 and in Ireland even
longer. The differences among these versions prove that even cheap print
based on older materials could reflect regional tastes. Chapbook histories
treat the recruitment of *Dorastus and Fawnia* to Scotland and Ireland, and
to children's literature, as a social drop. But to see the story's movement
from London to the provinces, from men to women, from mistresses to servants, from adults to children, as downward is reductive. As the romance
moved outward with the spread of literacy, its shape and function were
repeatedly transformed: new readers found new meanings and uses for the
work, which publishers' changes reflected. The success of *Pandosto* in a
number of competing versions demonstrates the diversification of the market for popular culture over the early modern period. Readers were not

FIGURE 3.16
Frontispiece and title page, *The Adventure {sic} of Dorastus and Fawnia*
(London: J. Mackenzie, 1810), shelfmark 12403.a.47.
BY PERMISSION OF THE BRITISH LIBRARY

simply content to consume whatever cultural leftovers they were offered, but made choices among several types of experience.[111]

That reading experience was, *pace* Burke, still one in which the gentle classes participated—first in their youth and, later on, nostalgically. At the start of this study, I was puzzled by the rarity of references to *Dorastus and Fawnia*, given that the chivalric texts that underwent similar adaptation were so frequently and lovingly mentioned by Spufford's humble auto-biographers and elite schoolboys.[112] In the seventeenth century, godly authors such as John Bunyan and Milton drew on chivalric romances while guiltily decrying their immorality; cannier male writers, like Kirkman, learned to model their own productions on those of the past. Later, respectable writers like Johnson and Boswell were bolder in recording qualified affection for the reading of their shared schoolboy past, although they were still circumspect about the influence of romance on their own writings. They canonized these guilty pleasures as timelessly antique, natively English, and the quaintest and humblest of material objects, or, as Boswell named his collection, "curious productions."

The titles these men mention are chivalric romances, some even older than *Dorastus and Fawnia*, but still considered virile reading for young boys.[113] At the risk of gender stereotyping, I would explain the absence of anecdotes from young males about reading *Dorastus and Fawnia* or *The Royal Shepherdess* as an indication that the story had been primarily constructed, by the eighteenth century, as preferred reading for girls. That identification had been both predicted and mocked as early as the Jacobean character; only now had literacy spread and print diversified sufficiently that cheaper titles really could be oriented to female readers, much less nonelite ones. The scenes of consumption predicted the romance's downward movement to female domestics, but the material record of *Dorastus and Fawnia* suggests that the important movement was outward, to classes and regions where women's literacy had once been rare and was now becoming less so. An appeal to women readers was barely imminent in *Pandosto* as Greene penned it; a long series of skillful and caring re-commodifications transformed *Dorastus and Fawnia* for their use. The story pleased and delighted its nonelite female readers, not because they contented themselves with undesirable material, but because it was re-commodified to meet their needs. That conversion also explains why its survival went unnoticed in men's chapbook reminiscences and was consistently underreported in Shakespeare studies.

Material alterations had carried the chapbook and garland versions of *Dorastus and Fawnia* so far afield that the Shakespearean scholars of the nineteenth century had no awareness of its contemporary popular life. In 1843, Collier published *Shakespeare's Library: A Collection of the Plays, Romances, Novels, Poems and Histories Employed by Shakespeare in the Composition of His Works*. Collier asserted that because Shakespeare "seems greater by comparison," "those who are best informed regarding the productions of his contemporaries and rivals are most ready to admit his immeasurable superiority to all of them"; "the instance before us"—*Dorastus and Fawnia*—"completely establishes" this claim (4:11). Collier is as certain of the aesthetic inferiority of *Dorastus and Fawnia* as of its historical distance:

believing he refers to a long-ago past, he comments that " 'Pandosto' appears to have been extraordinarily popular, and Mr Dyce enumerates twelve editions" (4:15). He did not realize that Stanhope's version of *Dorastus and Fawnia* was published that very year in Belfast, apparently still "extraordinarily popular" among those who felt no need to compare it to Shakespeare's play.

CHAPTER FOUR

The Romance of Service
The Readers of *Dorastus and Fawnia*, 1615–1762

Let Time's news
Be known when 'tis brought forth. A shepherd's daughter,
And what to her adheres, which follows after,
Is th'argument of Time.
                                    —The Winter's Tale, 4.1.26–29[1]

Scenes of consumption like those in seventeenth-century verse satires and prose characters recur in eighteenth-century novels and stage comedies, as nonelite readers are caught in the act of reading. The texts given to these staged readers are imaginative narratives, accepted as mimetic, cheaply available, and consumed for pleasure—and that is enough to condemn them in elite eyes. These scenes are unabashedly voyeuristic, as alleged horror at degraded popular taste is intermingled with eroticized interest in the pleasures experienced by the reader or buyer, and they disproportionately represent popular readers as women. Thus romance comes to be identified with this primal scene in which a lower-class woman, rapt with misdirected erotic desire, reads an indulgent text, unaware of the mocking but riveted men who have summoned her up. Beginning in the Jacobean period, women in service begin to appear repeatedly in such scenes, bearing the burden of pervasive doubts about practices of cultural consumption. Early modern economic theory conceived domestic servants as consuming national wealth, unlike agricultural servants, who were held to augment national wealth. Increasingly, however, especially after 1660, domestic servants were seen as necessary to their superiors' refined practices of consumption. Portrayals of servant women as misguided consumers of culture multiplied as consumption was feminized and as domestic service was slowly consigned to women.

Chapter 2 discussed the Overburian portrayal of 1615, in which a maid's reading of Greene layered trivializing eroticism over anxieties about the spread of literacy and of printed romances, themselves increasingly seen as commodified aspiration. Economic anxieties are shifted to the cultural register so that romances, not her position as a servant, lead the chambermaid to imagine herself as self-fashioned and mobile. The character thus portrayed the legitimate ambitions that induced the young to go into service as the fantasies of an oversexed and overreaching female—and at the same time wrote the romance as the inappropriate object of consumption that fanned her desires. Of course, certain material conditions may have led seventeenth-century observers to note increased servant literacy, especially in the metropolis. David Cressy has found that servants in Stuart London were "extraordinarily literate," taking on the "literary colouration of their masters." To some extent, servant literacy was actively advocated: some godly treatises urged that masters should teach servants to read, just as parents taught children; in other cases, servants were asked to read aloud, especially to their mistresses. Less officially, some servants may have borrowed pleasure reading from their masters' or mistresses' libraries. Through such practices, a household's romances could have crossed what J. Jean Hecht calls the "cultural nexus," the transfer of culture from master class to servant class.[2] For whenever a chambermaid *did* borrow her mistress's romance, it was the institution of service that enabled a woman without capital to familiarize herself with a costly cultural object (only after 1660 would such romances be available in the more affordable chapbook form).

Seventeenth- and eighteenth-century scenes of consumption allowed narrators to draw analogies between servant women readers and popular romances, between the inappropriate fantasies of women whose desires to read embraced pleasures sensuous, amorous, and perhaps socially ambitious and the romance texts that spurred such pleasures. Such analogies were redoubled, of course, by the unacknowledged enjoyment of the imaginers, also shaped by eros and social ambition. But the effect of these scenes always was to consolidate social privilege in emerging literary genres.

Because material distinctions between genres helped to drive this differentiation, the story of the servant readers of popular romance is also a story of the rise of the novel—and not the story that has been told before.[3]

In twentieth-century criticism, another kind of scene of consumption attempts to more sympathetically re-create the experiences of popular readers. As Carolyn Steedman movingly demonstrates in her classic *Landscape for a Good Woman*, insight into such a scene depends on the critic's willingness to admit that she has consumed popular literature herself: "I want to open the door of one of the terraced houses, in a mill town of the 1920s, show [critics] my mother and her longing, make [them] see the child of my imagination sitting by an empty grate, reading a tale that tells her a goose-girl can marry a king."[4] At the heart of any reception history is this fantasy of sharing the reading experiences of the past. For the student of early modern culture, this desire is particularly vain, since reading experiences can only be peered at through the lens of history. The fundamental impulse in studies of contemporary popular culture is similarly problematic: the hope of discovering what readers get out of their practices of consumption runs up against subjects unprepared, and not unjustly reluctant, to answer academic questions about their motives. In both models, the critic must accept a degree of estrangement; the danger is that the distance may breed contempt, so that the other cultural consumers' experiences are undervalued, and their motivations oversimplified.

Thus, any analysis of popular reading, however well intentioned, risks reproducing the evaluative structure of the scenes of consumption. Disapproval of nonelite reading practices on nakedly elitist grounds, as in the Overburian character, may be replaced by disapproval on ideological grounds, a tendency still troubling popular cultural studies. If fiction is wish fulfillment, consuming it is seen as denial; if, on the other hand, fiction works like ideology, consuming it is seen as false consciousness. But surely popular literary texts, not just canonical literary texts, have the potential to test alternative narratives against ideologies, to offer wishes that are at some level possibilities. We can unlearn the habit of encoding popular culture entirely as a system of social control that allows fantasies to certain groups only on the condition that fantasies and groups alike are scorned. And if our reconstruction must still identify cultural consumers by class and gender, how do we judge their experiences? If their reading is complicit with patriarchal or aristocratic interests, should we condemn it as the patriarchs did? Following Steedman's courageous work, this chapter refuses to disparage the reading choices of servant women on ideological grounds, since doing so can reinscribe the disapproval of consumption on patriarchal grounds.

Steedman has argued that critics often fail to understand the cultural lives of the nonelite because they have radically underestimated the complexities of their historical situations: "lacking [bourgeois] possessions of culture, working-class people have come to be seen, within the field of cultural criticism, as bearing the elemental simplicity of class-consciousness and little more" (13). Although materialist critics have sometimes dismissed the dreams of working-class girls and women, filtered through fairy tales, as mere fantasies, such longings for freedom, mobility through marriage, and material comfort constitute a critique, from women's position, of "the structures of political thought that have labelled this wanting as wrong" (23). Steedman counters critics' scenes of consumption with her own stories, as read and told in family history and autobiography, now reconstructed to reveal women's social, sexual, and economic realities. My project in this chapter is similar, for I read early modern scenes of consumption and modern critical acceptance of their claims as failures to imagine what romances might have meant to nonelite women readers.

Re-creating lost acts of consumption is particularly challenging in the case of early modern popular readers, who are not just distant or resistant but virtually unrecorded. How can we know who the consumers of *Pandosto* were and what led them to this text, among others? The question was posed in almost exactly that form by Charles Mish, in the article that first identified the story to scholars as a seventeenth-century best-seller: "Should we know what features separated *Pandosto* from the many similar romances from which it appears indistinguishable, we would be a long way toward understanding . . . popular taste."[5] The figures Mish compiled pointed to a limited survival from 1588 into the eighteenth century. My own work has found so many later editions that the afterlife of *Pandosto* has been doubled from Mish's estimate. This work must have filled some need, or rather needs, in order to have persisted for two and a half centuries, spread through the kingdom and even to the States, and merited adaptation in "novel," chapbook, and garland forms. While this evidence of survival did not strike Mish as positive—chapbooks to him were the "nadir" of circulation—today it seems compelling proof that Greene's romance was continually used, and in changing ways. The most obvious measure of that adaptability is the range of titles under which Greene's romance appeared. Given this variability, this chapter will refer to the story as *Dorastus and Fawnia*, since the lovers' names were the most enduring element in the titles of adaptations after 1635. That change also provokes a hypothesis that this chapter tests: did the new title, by swaying the balance of interest from the jealous king to his lost daughter, the shepherdess, and her princely wooer, signal a change in intended audience from elite adult men to young, perhaps socially aspirant women?

As in the rest of the book, this chapter surveys statistical and bibliographic evidence of the cultural uses of *Dorastus and Fawnia* side by side with anecdotal evidence drawn from literary texts. As in chapter 2, I reexamine familiar scenes of consumption offered in literary texts. For Mish as for Wells, the information from literary anecdotes discourages further inquiry: since *Dorastus and Fawnia* is mentioned as reading for maidservants in both Overbury's *Characters* (1615) and Samuel Richardson's *Clarissa* (1747–48), its proper readership is conclusively documented and its decline inevitable. But these representations, occurring centuries apart and in biased settings, cannot be taken as demographically accurate. Furthermore, this limited evidence does not align with the bibliographic record that more reliably proves the endurance of *Dorastus and Fawnia*. The fulltext format in which the story was published throughout the seventeenth century, and the individual readers who mention it, prove that its appeal was not *exclusively* to the female, young, and nonelite. Scenes of consumption figure readers of the romance as *uniformly* young female servants from the Jacobean period on, but how could *Dorastus and Fawnia* be said to degenerate if it was read by servant women from so early in its life?

Instead of accepting these scenes at face value, I read them as acts of distinction that degrade the widely popular romance by associating it with the lowest imaginable reader, or at least the lowest reader whose conjuring can give pleasure to the imaginer. *Dorastus and Fawnia* is portrayed as a mere romance, clumsily produced, out of fashion; its reader is imagined as female, ill-educated, not gentle-born, contemptible—but mobile and literate enough to be claiming elite attention. Her textual desires bespeak ambitions—erotic, marital, sartorial, chivalric, vocational, politically radical—that the elite imaginer wishes to discount.

Indeed, the pleasure the servant reader takes in her text often stands for a whole array of practices of consumption that the elite would deny to her social class. As consumption became the primary endeavor of the early modern household, ambivalence centered on the servant, omnipresent in the domestic sphere, and charged with clearing away consumption's dirty traces. Quite simply, the servant brought the problem of correlating status to consumption into the home. The desire to raise one's status through one's pattern of consumption, easily justified by the middle class, was contentious when expressed by a live-in worker emulating her employers' pretenses. In but not entirely of the family, the servant made social self-representation an issue. Accommodating the contrary ideologies of a status-based social order and an emerging class-based system, service was an institution under pressure: during the early modern period, it changed from an almost universal life-cycle experience to a permanent, degraded class position. Attempting to negotiate these contradictions, fictional representations of service in romances and in novels powerfully test the explanatory power of ideology; the regulation of servants' consumption of fiction—again, romances as well as novels—attests to its ideological power.

The claim that both romances and novels were potentially relevant to servants directly challenges the critical assumption that in the eighteenth century, only the novel represented servants with significant sensitivity to emergent ideologies of class.[6] In a massive formulation of *The Origins of the English Novel*, Michael McKeon has argued that the early modern shift from status-based to class-based service is analogous to and worked out in the transformation of romance to novelistic forms. Specifically, he links representations of servant protagonists to opposed ideological positions in early modern fiction. "Romance ideology" reveals servant-protagonists to be lost nobles, relying on honor and ability as signs of "inexpungeable nobility"; "progressive ideology," associated with the early novel, allows them to be heroes and heroines without noble birth, and ultimately attributes honor to commoners rather than nobles. Plots that exploit "the aristocratic romance convention of revealed noble parentage" serve aristocratic interests, while plots like that of Samuel Richardson's *Pamela* locate honor in those of ordinary birth and extraordinary virtue and justify emergent bourgeois ideologies of self-control.[7] In romance narratives, the apparent social contradiction of a servant with incommensurate gifts is resolved by the operations of an infallible hierarchy:

> the romance convention of discovered parentage mediates the threat of noncorrespondence by problematically isolating physical beauty and true nobility apart from inherited nobility, only to reconfirm the wholeness of honor at the end of the story.   (McKeon 133)

Novels, McKeon says, face questions of noncorrespondence more squarely, allowing the aspirations of the virtuous nonelite to be tested and even celebrated (although *Pamela* draws on the language of nobility to justify its hero-ine's virtues and rewards). He does not directly discuss *Dorastus and Fawnia*, but the story of Fawnia clearly fits the model of aristocratic romance. By McKeon's measure, the princess-as-shepherdess motif in *Dorastus and Faw-nia*, which appears to feed the dreams of shepherdesses, must be read as ful-filling the wishes of princesses—a reading that cannot account for the pop-ularity of *Dorastus and Fawnia* among Britain's rural readers. My analysis of Fawnia's status changes counters this view that the servant-revealed-as-noble motif in Elizabethan romances reduces them to conservative narra-tives; wish fulfillment, I suggest, is not inherently conservative.

For McKeon, representations of service become crucial testing points for generic change, since treatments of social ideologies, or "questions of virtue and truth," diverge widely between earlier romance forms and the new novel. He holds that romances with revealed-parentage plots become cul-tural dead ends in the seventeenth century, claiming their "incapacity" to address contemporary concerns (133). Briefly pondering "the problematic persistence of 'romance' " that also troubled Ian Watt in *The Rise of the Novel* (1957) and Fredric Jameson decades later, McKeon dismisses the entire genre as "in part . . . necessary" to provide the novel its "dialectical nega-tion," and in part an "optical illusion" of the history of critical categories.[8] These abstractions whisk the genre of romance from the remainder of his analysis:[9] Elizabethan romance and its disguised-servant plot are ideologi-cally redundant after 1600, and their persistence is an illusion. Yet for two and a half centuries after *Pandosto*'s initial publication, publishers found it profitable not only to reissue the romance but also to refit it for distribu-tion to the broader, poorer chapbook audience. We cannot explain the longevity of this Elizabethan romance by agreeing with chapbook historian Margaret Spufford that the seventeenth century's "second-hand" fictions "had above all no relevance" to nonelite readers.[10] Recognizing that they chose *Dorastus and Fawnia* from within a constrained field of cheap print, we must also recognize that the story continued to meet changing needs. One key to understanding this growing audience must be the likelihood of their partial identification with the mobility and ambitions of this princess-shepherdess.

Stories like Fawnia's, which I call "romances of service," did not become irrelevant as the novel rose or the aristocratic chain of being loosened. Rather, they made useful sites for authors, readers, characters, and observers to consider the uncertain basis of class and gender identities. Romances, like novels, provided examples of individuals whose anomalous, changing, or resistant status might challenge traditional ideologies. McKeon claims that romance ideologies were fading "fictions" that were "transmuted . . . into *servants* of other ideologies," a metaphor that is more apt than he realizes (133; emphasis added). For if aristocratic ideologies, including that of courtly service, gradually lost their explanatory force in early modern society, their reproductions within fiction lent themselves to new meanings, permitting oblique commentary upon social change. Romances of service were fictional mirrors that could be held up by working men and women in order to read social position not as innate or inalienable but as the product of contingent narratives.

In this chapter I speculatively reconstruct the interests of the later servant readers who found this Elizabethan romance of service relevant to their subordinate social positions. Especially in the two periods of its long life that I study closely here, readers' interpretations of *Dorastus and Fawnia* were shaped by the historical transformation of service from a life cycle to a permanent position of class and gender subordination.[11] I begin by placing the first scenes of servants reading Greene's romance in the context of the Jacobean crisis of mobility that undermined the traditional classification of servants as family members. Then, I consider how the story's possible meanings might have changed by the 1730s and 1740s, when domestic servants, now mostly female, worked as alienated labor and were recognized as lower class. In both periods, I argue, various class and gender groups explored the social construction of identity by reading this familiar romance in new ways.

I see the romance of service not as the opposite of the novel, but as another version of the story of noncorrespondence between virtue and social rank, another mimetic reflection on the mutability of social status. By the eighteenth century, the number of fictions that confronted social mutability was enormous and uncontained by generic labels. Whether called romances or novels, they were considered dangerous reading for women and for servants. Gradually, the respectability of the novel was articulated by discrediting the romance as material for "the young, the ignorant, and the idle"—particularly by those who feared that cheaper print forms made fiction too accessible to real servant women. In the mid-eighteenth century as in the Jacobean period, the possibility that a servant reader might raise herself (without, of course, the aid of revealed parentage) led writers for the elite to ridicule servant women reading print romances. The need for such distinctions grew as service itself gave these women the opportunity to read romances of service.

This chapter examines these scenes as interested constructions of readership; at the same time, it takes seriously the proposition that the reading of romances by servants was economically possible, sociologically likely, ideologically meaningful, and by definition critical of norms linking literacy to consumption. When a scene of consumption involves a romance of service, the problem of lower-class women's fiction reading is put in its most intense form. The scene imagines the servant girl's dream of marriage and freedom as, precisely, unimaginable. By dismissing her reading as a fulfillment of fantasy, the scene masks elite fears that the romance of service may tell her something all too true: that service is founded on an arbitrary system of social assignment, riddled with self-contradictions. Servant readers may not gain their ambitions without revealed parentage or lucky marriage, but they may see the thinness of ideology that keeps them where they are. As Steedman points out, fiction that is not journalistically lifelike can still tell readers that life shouldn't be like that. As critics, we have tended to regret the romance plot convention that resolves this apparent dissonance by identifying the heroine's disproportionate talents as unmistakable signs of high birth. But we may thus have underestimated the imaginative acts that created such heroines as experimental figures, representative of a newly volatile social order. These heroines' contradictions opened up imaginative possibilities for readers as well, encouraging them to distinguish worth from birth and talent from privilege.

TH' ARGUMENT OF TIME

In its 1588 form, Greene's romance is fully implicated in the logic of service: although Fawnia is not a servant, she works in husbandry for her adoptive father, a position that mirrors the servant's place as foster child in a household economy. That structural link to service is supported by several specific instances where Fawnia (as shepherdess) is offered the opportunity of employment in the court. Her suitor, Prince Dorastus, asks whether she would like to serve at Sicilia's court, before getting around to proposing marriage. Meanwhile, Porrus, fearful of her virtue, resolves to send her: "the King will take Fawnia into his service." In a transparently immoral offer, Pandosto (not recognizing Fawnia as his daughter) offers her a place of "dignities and riches" in exchange for her "consent."[12] All of these offers are treated as tantamount to prostitution, picking up on a submerged skepticism toward courtly service in Elizabethan England. Even in the first generation of the romance plot, problems of service come to the forefront, as the cupbearer Franion, who decides to disobey Pandosto's various murderous orders, acts within an ongoing debate about the nature of proper service to a corrupt master.[13]

Questions about servant mobility are also implicit in the second generation's love story (increasingly central as *Pandosto* became *Dorastus and Fawnia*), which flirts at length with the possibility that a shepherd's daughter may be a figure of perfect maidenhood, fit to marry a prince. Even before Fawnia's royal identity is disclosed, she appears to offer an idealized resolution of social tensions, defusing the problem of ambition that went along with portrayals of talented servants. Like other working heroines of late Elizabethan romance, she is true to *both* her birth and her position in life. This child of the king of Bohemia, banished as a newborn, has grown up as a simple Sicilian shepherdess, but she has attained "exquisite perfection, both of body and mind." Her ultimate gift is the "submiss modesty" with which she willingly "humble[s] herself as bec[omes] a country maid and the daughter of a poor shepherd"—which, of course, she is not. Indeed, Greene tells his readers, her performance is so exemplary, and her grace in serving others so exceptional, that they should "betray that she was born of some high parentage" (Salzman, *Elizabethan*, 176). If the ideals of service were thought to be properly realized only by those born to be served, the excellence of Fawnia's service would have betrayed her true identity to sixteenth-century readers.[14]

Only that identity, it appears, could justify the extraordinary opportunities that the narrative grants its heroine. Fawnia's movements from infancy to maidenhood to marriage, from princess to shepherdess to princess again, are indeed the stuff of romance. But these conventions are questioned, since Greene shows Fawnia herself to be keenly aware that social barriers would normally constrain her mobility. Her birth, she tells Prince Dorastus, is "so base" that she is "unfit to be a wife to a poor farmer" (Salzman, *Elizabethan*, 185). When the prince comes in shepherd's attire to court her, she argues that "rich clothing make not princes, nor homely attire beggars"; this remark, although ironic in light of her own improbable disguise, reveals her sense that social status is essential and absolute. Even her speech accepting the prince's proposal hesitates over that sense: "Beggars' thoughts ought not to reach so far as kings, and yet my desires reach as high as princes" (Salzman, *Elizabethan*, 188). Thus, fabulous as it may be, Fawnia's royal espousal is framed within the contemporary ideology that would forbid it. Like her maiden rise, her infant fall in status took place within existing ideologies of social fitness: Porrus adopted the foundling surreptitiously because her furnishings indicated her proper station was higher. Both of Fawnia's shifts between gentle and servant status are presented as ambitious changes deliberately undertaken within a system that ordains fixity.[15] They are graphed as imaginative transpositions of the much-observed rise in social mobility of the late sixteenth century. Above all, we can see Fawnia's mutability as the fictive analogue of the remarkable mobility of early modern youth in geography, employment, marriage, and social class, institutionalized through the early modern practice of youth service.[16]

In her wide-ranging study of early modern English adolescence, Ilana Krausman Ben-Amos points out that youthful characters in popular literature may have served to "symbolise hopes for a better material life."[17] That symbolism was intensified when the young were servants, for the radical changes in individual circumstance wrought by entry into and exit from service made it a synecdoche of the period's social mobility. In the late sixteenth century, such work was common to youths in almost every status group; it was required of all young people not employed by their parents or as apprentices.[18] Life-cycle service launched young men and women on the social trajectories, both upward and downward, that comprised much of the period's social instability. Although the practice was said to maintain demographic equilibrium among families disordered by death, poverty, remarriage, or land redistribution, it also produced disequilibrium by breaking family ties and enabling self-advancement.[19]

While contemporary social theory denied the possibility of mobility and downplayed the role of youth service in either regulating or producing it, romance plots indirectly represented these forces of change. Elizabethan romances used chivalric motifs of courtly service and discovered parentage to address the tensions of social dependence and the inconsistencies between individual birth and individual fortune. Precisely because, in Elizabethan England, service was *not* a permanent status but a temporary state, these fictions about servants' social mobility enabled authors and readers to consider the mutability of individual status without directly challenging the dominant ideology of fixed hierarchy.[20]

After the Restoration, however, servants' exits to marriage and independence were increasingly barred by economic obstacles; by the eighteenth century, service, especially domestic service, was relegated to women of low birth as a permanent class position.[21] As the master-servant relationship became more obviously exploitative, romances of service served new purposes for lower-class readers. They still depicted boundary crossings that could feed readers' doubts about the much-troubled equation of worth and birth, but the role models that they offered, once fostering hope and ambition, increasingly urged calculation and caution. A fantasy grounded in real hopes of advancement became a moral fable enabling female servants to balance their dreams of self-advancement against their knowledge of their vulnerability.

Although the meanings of *Dorastus and Fawnia*, as of any text, were reproduced repeatedly as it was placed in the hands of new readers, no direct record of those interpretations exists. Yet the possible meanings of this romance of service are legible in its successive textual adaptations, in which publishers reflected the interests of its changing audiences and their experiences of social differences; and in literary scenes of consumption, in which elite observers pictured the servants' romance reading as the dispersion of cultural cast-offs, and constructed their own narratives of servant readers' subordination.

Historians of the novel often have taken the early modern elite's animadversions on romances and popular readers at face value, although the work of William Warner and Patrick Brantlinger begins to undo the novel's self-made myths.[22] But the scenes of consumption that give *Dorastus and Fawnia* to a servant audience, read in their social specificity, are strongly ideological constructions. Once again, they enact distinction in the face of a growing readership, denigrating both romance reading and socially subordinated groups by identifying them with each other. Over the seventeenth and eighteenth centuries, women and servants were increasingly literate, but increasingly marginalized from employment and property ownership. Simultaneously, nonelite women readers were portrayed as receptacles for trickling cultural runoff. The romances consumed by women and servants were taken as further evidence of their cultural, and hence social, inferiority. Thus, elite observers responded to the romance's expanded audience with their own relational narratives, which sought to confine those aspirant readers to fixed social positions. This antimimetic critique of popular readership, picking up on the old Platonic arguments, was the ideological counterpart to material distinctions. Together, ideological and material differentiation aided in the formulation of the novel as a genre specifically opposed to popular romance.

THE TEMPORARY SHEPHERDESS
AND THE HAPPY MILKMAID

In Elizabethan England, youth service was a matter of law and custom. According to the Statute of Artificers (1350–51), all unmarried men and

women below gentle status and not in apprenticeship or domestic service
were expected to lend their labor to service in husbandry. Although practices varied with locality and social rank, most young people left their families to work in other households. Tudor social theories claimed that a master's children and his servants were equivalent in status, alike members in
his "family" of dependents, but Elizabethan parents plainly did differentiate between progeny and employees. Still, like wives and children, servants
did not comprise a status category of their own but were defined in relation
to their masters; they, too, were, as social historian Ann Kussmaul has put
it, "politically invisible" (9). The fact that servants took on their master's
status (and even, sometimes, married into his family) made them, in effect,
social chameleons. Only upon exiting service into marriage, and possibly
property ownership, did an individual acquire a permanent rank. Nonetheless, the placement of servants in households could cut across status categories in ways that exacerbated the tensions in existing ideologies of social
status.[23]

The contradictory position of the servant, within but not born into the
family, aspirant but dependent, made service a subject for anxiety in Elizabethan social theory. Servants were required to throw over their birth status and adopt that of their new household. Service demanded what social
theory supposedly forbade: refashioning one's identity. This mandate informs the romance ideology of discovered parentage. In the patriarchal
logic of service, the servant's father was replaced by her master; in the
romance of service, the servant's master/father might be replaced by a king.
The motif, however fantastic, recurred in early modern fiction because the
movement from household of birth to household of service was a nearly universal experience of early modern youth. It survived in the fantasies of the
nineteenth century, perhaps transmitted via fairy tales, and was reinvented
by Sigmund Freud as the tellingly named "family romance"—the "phan-
tasy in which both [the child's] parents are replaced by others of better
birth," perhaps even nobles.[24] Notably, Francis Kirkman's formative statements on romance reading connect his interest in popular print romance to
the family romance fantasies of his boyhood (see chapter 3).

The story of Fawnia not only follows a family romance archetype but
also locates it within the Elizabethan institution of service. Of course Fawnia is not a servant, but because she has been taken into a family other than
her own, early modern readers would have experienced her life story as that
of a servant—especially if they themselves worked in service. Fawnia's
placement, like that of most Elizabethan servants, was in husbandry: under

the guardianship of Porrus, she is a "temporary shepherdess" whose herd-
ing duties are carefully observed.[25] Like servants in husbandry, she uses her
post to find a mate and leaves service to marry (although her marriage is
atypically lofty). Until then, Fawnia remains loyal to her vocation, telling
Dorastus, "I am a shepherd."[26] Greene emphasizes that she is unwilling to
"serve a courtly mistress": "I am born to toil for the court, not in the court,
my nature unfit for their nurture" (184). These compunctions are not con-
tradicted by her speedy acceptance of the prince's marriage proposal: this
romance reminds its readers that the ends of service are making one's match
and following one's fortune.

Like an early modern servant, Fawnia is both securely dependent in a
familial household economy and somehow out of place, not truly a member of the family. She is unaware, of course, that she has been fostered out,
but readers can never forget it because Greene repeatedly stresses her superiority. Never, in her many soliloquies or in dialogue with Dorastus, does
she refer to Porrus and Mopsa as her parents. She assumes the freedom to
arrange her own match that was the great advantage (or, to others, threat)
of youth service.

The contradictions of her double identity also transform the social position of her adoptive father, Porrus, who represents a different kind of hired
labor, a "mercenary . . . who got his living by other men's flocks": not even
a servant in husbandry but a wage laborer.[27] Agricultural wage laborers in
early modern England were bitterly poor, seldom earning enough to marry
and raise children. But Porrus and his wife, Mopsa, have an advantage that
most lacked: the gold found in Fawnia's mantle (a precocious dowry).
Greene explains that with the gold, Porrus "got a small flock of sheep,
which when Fawnia (for so they named the child) came to the age of ten
years, he set her to keep, and she with such diligence performed her charge
as the sheep prospered marvellously under her hand" (Salzman, *Elizabethan*,
176). Fawnia presents a double benefit: the princess's gold (kept secret from
her) as well as the young shepherdess's labor, a point underlined as the sentence names Fawnia for the sheep she both funds and tends. Greene is quite
explicit in pointing out that the value of her labor exceeds the cost of her
maintenance and moves Porrus from propertylessness to property ownership: "fortune so favoured him in having no charge but Fawnia that he
began to purchase land" (Salzman, *Elizabethan*, 176). Porrus is able to rise
from a position below service (wage laborer for an unseen master) to a position of mastery,[28] thanks to Fawnia's fall: his "discovery" of this valuable
baby is the inverse of her later discovery of her true parentage. Fawnia's

value to her master fantastically exaggerates the economic productivity of the servant in husbandry.

The productivity alleged to divide the servant in husbandry from the household servant extended to servant reading practices in early portrayals. Fawnia, who is never described as literate although her speech matches her royal lover's rather than her parents', is a productive worker in husbandry who does not waste time in reading. Shakespeare's Perdita, whose pastoral labor has enriched her adoptive father, betrays no interest in the narrative blandishments of the ballad seller. Even the Overburian character defends the woman working in husbandry by comparison to the parasitic household servant, for the next set of *Characters* published under Overbury's name added the chambermaid's counterpart, "a fayre and happy milke-mayd."[29] This female servant is free of romantic notions and social ambitions: "She makes her hand hard with labour, and her heart soft with pittie: and when winter evenings fall early (sitting at her merry wheele) she sings a defiance to the giddy *Wheele of Fortune*." The happy country maid eschews print narratives for the pleasures of work, and reconciles herself to her station in life rather than dreaming of being "a Ladie errant." The virtuous, old-fashioned servant in husbandry is contrasted to the loose, newfangled chambermaid, one of an emerging class of former country girls laboring—sometimes in more than one sense—in London houses.[30] The chambermaid likes the country, "but she holdes *London* the goodliest Forrest . . . to shelter a great Bellie" (Paylor 56). Thus, Overbury's ambitious chambermaid is a scapegoat for the conspicuous leisure of the householders who maintain her in order to enhance their own social positions.[31]

IMPROBABILITY, IF NOT IMPOSSIBILITY

By the mid-eighteenth century, the position of servants was no longer equivocal but dropping rapidly. Demographic, economic, agricultural, and ideological changes reduced the opportunities for servants to move upward upon exiting service: the in-dwelling servant in husbandry was replaced by the cheaper day laborer (mostly male), and youths in the household were replaced by a permanent class of domestic servants (mostly female). According to Amussen, "the social and economic gap between servant-supplying and servant-hiring families widened, stretching to the breaking point the notion that servants became members of their employers' families" (158). The reductions in opportunity were particularly devastating for women. Their wage-earning potential dwindled as they were denied skilled outdoor work and shunted into menial domestic roles.[32] As agricultural labor was masculinized and domestic service feminized, Fawnia's pastoral duties became increasingly remote from the work experiences of most romance readers.

Implicit in Fawnia's story, and indirectly in Porrus's, was a real possibility of self-improvement through service, a period of training and saving for a more independent life. In the eighteenth century, as Bridget Hill has pointed out, agricultural service offered much less hope of social movement: "At the end of service there was still the likelihood of marriage, and still the possibility of setting up an independent household, but few [servants in husbandry] expected to be masters and mistresses taking in servants in husbandry in their turn" (83). Many could hardly afford to marry, much less hope for the self-advancement that the romance of service had so spectacularly dramatized. This foreclosure of opportunity further divided servants from the master's family, a term now redefined to exclude hired workers. Neither ability nor training would be sufficient to cross the yawning "social gap between the experience of servants and family members" (Amussen 158).[33] The gap also transformed the significance of the romance of service, reducing the psychological force of its regained-parent plot and exposing the arbitrary power of the patriarch/employer. Class separation invited the employer to *be* arbitrary, for servants, increasingly seen as outside the family, were no longer protected under the umbrella of paternalism.

In light of service's deteriorating status and security, lower-class readers' interests in the romance of service were bound to change. Fawnia's experience of leaping social gulfs may have moved further from rural readers' practical ambitions. But her romance of service was still an urgently useful exploration of subordination and mobility. In the chapbook redactions of *Dorastus and Fawnia*, discussed in chapter 3, shortening the story emphasized characters in service: Franion, Porrus, Mopsa, and repeatedly, Fawnia. Her role is most remarkable in a full-length modernization—not a condensation—Stanhope's The *Fortunate Lovers* (before 1735), which registered the changing place of service by heightening both the social pressures toward subservience and servants' impulses to resist them.

Stanhope's *Fortunate Lovers* was the first version of *Pandosto* to disapprove explicitly of social mobility—which suggests that servants may have been among the intended audience. Stanhope's prefatory summary of the story's "Rules of Morality" criticizes Porrus's improvised social rise: "was it fair or honest in him to conceal the Riches of Fawnia, and convert part of them to

his own use?"[34] Social mobility appears to be won only by those who are
unfair and dishonest. Stanhope's interpretation echoes the middle-class
concern about the ambitions of servants that, paradoxically, heightened as
social divisions became more rigid. If, as Bridget Hill puts it, "servants had
become inferiors who must be kept in their place," then their hopes of self-
improvement were anomalous and their pretenses absurd.[35]

The body of *The Fortunate Lovers* contradicts Stanhope's prefatory claim,
however, fully indulging the shepherdess Fawnia in her ambitious courtship
with the prince and making her more forceful in pressing him toward honorable marriage. Stanhope's version is thus complicit with the new form that
the eighteenth century lent to the "myth of social betterment through service." Now, when few female domestics found prosperity through matches
with their peers, they were accused of soliciting the attentions of their masters. The servant's main weapon was consumption: fine dress would allow
her to compete erotically with her social betters, or so the latter claimed. For
most servants, of course, neither fashion nor wiles nor virtue was sufficient to
overleap the socioeconomic barriers between them and their masters.[36]
Employers' fantasies of the preying maidservant simply confirm that with
such labor becoming a permanent class position, the female domestic's one
remaining prospect for self-betterment was an erotic gamble. Stanhope's
revisions to *Dorastus and Fawnia* admit just how a female servant might have
to negotiate in order to change her position, rewriting Fawnia's euphuistic
sighings about the hopelessness of cross-class love into a logical assessment
of her chances. Greene's Fawnia considered the "impossibility" of her love
for Dorastus, but Stanhope's considers "the Improbability, if not Impossibility of obtaining her Desire." A new peroration sharpens her awareness of
the obstacle of class difference: "O the Gods! Why did you give me a Soul
capable of the most noble Passion, and not a Fortune to answer my desire[?]"
(Stanhope 24).

The hope of a marital long shot, fulfilled for Fawnia, in daily life must
often have exacerbated female servants' vulnerability to their masters' ex-
tramarital abuses. As Stone puts it, maids were "the most exploited, and
most defenceless" women of the eighteenth century. Hill comments that
"What has been called 'the eroticism of inequality' may in part explain the
frequency with which masters are found seducing their dependent
menials"; she excerpts conduct books for female servants advising "circum-
spection" in dealings with male employers and co-workers (*Women and
Work*, 146, 137, 234–35). Women's increased vulnerability was produced
by contradictory ideologies: employers still held patriarchal authority over

servants, but the lapse of paternalism in practice left servants with little societal or legal protection.[37] This is not to say that Jacobean servants were not sometimes abused, but that their abuses had been more successfully prosecuted, as a case involving one of the *Pandosto*s demonstrates.[38]

Stanhope's revision reflects the changes that balanced the destiny of a mid-eighteenth-century female domestic servant between remote dreams and immediate risks. It responds to the increase in risk by expanding and politicizing the scenes in which Fawnia defends her vulnerable social position and her threatened sexual honor. Near the end of the romance, Fawnia has fled (with Dorastus and Porrus) to the court of Pandosto, who lusts after her, unaware of either her humble upbringing or their actual relationship. Stanhope's defense of Fawnia is longer than Greene's, and newly "stinging and resolute" (47): this Fawnia recognizes that the king has "Power," but charges that he has "exercised it, in an arbitrary manner upon the Innocent," likening his attempted seduction to an army's massacre of "a small Village, that is weak and defenceless" (50–51). She refuses Pandosto's advances in terms that ringingly assert the sovereignty of the individual: "I have a Monarch's Soul, though the Gods have been pleased to cover it with Plebean Clay."[39] Despite the conservative position advocated in Stanhope's preface, the body of his modernization demonstrates how political arguments might be appropriated by those in service to resist the arbitrariness of their masters. Stanhope resituates the romance within the period's emergent discourse of the dominion of the individual, making it applicable to women and available to a servant readership.

The lesson in self-defense intensifies when Pandosto learns of Fawnia's ignoble birth. His frustrated lust turns to anger, and he condemns her and Porrus to death. Again, Stanhope expands Fawnia's role to demonstrate both her required submissiveness and her exceptional resistance. She exonerates the men to whom she owes obedience—her lover, Dorastus, and her guardian, Porrus. Then she again criticizes Pandosto's misuse of his paternal power: "Who art thou, King Pandosto, who judgest[?]" (Stanhope 56). Thus, Stanhope gives Fawnia a heroic assertion of the dignity of the powerless in the face of power, just before the secret of her noble status is revealed. The situation, with a panoply of patriarchs that includes Fawnia's apparent father, actual father, and future husband, exposes how women affirm patriarchy's normative power, but also how they can resist its abuse. Indeed, Stanhope's moral lesson for the servant reader might be that the master who seduces a servant, in violating ideologies of paternalism, is driven by a desire as incestuous as Pandosto's "abandoned and lascivious" lust for his daughter (51). Since the old paternalistic ideologies apparently never extended the incest taboo to master-servant relations (see Griffiths 269), Stanhope's idealized paternalism is not conservative but revisionist.

In its championing of female self-defense, Stanhope's adaptation brings out themes that were also coming to dominate more exclusive literary forms. Critics of the eighteenth-century novel have sometimes argued that its obsession with essentialized female virtue worked to entrap its female subjects as much as to empower them: the novel creates the woman as victim so that readers may enjoy the spectacle of her resistance. More specifically, the novelistic *topos* that places a lower-class woman in the hands of an aristocratic seducer has been read as an eighteenth-century form of class fantasy.[40] These criticisms do not apply to *The Fortunate Lovers*, since the threat of seduction had faced Fawnia for more than a century. All that Stanhope added in his version was the force and extent of her resistance. It is harder than usual to argue that *this* eighteenth-century author's idealization objectifies his heroine.

Rather, it could be argued that Greene's Fawnia is more trapped than Stanhope's in seamless gender ideology, rescued from exploitation by fortune because she has no way to rescue herself. If this localized modernization of an existing tale requires female resistance as a raised standard, it also demonstrates how that resistance can be conducted successfully. Stanhope's heroine appropriates the eighteenth century's newly heightened sexual essentialism and uses it to stave off the age-old threat of "constrained love" (Salzman, *Elizabethan*, 185). His adaptation offers women readers the possibility of resisting the misuse of class and gender privilege, of drawing on ethical argument when social and legal sanctions are no longer available. Thus, it reminds us not only that the ideological problems seen in *Pandosto* since the 1580s could still entrap eighteenth-century readers but also that emergent political and gender ideologies could be brought to the text. When a shepherdess informs a king that he and she alike have "Monarch's Souls," she is indeed demonstrating the usefulness of new codes.[41]

The Fortunate Lovers advised lower-class readers to be cautious in their hopes for wealth and advancement; it urged women to observe newly formalized conventions of subordinate behavior while defending their virtues staunchly.[42] However, the reputation of chapbook romances among the servant-employing classes was exactly the opposite. In the tradition of the Overburian character, elite discourse continued to blame maids, not masters, for cross-class sexual activities, which, like undue social ambitions, were still said to be fostered by romance reading. Stanhope anticipated such antimimetic criticism in his preface, which insists that the book teaches the *errors* of social aspirations and disobedience. By my reading, the preface simply deflects attention away from the markedly independent actions of its servant heroine, recognizing the story's didactic force but downplaying the centrality of that nonsubmissive Fawnia with whom nonelite female readers could identify.

SIMPLE HISTORY

How did elite audiences of the 1730s and 1740s perceive the readers of such new fictional forms as Stanhope's moralized romance and the even cheaper chapbook redactions of *Dorastus and Fawnia*? Critics have assumed that the socioeconomic forces that segregated England's genders and classes during and after the Restoration did much to segregate print culture as well. But if elite males were thus able to ignore certain cheap romances, they were not unaware that such forms existed, any more than eighteenth-century playgoers were unaware of the existence of drolls at fairs. The constant claims for segregation in eighteenth-century practices of consumption do not prove that it was achieved, but that it was increasingly *sought* by the elite. As old regional, status, and church orders weakened, cultural consumption remained a primary field of social differentiation.[43] Women, without many economic and legal resources, could join men in consuming cultural and material goods to an extent that disturbed elite males. Even nonelite women could dabble in the "luxuries" that trade was making increasingly affordable and advertising increasingly desirable: clothing, tea, and printed entertainments.

The centrality of consumption to women's social status was, in one sense, a measure of all women's marginalization: the "undermining of the family economy" meant that "women lost certain roles in economic production [as] they took on new and subordinated roles in economic consumption." In fact, consumption, not production, was the primary economic activity of most English households by the eighteenth century, but gender ideologies denied its centrality, even as an indicator of status. Like leisure and romance reading, consumption was essentialized and ridiculed as fundamentally feminine. Similar axiologies continued to class domestic servants as agents of consumption, not production. Servants, who devoted their human capital to displaying the status of their masters and mistresses, were said to be "consum[ing] without mercy the produce of the state, with very little return of advantageous labour."[44] At the same time, women servants were being driven out of "productive" agricultural work by both restructured labor practices and new gender ideologies. Increasingly, outdoor work was for men, and domestic service was for women. The traditional charge that domestic labor was less productive than husbandry combined with the feminization of the domestic workforce to re-form the female domestic servant as the embodiment of idle consumption.

Male property owners and female consumers invested heavily in the development of commodity culture, then complained when they saw similar commodities made available to their economic and social inferiors. They were especially worried that servants bought fashionable clothes and drank tea, for they saw such "mimetic venture[s]" as emulating tastes they considered their own prerogative. Despite the complaints that "plain country-Joan is now turn'd into a fine London-madam," there was little danger that emulation actually would produce mobility.[45] Employers knew that lower-class consumption of dresses, tea, and fiction could breach well-guarded socioeconomic gates only symbolically. But of the three, fiction could most effectively demonstrate to lower-class consumers that status itself was "mimetic," a means for re-presenting individuals through their symbolic consumption. Ian Watt notes "how many contemporary declamations against the increased leisure, luxury and literary pretensions of the lower orders specifically refer to . . . domestic servants." He attributes this pattern to the size and "conspicuous literacy" of the occupational group, adding that they "were, as ever, peculiarly likely" to imitate "their betters" in "conspicuous leisure" (47). Watt does not inquire into the *motives* of these declamations, but his reference to Pamela as the "culture-heroine" of servant literacy should remind us that servants' fiction reading was seen as both a symptom of and an incitement to the questioning of class segregation.

In the mid-eighteenth century, a new set of scenes of consumption, involving servant women and works like *Dorastus and Fawnia*, worked to forestall such questioning. These scenes seemed to endorse elite commentators' cultural preferences as superior to those of foolish and idle domestics, especially women domestics. Mildly salacious references to private pleasure reading enabled male writers to excuse their own bookish indulgences by blaming women for fiction's excesses (the attack extended to women romance writers, discounting one of the few areas in which educated women had attained cultural and economic independence). Ultimately, the feminization and degradation of the romance aided the critical codification of a new genre, more moralized and yet more "rational" and masculine: the novel.[46] As authors raised the novel, they debased the romance as reading material fit only for the uneducated, prurient, and credulous. The inherited prejudice against prenovelistic fiction has blocked even twentieth-century literary historians from seeing romance's continued influence and social relevance. An outpouring of criticism has established the substantiality of romances by eighteenth-century women, but we have not overcome the assumption that the reading of other, *pre*-eighteenth century romance texts was a sign of degradation in eighteenth-century England.

The pivotal figure in the negotiation between older romance forms and the emergent novel is Samuel Richardson. He provided much of the moral justification for the distinction that would later be made between novel and romance, although he himself eschewed both names. He refused to call *Clarissa* (1747–48) either "a light Novel, or transitory Romance," but in a crucial scene, he marks a class distinction between his own work and popular romance, taking *Dorastus and Fawnia* as his example.[47] Lovelace is recounting, in a letter to his friend Belford, the midnight events that have brought Clarissa into his arms:

> I was alarmed by a . . . confused buzz of mixed voices. . . . Downstairs ran Dorcas, and at my door . . . cried out: Fire! Fire! . . . I cried out, Where? Where? almost as much terrified as the wench: while she, more than half undressed . . . pointed upstairs.
>
> I was there in a moment, and found all owing to the carelessness of Mrs. Sinclair's cook-maid, who, having set up to read the simple history of Dorastus and Faunia when she should have been in bed, had set fire to an old pair of calico window-curtains.   (Richardson 261–62)

The confusion gives Lovelace a chance to clasp an underdressed Clarissa, although he fails to press his advantage; still, the atmosphere of sexual threat contributes to the derisiveness of even this glancing reference to popular romance. She has been "careless" in her cultural choices, careless with her candle, and careless of her labor power by reading when she should have been sleeping (one eighteenth-century conduct book told servants: "when you hired yourselves, you sold all your time to your masters"[48]). "Simple" parodies the various adjectives, such as "pleasant and delightful," that made up the titles of chapbook versions of *Dorastus and Fawnia*.[49] The spelling "Faunia" was first used in the Aldermary Churchyard chapbooks, and may identify the cook-maid's reading as one of that prolific firm's illustrated condensations.

This appearance of *Dorastus and Fawnia* in the midst of Lovelace's stirring tale is as suspect, narratologically and ideologically, as Lovelace's sexual intentions. For one thing, it echoes a similar mention of romance in *Gulliver's Travels* (1726), which Richardson knew and admired. Gulliver tells the tale of the fire in Lilliput that he so obligingly extinguished:

> I was alarmed at midnight with . . . cries . . . at my door. . . . several of the emperor's court . . . intreated me to come immediately to the palace, where her Imperial Majesty's apartment was on fire, by the carelessness of a maid of honour who fell asleep while she was reading a romance.[50]

Swift and Richardson alike set the destructive "carelessness" of the reading maid in contrast to the urgent loyalty of those who raise the alarm (courtiers, Dorcas) and to the prompt, "heroic" action of the narrators (Lovelace, Gulliver). But Richardson's echo of Swift sharpens the attack on the romance. In Swift's tall tale, the unnamed romance merely stands for the pettiness of court society, since his late-night reader is a maid of honor, a member of the court. The reader in *Clarissa* is a cook-maid who serves as housekeeper, and her immersion in fiction is a failure in her duties that distinguishes her from the conscientious audience addressed by the novel. Unlike Swift, Richardson chose carefully among available titles, drawing on his lifelong career as a printer. He must have expected some of his readers to recognize *Dorastus and Fawnia* from drolls or chapbooks (why else mention this particular name?)—but the social dynamics of this little story imply that readers who undertook his multivolume "History of a Young Lady" should not be satisfied by any "simple history."

Richardson's reference to *Dorastus and Fawnia* is further overdetermined: epistemologically, the events of this story *cannot* have taken place. The vivid immediacy of Lovelace's description of the alarm encourages readers to forget what they, like Clarissa, know to be true: the fire is Lovelace's "plot."[51] While Lovelace swears that "Upon my soul, madam, the fire was real. *(And so it was, Jack!)*," the scoundrel planned the evening's events in advance: "all agreed upon between the women and me" (265, 261). The fire may have happened, but it was certainly not "owing to carelessness." Since the cook-maid, like Dorcas and Mrs. Sinclair, serves him in this plot (as well as the larger pretense about the nature of the household), Lovelace's criticism of her carelessness is without basis, and indeed egregious. With the convincing delivery of this unmotivated fiction about a romance-reading servant, Lovelace momentarily deceives Belford as he did Clarissa, and Richardson misleads his readers.

Thus, even as Richardson implies his abstinence from romance, he indulges Lovelace in blatant fiction making for its own sake. In turn, Lovelace indulges his own pleasure in fiction making, exceeding the exigencies of his plot against Clarissa, by using the service of lower-class women. Ironically, Richardson allows Lovelace to create a fiction that projects their shared obsession with elaborate fantasies onto those servants. If the wench Dorcas mirrors Clarissa much as maids mirrored their mistresses' tastes for fiction in previous voyeuristic antifictional anecdotes, the attack on the cook-maid's reading parodies the mirroring motif. Richardson's fiction about servants' taste for fiction differentiates his purified, literary proto-novel from popular romance, separating the two genres as, respectively, bourgeois and humble, modern and dated, virtuous and self-indulgent, productive and idle.

Dorastus and Fawnia was a resonant title for Richardson to summon up, given its own complex negotiation of hierarchies of readers. Thematically, it redoubles the tension between heroic service and sexual exploitation staged in Lovelace's plot, for Greene's lovers, like Richardson's, permitted readers to compare abusive paternalism to the decorum of feminine gentility. The history of *Dorastus and Fawnia* was far from simple, its ideological aptness far from faded; in the 1740s, its meanings were still multiplying. Whether read in chapbook or modernized adaptation, seen in festive droll or theatrical adaptation, propped up on kitchen shelves or nodded to in famous novels, the romance continued to offer its readers alternate constructions of social identity and class difference. Even in the mid-eighteenth century, the question posed by Fawnia's ambiguous place in service—could servants become mistresses through hard work, fortunate marriage, or the consumption of fashionable commodities?—was still urgent and unanswered. The complex history of Greene's romance thus belies McKeon's characterization of the romance genre as escapist and irrelevant to early modern society. The story of this maiden whose personal graces exceed her low social status encouraged early modern readers to recognize the integrity of the dependent within ideologies disseminated by the powerful. That many of those readers were the real-life equivalents of Steedman's "goose-girl" makes it all the more important that they dreamed of marrying a prince, learned to refuse a king, or dared to read when they should have been sleeping.

INCONSPICUOUS POPULAR LITERACY

To explain why Richardson might have gone out of his way to plant this self-consuming reference to the "simple History of Dorastus and Faunia" in his massive history, *Clarissa*, I turn to another context: Richardson's work as a printer, which gave him a unique vantage on the status of fiction as a material commodity. At several points in this study, I have drawn on influential articulations of elite and popular literature by booksellers and writers who themselves straddle both categories and whose work gives them an intense awareness of the materiality of print and of the ways its forms accrue social meaning. Chettle, Nashe, Kirkman, Langbaine, and Richardson sense that a writer's attention to his narrative is paralleled by a printer's attention to its printed form and a publisher's attention to its marketability. They are also frank about the effect of publication success on the class position of the author or publisher, for worse or for better, as shown by their own social trajectories. Kirkman saw his career as bookseller/writer as approximating his own dreams of "family romance." I suggest that Richardson did as well, and that his dreams of class transposition inform *Clarissa*'s reference to romance and its similar ideologies. *Clarissa* has more in common with "the simple history of Dorastus and Faunia" than Richardson would admit; the link can be made by way of his *Pamela, or Virtue Rewarded* (1740–41).

The hints that Richardson left of his early life all involve storytelling, love, and virtuous aspiration to social advancement, themes that seem to have been united in Richardson's mind even before *Pamela* worked out a new relationship among them. Biographical criticism has recognized this thematic continuity, but perhaps not the extent to which Pamela's class transposition might be connected to Richardson's own. It also has recognized the presence of romance under *Pamela*'s "realist" narrative, but done little to connect it to the presence of popular books in Richardson's career as stationer. Richardson went out of his way to express his opposition to the fashionable novels, short romances, and "secret histories" published by the fashionable writers of his day. He said far less about popular romances, which were even further from respectability. Nonetheless, they recur in his biography and inform *Pamela*. The heroine's "conspicuous literacy" is tied to an awareness of popular literature that Richardson carefully hid—his own inconspicuous popular literacy.

The social trajectory of Richardson's own youth parallels Pamela's. Her parents suffer some obscure financial embarrassment and send their daughter from the country into service in the hope that she will do better.

Richardson's father had a mysterious financial crisis that brought the family to the country in Richardson's boyhood; on their return to London, they managed to find Richardson an apprenticeship with a printer. Penniless Pamela, trained by old Lady B., marries her son and becomes a lady herself; penniless Richardson, trained by printer John Wilde, married his daughter and became a master printer. Their stories fit McKeon's definition of progressive ideology: Pamela marries into the aristocracy rather than proving born to it; the apprentice Richardson makes good, as did the citizen heroes of Thomas Deloney's novels.

Still, beneath those events are hints of the romance narrative that progressive ideology supposedly eschews. *Pamela* has been heralded for rewarding the aspirations of its servant heroine with marriage rather than revealed parentage. But Richardson's later revisions of *Pamela* back away from the clarity of that ideological breakthrough, gradually elevating the gentility of her impoverished parents and turning her into a noble figure exiled in service, a slightly more bourgeois version of the aristocratic myth rather than its direct opposite.[52] D. C. Muecke holds that "Pamela is no more a real servant than Cinderella was," since she has the name of a romance heroine, "an education beyond her situation," and the beauty "of a lady"; furthermore, she knows it, since "she consistently maintains a certain distinction between herself and the other lower servants."[53]

Richardson's hints about his early life are haunted by his own family romance fantasy: the memory of a "Correspondence with a Gentleman greatly my Superior in Degree, and of ample Fortunes, who had he lived, intended high things for me."[54] Like Kirkman, Richardson dreamed of a patron more glorious than either his father or his master, and found those fantasies confirmed in his earliest reading and reproducible in his own storytelling. He was noticeably evasive about the reading of his youth—after all, he had less education than even Kirkman—but his first recollection of storytelling (in a 1753 letter to his Dutch translator, Johannes Stinstra) gives a hint. He would tell his less book-loving "Schoolfellows" "Stories as they phrased it": some "from my Reading as true; others from my Head, as mere Invention." Whether his "Stories" were read or imagined, true histories or "pleasant," was of little importance: what Richardson and his eager auditors wanted was a story that "affected them." Richardson's example points to chapbooks as his model: "One of them, particularly, I remember, was for putting me to write a History, as he called it, on the model of Tommy Potts; I now forget what it was; only, that it was of a Servant-Man preferred by a fine young Lady (for his Goodness) to a Lord, who was a Libertine." The story anticipates that of Pamela, rewarded for her virtue, although here the servant is male, like the storyteller and his listeners. Having hinted that chapbook fantasies stand at the core of his authorial practice, Richardson quickly backs off: "All my Stories carried with them I am bold to say an useful Moral" (Eaves and Kimpel, *Richardson*, 9).

A number of critics have noticed traces of chapbook romance in *Pamela*. Margaret Anne Doody long ago noted that the heroine's "low style" is consonant with chapbook courtship manuals and fables.[55] More specifically, Muecke identifies the chivalric tale of *Guy of Warwick* as an intertext throughout the novel, but especially in the Lincolnshire episodes, where Pamela's main oppressors, the Swiss factotum Monsieur Colbrand and a cow, parody Guy's opponents, Giant Colbrand and a bull.[56] At one level, these stories are present as characterization, like the country artlessness of Pamela's speech. Chapbook literacy is the cultural literacy of a servant. But of course Richardson says repeatedly that Pamela's education by her parents and by Lady B. has exposed her only to virtuous and good books. In this she can be compared to her "brother," the hero of *Joseph Andrews*, who has read the Bible and *The Whole Duty of Man*. Joseph's "biographer," on the other hand, commends to readers of the Andrews family romances a Kirkmanesque curriculum of popular romances, grandly redescribed:

> our own Language affords many [biographies] of excellent Use and Instruction, finely calculated to sow the Seeds of Virtue in Youth, and very easy to be comprehended by Persons of moderate Capacity. Such are the History of . . . an Earl of *Warwick*, whose Christian names was *Guy*; the Lives of *Argalus* and *Parthenia*, and above all, the History of those seven worthy Personages, the Champions of Christendom.[57]

Fielding accurately parodies the educational claims of the popular romances, an indication (if we needed one) that they were widely known. Whatever Richardson felt about Fielding, he probably would have agreed that such claims were horrifying. Only once is Pamela's cheap-print literacy conspicuous, at that desperate, suicidal moment when she expresses dread that her story will be made up into ballads.

This is not to say that Pamela is not identified with popular literacy. In the early stages of the novel, she is linked to the higher end of popular reading for women, the feverish romances that Richardson reviled.[58] But to protect her virtue as reader, the presence of these romances as the subtext to Mr. B.'s advance is never made explicit in Pamela's own speech or self-characterization. She has likened herself to no less classical a figure than Lucretia when Mr. B. brings down her cultural pretenses: "O, my good girl, you are well read, I see; and we shall make out between us, before we have done, a pretty story in romance."[59] Here is the familiar accusation that the servant reader's desires have been inflamed by reading a "pretty," or simple, or delectable, romance. And as in the more fully developed scenes of consumption, the accusation is most reliable in proving that Mr. B. himself knows his romance plots.

In this case, however, Mr. B.'s association of the servant reader with popular romance seems entirely justified, for the rhetoric that Pamela employs in her most high-flown moments seems to come directly out of *Dorastus and Fawnia* and its revisions. She writes to Mr. Williams that her fears of Mr. B. are not vain: "my Soul is of equal Importance with the Soul of a Princess; though my Quality is inferior to that of the meanest Slave" (141). The structure of that line, and others where she proffers her life over her virtue, hearkens back to Fawnia's antitheses, as in her striking assertion to Dorastus: "mine honesty is such as I had rather die than be a concubine, even to a king, and my birth is so base as I am unfit to be a wife to a poor farmer" (Salzman, *Elizabethan*, 185). Pamela's statement resembles that of her near-contemporary, Stanhope's Fawnia, even more closely: "I have a Monarch's Soul, though the Gods have been pleased to cover it with Plebean Clay" (Stanhope 47). *Pamela* extends the romance's exploration of the rhetoric of female virtue imperiled, its peculiar blend of antithetical balderdash and impassioned proto-democratic principle. Perhaps that is because it is, despite Richardson's prefatory denials and epistolary innovations, still a romance at heart.

I am hardly the first to call *Pamela* a romance. When Richardson denied that categorization, he still did not know what else to substitute. The lines claiming *Pamela*'s generic distinction were hard to draw. Furthermore, Richardson's practice as large-scale commercial printer tied him, throughout his life, to the full range of the fiction market in all its dubious heterogeneity, so he could never get very far away from romances or cheap print. For example, Richardson clearly wished to distinguish himself from another author/bookseller, Eliza Haywood (to whom he had economic links, having printed at least one of her titles).[60] In response to accusations that his story was no better than those it aimed to replace, he published later editions of *Pamela* with a preface, quoting a few critical responses and several fulsome letters of praise from his friend Aaron Hill. Hill sought to answer objections to *Pamela* much as Stanhope had sought to answer objections to *The Fortu-nate Lovers* in his own preface—which is not surprising, since Stanhope (under his real name, William Bond) had been coeditor with Hill of the short-lived *Plain Dealer*, printed by Samuel Richardson (Eaves and Kimpel, *Richardson*, 37–41; Sale 48–51). The 1735 edition of *Dorastus and Fawnia* had carried Stanhope's defense and an ad for Haywood's *Secret Histories*; *Pamela* appeared with Hill's defense and the author's preface, which were widely perceived as Richardson's shameless self-advertisement.

Richardson's preface comments that the "incomparable Writer" Hill had been particularly helpful in addressing "an Objection, that is more material than any we have mention'd": did this story invite all the young men in the world to marry serving maids? (19). No, Hill replied, "the *moral meaning of* PAMELA's Good-fortune, far from tempting young Gentlemen to marry *such* Maids as are to be found in their Families, is by teaching Maids to *deserve to be Mistresses*, to stir up Mistresses *to support their Distinc-tion*" (21). Hill's ingenious answer lets slip the circumstances that render "Distinction" a "material" necessity: this book will be read by "young Gen-tlemen," "Mistresses," *and* "Maids." It risks teaching maids ambition for the sake of teaching their mistresses virtue (assuming that the mistresses are inherently more likely than the servants to attain either). Hill locates the impetus for class distinctions on moral grounds *within* the lack of dis-tinction on cultural grounds. Because *Pamela* is popular in the inclusive sense (and the size and breadth of its audience were certainly unprece-dented), distinction must arise from the variant cultural uses that readers make of it. Once consumed, *Pamela* will re-produce class distinctions, albeit on slightly more meritocratic lines.

Hill's moralizations confirm that *Pamela* raised middle-class anxieties about fiction consumption among lower-class women. Richardson's char-acterization of his heroine had tried to head them off. Although Pamela is conspicuously literate, she is set apart from the women in scenes of con-sumption, for she is not a reader but a *writer*—of letters. The famous episode in which Mr. B. finds Pamela writing transforms the scene of romance consumption into a scene of romance *production*. In the continua-tion, Pamela's relationship to literacy is carefully regulated. She gives oral book reports to her husband, distributes the Bible and *The Whole Duty of Man* to their tenants, and, having studied Locke's educational theories, *tells* nursery tales to her children, their nurses, and a maid doing needlework. Mrs. Pamela B. raises children and servants on a model of morality and orality, not literacy. Thus, Richardson started *Pamela* as a romance, rooted in cheap print, and tried to transform it into a tale, confined to the orality of the family circle. The attempt recalls how *The Winter's Tale* rendered *Pandosto* as oral. As Warner shows, the "media event" *Pamela* launched proved beyond Richardson's control (*Licensing* 178).

The expulsion of cheap print from Pamela's experience can be set against Richardson's initial conception of *Pamela*, a landmark of print culture made in a family shaped by the print trade. *Pamela* originated as a commissioned work, a book of sample letters specifically designed for "those Country Readers who were unable to indite for themselves." Richardson was hired to write it by the publishers Charles Rivington and John Osborne, for whom he had previously printed. At first, the book was strictly functional. Then Richardson started writing letters advising "handsome Girls, who were obliged to go out to Service . . . how to avoid the Snares that might be laid against their Virtue," and found his imagination fired by the memory of an old story about an upwardly mobile serving maid. He began scribbling his story in November 1739 and finished the following January. His confidence was bolstered when his wife and a family member began coming nightly to his "little closet," eager to "hear a little more of Pamela" (Eaves and Kimpel, *Richardson*, 90–91).

The two women who comprised the first audience for *Pamela*, when it was still a winter's tale read aloud in the family circle, were Richardson's second wife, Elizabeth Leake, daughter of a printer; and Elizabeth Midwinter, daughter of the Edward Midwinter who had published Stanhope's *The Fortunate and Unfortunate Lovers* in 1735. As Spufford has shown using Midwinter's estate papers, Elizabeth was evidently raised as a lady, with a maid of her own. Yet the Midwinter clientele was quite frankly popular; his shop was often barraged by hawkers and chapmen eager for new material (Spufford 90–91). When Midwinter died in 1736, Elizabeth was his heir (Midwinter's only son was by *his* maid), and was placed in wardship to John Osborne, future copublisher of *Pamela*. But it was the Richardsons who effectively adopted her, for she was included in Francis Hayman's portrait of the family in 1741, wearing a splendid satin dress (see Eaves and Kimpel, *Richardson*, plate III), and Richardson arranged for her marriage settlement—to Lord Francis Gosling.[61] Osborne's commission and Osborne's ward came to Richardson together, facilitating the production of his book much as Fawnia and her gold facilitated Porrus's rise. Elizabeth, this young orphan, daughter of one hardworking printer and adopted by another, ended up marrying a lord. In 1736, did she bring a copy of *The Fortunate Lovers* with her to the Richardsons'? Would she have conceived of the relationship between her father's title and Richardson's innovative epistolary novel? What did the daughter of a chapbook publisher think of *Pamela*'s conspicuous literacy? And did she connect Fawnia's rise or Pamela's rise to her own?

RICHARDSON'S NEGOTIATIONS WITH popular romance during the writing of *Pamela* are the prehistory, then, to the rejection of popular romance in *Clarissa*'s scene of consumption. The fire scene, like the Jacobean scenes, supports material distinctions between fictional genres, but its workings are subtler, cleverly and multiply displaced onto an anonymous character, an unreliable narrator, and a nonexistent set of events. Why did Richardson invoke the cultural bar against fiction consumption in lower-class women in a novel about the supremely well-read, virtuous, and self-abnegating Clarissa? The answer must turn on his own involvement in furnishing cheap reading material to lower-class women, whether *Pamela*, a fiction that, in comparison to *Clarissa*, looked romantically incendiary, or earlier romances that, next to the substantial *Clarissa* that Richardson published for himself, looked lowbrow and flimsy. The "simple history of Dorastus and Faunia" was cousin to the popular romances that Richardson had made material: *Pamela*; *The Famous History of Tom a Lincolne*, which John Wilde printed during Richardson's apprenticeship; the condensation of *Gulliver's Travels* that was one of young Richardson's first independent products. And Mrs. Sinclair's cook-maid was kin (bad kin, to be sure), to Richardson the young romance reader. For as a young apprentice, Richardson had read in his room by candlelight, worrying about his master's disapproval. Of course, he was more vigilant than the cook-maid: "I took Care, that even my Candle was of my own purchasing, that I might not in the most trifling Instance make my Master a Sufferer." Of course, he did not "disable myself by Watching, or Sitting-up" too late to be able "to perform my Duty to him in the Day-time" (Eaves and Kimpel, *Richardson*, 11). Richardson knew better than to read when he should have been sleeping. He had taught himself to regulate his own consumption of romances, but he could not stop producing them.

Richardson's scene of consumption in *Clarissa* projected his own reading pleasures onto an anonymous servant woman and into a state of epistemological uncertainty. This scene revealed itself as staged, yet for two centuries, no one noticed. It was Richardson, printer and autodidact, who discovered how effectively literary art could mask material distinctions.

A PLEASANTER HISTORY BY HALF

Similar urbanity attends the last scene of consumption involving *Dorastus and Fawnia*, suggesting that by the second half of the eighteenth century, cheap print and servant readers could be treated at something of a picturesque distance, softened by sentimentalization of the reading experience. The scene comes in the Irish dramatist Isaac Bickerstaff's first and most successful comic opera, *Love in a Village*, first performed at Covent Garden in 1762 and produced there a solid 183 times. Bickerstaff later published another successful comic opera, *The Maid of the Mill* (1765), loosely based on *Pamela*.

The "opera"—we might call it a musical—opens at the country estate of Justice Woodcock, where his daughter Lucinda is sheltering her friend Rossetta in "the character of a chambermaid." Rossetta is in disguise because she has run away from her father's house, horrified that he has arranged to marry her to the unseen son of an affable stranger. Lucinda treats Rossetta as an equal, but hints at her continued dismay at Rossetta's social drop. Rossetta reminds Lucinda that "It is the only character, my dear, in which I could hope to lie concealed," the final phrase blending the play's pleasures of country torpor, role-playing, deceit, and seduction.[62] Luckily, Rossetta finds her disguise an asset: "I have had so many admirers since I commenced Abigail, that I am quite charmed with my situation" (5). The admirer she cares for, against her better judgment, is Thomas, the Woodcocks' new gardener.

In the next scene, Thomas obligingly explains to the audience that he, too, has adopted a servant disguise to evade an arranged marriage. He says that marrying the Woodcocks' chambermaid is "impossible," then sings a pastoral air about that forbidden fantasy, reminiscent of Macnamara Morgan:

> Oh! had I been by fate decreed
> Some humble cottage swain;
> In fair Rossetta's sight to feed,
> My sheep upon the plain.

What bliss had I been born to taste,
Which now I ne'er must know.

(7)

He amplifies the problem: "prudence" prevents his marrying so low, "honour" his "making a mistress of her" (9).[63] He turns out to be more honorable (in modern eyes, at least), than Rossetta's own father, Hawthorne, who comes to visit Woodcock. Hawthorne sings of Woodcock's right "to toy and to kiss" with his chambermaid, not realizing who this maid really is (41). By act 3, scene 1, the too-indulgent Hawthorne and Sir William Meadows (father of "Thomas") realize that the disguised lovers are in fact the children they intended to pair off. When they ask Rossetta whether she has loved the "gardener," she too places class prudence before passion: "had I not look'd upon him as a person so much below me, I should have had no objection to receiving his courtship." She then changes her claim, slipping belatedly into the high-flown antitheses of romance: "I assure you Sir William, in my own opinion, I should prefer a gardener, with your son's good qualities, to a knight of the shire without them." She sings:

'Tis not wealth, it is not birth,
Can value to the soul convey;
Minds possess superior worth,
Which chance nor gives, nor takes away.

(55)

But that protest seems insincere, given the knowledge of all parties that Rossetta need make no such choice. It is perfectly safe, then, for Rossetta's father to comment of the match:

Why Sir William it is romance, a novel, a pleasanter history by half, than the loves of Dorastus and Faunia; we shall have ballads made of it within these two months, setting forth, how a young 'squire became a serving man of low degree: and it will be stuck up with Margret's ghost, and the Spanish lady, against the walls of every cottage in the country. (52)

The courtship is pleasanter by half because *both* halves of the pair seemed low—and neither proved to be. The opera's doubling of discovered parentage overtops romance ideology.

By the mid-eighteenth century, drama had lost some critical perspective toward the marriage market, devising elaborate plots that magically justify the arranged marriages that Restoration drama's youth had successfully plotted to evade. In Bickerstaff's opera, those resolutions take on an almost deliberately arbitrary tone, perhaps even calling attention to their own artifice. Justice Woodcock is persuaded to accept Lucinda's chosen marriage to a young man of perfectly appropriate birth—by the reward of a song and a kiss from Rossetta. Then Rossetta says to Hodge, a servant besotted with her, who has hard-heartedly sacrificed to the London streets Margery, the *real* serving maid he has gotten in trouble, "Oh lord Hodge! I beg your pardon; I protest I forgot; but I must reconcile you and Madge I think; and give you a wedding dinner to make you amends" (73). The very arbitrariness and heedlessness of fortune that Greene's heroines (and heroes) had bewailed is now located within the heroine's actions and lapses, and only enhances her charms.

Woodcock's maiden sister blames this arbitrariness on female literacy, of all things, telling Lucinda that her love is "mighty pretty romantick stuff! but you learn it out of your play books, and novels. Girls in my time, had other employments, we work'd at our needles, and kept ourselves from idle thoughts. . . . Ah! I never knew a woman come to good, that was fond of reading" (60). The play's ambivalence toward fashionable, feminized literacy may be linked to the ambivalence of Bickerstaff (a young man himself, recently arrived from Dublin) toward the fashionable literacy he was exploiting. But it is popular literature that is singled out in Hawthorne's whimsical remark—cheap print turns the adventures of young gentlefolk into entertainment and wallpaper for the populace, and profit for ballad publishers.

That kind of commodification was hardly news to Bickerstaff. In the 1763 edition of the play, a brief prefatory "advertisement" disingenuously underestimates the extent of the opera's debt to Charles Johnson's *The Village Opera* (1729), which was the whole plot, not the stated "incident or two" ([A4]). Although his collaborator's music won the day in this case of questionable authorship, Bickerstaff was thereafter continually getting caught in the gray area between adaptation and plagiarism, a problem doubly registered in the front matter of *The Maid of the Mill*. A two-page preface carefully explains its indebtedness to Richardson's *Pamela* for its central situation, fleshed out with theatrical foils. And leaf A4, without any heading, contains a new advertisement: "This Opera is entered at STATIONERS HALL, and whoever presumes to Print the Songs, or any Part of them, will be prosecuted by the Proprietors." The notice threatens those who would do exactly what Hawthorne had predicted the ballad publishers would with the plot of *Love in a Village*. The offer, made in jest, of turning experiences into commercial profit must reflect Bickerstaff's own sense of the voracity of the publishing market.

Indeed, Bickerstaff's reference to *Dorastus and Fawnia*, unlike the other anecdotes I have discussed, may have opened up boundaries between fields of cultural consumption rather than seeking to close them, making a gentle but contextually dense joke about the broad cultural diffusion of both romances of service and fabulous entertainment. The play's plot is itself reminiscent of *The Winter's Tale*, which Bickerstaff had probably read; so is act 1's rural laborer's fair.[64] The opera, and particularly the hero's pastoral songs, may well have emulated the softened pastoral elements of new adaptations of Shakespeare's play. Bickerstaff came to London in 1755, which means that he could have seen either the Morgan adaptation, *The Sheep-Shearing*, which had been a success in London and Dublin in 1754–55, or David Garrick's *Florizel and Perdita, a Dramatic Pastoral*, presented at Drury Lane from 1756–62.

The actor playing Justice Woodcock, father of Lucinda and straight man to Hawthorne, was Ned Shuter, whom Arthur Scouten calls "the famous low comedian."[65] Beginning in 1754, Shuter had also taken the role of Autolycus, the scoundrel ballad seller, in Morgan's adaptation of *The Winter's Tale* at Covent Garden. Miss Brent, who played Rossetta in 1762, had played Perdita in 1760–62. Meanwhile, an actor named Richard Yates originated the role of Autolycus in David Garrick's adaptation, beginning in 1756 and mounted again at Drury Lane in 1762. But in previous summers, another Richard Yates (theater historians are still sorting out the two) mounted drolls (short playlets) at fairs, as an alternative to the patent theaters; at Bartholomew Fair, Yates's company had performed *Dorastus and Fawnia* in May 1749 (no cast list survives). The coincidence is a reminder of the pattern in earlier drolls: the one surviving advertisement for a droll *Dorastus and Fawnia* freely intermixes names from *The Winter's Tale* (see chapter 3).[66]

Dorastus and Fawnia may have been cited in *Love in a Village* as a famous love story sold as a ballad, but it was also remembered by cast members, and by many in their audience, as a famous love story to be viewed in a context of cultural mixing. At the fair, all classes famously re-created themselves: an account of the droll audience at Bartholomew Fair in 1739 comments that "The chambermaid and Countess sit / Alike admirers of the wit"[67]; the tastes of all women (but probably not all men) are considered equal. Hecht reports a similar "convergence of classes" in the London play-houses at mid-century; one 1747 description said that the *"Middle Gallery"* of London playhouses was occupied by "Citizens Wives and Daughters, together with the *Abigails*, Serving-men . . . and Apprentices" (201). Cul-tural mixing built the cast list for the droll of *Dorastus and Fawnia*, dis-cussed in chapter 3. In the other direction, popular culture was still being brought into the theaters, especially by comic stars: in 1765, Shuter gave a speciality performance before Thomas Hull's *Spanish Lady* (the lady men-tioned by Hawthorne?), singing "snatches from a dozen popular old bal-lads."[68] By the 1770s, it was possible for Henry Walton to paint "A Pretty Maid Buying a Love-Song" (1778), treating a ballad-selling scene as an object of beauty rather than horror. The discovery of the folk had become a matter of fashion, and the edge was off distinction.

Was Bickerstaff's opera doing the work of distinction, and if so, how, and among whom? It portrays the country as a place where property own-ers and their servants share popular literacy. Of course, this inclusive stag-ing of popular consumption may mark another line of distinction, present-ing country literacy as provincial to its London audience. In any case, the romance is far less of a threat in this scene than in my earlier examples; it is associated with the past (the ballads mentioned are titles that had attracted interest in periodicals) but also allowed to occupy the present and approximate the other "romances" or "novels" of its day. That degree of comfort, I argue, reflects the existence of a securely *literary* tradition for Bickerstaff's treatment of romance narrative. Bickerstaff chose *Dorastus and Fawnia* because he could count on much of his audience having knowledge of it either directly or through literary texts that would validate his work. He alludes simultaneously to *Dorastus and Fawnia* and to *Clarissa* (and per-haps to *The Winter's Tale*). In part, *Dorastus and Fawnia* is invoked because it has been invoked by other authors before, authors of value to Bickerstaff as he develops the somewhat "low" form of the comic opera. To summon up *Dorastus and Fawnia* in 1762 is to admit a long history of acts of dis-tinction in which it served to mark the boundary between elite and popu-lar literatures.

Pleasantly enough, *Love in a Village* can be documented as being popu-lar among servants, unlike my other romances of service. In her study of servant readership in the mid-eighteenth century, Jan Fergus shows that one Rugby bookshop sold copies of *Love in a Village* to both a male and a female servant.[69] For once, an anecdotal claim about readership—predict-

ing that this love story will be known in "every cottage in the country"—
can be confirmed by documentary evidence. Fergus notes that while the
play was popular with schoolboys and girls, its plot "might have a particular appeal for servants" and poorer youth. Apparently, nonelite readers
enjoyed a play that featured a double-discovered parentage plot for the gentle and carelessly neglected the minor plot involving domestic servants. It
is almost disappointing that servants enjoyed this particular romance of
service, which seems like the most unrealistic wish fulfillment. But perhaps
its self-reflexive defense of even such thin fictions was part of its popular
appeal. When readers have little expectation of real advancement, might
they not take pleasure in seeing patently fictional wishes come true?

I have argued that the denigration of popular print and the discovery of "folk" culture are reciprocal, and that the elite disavowal of popular print was selective. Educated writers throughout the eighteenth century had sufficient privilege to express lingering nostalgia for the chivalric romances that they associated with a shared schoolboy past.[1] But the same reading material, in the hands of the nonelite, provoked ridicule or contempt: lower-class reading experiences were misrepresented in scenes of consumption or written out of the cultural record. Among Britain's nonelite readers, those of early nineteenth-century Ireland bore the brunt of elite disavowal of popular romance. The same texts that English writers of the eighteenth century had celebrated as favorites from their youth were explicitly condemned by government and charitable society reformers as unsuitable for Irish children. Once more, the reading of *Dorastus and Fawnia* was figured as a scandal, but this time it was a crisis of ideological control over the children of the colonized and the poor.

The crisis emerged from a series of investigations into the state of education in Ireland, culminating in the Parliamentary act of 1832 establishing national schools. From about 1780 to 1830, English parliamentary and charitable committees investigated English-language schools in Ireland's counties, as they existed under various inadequate forms of sponsorship. When these reports turned to textbooks, their prose broke down into horrified catalogues of the inappropriate and immoral books being used to teach English. The pattern was already familiar when Hely Dutton wrote in his *Statistical Survey of the County of Clare* (1808):

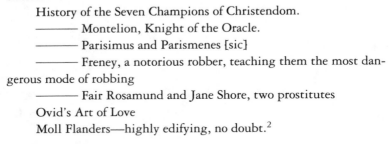

> The state of education may be easily appreciated, when it is known that, with the exception of a few universal spelling books, the general cottage classics are:
>
> History of the Seven Champions of Christendom.
> ———— Montelion, Knight of the Oracle.
> ———— Parisimus and Parismenes [sic]
> ———— Freney, a notorious robber, teaching them the most dangerous mode of robbing
> ———— Fair Rosamund and Jane Shore, two prostitutes
> Ovid's Art of Love
> Moll Flanders—highly edifying, no doubt.[2]

The core of Dutton's list is a group of chivalric "histories" that recalls Kirkman's 1671 curriculum in popular romance—and his claim that one history, *Seven Wise Masters*, was used to teach reading in Ireland (see chapter 3).

Unlike Kirkman, Dutton and those who confirmed his findings in other counties found nothing to celebrate about Irish popular reading. William Shaw Mason's *Parochial Survey of Ireland* (1814–19) reported that in one parish, "the books for those advanced to reading, are generally those sold by pedlars of odd volumes of novels," while in another, the reading materials for schoolchildren were "not calculated to impress on their tender minds either a sense of religion or virtue; they are generally story-books, or some vulgar ill-written histories" (Dowling 82). So strong was this consensus that a visitor to County Clare in 1816 could simply assert that the "books are as worthless as they have been observed to be in other parts of Ireland" (Dowling 80). Reports of hearings show that schoolmasters and pastors were asked whether their students had been reading the inspectors' *bêtes noires*—criminal biographies, works of Catholic devotion, and the old-fashioned manual of sexual pleasures called *Aristotle's Masterpiece*.[3]

The fullest list of unsuitable textbooks, and the one that most amply demonstrates the nature of the objection to Irish popular reading, was compiled as an appendix to the First Report to the Commissioners on Education in Ireland in 1825.[4] This appendix seems to constitute a full list of the books available for purchase in Ireland (its reprinting in Patrick John Dowling's *The Hedge Schools of Ireland* runs to six pages), its contents and miscellaneity strikingly recalling the catalogues found in the backs of chapbooks. It is divided into "Religious Works" and "Works of Entertainment, Histories, Tales, Etc." The latter category includes those criminal biographies and *Aristotle's Masterpiece*; the perennial chivalric romances, *Seven Wise Masters*, *Montelyon*, *Parismus and Parismenos*, and *Don Bellianis*; and such widely admired works of English polite culture as Locke's essays, a book of essays on Shakespeare, Lennox's *Female Quixote*, Fielding's *Joseph Andrews*, and Richardson's *Pamela*, *Clarissa*, and *Charles Grandison* (Dowling 154–61). Also on the list is something called "Dorastus and Gavora," which, since it is closely preceded by "Hero and Leander," I can identify as Stanhope's The *Fortunate and Unfortunate Lovers* (Dowling 158).

Under that title and various subtitles, Stanhope's retelling of Greene's romance is extant in Irish imprints from 1793/4 (Dublin), circa 1800 (n.p.), and 1843 (Belfast). These three copies are clearly drops in an ocean of Irish editions. J.R.R. Adams, surveying popular literature from Ulster's presses through booksellers' advertisements on the backs of extant titles, notes that *The Fortunate and Unfortunate Lovers* was clearly a staple work. J. Magee of Belfast advertised it in 1752, 1753, 1763, 1764, 1765, 1766, 1767, 1780, 1781, 1782, and 1784. It was also advertised between 1835 and 1850 by Joseph Smyth of Belfast, whose cheap issues often coordinated with those of C. M. Warren of Dublin. Finally, it was advertised by John Simms and James M'Intyre, who published many familiar cheap titles from 1836 to 1842 before they began innovative, large-scale publication of full-length novels in cheap, uniform format.[5] The 1843 edition of Stanhope in the British Library, marked "Belfast: the booksellers," may be theirs or an unknown competitor's. It was the mass-produced novels of Simms and M'Intyre and their English competitors, and at the other end of the scale the illustrated newspaper, that finally defeated the chapbook format and the old titles that had survived for three centuries. Steam presses, stereotyping, and cheap paper allowed them to produce bulky novels, complete with illustrated paper covers, for the price of the older, smaller chapbooks.

What were all these books doing in Irish schools, how long had they been there, and what about them provoked such outrage? Dowling's study offers a plausible explanation of their uses. Most of the books were found in hedge schools, village academies run by a single independent teacher/headmaster who was paid by parents (a pittance, usually) for instructing children in the three Rs, including reading knowledge in English, and often in Latin. Students reached basic literacy by using hornbooks at first, and spelling books or primers later; beyond that, there were no extant textbooks for young readers in English as a second language, and no money with which to buy them.

Children brought in whatever "cottage classics" their homes could provide. Dowling explains, "Parents undoubtedly bought some of the books, for they were the cheapest on the market, and handed them on to their children when the latter required something to read from at school. In fact *it was these books, or nothing*" (Dowling 82, emphasis added). The books were probably also used for what modern educators call "free reading," since the conditions of a one-room (or even outdoor) schoolhouse demanded material that would hold the attention of advanced students while the teacher worked with beginners. In that context, Dowling suggests, many of these books would have done much to promote interest in reading (87).

How long had this practice continued? Dowling does not speculate, and other sources on British popular reading have been uncertain whether to believe the claims for the educational use of popular fiction in Ireland. Niall Ó Ciosáin's *Print and Popular Culture in Ireland, 1750–1850* maintains that the reporters' interest in popular reading as "part of an explanation of social disorder in Ireland" does not "discount their testimony" that the books were used, and quotes other Irish sources that corroborate the practice.[6] What is less certain is how early the practice became widespread. Kirkman's assertion that Irish "Children are in general put to read in" *Seven Wise Masters* after attaining basic "Knowledge of Letters" is seen by Paul Salzman as "an inadvertent admission of the true level of these romances."[7] Margaret Spufford, reconstructing the uses of cheap print in seventeenth-century England, touches on claims for the Irish practice:

> The preface of Pepys's threepenny abbreviated version of *The Seven Wise Masters* made the unusual claim, "of all Histories of this nature, this exceeds, being held in such esteem in Ireland, that it is of the chiefest use in all the English Schools for introducing Children to the understanding of good letters." The claim would appear wildly improbable, despite the fact that Irish chapmen were often specifically appealed to in the advertising of the publisher-booksellers, if it were not for the astonishing evidence provided by Hely Dutton writing of County Clare in 1808. . . . If the [romances] were there in the nineteenth century, they may well, in view of the advertising, have been there in the seventeenth century also. (Spufford 74)

The thinness of records for the Irish book trade makes it difficult to establish exactly when and how widely popular fiction became available in Ireland. But the convergence among the advertisements in Pepys's chapbook from the 1680s, Kirkman's claims in the 1670s, and the findings of school inspectors in the early 1800s is unmistakable. The reading of popular fiction had been established in Ireland for centuries before it came to the administrators' attention.

What was the horror toward which these administrators' lists gesture? Like most catalogues of condemned books, the lists treated wildly various works as an undifferentiated mass of unacceptable material. The lists included a number of works highly valued in the libraries of the educated, but the investigators had no interest in making fine distinctions when it came to popular reading. Adams, writing about Ulster, notes that

> Contemporary critics of popular reading material almost totally ignored any distinction between different types of such material: either it was officially approved and written by the commonality's betters with some sort of moral uplift as the ultimate aim, or it was to be utterly and uncritically condemned, whether it was a medieval romance or *Nocturnal revels*. (Adams 99)

The catalogues characteristically specified charges against some books and damned others by association. Perhaps some books were too criminal, others too high-flown; they were all unthinkable. As Ó Ciosáin points out, in a period of social unrest, reporters had every motivation to "constru[e] as seditious" books that were not.

The reformers' inability to discriminate suggests that they were particularly disturbed to find reading material varied enough to allow for popular choice. The absence of graded readers raised the specter of an educational experience that was neither supervised nor uniform. Poor supervision was a constant complaint; as the reports argued at length, Irish schools were insufficiently disciplined, mainly because their practices had been determined by the Irish themselves. Free reading exemplified that lack of control. That students should volunteer their own titles, that their literacy should be turned to voluntary pleasures, that these readings might encourage aspiration to further voluntary pleasures—all were quite unacceptable.[8] Thus children became the objects of the recurring Platonic critique of mimesis consumed for pleasure. Even more than women, servants, or "simple persons," children were perceived as impressionable. And as the pleasures of romance had been associated with women and the ambitions of romance with servants, so now the supposed immaturity of romance was associated with children who were both poor and of an allegedly inferior "race." Their consumption of fantastic romances threatened their compliance as colonial subjects and as future workers and servants for the metropolis.

The inspections did not admit the extent to which the problem of free reading in an unfree Ireland was a problem created by English policies—policies even more shortsighted than those concerning the literacy of the English lower classes. The history of the Irish book trade reflected English disregard for Irish literacy, and the history of the hedge schools reflected English repression of Irish educational efforts. The book trade was tightly controlled by English interests even in the early modern period, as M. Pollard demonstrates in a detailed study of the trade in Dublin.[9] Under Elizabeth, English-language primers had been brought to Ireland in a deliberate effort to supersede the Gaelic culture of the bard schools; famously, precious old manuscripts were cut up to make covers for those primers.[10] The King's Printer's Monopoly, which was in almost continuous force from 1604 to 1732, restricted Irish publishing to a single press under royal supervision; its output was mainly proclamations, primers, and the like. It was possible, but not encouraged, to bring in English books; that irregular trade has left few traces. One early instance is telling: in 1575, a Cork merchant imported "250 small or children's books" and "12 *Wise Masters*" along with hornbooks and grammars (Pollard 34).

The Jacobean boom in colonial investments led to a brief experiment in which the London stationers persuaded King James to substitute for the King's Printer a joint venture in their mutual interest. From 1618 to 1641, the Stationers maintained the "Irish Stock," a monopoly in book production (mainly of primers) that paralleled the cultivation of Ireland as "plantations" for English investment.[11] As Pollard argues, the Stationers' expectation of profit is our "best evidence . . . that a promising trade in books in Ireland was already in existence" (36). But financial mismanagement and other problems dogged the effort, and the Civil War did it in. In a 1637 letter to Charles I, a young aristocrat argued that he should be given a share in the Irish stock, since he would ensure that Ireland got what it really needed, an Irish-language Bible that would suitably indoctrinate the populace. The lack of one was working, he claimed, "to ye great hurt and prejudice of ye breeding of youth in that State, who in their yonger yeares and beginnings are forced to drinke in, or season themselves wth fabulouse & unprofitable tale Bookes & Storyes." English-language texts were just as bad, he added, since the stationers had been importing "severall fabulous Historyes out of England [and] selling them at Excessive Rates throwout ye whole kingdome, soe yt youth being educated thereby, rather did cherish vice then Establish vertue and Religion."[12] This proposal was ignored. In 1638, four young booksellers from London set up shop in Dublin, justifying their efforts as colonial control. This venture, too, quickly collapsed (Pollard 38–39).

Beginning in the 1680s, a native book trade sprang up in Dublin, in spite of the monopoly. Although it was well established by 1700, the Irish demand for books far outstripped the supply. The overall shortage of books in Ireland became a topic for English scorn and Irish complaint, and popular fiction titles of English origin were relied on to help fill the void. In 1729, James Arbuckle wrote cuttingly in the *Dublin Tribune* of a Protestant Irish Gentleman who had absolutely no "Furniture" of books. The biggest book collection in the household was likely to belong to his wife's "Woman," who might keep

> a *Robinson Crusoe, Gulliver's* Travels, and *Aristotle's* Master-piece, both for her own Edification, and the instruction of the young Ladies, as soon as they are grown up; not to mention *Tommy Pots, Jack* the *Giant-killer,* the *Cobler* of *Canterbury,* and several other notable Pieces of Literature carried about in the Baskets of itinerant Pedlars, for the Improvement of his Majesty's Liege People.   (Pollard 221)

The scale of the cheap-print trade may have been considerable. One surviving inventory, of a relatively impoverished Quaker chapman who died in 1736, lists 2,050 copies of *Mol Flanders* [sic], 2,026 of *Aristotle's Masterpiece,* and 2,050 copies of *Argalus and Parthenia,* along with "850 damaged Argalus's . . . Valued as waste paper being useless" from water damage (Pollard 219). Not surprisingly, some of the Irish themselves saw the importation of English popular reading as unwholesome. A 1735 advertisement by the Catholic bookseller James Hoey justified Mother Goose and Cinderella as better reading for schools than *Don Bellianis* and *Parismus,* his preference for fairy tales reflecting French taste. Hoey quoted a "Rev. Walker" as fulminating that "the reading of old immoral, ridiculous Romances . . . *has a potent Domination over Children, and a malignant Influence on all their future learning*" (Pollard 222).

Meanwhile, Irish book-trade conditions made Shakespeare hard to come by. As late as 1767–68, the wife of the Right Honorable Richard Jackson bought her set of Shakespeare second hand (Pollard 218). The first Dublin edition of his works was from 1725, "almost needless to add, a piracy," Jaggard's *Shakespeare Bibliography* would later sniff.[13] The Irish held that English copyright law did not extend to Ireland, technically a foreign country, so publishing English copies there was not illegal so long as the books were not smuggled. The English were quick to charge that they *were* smuggled, when in fact books could be made more cheaply in Dublin than under the London Stationers' Company regulations (Pollard 224). Most products of eighteenth-century Dublin presses were reprints of older titles by English authors, since profits were too small to attract successful Irish authors.[14] Eighteenth-century Dublin book publishers therefore made the most of reprint publishing and became innovators in cheap publication. They "chose the most readable and popular material from London publications and offered it to a wider readership than the expensive London book could command" (Pollard v).[15] Ironically, then, the earlier book trade restrictions cleared the way for Ireland to develop mass-market publishing of both literary and popular works.

The growth of a cheap popular press, positive from a modern perspective, was considered dangerous in Ireland because it accompanied a stunted educational system. Here, even more than for the book trade, English policies must be blamed. Schooling by Catholic instructors was technically illegal until the Catholic Emancipation Bill of 1829 (Dowling 23, 31). Repression of Irish schools was particularly harsh under Cromwell's protectorate and under the Penal Laws enacted upon the accession of William III. Later, procedures for licensing schoolmasters theoretically eased the possibility of education, but certainly did not raise standards or provide funding. In hindsight, the surprising feature of this bar was that it discouraged not only the teaching of Latin and Gaelic but even the teaching of English. As the Irish statesman Edmund Burke wrote of the 1745 Act to Prevent Foreign Education, "To render men patient under a deprivation of all the rights of human nature, everything which could give them a knowledge or feeling of these rights was rationally forbidden" (quoted in Dowling 24).

The Irish responded by inventing the hedge schools. Dowling is partisan, but the ubiquity of the schools supports his claim that Irish parents were passionate in wanting their children to attain literacy regardless of obstacles or costs.[16] The schools were persecuted as breeding grounds for Catholicism (many masters were Catholic), as drains on population (because they sometimes fed students to Continental academies), and as sites for local resistance. Their name reflected their marginal status: classes were held on roadsides, outdoors, or in rough huts, so that no householder risked prosecution for sheltering the illegal enterprise of education. Dowling concludes that the hedge schools "rendered possible . . . the conduct of a kind of guerilla warfare in education" (48), against the "deprivation" of "rights of knowledge" noted by Burke.

Because the hedge schools were illegal, no one could be bothered to publish suitable readers for them. The Bible—the most common first reader in England—was too divisive to be encouraged, and texts devised by one religious interest or the other were bound to meet opposition at some level. Even classical history was too dangerous, according to an 1808 letter addressed to a parliamentary committee by Richard Lovell Edgeworth: "such abridgments of these histories as I have seen are certainly improper; to inculcate democracy and a foolish hankering after undefined liberty, is not necessary in Ireland." Instead, he recommended works that imparted "piety and morality, and industry" (Dowling 85). Yet there was little interest in devising such works for Irish schools until the end of the eighteenth century. In the meantime, Irish students used what they had, turning to popular fiction.

Alternative schools designed by English reformers restored the rights of knowledge only partially, since they sought strict control over the texts to which literacy gave access. The worst of these were the shameful, for-profit Charter schools set up by a grant from the English government in the late eighteenth century. These were conceived of as a direct challenge to Catholicism and, since they were effectively workhouses, as an instrument of labor control. But they were also a challenge to Irish popular culture. The students were given a Bible, a primer, and a *Whole Duty of Man*—this was often the extent of their education—while the grants to those who ran Charter schools were derived from a tax on chapmen and hawkers (Pollard 11). Thus, the costs of this approved site of minimal literacy were borne by those who provided nonapproved reading alternatives.

An even cannier attack on the popular press was evident in the work of the nonsectarian Kildare Place Society, founded in 1814–15. The Society "was horrified by the material in use in the common pay or hedge schools," and "felt that it was of little use teaching the Irish to read if they then rushed to their local chapman and bought copies of undesirable writings" (Adams 99–100). However, since the Society's policies "deprived it of the Bible as a basis for the curriculum," and also ruled out Anglican textbooks, "the only alternative was to write, print, bind, and distribute material in direct competition with the pernicious literature, alongside it, through the same outlets," and in the same formats (Adams 100). Drawing on the example of Hannah More's *Cheap Repository Tracts*, considered a great success in England, the Society wrote its own tracts.[17] Besides donating a complete set to each approved school, the Society distributed them via the chapbook network, calculating that their "protective mimicry" of the chapbook format would help them find readers (Adams 100). They also sold the tracts at wholesale prices designed to undercut the trade's chapbooks (Dowling 82). In this, Kildare Place titles did not succeed; indeed, chapbook sellers actually advertised Kildare titles indiscriminately on the backs of their own volumes, absorbing the purified material into the condemned canon (Adams 100–5, 140, 151).

The voracity of the appetite for print in Ireland was interpreted as yet another instance in which popular readers, faced with limited cultural options, showed no ability to discriminate. As ever, that interpretation is unfounded, for Irish readers clearly saw differences among the materials and expressed their preferences through their purchases. On one side, Adams notes that Kildare Place found that preachy titles failed immediately (Adams 104). The Society also suppressed any marks of charitable origins on the tracts, accurately foreseeing the resistance of their intended converts (Adams 100). On the other side, Irish readers selected works from the English popular canon that best fit their tastes. Ó Ciosáin proposes that chivalric romances were popular because their emphasis on heroism and "the importance of blood and descent" spoke to preexisting Irish values (83); this theory is borne out by a preference for native heroes. Adams notes that *Guy of Warwick* and *Palmerin of England* were not popular in Ulster, presumably because they served English patriotic ends.[18] Throughout Ireland, the most successful chivalric romances included Irish heroes, as Kirkman anticipated when he added an Irish spin-off to *Don Bellianis of Greece*. The *Seven Champions*, of course, featured St. Patrick of Ireland, warring, wenching, and slaying dragons. In their nonchivalric romances, too, Irish readers made definite choices, for instance taking more of an interest in Arabian tales than English popular readers did. If previous versions of *Dorastus and Fawnia*, or for that matter the *Royal Courtly Garland*, were brought to Ireland, no trace has survived. But *The Fortunate and Unfortunate Lovers, or New Arabian Tales*, imported by 1752 if not earlier and thus within a generation of its English debut, lasted ninety years in the popular canon. Selling at sixpence, *The Fortunate and Unfortunate Lovers* was in the highest price bracket for a chapbook.[19]

Romances from England were used in the schools because nothing else was available, but they continued to succeed in print because they reflected

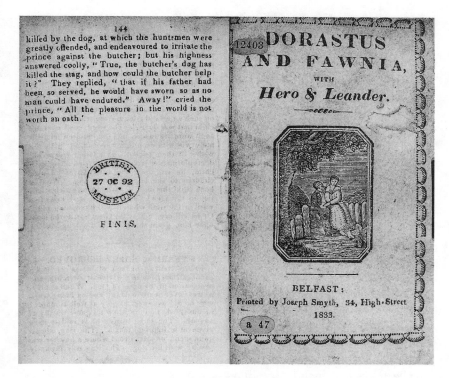

144

killed by the dog, at which the huntsmen were greatly offended, and endeavoured to irritate the prince against the butcher; but his highness answered coolly, "True, the butcher's dog has killed the stag, and how could the butcher help it?" They replied, "that if his father had been so served, he would have sworn so as no man could have endured." Away!" cried the prince, "All the pleasure in the world is not worth an oath.'

FINIS,

12403 DORASTUS AND FAWNIA,

WITH

Hero & Leander.

BELFAST:

Printed by Joseph Smyth, 34, High-Street 1833.

a 47

FIGURE E.I

Cover, *Dorastus and Fawnia, with Hero and Leander* (Belfast: J. Smyth, 1833), bound with 1843 edition.

BY PERMISSION OF THE BRITISH LIBRARY (SHELFMARK 12403.A.47)

regional interests and popular tastes. The irony missed by English critics is that in the case of *The Fortunate and Unfortunate Lovers*, Irish readers selected a work that had already been given a moralistic coating. Stanhope's romance appeared with its preface condemning the well-meaning disobedience of the lovers and with a closing verse saluting the workings of providence. On the surface, the book appeared to be all that the reformers could ask, although none of the surveyors apparently opened it to consider its contents. However, if it had, like the Kildare Place tracts, depicted characters meekly accepting their state of cultural deprivation, it never would have done so well on the open market. Instead, as I have suggested, Stanhope's romance voiced vigorous opposition to misuse of power, in terms available to male and female readers. Fawnia's retort to her host (and father) Pandosto, as he threatens her virtue and the lives of his Sicilian visitors, is especially interesting in an Irish context:

> I know thou hast Power, and am too sensible that you have exercised it, in an arbitrary manner upon the Innocent. . . . Know thou Sovereign of *Bohemia*, that though the Body is subject to Victory, yet the Mind is not be subdued with Conquest. . . . Is it any Honour, think you, to draw down a whole Army against a small Village, that is weak and defence-less, and to ransack a poor inoffensive People, who cannot defend them-selves? much less is it honourable to seduce an innocent Maiden, or to compel her by Force and superior Strength.   (Stanhope 50–51)

Stanhope's text had genteel, moralizing intentions, but it could not sustain the complete servility that the school inspectors had in mind. Fawnia's stand was a potentially powerful rhetorical claim, presented to schoolboys and girls in "their yonger yeares and beginnings" and placed in the mouth of a young woman, with whom other young women readers might be eager to identify. Stanhope's rhetoric is not rigorous political theory, but its empha-sis on an unsubdued "Mind" even in a subjected political "Body" would have justified the concerns of inspectors had they bothered to read the text.

The attacks on Irish free reading were, I have suggested, not selective about the literary value or class origins of the books, and thus would have found nothing redeeming in the evident gentility of Stanhope's. If the inspectors did discriminate, it was in identifying those texts most likely to cause political inflammation. Edgeworth's letter of 1808 demonstrates that political theory was condemned wherever it was recognized. Dowling defends the range of works listed in the 1825 First Report to the Com-missioners, on the grounds that they would have aided students in "acquir-ing a taste for literature and history" (Dowling 87). Such taste was itself to be feared, as fostering desire for class advancement and political rights. Popular literature was perfectly capable of fostering the same dangerous desires, as a few commentators admitted: in his *Projects for Re-establishing the Internal Peace and Tranquility of Ireland* (Dublin, 1799), Whitney Stokes wrote:

> The lower classes in Ireland, until within these few years confined their purchases of books to a particular kind, called Burtons, which they got for six pence halfpenny a piece. . . . Some will think romances innocent,

but these works contribute greatly to keep alive a false admiration of courage, a spirit of war and revenge, and a love of adventure so incompatible with the happiness of mankind. (Pollard 222)[20]

Stokes's language answers Stanhope's: the romance that protests the rights of the "innocent" is not, itself, politically innocent. One instance of "courage" fostered by romance reading may be Burke himself, who "confessed in the House of Commons" that "a very favourite study" of his youth had been "the old romances, Palmerin of England and Don Belianis [sic] of Greece."[21]

The clearest link between the political threat of Irish free reading and *Dorastus and Fawnia* was in William Carleton's *Traits and Stories of the Irish Peasantry* (London, 4th ed., 1836):

> The matter placed in their hands was of a most inflammatory and pernicious nature, as regarded politics; and as far as religion and morality were concerned, nothing could be more gross and superstitious than the books which circulated among them. . . . Their weapons of controversy were drawn from [popular Catholic works]. The books of amusement read in these schools . . . were, the Seven Champions of Christendom, the Seven Wise Masters and mistresses of Rome, Don Belianis of Greece, the Royal Fairy Tales, the Arabian Nights Entertainments, Valentine and Orson, Gesta Romanorum, Dorastus and Faunia, the History of Reynard the Fox . . . Parismus and Parismenos; along with others, the name of which shall not appear upon these pages.
>
> (quoted in Dowling 80–81)

"Dorastus and Faunia" appears in this roll call of objectionable material as mere "amusement." But if my analysis has been correct, its pleasures cannot be firmly separated from its potential to furnish "weapons of controversy." The threat of free reading was continuous with the threat of political and doctrinal free thought. If nothing else, the reading of romances, that "amusement" that Irish children shared with their parents, was an oppositional claim of a right to pleasure in literacy.

In condemning those pleasures, Ireland's self-appointed reformers drew on the long history of material distinctions that I have traced in this book. Educated English writers had been reproving the reading of cheap print in their own nation for centuries; only in Ireland could they hope to repress it.[22] The reformers condemned popular romance as reproducible "matter," with all the power of print. As in Shakespeare's portrayal of gullible Mopsa, Carleton condemns "political and religious ballads of the vilest doggerel" to be found "in the hands of young and old, and, of course, fixed in their credulity" (quoted in Dowling 81). Reformers also denounced fiction for being imaginary, for inviting a countenancing of other worlds, other lives, other ambitions, against a social order that urged unquestioning contentment. To consume fiction was, once more, to replace the fictions of dominant ideologies. In 1808, Edgeworth blamed popular "abridgments" for causing a "foolish hankering after undefined liberty." As the father of Maria Edgeworth, who had published an Arabian tale in 1804, he knew that the power and appeal of reading was international and cross-class. Desiring to read was only "foolish" for those to whom no further liberties would be extended. Every elite condemnation confirmed that popular reading was analogous to other popular freedoms, and that in choosing their reading material, popular audiences were engaged in political acts.

APPENDICES

APPENDICES

APPENDIX A: *Pandosto* Prose Versions

Date	Short Title	Author[1]
1588	Pandosto. The Triumph of Time.	RG
1592	Pandosto. The Triumph of Time.	RG
1595	Pandosto. The Triumph of Time.	RG
1600	Pandosto. The Triumph of Time.	RG
1607	Pandosto. The Triumph of Time.	RG
1609	Pandosto. The Triumph of Time.	RG
1614	Pandosto. The Triumph of Time.	RG
1619	Pandosto. The Triumph of Time.	RG
1629	Pandosto. The Triumph of Time.	RG
1632	Pandosto. The Triumph of Time.	RG
1635?	The pleasant historie of Dorastus and Fawnia	RG
1636	The pleasant historie of Dorastus and Fawnia	RG
1640?	[The pleasant historie] no title page	[RG]
1648	The pleasant historie of Dorastus and Fawnia	RG
1655	The pleasant historie of Dorastus and Fawnia	RG
1664	The pleasant historie of Dorastus and Fawnia	RG
1677	The pleasant historie of Dorastus and Fawnia	RG
1680?	The delightful history of Dorastus and Fawnia	anon.
1684	The pleasant historie of Dorastus and Fawnia	RG
1688	The pleasant historie of Dorastus and Fawnia	RG
1690?	The pleasant historie of Dorastus and Fawnia	RG
1696/1700	The pleasant and delightful hist. of Dorastus, with Josephus	RG
1700?	The pleasant and delightful hist. of Dorastus	RG
1700?	The pleasant and delightful hist. of Dorastus	RG
1700?	The history of Dorastus and Fawnia	anon.
1703	The pleasant and delightful hist. of Dorastus	RG
1705?	The pleasant and delightful hist. of Dorastus, with Josephus	RG
1727?/35	The fortunate and unfortunate lovers	HS
1735	The fortunate and unfortunate lovers	HS
1750?	The pleasant and delightful hist. of Dorastus	RG
1762?	The pleasant and delightful hist. of Dorastus, with Josephus	RG
1730–60	The history of Dorastus and Fawnia	anon.
1730–70?	The history of Dorastus and Faunia	anon.
1775?	The history of Dorastus and Faunia	anon.
1775?	The history of Dorastus and Faunia	anon.
1770–90	The history of Dorastus and Fannia [sic]	anon.
1793[4]	The fortunate and unfortunate lovers/New Arabian tale	HS
1795	The history of Dorastus and Fawnia	anon.
1796	The royal shepherdess/German princess	anon.
1800?	The fortunate and unfortunate lovers/New Arabian tale	anon.
1807	Dorastus and Fawnia/German princess	anon.
1800–20	The royal shepherdess/Dorastus and Fawnia/German Princess	anon.
1810?	The adventure of Dorastus and Fawnia	anon.
1812	Dorastus and Fawnia/German princess	anon.
1843	The fortunate and unfortunate lovers/New Arabian tale	anon.

[1]As given on title page: Robert Greene (or a variant); Hugh Stanhope; or anonymous.

[2]As given on title page.

[3]As entered in, successively, *Short-Title Catalogue*, Wing, *English Short-Title Catalogue* on CD-ROM, and *Nineteenth-Century Short-Title Catalogue*; or in holdings catalogues for the Folger Shakespeare Library, the Harding Collection at the Bodleian, Houghton Library at Harvard, the Lauriston Castle Collection at the National Library of Scotland, or the Newberry Library, Chicago.

Publisher[2]	Reference[3]	Library	Format	Collation
T. Orwin for T. Cadman	12285	British	4o	A-G4/56p
[R. Field] for J. B[rome]	12286	Folger Shakespeare	4o	A-G4
[V. Simmes] for J. B[rome]	12287	Huntington	4o	A-G4/56p
[R. Bradock] for J. B[rome]	12287.5	Biblioteka Gdanska	4o	A-G4
[T. Purfoot] for G. Potter	12288	Bodleian; Houghton	4o	A-G4/56p
W. Stansby for G. Potter	12288.5	Folger	4o	A-G4
T. C[reede] for G. Potter, sold J. Tap	12289	British	4o	A-G4/56p
E. All-de for G. P[otter], sold by J. Tap	12289.5	Huntington	4o	A-G4/56p
T. P[urfoot] for F. Faulkener	12290	Bodleian	4o	A-G4
T. P[urfoot] for F. Faulkner	12291	British	4o	A-G4/56p
T. P[urfoot] f. F. Faulkner	12291.5	Folger	4o	A-G4
[E. Purslowe] f. F. Faulkner	12292	British; Folger	4o	A-G4/56p
?	12292.5	Folger	4o	A?-G4
For F. Faulkner	G1833	British; Folger	4o	53p
For Edward Blackmore	G1834	Trinity College, Cambridge	4o	
R. Ibbitson, J. Wright, W. Thackery	G1835	Trinity College, Cambridge	4o	
For J. Wright, sold by J. Clarke	G1836	British	4o	54p
For C. Dennison	G1827bA	Magdalene College, Cambridge	12mo	2+20p
By H. Brugis for Clarke, Thackery, Passinger	G1836A	Folger	4o	A-G4/56p
For G. Conyers	G1837	British, Magdalene	4o	56p
By J.W. for G. Conyers	G1838	Bodleian	4o	
For G. Conyers	G1832	British; Folger; Newberry	8o	A-E8/78p
W. O[nley]. for G. C[onyers]	G1838A	Folger	8o	96p
By W[m]. O[nley].	G1832A	Newberry	8o	
For J. Blare	G1827A	Folger	8o	A-B4/16p
By W. O[nley] for G. Conyers	ESTC	British, NLS; Houghton	8o	48p
For G. Conyers	ESTC	Bodleian	8o	2+78p
For E. Midwinter	ESTC	Clark, UCLA	12mo	138p
For A. Bettesworth, C. Hitch	ESTC	British; Folger, Lilly	12mo	A-G6
For Woodgate and Brookes	ESTC	British; NLS	12mo	4+116
For Woodgate and Brookes	Folger	Folger	24mo	A-E12
Newcastle: John White	Harding	Bodleian	8o	16p
Aldermary, London	Harding	Bodleian	long 12mo	24p
Aldermary/Bow Lane, Londou [sic]	ESTC	National of Scotland	12mo	24p
Printed and sold in London	ESTC	Bodleian	12mo	24p
Bow church yard	Houghton	Houghton	12mo	24p
Dublin: William Jones	ESTC	British	18mo	180p
J. White/Charles-river bridge	ESTC	Boston Public	18mo	24p
Stirling/C. Randall	Houghton	Houghton	12mo	24p
The booksellers	ESTC	National of Ireland	18mo	143+1p
Glasgow: J. and M. Robertson	Lauriston	National of Scotland	12mo	24p
Edinburgh: J. Morren	Harding	Bodleian	12mo	24p
London	19STC	British	12mo	146p
Darlington: W. Appleton	Newberry	Newberry	12mo	24p
Belfast	19STC	British	12mo	47p

APPENDIX B: *Pandosto* Verse Versions

Date	Short Title	Author[1]	Publisher[2]
1595	The Fissher-mans Tale	Sabie, Francis	London: R. Johnes
1595	Flora's Fortune	Sabie, Francis	London: R. Johnes
1663?	The jealous Duke, and the injur'd Dutchess[4]	Jordan, Thomas	London: by R.W[ood] for Elizabeth Andrews
1663?	The jealous Duke [in Royal Arbour of Loyal Poesie]	Jordan, Thomas	London: E. Andrews
1672	Fortunes Tennis-ball	S.S.	London: A. P[urslowe] for Th. Vere
1688	Fortunes Tennis-ball	S.S.	London: A. M. for J. Deacon
1705?	The most excellent history of Dorastus and Fawnia	anon.	Edinburgh?
1750?	The royal courtly garland/how a King	anon.	London
1750?	The royal courtly garland/joy after sorrow	anon.	Aldermary
1760?	The royal courtly garland/joy after sorrow	anon.	Bow-church-yard
1765?	The royal courtly garland/how a King	anon.	Coventry?
1770?	The royal courtly garland, in 6 parts	anon.	Newcastle?
1775?	The royal courtly garland, in 6 parts	anon.	Newcastle
1775?	The royal courtly garland/joy after sorrow	anon.	Tewkesbury, Gloucester, Cheltenham
l/e 1792	The royal courtly garland/joy after/6 parts	anon.	Glasgow?
1800?	The royal courtly garland, in 6 parts	anon.	London?
1800?	The royal courtly garland/joy after sorrow	anon.	?
1800?	The royal courtly garland/joy after sorrow	anon.	?

[1]As given on title page.

[2]As given on title page.

[3]As entered in, successively, *Short-Title Catalogue*, Wing, *English Short-Title Catalogue* on CD-ROM, or holdings catalogues of the Newberry Library, Chicago.

[4]In *A Royal Arbor of Loyal Poesie*.

[5]Out of 8+80+72 in volume.

Library	Format	Collation
British	4o	
British	4o	
British	8o	5p[5]
	8o	5p
Huntington	8o	24p
Bodleian	8o	24p
National of Scotland	8o	18p
Cambridge	1/2mo?/oblong	1sheet
Bodleian; Houghton	1/2mo?/oblong	1sheet
Houghton	1/2mo.	1sheet
British	16mo.	8p
British; Folger	12mo.	8p
British	12mo.	8p
British, NLS; Huntington	12mo.	8p
Glasgow University	8o	8p
British	16mo.	8p
British	12mo.	8p
Newberry		8p

NOTES

Introduction

1. This book thus complements Adrian Johns's *The Nature of the Book: Print and Knowledge in the Making* (Chicago: University of Chicago Press, 1998), which maintains that "the very identity of print itself has had to be *made*" (2). Johns traces print's changing epistemological force in a wide array of scientific, philosophical, and literary texts of the late seventeenth and eighteenth centuries.

2. Fredric Jameson, "Magical Narratives: Romance as Genre," *New Literary History* 7 (1975): 161. Also see Michael McKeon, *The Origins of the Novel 1600–1740* (Baltimore: Johns Hopkins University Press, 1987), 2–4, 19. For Jameson and McKeon, the persistence of romance in popular genres is anomalous because romance carries feudal ideologies irrelevant to later cultures, but I contend that *Pandosto*'s ideological significance is continually transformed by its later uses, not fixed at the work's origin. The critique of popular romance "wish fulfillment" is engaged fully in chapter 4.

3. Margaret Spufford, *Small Books and Pleasant Histories: Popular Fiction and Its Readership in Seventeenth-Century England* (Athens: University of Georgia Press, 1982), identifies "histories" as the term used by booksellers in the 1680s to denominate longer books in quarto (twenty-four-page quartos were "double-books," while smaller formats were "small merry books" or "small godly books") (93, 96, 262–67). The common phrase "pleasant histories" suggests that works in this format were predominantly entertaining narratives, more or less fictional, but the category is one of price, not genre.

4. In 1587, Stationers' Company regulations set a maximum of 1,250–1,500 copies per setting of type. After 1635, the maximum edition size was raised to 1,500–2,000. After the Restoration, no maximum was enforced, but through the eighteenth century, high paper costs encouraged publishers to keep editions small for

all but the most proven genres and titles. See Richard Altick, *The English Common Reader* (Chicago: University of Chicago Press, 1957), 19–22. Chapbook publishers might, of course, have disregarded these limits even earlier. On book sharing, see Spufford 110; Tessa Watt, *Cheap Print and Popular Piety, 1550–1640* (Cambridge: Cambridge University Press, 1991), 7.

5. In Mish's list, it ranks third overall (after Aesop's *Fables* and Bunyan's *Pilgrim's Progress*), and first among nondidactic works. Charles Mish, "Best Sellers in Seventeenth-Century Fiction," *Publications of the Bibliographical Society of America* 47 (1953): 360. A better term than "best seller" might be "steady seller," used by David D. Hall to denote devotional works that were perennials in the early American press, unnoticed critically but vividly remembered by individual readers. See "The Uses of Literacy in New England, 1600–1850," in *Cultures of Print: Essays in the History of the Book* (Amherst: University of Massachusetts Press, 1996), 61–64.

6. These lost editions may include a possible first edition of circa 1585 (see chapter 1) and reissues by large-scale publishers in the eighteenth and nineteenth centuries (see chapter 3 and epilogue).

7. Mish, for example, sees the taste of seventeenth-century readers for older works as "somewhat retarded culturally" ("Best Sellers" 361), even though his method of counting editions is bound to favor older works. He says that the persistent older romances make up a "subliterary tradition" (373).

8. Spufford differs in presenting a careful analysis of Autolycus's wares (116–17).

9. William Shakespeare, *The Winter's Tale*, Arden edition, ed. J.H.P. Pafford (New York: Routledge, 1963), 4.3.26 and 4.4.261–62. In their literal context, Autolycus's "unconsidered trifles" are stolen linens, not ballads.

10. Paul Salzman, ed., *An Anthology of Elizabethan Prose Fiction* (New York: Oxford University Press, 1987), 169. Further references to Salzman's edition of *Pandosto* will be cited parenthetically as Salzman, *Elizabethan*.

11. On the resonance of the lost child theme with early modern family anxieties, especially as they play out in *The Winter's Tale*, see Frances E. Dolan, *Dangerous Familiars: Representations of Domestic Crime in England, 1550–1700* (Ithaca, NY: Cornell University Press, 1994), 121–70.

12. Stanley Wells, *Shakespeare: A Life in Drama* (New York: Norton, 1995), 338–39. Further editions cited as Wells, *Shakespeare*. An earlier version of this account is Wells's important essay, "Shakespeare and Romance" in *Later Shakespeare*, Stratford-Upon-Avon Studies 8 (New York: St. Martin's Press, 1967), 64. Wells's dissertation, *"Perymedes the Blacksmith" and "Pandosto" by Robert Greene: A Critical Edition* (1962; reprint, New York: Garland, 1988), has been a constant resource for this study.

13. Wells goes on to comment, "Probably [*Pandosto*] owed its popularity to its presentation of basic human situations in an undemanding manner, and it may well be this very quality that recommended it to Shakespeare as the basis for a play": curiously, what is "undemanding" in Greene becomes universal in Shakespeare (*Shakespeare* 339).

14. Gerard Genette, *Paratexts: Thresholds of Interpretation*, trans. Jane E. Lewin (Cambridge: Cambridge University Press, 1987), 1.

15. Ibid., 2. Genette's model thus embraces both the materiality (printing, graphic qualities, and authorial presentation) fundamental to book history and the concern with the context of interpretation that motivates the reception theories of Hans Robert Jauss and Wolfgang Iser. Genette's taxonomy of the paratext assumes that the text itself remains stable, an assumption that does not hold for early modern texts or for much-adapted popular publications. Therefore, I have adopted his vocabulary only loosely in this book.

16. Most of the evidence for Elizabethan nonelite women as readers of romance was assembled by Louis B. Wright in *Middle-class Culture in Elizabethan England* (Chapel Hill: University of North Carolina Press, 1935), 103–18; also see Caroline Lucas, *Writing for Women: The Example of Woman as Reader in Elizabethan Romance* (Milton Keynes: Open University Press, 1989), 14–18. Suzanne W. Hull assembles evidence from title pages and dedications in *Chaste, Silent & Obedient: English Books for Women, 1475–1640* (San Marino, CA: Huntington Library, 1982). Recent critical work continues to explore the association between romance and women readers or auditors, including Paul Salzman, *English Prose Fiction, 1558–1700* (Oxford: Clarendon Press, 1985); Helen Hackett, " 'Yet Tell Me Some Such Fiction': Lady Mary Wroth's *Urania* and the 'Femininity' of Romance," in *Women, Texts and Histories 1575–1760*, eds. Clare Brant and Diane Purkiss (New York: Routledge, 1992), 39–68; Constance C. Relihan, *Fashioning Authority: The Development of Elizabethan Novelistic Discourse* (Kent, OH: Kent State University Press, 1994); Constance C. Relihan, ed., *Framing Elizabethan Fictions* (Kent, OH: Kent State University Press, 1996); Jacqueline Pearson, "Women Reading, Reading Women," in *Women and Literature in Britain, 1500–1700* (Cambridge: Cambridge University Press, 1996), 80–99; and Jacqueline Pearson, *Women's Reading in Britain, 1750–1835* (Cambridge: Cambridge University Press, 1999). Helen Hackett's *Women and Romance Fiction in the English Renaissance* (Cambridge: Cambridge University Press, 2000) engages repeatedly with my concerns; I regret that it appeared only as this book went to press.

17. This argument contests Pierre Bourdieu's sweeping claim that working-class culture is defined by a "taste for the necessary" in *Distinction: A Social Critique of the Judgement of Taste*, trans. Richard Nice (Cambridge: Harvard University Press, 1984), 178. The choices among goods available to the nonelite may resist detection by elite analysts to whom the entire range appears unthinkable. An influential interrogation of that problem is Janice A. Radway's landmark *Reading the Romance: Women, Patriarchy, and Popular Literature* (Chapel Hill: University of North Carolina Press, 1984).

18. Bourdieu addresses the seventeenth-century rise of taste-monitoring institutions on 277 and 588*n*2.

19. Bourdieu seems to regard distinction as characteristic of modern cultures, and refers to it in passing as having "gone on unceasingly, from the seventeenth century to the present day" (2). Presumably he links the beginning of distinction to the rise of classical aesthetic theory. I do not assume that distinction originated in the early modern period, but certainly habits of social differentiation through cultural consumption became more urgent and more elaborated as the rise of mercantile wealth and the spread of print quickened the pace of change.

20. My book concentrates on the expansion of print rather than the growth of literacy because the latter is notoriously hard to measure, while the former is amply evident. On the expansion of the book trade during Elizabeth's reign, see H. S. Bennett, *English Books and Readers 1558–1603* (Cambridge: Cambridge University Press, 1965), 269–71. Also obvious are the explosion of unregulated printing during the Interregnum and the ever-growing numbers of presses operating in London and provincial towns after 1660. As for literacy, Spufford argues that the scale of chapbook publication after 1660, as well as autobiographical evidence left by nonelite readers, supports estimates of basic literacy rates substantially higher than David Cressy's, based solely on the ability to sign (19–37; cf. David Cressy, *Literacy and the Social Order* [Cambridge: Cambridge University Press, 1980]). Spufford is interested in those with only primary instruction in reading (and not instruction in writing, which was rarer), whom she sees as the target audience for the cheapest chapbooks. Work on women's literacy is valuable in thinking about the practices of those who could read but not sign; see, for example, Pearson. Obviously, rising literacy rates cannot be extrapolated directly from rising book production. For one thing, it seems that among the well-off, book ownership per capita rose strikingly during the seventeenth century. Furthermore, literacy rates varied tremendously throughout the period of this study, not just by class but also by region, occupation, and gender.

21. Romance was conventionally justified as both pleasurable and profitable. Without discounting practices of reading romances as exemplary, this study focuses on the debate over pleasure-reading that was fundamental to objections to the spread of romance.

22. The shape of my argument requires that I use the terms "elite" and "popular" while I argue for their constructedness. Bourdieu's work does not reduce the dynamics of distinction to only two poles, but recognizes a more complex system of differentiation in twentieth-century culture. I use these terms to denominate positions in cultural evaluation rather than reductive social categories, and my treatments of individual authors recognize their unique positions and audiences. The phrase "writers for the elite" acknowledges that writers who expressed elite tastes were often themselves in precarious socioeconomic positions. By the nineteenth century, the differentiation of literary and scholarly spheres makes "the elite" a less useful term. On this point, see Jonathan Brody Kramnick, *Making the English Canon: Print-Capitalism and the Cultural Past, 1700–1770* (Cambridge: Cambridge University Press, 1998), and Trevor Ross, *The Making of the English Literary Canon* (Montreal: McGill-Queen's University Press, 1998).

23. Important landmarks in editorial revisionism include Donald F. McKenzie, *Bibliography and the Sociology of Texts*, The Panizzi Lectures, 1985 (London: British Library, 1986); Margreta de Grazia and Peter Stallybrass, "The Materiality of the Shakespearean Text," *Shakespeare Quarterly* 44 (1987): 255–83; Randall McLeod, "The very names of the Persons: Editing and the Invention of Dramatick Character" in *Staging the Renaissance: Essays on Elizabethan and Jacobean Bibliography*, ed. David Scott Kastan and Peter Stallybrass (New York: Routledge, 1991), 88–96; Stephen Orgel, "What Is a Text?," in *Staging the Renaissance*, 83–87; and Andrew Murphy, ed., *The Renaissance Text: Theory, Editing, Textuality* (Manchester: Manchester University Press, 2000).

Scholarship has been particularly rich on English print's relationship to manuscript, as in Arthur Marotti's *Manuscript, Print, and the English Renaissance Lyric* (Ithaca: Cornell University Press, 1995); W. H. Woudhuysen's *Sir Philip Sidney and the Circulation of Manuscripts, 1558–1640* (Oxford: Clarendon Press, 1996); Harold Love's *Scribal Publication in Seventeenth-Century England* (Oxford: Clarendon Press, 1993); and Margaret Ezell's *Social Authorship and the Advent of Print* (Baltimore: The Johns Hopkins University Press, 1999); and to gender and sexuality, as in Wendy Wall, *The Imprint of Gender: Authorship and Publication in the English Renaissance* (Ithaca: Cornell University Press, 1993); Jeffrey Masten's *Textual Intercourse: Collaboration, Authorship, and Sexualities in Renaissance Drama* (Cambridge: Cambridge University Press, 1997); and Margreta de Grazia, "Imprints: Shakespeare, Gutenberg and Descartes" in *Alternative Shakespeares 2*, ed. Terence Hawkes (New York: Routledge, 1996), 63–94.

24. Recent books by literary scholars that address popular texts include Dolan's *Dangerous Familiars*; Nigel Wheale's *Writing and Society: Literacy, Print and Politics in Britain 1590–1660* (New York: Routledge, 2000); and Mark Thornton Burnett, *Masters and Servants in English Renaissance Drama and Culture* (New York: St. Martin's, 1997). Also see Burnett's "Popular Culture in the English Renaissance," in *Writing and the English Renaissance*, eds. William Zunder and Suzanne Trill (London: Longman, 1996), 106–22; Naomi C. Liebler, "Elizabethan Pulp Fiction: The Example of Richard Johnson," *Critical Survey* 12 (2) (2000): 71–87; Garrett Sullivan and Linda Woodbridge, "Popular Culure in Print," in *The Cambridge Companion to English Renaissance Literature, 1500–1600*, ed. Arthur F. Kinney (Cambridge: Cambridge University Press, 2000), 265–86. The research of Victor Neuburg, Roger Thompson, and Pat Rogers on chapbooks, particularly in the eighteenth century, is cited in chapter 3. John Simons holds that these "little paper objects" convey a wide "range of literate experiences" and "affective value"; see *Guy of Warwick and Other Chapbook Romances: Six Tales from the Popular Literature of Pre-Industrial England* (Exeter: University of Exeter Press, 1998), 2. For historians' accounts, see Tim Harris, ed., *Popular Culture in England, c. 1500–1850* (New York: St. Martin's, 1995), and Barry Reay, ed., *Popular Culture in Seventeenth-Century England* (London: Croom Helm, 1985); for folklorists', Cathy Lynn Preston and Michael J. Preston, eds., *The Other Print Tradition: Essays on Chapbooks, Broadsides, and Related Ephemera* (New York: Garland, 1995).

25. Elite writers refer more often to chivalric romances than to *Pandosto*, which may have found its audience increasingly among women, who were less likely to publish accounts of their youthful reading. However, I am cautious about claiming *Pandosto* as a text for women, given the slipperiness of generic sorting within the romance field and the ideological force of period claims about gendered readership. Many women have signed copies of *Pandosto*, but I am not aware of any early woman writer who recalls reading it as a child. It is not mentioned by the first Englishwoman to claim romance as a female tradition, Clara Reeve, in *The Progress of Romance* (London, 1785). Charlotte Lennox's comparison of *Pandosto* to *The Winter's Tale* in *Shakespear Illustrated* (London, 1753–54) does not indicate when she first encountered the story (see chapter 3), and it is not mentioned in her *Female Quixote* (1752).

26. That popular literature should be defined to include high-ranking readers has been a point of consensus among recent historians of early modern popular culture. Daniel Cohen acutely describes his early American popular audience as the "extensive, in some cases massive, audience of readers, not necessarily confined to (although generally not excluding) the wealthy, the classically educated, or the professionally trained," but "undoubtedly" including "children, servants, farmers, apprentices, artisans, mechanics, and housewives." See Cohen, *Pillars of Salt, Monuments of Grace: New England Crime Literature and the Origins of American Popular Culture, 1674–1800* (Oxford: Oxford University Press, 1993), ix. Although the early modern English reading audience is not "massive," Cohen's model of popular readership as "extensive" and diverse seems useful.

27. The phrase alludes to Chartier's *The Cultural Uses of Print in Early Modern France*, trans. Lydia G. Cochrane (Princeton: Princeton University Press, 1987). Also see Roger Chartier, *The Order of Books: Readers, Authors, and Libraries in Europe Between the Fourteenth and Eighteenth Centuries*, trans. Lydia G. Cochrane (Stanford: Stanford University Press, 1994); and Roger Chartier, ed., *The Culture of Print: Power and the Uses of Print in Early Modern Europe*, trans. Lydia G. Cochrane (Princeton: Princeton University Press, 1989), especially "The Hanged Woman Miraculously Saved: An *occasionnel*," 59–91. On England, see James Raven, Helen Small, and Naomi Tadmor, eds., *The Practice and Representation of Reading in England* (Cambridge: Cambridge University Press, 1996); Eamon Duffy, "The Godly and the Multitude in Stuart England," *The Seventeenth Century* 1 (1986): 31–55.

28. Roger Chartier, "Popular Appropriations: The Readers and Their Books," in *Forms and Meanings: Texts, Performances, and Audiences from Codex to Computer* (Philadelphia: University of Pennsylvania Press, 1995), 94. Further references will be cited parenthetically as Chartier, "Popular."

29. Chartier draws this opposition from D. F. McKenzie; see "Popular," 275.

30. Roger Chartier, "Reading Matter and 'Popular' Reading," in *A History of Reading in the West*, eds. Gugliemo Cavallo and Roger Chartier, trans. Lydia G. Cochrane (Amherst: University of Massachusetts Press, 1999). Further references will be cited parenthetically as Chartier, "Reading." For example, Chartier argues that peasant literacy's "decontextualization of fragments" may be comparable to the elite practice of extracting aphorisms in commonplace books rather than an exclusively popular way of reading ("Reading," 282). Scott C. Shershow, *Puppets and "Popular" Culture* (Ithaca, NY: Cornell University Press, 1995), makes a fascinating and theoretically sophisticated case for treating the category of the popular with the suspicion signaled by his quotation marks around the word.

31. Chartier, "Reading," 283. As an example, he holds up Lisa Jardine and Anthony Grafton's " 'Studied for Action': How Gabriel Harvey read his Livy," *Past and Present* 129 (Nov. 1990): 30–78.

32. Peter Burke, *Popular Culture in Early Modern Europe* (New York: Harper Torchbooks, Harper & Row, 1978).

33. "Axiologies" invokes Barbara Herrnstein Smith's *Contingencies of Value* (Cambridge, MA: Harvard University Press, 1988). Smith's searching interrogation of the violence done when socially contingent hierarchies of value are naturalized is fundamental to this project.

34. Among serious scholars of Elizabethan prose fiction, *Pandosto*'s critical standing is high, but it is also the link to *The Winter's Tale* that keeps this romance in frequent scholarly republication (in fiction anthologies and with the play). *Pandosto* was mounted and enthusiastically received during the new Globe's opening season in 1997, in a single staged reading at the Globe's Education Centre associated with the mainstage production of *The Winter's Tale*. Greene's goddess Fortune was smiling when this production was scheduled during my fleeting visit to London in July 1997. I thank Rosemary Linnell of the Globe Education Centre for giving me a copy of her ingenious script.

35. In some critical statements, this romance tradition is derived from the Continental Renaissance; in others, from a formal or religious archetype. For archetypal Shakespearean romance, see two seminal essays, G. Wilson Knight, "Great Creating Nature" (1947) and Northrop Frye, "Recognition in *The Winter's Tale*" (1963). Both are reprinted in *Shakespeare: "The Winter's Tale": A Casebook*, ed. Kenneth Muir (1969; reprint, Nashville, TN: Aurora, 1970), 136–50 and 184–97. The best articulation of the genre is still Wells, "Shakespeare and Romance," although Stephen Orgel's introductions to *The Tempest* and *The Winter's Tale* for Oxford, The World's Classics, are suggestive. Some critics now propose treating the late plays as tragicomedies, a generic name that was current in the period. Several essays in Nancy Klein Maguire, ed., *Renaissance Tragicomedy: Explorations in Genre and Politics* (New York: AMS Press, 1987), usefully discuss the late plays in relation to Guarinian and Fletcherian tragicomedy.

36. Diana E. Henderson and James Siemon, in "Reading Vernacular Literature," in *A Companion to Shakespeare*, ed. David Scott Kastan (Oxford: Blackwell, 1999), 206–20, recently proposed a historicized intertextuality as an approach to early modern romance. They urge that "we emphasize connections, rather than differences, between Shakespeare's writing and the literary landscape of his day," avoiding "easy categorization of 'high' or 'popular' culture" (207). If, for instance, we dismiss chivalric romances as an "outmoded fad," we will be blind to their cultural centrality and thus "miss the extent to which those works we *have* canonized would have been perceived as part of this romance phenomenon, valued less for their individuated authorial perspectives than for their fulfillment and play with generic expectations" (217).

37. Gary Taylor, *Reinventing Shakespeare: A Cultural History from the Restoration to the Present* (New York: Oxford University Press, 1989); Margreta de Grazia, *Shakespeare Verbatim: The Reproduction of Authenticity and the 1790 Apparatus* (Oxford: Clarendon Press, 1991); Jonathan Bate, *The Genius of Shakespeare* (New York: Oxford University Press, 1998). Also see Jean I. Marsden, ed., *The Appropriation of Shakespeare: Post-Renaissance Reconstructions of the Work and the Myth* (New York: St. Martin's Press, 1991).

38. Michael Dobson, *The Making of the National Poet: Shakespeare, Adaptation and Authorship, 1660–1769* (Oxford: Clarendon Press, 1992); Jean I. Marsden, *The Re-Imagined Text: Shakespeare, Adaptation, and Eighteenth-Century Literary Theory* (Lexington: University Press of Kentucky, 1995); Paulina Kewes, *Adaptation and Authorship: Writing for the Stage in England, 1660–1710* (Oxford, Clarendon Press, 1998).

Because I am treating all published texts as commodities, I have coined the term "re-commodification" for a text significantly reshaped by publishers for a new audience, appealing to new systems of value. Retitling and condensation are two types of re-commodification that are especially important to the later history of *Pandosto*, and will be discussed in chapter 3.

39. Michael McKeon, *The Origins of the English Novel, 1600–1740* (Baltimore: The Johns Hopkins University Press, 1987); J. Paul Hunter, *Before Novels: The Cultural Contexts of Eighteenth-Century English Fiction* (New York: Norton, 1990); and William B. Warner, *Licensing Entertainment: The Elevation of Novel Reading in Britain, 1684–1750* (Berkeley: University of California Press, 1998).

40. Margaret Anne Doody, *A Natural Passion: A Study of the Novels of Samuel Richardson* (Oxford: Clarendon Press, 1974), 33–34.

41. Lorna Hutson, *The Usurer's Daughter: Male Friendship and Fictions of Women in Sixteenth-Century England* (London: Routledge, 1994). Also see Donald Beecher, ed., *Critical Approaches to Renaissance Prose Fiction, 1520–1640* (Ottawa: Dovehouse Editions, 1998).

1. *"Growne so ordinarie": Producing Robert Greene's* Pandosto *and Sir Philip Sidney's* Arcadia, 1585–92

1. Alexander B. Grosart, ed., *The Life and Complete Works in Prose and Verse of Robert Greene*, 12 vols. (London: 1881–83), 12:172–73. Further references to Greene's works in Grosart's edition will be cited parenthetically as Grosart.

2. Pierre Bourdieu, "The Field of Cultural Production," *Poetics* 12 (1983): 341.

3. Arundell Esdaile, *A List of English Tales and Prose Romances Printed Before 1740* (London: Bibliographical Society, 1912), xix.

4. John Clark Jordan, *Robert Greene* (New York: Oxford University Press, 1915), 19.

5. Paul Salzman, *English Prose Fiction 1558–1700* (Oxford: Clarendon Press, 1985), 61. Further references will be cited parenthetically as Salzman, *English Prose Fiction*.

6. In his 1961 critical edition of *Pandosto*, the lengthiest appraisal of its importance before this book, Stanley Wells offered the following explanation of its success: "Drawing, consciously or not, on many different literary traditions, and bringing together in one work a variety of popular motifs, Greene *provides* his readers with, if not true imaginative stimulation, at any rate the raw material of day-dream and romance" (*"Perymedes the Blacksmith" and "Pandosto" by Robert Greene. A Critical Edition* [1961; New York: Garland, 1988], lxxxv, emphasis added).

7. Louis Wright comments that Greene *"naturally* took advantage of the great demand for romantic stories" and the taste for "sugary talk of love" in an "idealized

Arcadian world" (*Middle-class Culture in Elizabethan England* [Chapel Hill: University of North Carolina Press, 1935], 384–85, emphasis added). Samuel Lee Wolff assumes that Greene wrote in the *novelle* form because "its emphasis on what happened, its want of profound characterization, its want of complication in plot, . . . made a broad popular appeal" (*The Greek Romances in Elizabethan Prose Fiction* [New York: Columbia University Press, 1912], 370).

8. Charles W. Crupi remarks that "the Greene of tradition is calculating in seducing his readers but careless in managing his art," a myth that "interfere[s] with taking the works seriously," but then blames this "denigration" on "Greene's career as a popular writer" (*Robert Greene* [Boston: G. K. Hall, 1986], 143). Brenda Cantar usefully treats even the view of Greene as a "popular writer" as constructed by tradition, since it was other pamphleteers who forged his "reputation as a derivative hack—slaving away in an Elizabethan Grub Street garret, churning out pamphlets to meet a rising demand for the printed word, and his own need of money" ("Introduction," *Menaphon*, by Robert Greene [Ottawa: Dovehouse Editions, 1996], 20). Sandra Clark points out that the scholarly image of Greene has been shaped largely by the testimony of Gabriel Harvey, which he himself admitted was "hearsay" (*The Elizabethan Pamphleteers: Popular Moralistic Pamphlets 1580–1640* [Rutherford, NJ: Fairleigh Dickinson University Press, 1983], 47).

9. The number is approximate because bibliographers differ on how to count some multipart items. It is also debatable how many of these works should be treated as fiction. Since fiction is my subject, I pay little attention to a few items, such as translations and topical pamphlets, that are not narrative; but I do include Greene's final works, in which fiction and autobiography become indistinguishable. Also omitted from this count, and my analysis, are the plays, which were not published in Greene's lifetime.

10. Walter Davis, *Idea and Act in Elizabethan Fiction* (Princeton: Princeton University Press, 1969), 139.

11. Alexander B. Grosart, ed., *The Works of Gabriel Harvey*, 3 vols. (1884–85; reprint, New York: AMS Press, 1996), 1:162.

12. This list does not include reading because I consider that activity under the topic of reproduction (see chapter 4). Most producers of *Pandosto* of course also read it and re-produced it in their own experience; but not every reader left textual traces, and it is those marks that constitute production. This chapter reconstructs some signals that might have shaped those unrecorded early reproductions.

13. See, for example, Arthur F. Marotti, *Manuscript, Print, and the English Renaissance Lyric* (Ithaca: Cornell University Press, 1995); Jeffrey Masten, *Textual Intercourse: Collaboration, Authorship, and Sexualities in Renaissance Drama* (Cambridge: Cambridge University Press, 1997); Richard C. Newton, "Jonson and the (Re)-invention of the Book," in *Classic and Cavalier: Essays on Jonson and the Sons of Ben*, eds. Claude J. Summers and Ted-Larry Pebworth (Pittsburgh: University of Pittsburgh Press, 1982), 31–55; Kevin Pask, *The Emergence of the English Author* (Cambridge: Cambridge University Press, 1996); and Wendy Wall, *The Imprint of Gender: Authorship and Publication*

in the English Renaissance (Ithaca: Cornell University Press, 1993). A rare study of a popular author is historian Bernard Capp's *The World of John Taylor the Water-Poet* (Oxford: Clarendon Press, 1994).

14. Saunders quotes the scholar Gabriel Harvey's horror at being "reckonid in the Baccheroule of Inglish Rimers" in "The Stigma of Print: A Study in the Social Bases of Tudor Poetry" (*Essays in Criticism* 1 [1951]: 155). As I will show, Harvey knew more about writing for pay than he admitted. Also see Stephen W. May, "Tudor Aristocrats and the Mythical 'Stigma of Print.' " *Renaissance Papers* 1980 [1981]: 11–18; and Wall.

15. Alexandra Halasz, *The Marketplace of Print: Pamphlets and the Public Sphere in Early Modern England* (Cambridge: Cambridge University Press, 1997), 7. Also see Cedric C. Brown, ed., *Patronage, Politics, and Literary Traditions in England, 1558–1658* (Detroit, MI: Wayne State University Press, 1991).

16. H. R. Woudhuysen, *Sir Philip Sidney and the Circulation of Manuscripts, 1558–1640* (Oxford: Clarendon Press, 1996), 8.

17. Tarlton had just died in 1588. For the use of Tarlton's name in jestbooks (most now lost) during his lifetime, and for the posthumous use of his image on alehouse signs, see Alan and Veronica Palmer, *Who's Who in Shakespeare's England* (New York: St. Martin's, 1981), 248. Harvey obsessively associated Greene with Tarlton's clowning authorship, and echoed a common expression when he said that Greene had died and "gone to Tarleton" (Grosart 1:167).

18. The authorial possessive was more common in titles to books of practical instruction, writers of which were assumed to have some prior authority.

19. See *The Elizabethan Prodigals* (Berkeley: University of California Press, 1984), 79–104. For writers unable to find clerical or court appointments, Helgerson argues, the narrative of the prodigal son became a way of imagining their return to ideals of service to God and nation. There is no record of Greene pursuing any career other than writing, although he did exploit his connections to the court, at the universities, and in the law courts early in his career.

20. Their findings tangle psychological interpretation with problems in dating the pamphlets (see ibid., 99; Crupi 14–16).

21. Marlowe's personal life may have inspired Greene, but again furnished no textual precedent.

22. Grosart, ed., *The Works of Gabriel Harvey*, 1:168–69, emphasis added. Alexandra Halasz uses this passage to show how Harvey "creates the biography of Greene as a degraded author" (105).

23. I use masculine pronouns because my instances are male; early modern woman writers faced distinct challenges in both position and disposition.

24. Much of that work has already been done in Sidney's case by recent studies of his reputation. See Woudhuysen, *Sir Philip Sidney*; Dennis Kay, "Introduction," in *Sir Philip Sidney: An Anthology of Modern Criticism*, ed. Dennis Kay (Oxford: Oxford University Press, 1987), 3–41; Martin Garrett, *Sidney: The Critical Heritage* (New York:

Routledge, 1996). Also see Alan Hager, "The Exemplary Mirage," reprinted in Kay (45–60); and Pask, 53–82.

25. The *New Arcadia* has some generic features, such as its epic scale, that signal Sidney's effort to re-position the work as a weightier romance than the *Old Arcadia*.

26. Around 1600, a fad for poetic anthologies brought lines from the two authors side by side (in *England's Parnassus*, *England's Helicon*, *Bel-vedere*).

27. From *Foure Letters and certaine Sonnets: Especially touching Robert Greene, and other parties, by him abused* (1592); excerpted in *Elizabethan Critical Essays*, ed. G. Gregory Smith, 2 vols. (London: Oxford University Press, 1904), 2:231.

28. See Peter Lindenbaum, "Sidney's *Arcadia* as Cultural Monument and Proto-Novel," in *Texts and Cultural Change in Early Modern England*, eds. Cedric C. Brown and Arthur F. Marotti (New York: St. Martin's Press, 1997), 91. My thanks to Peter Lindenbaum for sharing this work with me from an early date.

29. Julius Lloyd, *The Life of Sir Philip Sidney* (London: Longman, Green, Longman, Roberts, and Green, 1862), 101.

30. Alan Stewart argues that "on the Continent, . . . Philip Sidney was a name to conjure with, long before his death" in *Sir Philip Sidney: A Double Life* (London: Chatto & Windus, 2000), 6.

31. Gabriel Harvey's phrase was echoed by later defenders of Greene. See *Foure Letters and Certaine Sonnets*, ed. G. B. Harrison (London: John Lane, 1923), 21.

32. In an essay that regrettably appeared after this chapter was written, Derek B. Alwes demonstrates how much can be learned by analyzing Greene's dedications in juxtaposition ("Robert Greene's Duelling Dedications," *English Literary Renaissance* 30 [2000]: 373–95).

33. Robert Greene, *Pandosto* (1588), A2–A2v, emphasis added. There is no evidence that the dedicatee, "the Right Honorable George Clifford Earle of Cumberland" (born in 1558 and always somewhat roisterous) provided any shrouding or patronage, although Greene's reference to "Philip of Macedon," who deigned "to take a bunche of grapes of a country pesant," makes the financial motive clear.

34. Juliet Fleming, "The Ladies' Text," in *Sexuality and Gender in Early Modern Europe*, ed. James Grantham Turner (Cambridge: Cambridge University Press, 1993). Also see Wall, 1–22, for its manifestation in print.

35. These instances are cited and discussed by Katherine Duncan-Jones in "Philip Sidney's Toys," in Kay, ed., *Sir Philip Sidney*, 61–80.

36. Katherine Duncan-Jones synchronizes the *Old Arcadia*'s conception with his sister's pregnancy in *Sir Philip Sidney, Courtier Poet* (New Haven: Yale University Press, 1991), 168.

37. John Buxton, *Elizabethan Taste* (1963; reprint, New Jersey [sic]: Humanities Press, 1983), 255. The academic drama *The Return from Parnassus* (ca. 1600) says it is a "Christmas toy," which means that it aspires to brilliance, but of a more pleasurable than scholarly sort.

38. From Raphael Holinshed, *The Third Volume of Chronicles* (London, 1587); quoted in Garrett 113.

39. P. J. Croft, "Sir John Harington's Manuscript of Sir Philip Sidney's *Arcadia*" in *Literary Autographs*, eds. Stephen Parks and P. J. Croft (Los Angeles: William Andrews Clark Memorial Library, 1983), 46, 67–69.

40. Greene's sequel to *Mamillia*, itself entered in 1583, apologizes for a two-year lapse since the first part (René Pruvost, *Robert Greene et ses romans* [Paris: Publications de la Faculté des Lettres D'Alger, 1938], 100).

41. *Euphues* is quoted from Paul Salzman, ed., *An Anthology of Elizabethan Prose Fiction* (New York: Oxford University Press, 1987), 150. In all, there were fifteen editions of part 1, published by 1617, and four more, combined with the sequel, by 1636. Mish, observing that this "concentrated appeal" evaporated after 1636, decided that *Euphues* had been a passing "literary mode" rather than a "genuinely popular book" like *Pandosto*, with some twenty seventeenth-century editions to Lyly's ten ("Best Sellers in Seventeenth-Century Fiction," *Publications of the Bibliographical Society of America* 47 [1953]: 367).

42. Greene did not invent the strategy; he probably borrowed it from the multi-part *Amadis*, or from controversial tracts. He was not even the first to use the device in an English romance—that was Brian Melbancke, in *Philotimus* (1582). But Melbancke, unlike Greene, never delivered.

43. Brian Melbancke, Greene's classmate at St. John's, had published his own Euphuistic romance, *Philotimus. The Warre betwixt Nature and Fortune*, in 1582. Roger Ward, who published *Philotimus*, may have been the first publisher of *Pandosto*; see discussion in this chapter. Melbancke was a pensioner, not a sizar. Hyder E. Rollins has pointed out that the book is cobbled together, even setting borrowed lines of verse as prose, with results that are far more ungainly than anything Greene wrote ("Notes on Brian Melbanck's [sic] 'Philotimus,' " *Studies in Philology* 1 [1929]: 40–57). Its context is not that of coterie authorship. One possible coterie author was Henry Constable, the only fellow commoner in Greene's class, whose sonnet sequence *Diana* was published in 1592, signed only with his initials.

44. Suzanne W. Hull, *Chaste, Silent, and Obedient* (San Marino, CA: Huntington Library, 1984), 193, 197. A very brief verse romance from 1605 revives this dubious claim: "Rebuke him Madam, who deludes your Toy, / Tis made for Ladies, not for Lordes to see" (184).

45. An Elizabethan female subculture is imagined by stationer Edward Blount, who in 1636 tried unsuccessfully to revive the euphuistic fad that had been so profitable a generation before: "*Euphues* and his *England* began first, that language: All our Ladies were then his Schollers; And that Beautie in Court, which could not Parley Euphueisme, was as little regarded: as which now there, speakes not French" (Esdaile, *A List of English Tales*, xix).

46. Many of these instances were gathered by Louis B. Wright in *Middle-class Culture in Elizabethan England*, 111–13 and "The Reading of Renaissance English

Women," *Studies in Philology* 28 (1931): 139–56. All of Wright's examples are repeated in Caroline Lucas, *Writing for Women: The Example of Woman as Reader in Elizabethan Romance* (Milton Keynes: Open University Press, 1989), 15–16.

47. After Greene's death, an enthusiast used terms that made Lyly's erotic implications completely explicit when he urged the mourning of Greene by

> yee dainty Damsels of renowne,
> That long to dallie, with your loved Lords:
> And you brave Gallant, worthy noble Lords,
> That love to dandle in your Ladies lapps.

Greenes Newes Both from Heaven and Hell . . . and Greenes Funeralls, ed. R. B. McKerrow (1911; reprint, Stratford-upon-Avon: The Shakespeare Head, 1922), 74. Further references will be cited parenthetically as McKerrow, *Greenes Newes*.

48. R. B. McKerrow, ed., *Works of Thomas Nashe*, rev. F. P. Wilson (Oxford: Blackwell, 1958), 3:329. Further references will be cited parenthetically as McKerrow, *Nashe*.

49. Interestingly, when the *Disputation* was retitled *Theeves Falling Out* in the 1610s, Greene's full name was given on the title page. There was also a new illustration, replacing the rabbits with three humans (presumably criminal) arguing over a book (presumably this one). Greene could have been involved in the preparation of the earliest custom illustrations, since there is one (a card-shark rabbit) on *A Notable Discovery of Coosenage*, first published in 1591.

50. By 1590, the date of this epistle, Clifford's sea voyages had made him a hero in some eyes and a buccaneer in others. These exploits began in 1586, too late to be reflected in the *Pandosto* epistle if it was drafted for a 1585 edition. A later witness to Clifford's virtue reports that on one of his voyages, he threatened a "young gallant" who was "reading Orlando Furioso" during morning prayers that he would "cast his book overboard and turn himself out of the ship" (1595 report, quoted in George C. Williamson, *George, Third Earl of Cumberland {1558–1605}: His Life and His Voyages* [Cambridge: Cambridge University Press, 1920], 281). Presumably, this book is Ariosto's romance and not Greene's play, but the incident does not portray Clifford as a likely patron for Greene.

51. Philip Sidney, *An Apology for Poetry*, ed. Forrest G. Robinson (Indianapolis: Bobbs-Merrill, 1970), 5.

52. *Howell His Devises, for his owne exercise, and his Friends pleasure* (London, 1581), quoted in Garrett 95.

53. For a portrait of Sidney as a young patron, see Duncan-Jones, *Sir Philip Sidney*, 229.

54. For other imitative titles, see Pask, 183*n*47.

55. Both Nashe and Harvey may have been employed to correct press. Part 2 of *The Return from Parnassus* (1600?) features Ingenioso, a university wit, negotiating the sale of his pamphlet to John Danter for £2, and being warned never to become a press corrector.

56. Preface to *The Second Part of the French Academie by Peter de la Primaudaye* (2nd ed., 1594), B1^r; quoted in Crupi 150–51*n*44. But then, if authors did indeed hold plagiarism against each other (still an area of critical uncertainty and a sore point for Greene scholars), Bowes would have had ample reason to complain of Greene, who in some of his romances repeated almost as much from the first part of Bowes's translation of the conduct book as he did from his own prior romances.

57. Pruvost takes a 1588 entrance of "the complaint of tyme" in the Stationers' Register to be *Pandosto*, but the revised S.T.C. linked that entry to a tract by John Carpenter. The ever-inventive John Payne Collier did propose a lost first edition of *Pandosto*, on the grounds that the textual errors in the 1588 edition were typical of a reprint (*Shakespeare's Library* [1843; reprint, London: Reeves and Turner, 1875], 4:12–13). In this case his imaginings may have been right.

58. Alexander Rodger, "Roger Ward's Shrewsbury Stock: An Inventory of 1585," *The Library* 5th ser., 13 (1958): 264. This claim was endorsed by Paul Salzman in his 1987 edition of the romance (*Elizabethan*, xxvii).

59. Booksellers made more profit on books they had printed or published than on those they bought wholesale from other stationers.

60. On 4 October 1591 *Endymion* and *Midas* were entered to her, Gabriel Cawood assigned his copy for *Gallathea*, and all three were printed within a year "for the widdowe Broome." Brome was not given copies in Lyly and Greene because they were suitable for a woman but because they were expected to sell. However, Cawood did not give up his still-profitable hold on the two parts of *Euphues*.

61. This edition, now in Gdansk, is listed in volume 3 of the revised S.T.C.

62. E. H. Miller, *The Professional Writer in Elizabethan England* (Cambridge: Harvard University Press, 1959), 153. *Greenes Mourning Garment* and *Philomela* were also entered to Wolfe but apparently first published by others.

63. Ibid., 155. Miller uses Greene as his prototypical hack but surmises that *Quip* might have been sold for as much as £5, assuming a very strong bargaining position. For an update, see Peter W. M. Blayney, "The Publication of Playbooks," in *A New History of Early English Drama*, eds. John D. Cox and David Scott Kastan (New York: Columbia University Press, 1997), 383–422.

64. Another argument for a later date rests on Samuel Lee Wolff's work on Greene and the Greek romances. Comparing verbal echoes in Greene's story of pastoral adoption to versions of Longus's *Daphnis and Chloe*, Wolff finds that the comic handling of the shepherd parents must have been based on Angel Daye's 1587 translation (448). However, the echoes are not so close that Greene could not have made these changes independently (or even influenced Daye).

65. This early analysis comes from manuscript notes on Sidney's rhetoric made by John Hoskyns ca. 1599–1600 (quoted in Garrett 155). On Greene's work with Greek romance see Wolff and Arthur F. Kinney, *Humanist Poetics: Thought, Rhetoric and Fiction in Sixteenth-Century England* (Amherst: University of Massachusetts Press, 1986), 222.

66. Woudhuysen also wonders whether Clifford might have shared his copy of the manuscript with Greene, a scenario I find unlikely. If Greene had seen this manuscript in the 1580s, with its first page headed "The first Booke or Acte of the Countess of Pembrookes Arcadia," he would have picked up on that titular pattern sooner.

67. See Wolff 443, and Abraham Fraunce, *The Arcadian Rhetorike*, ed. Ethel Seaton (Oxford: Basil Blackwell, 1950), e.g., 20, 23, 79, 116, 123.

68. I rely on Woudhuysen's lucid reconstruction of the *Arcadia*'s early publication (I hope without a similar bias against the Countess) and his analysis of Greville's letter (224–41, 416–21).

69. Michael Brennan, *Literary Patronage in the English Renaissance: The Pembroke Family* (New York: Routledge, 1988), 58. Also see his "William Ponsonby: Elizabethan Stationer," *Analytic and Enumerative Bibliography* 7 (1983): 91–100.

70. Victor Skretkowicz, "Building Sidney's Reputation: Texts and Editions of the Arcadia" in *Sir Philip Sidney: 1586 and the Creation of a Legend*, eds. Jan Van Dorsten, Dominic Baker-Smith, and Arthur F. Kinney (Leiden: E. J. Brill/Leiden University Press, 1986), 122, emphasis added.

71. "A Dedication to Sir Philip Sidney" (written 1604–12, published 1652) in *The Prose Works of Fulke Greville*, ed. John Gouws (Oxford: Oxford University Press, 1986), 11.

72. Even this is exaggerated: only a very idle reader would take all day to read fourteen execrable "sonnets" (McKerrow, *Greenes Newes*, 69).

73. *Henrie Chettle, Kind-Hartes Dream; William Kemp, Nine Daies Wonder*, ed. G. B. Harrison. (London: The Bodley Head, 1923), 5–6.

74. René Pruvost, not getting the joke, calls this a "bizarre capuchon" (551).

75. A few poems by Dickenson went into *England's Helicon* (1600), the influential anthology of pastoral poetry that also included liberal selections from the eclogues of Sidney and Greene.

76. See Smith, 2:308–9 for the list of books censured. The only Elizabethan romance listed is *Ornatus and Artesia* (Emanuel Forde, c. 1598?), presumably for its eroticism.

77. Quoted in Pruvost 43*n*7.

2. *Social Things: Commodifying* Pandosto, 1592–1640

1. Karl Marx, *Capital, vol. 1*, in *The Marx/Engels Reader*, ed. Robert C. Tucker (New York: Norton, 1978), 320–21.

2. Tessa Watt, *Cheap Print and Popular Piety, 1550–1640* (Cambridge: Cambridge University Press, 1991), 278.

3. For critiques of the ballad through the Elizabethan and Jacobean periods, see Natascha Wurzbach, *The Rise of the English Street Ballad, 1550–1650*, trans. Gayna Walls (Cambridge: Cambridge University Press, 1990); Tessa Watt, "Publisher, Pedlar, Pot-Poet: The Changing Character of the Broadside Trade, 1550–1640," in *Spreading the Word: The Distribution Networks of Print, 1550–1850*, eds. Robin Myers and

Michael Harris (Detroit: Omnigraphics, 1990); and Sharon Achinstein, "Audiences and Authors: Ballads and the Making of English Renaissance Literary Culture," *Journal of Medieval and Renaissance Studies* 22 (1992): 311–26.

4. During this era, aside from major works in folio, the most elite and the most functional of texts alike appeared in quarto format, unbound. An unbound quarto cost more than a ballad but significantly less than a folio; it was beyond the reach of the poorest but not beneath the dignity of the rich. As I will show, there is ample evidence that well-educated readers happily bought quarto romances for pleasure reading and maintained them in their home libraries. Most of the writers for the elite whom I quote in this chapter themselves published in quarto, although some fashionable works of light reading appeared in octavo.

5. Charles Mish counted individual editions of early fiction and drama to 1640 and concluded that the publication of fiction surged upward from 1576 to 1580, while drama publication rose rapidly after 1591 and never lost its dominance ("Comparative Popularity of Early Fiction and Drama," *Notes and Queries* [21 June 1952]: 269–70). Mish does not count unpublished plays.

6. The most familiar instances of scorn directed at printed romance involve chivalric romances. Of course they made ready targets, being of dubious origin (sometimes foreign), overly long, and much imitated. Criticism of them was socially driven: they offered forbidden pleasures to too many readers. Roger Ascham's *The Scholemaster* (1570) notes that "the whole pleasure" of *"Morte Arthure"* "standeth in two speciall poyntes, in open mans slaughter and bold bawdrye"; he shuddered to think "what toyes the dayly readying of such a book may worke in the will of a yong jentleman, or a yong mayde, that liveth welthelie and idlelie" (G. Gregory Smith, ed., *Elizabethan Critical Essays*, 2 vols. [Oxford: Oxford University Press, 1904], 1:4). Generations later, men of comparable rank decried citizens' taste for such romances. Like the works themselves, the habit of scorning the romances was borrowed from the Continent; Francis Meres listed translated and domestic chivalric romances in *Palladis Tamia* (1598) as books "to be censured of," as Lord De La Noue had censured *Amadis* (Smith 2:308). See Robert P. Adams, "Bold Bawdry and Open Manslaughter: The English New Humanist Attack on Medieval Romance," *Huntington Library Quarterly* 23 (1959/60): 33–48.

7. Trevor Ross, in an unusual and sophisticated reading, considers the humanist "blacklisting" of romance as "a negative form of canon-making, one that emanated from a fear of plurality, of the heresy of allowing everyone to choose what to read," in *The Making of the English Literary Canon* (Montreal & Kingston: McGill-Queen's University Press, 1998), 79.

8. Diana E. Henderson and James Siemon, "Reading Vernacular Literature," in *A Companion to Shakespeare*, ed. David Scott Kastan (Malden, MA: Basil Blackwell, 1999), 211.

9. From Juan Luis Vives, *Instruction of a Christian Woman*, translated 1540; cited in Ross, 82.

10. J.H.P. Pafford, ed., *The Winter's Tale*, The Arden Edition (London: Methuen, 1963), 4.3.26. Further references to the play cite this edition.

11. The Stationers' Company ordinance of 1598 fixed the maximum retail price of printed books, based on the number of signatures and the typeface chosen, with exceptions allowed for dense or complicated works. These variables corresponded to the capital costs (paper) and the labor costs (presswork and composition). This maximum was not changed until 1635, although prices for most other goods doubled over that period. See Francis Johnson, "Notes on English Retail Book-prices, 1550–1640," *The Library* 5th ser., 5.2 (1950): 84, 93. As long as *Pandosto* remained a straightforward quarto fitted neatly into seven sheets, its unbound cost could not vary much.

12. Texts consulted on Chadwyck-Healey's full-text database of *Early English Prose Fiction* (London: Chadwyck-Healey, 1997). Hind's *Eliosto Libidinoso* (1606) also imitates Greene; for its allusions to Sidney and Lyly, see Paul Salzman, *English Prose Fiction 1558–1700, A Critical History* (Oxford: Clarendon, 1985), 135. For Bettie, see John S. Weld, "W. Bettie's *Titana and Theseus*," *Philological Quarterly* 26 (1947): 36. Both cases of borrowing stand out as excessive even given the conventionalized nature of pastoral romance and the acceptance of imitation in the period.

13. Charles Mish, "English Short Fiction in the Seventeenth Century," *Studies in Short Fiction* 6 (1969): 234.

14. Sabie's poems add a good bit of material; they are more than versifications of Greene's story. Sabie himself was subjected to an amusing rewriting: the young gentleman John Ramsey copied out Sabie's verses into his commonplace book (Bodleian Douce 280), perhaps while home from boarding school in 1596, and signed his name in place of Sabie's. See Edward Doughtie, "John Ramsey's Manuscript as a Personal and Family Document," *New Ways of Looking at Old Texts: Papers of the Renaissance English Text Society, 1985–1991*, ed. W. Speed Hill (Binghamton, NY: Medieval and Renaissance Texts and Studies, 1993), 285.

15. The *Arcadia* was translated into French in 1624. See J. J. Jusserand, *Shakespeare in France* (London: T. Fisher Unwin, 1899), 121.

16. See René Pruvost, *Robert Greene et ses romans* (Paris: Publications de la Faculté des Lettres D'Alger, 1938), 287; Jusserand, *Shakespeare in France*, 40–44, 69–73; J. J. Jusserand, *An Introduction to Shakespeare's "The Winter's Tale"* (Cambridge, MA: [Harvard] University Press, 1907), xxviii–xxxviii. The second half of Puget de La Serre's two-day prose drama is reprinted in *Greene's 'Pandosto' or 'Dorastus and Fawnia' Being the Original of Shakespeare's 'Winter's Tale'*, ed. P. G. Thomas (New York: Duffield, 1907), 107–47. The play's first day may have been tragic, but the second day is tragicomic, ending not with a statue scene or suicide but with a brief recognition scene and the king's blessing of the lovers (147). On the polishing of the style in Regnault, see Henri Potez, "Le premier Roman anglais Traduit en français," *Revue d'Histoire littéraire de la France* 11 (1904): 45. To my knowledge, the only earlier extant translation from English literature into French was of Bacon's *Essays* (1611).

17. The scenery designs, from a sketchbook by Laurent Mahelot, are reproduced in Jusserand, *Shakespeare in France*; Jusserand, *Introduction*; and Thomas, *Greene's 'Pandosto.'* It is unclear which productions used them.

18. Jusserand, *Introduction*, also reproduces an illustration from a third French translation of 1722, which transferred the action to new locations and again did not mention Greene.

19. Richard Abbott and Helen Wilcox translated the WorldCat entry (Dublin, OH: Online Computer Library Center, 1992–2001). The subtitle is "the second part," recalling the two-part French *Pandoste* of 1631. The Dutch title *Dorastus en Fauniaas* does not follow its model, however. It might reflect either the French prose translations or English editions of Greene's romance of the 1630s, with "Dorastus and Fawnia" as their title. Copies are held at the Linkoping Stadsbibliothek in Sweden and the British Library. I have not located a copy of the first part, but this part spans from Fawnia's courtship to her reunion with her father.

20. D. F. McKenzie, "Printers of the Mind: Some Notes on Bibliographical Theories and Printing-House Practices," *Studies in Bibliography* 22 (1969): 13. Margreta de Grazia and Peter Stallybrass quote this phrase in "The Materiality of the Shakespearean Text," *Shakespeare Quarterly* 44 (1993): 259. The stability of *Pandosto* is particularly striking in contrast to the instability they note in Shakespearean play-texts.

21. Akihiro Yamada, in his study *Thomas Creede: Printer to Shakespeare and His Contemporaries* (Tokyo: Meisei University Press, 1994), discusses "compositorial fidelity to copy" in plans, including Greene's, printed by Creede (190–202). Wells's dissertation (*"Perymedes the Blacksmith" and "Pandosto" by Robert Greene: A Criticial Edition* [1962; reprint, New York: Garland, 1988]) contains bibliographical collations of editions to 1640, but there is no variorum edition.

22. It is always possible that Shakespeare read the 1607 or 1609 edition but independently revised the oracle, accidentally concurring with Greene's original, less threatening formulation.

23. See Peter W.M. Blayney, *The Bookshops in Paul's Cross Churchyard* (London: Bibliographical Society, 1990), 67.

24. See Brenda Cantar, ed., *Menaphon* (Ottawa: Dovehouse Editions, 1996), 28, on Greene's diverse audience. For the older view, see Louis B. Wright's *Middle-class Culture in Elizabethan England* (Chapel Hill: University of North Carolina Press, 1935), 115. Two of Greene's nonromance pamphlets, *Groatsworth of Wit* and *Quip for an Upstart Courtier*, long remained familiar to elite audiences. Robert Burton owned a copy of each (Nicolas K. Kiessling, ed., *The Library of Robert Burton* [Oxford: Oxford Bibliographical Society, 1988], 134). In one of his 1608 epigrams, Richard Middleton alludes to Greene's *Quip* in order to criticize a social upstart: "For *Robert Greene* doth say, and wisely scan, / A velvet slop makes not a gentleman" (quoted in J. Payne Collier, *A Bibliographical and Critical Account of the Rarest Books in the English Language*, 2 vols. [London: Joseph Lilly, 1865], 2:84).

25. French Rowe Fogle, *A Critical Study of William Drummond of Hawthornden* (New York: King's Crown Press, 1952), 1–6, 179–80.

26. Her copy, now in the British Library, is of the c. 1583 edition of the second part (not the first part, dedicated to "the ladies of Englande"). See Paul Morgan, "Fraunces Wolfreston and 'Hor Bouks': A Seventeenth-Century Woman Book-Collector," *The Library* 6th ser., 11 (1989): 198, 214. Her husband's unfitness means that this library was selected, maintained, and used primarily by Wolfreston. Morgan carefully explains that although the books include many "of types that can only be described as leisure reading," they are "superior in quality to the popular fiction and ballads sold by travelling chapmen and pedlars like Autolycus" (209, 210); but in fact she owned many jestbooks that would have been quite inexpensive. Her copy of the 1640 edition of a best-selling Jacobean romance, Emanuel Forde's *Famous Historie of Montelyon*, was passed on to her eldest son, who marked it as "his Booke" in 1652. A more distant descendant signed it in 1761. See Johan Gerritsen, "*Venus* Preserved: Some Notes on Frances Wolfreston," in *English Studies Presented to R. W. Zandvoort*; supplement to *English Studies* [Amsterdam] 45 (1964): 272.

27. Thus three of *Menaphon*'s five editions were brought to central Europe. Several other Greene titles printed in this era are held in Vienna's National Library, and the University of Göttingen owns a 1617 edition (the last) of *Arbasto*.

28. T. A. Birrell, "Light Literature in 17th-century Gentlemen's Libraries," in *Property of a Gentleman: The Formation, Organisation and Dispersal of the Private Library, 1620–1920*, eds. Robin Myers and Michael Harris (Winchester: St. Paul's Bibliographies, 1991), 116.

29. Henry Thomas, *Spanish and Portuguese Romances of Chivalry* (Cambridge: Cambridge University Press, 1920), 283–94. Also see Arthur B. Ferguson, *The Chivalric Tradition in Renaissance England* (Washington, D.C.: Folger Shakespeare Library, 1986); Mary Patchell, *The Palmerin Romances in Elizabethan Prose Fiction* (New York: Columbia University Press, 1947).

30. David Cressy, *Literacy and the Social Order: Reading and Writing in Tudor and Stuart England* (Cambridge: Cambridge University Press, 1980). Tessa Watt points out that although Cressy's statistics measure writing ability and thus underestimate reading ability, the demographic pattern he charts probably fits both skills ("Publisher, Pedlar, Pot-Poet," 63–64).

31. Over this period, Cressy reports a substantial although irregular drop in illiteracy across all occupational, geographical, and gender groups. Illiteracy among tradesmen and craftsmen in London and Middlesex dropped from 41 percent in the 1580s to 30 percent in the 1610s (146). Among this "middle of the range," the rise of literacy apparently stagnated late in Elizabeth's reign, but more than recovered under James (124, 169–70). Cressy finds the population of London "decidedly more literate" than the average, and domestic servants in particular enjoyed conditions favoring literacy (4, 124, 130).

32. Quoted in W. J. Paylor, *The Overburian Characters*. The Percy Reprints 13. (1936; New York: AMS Press, 1977), 43.

33. A year later, Ben Jonson would be mocked for publishing his folio of plays as "Works." *A Wife* reached seventeen editions by 1664.

34. See David Lindley, *The Trials of Frances Howard* (New York: Routledge, 1994).

35. Throughout the early modern period, domestic service allowed would-be readers of modest origin better access to reading instruction, household books to borrow, and candles.

36. Alexandra Halasz perceptively discusses this passage from Marx, pointing out that commodities—goods encoding social relationships—are not unique to capitalism, but under capitalism, those relationships become abstracted or alienated. Discourse had been exchanged as commodity before print, but the conditions that produced printed books were newly alienated (*The Marketplace of Print: Pamphlets and the Public Sphere in Early Modern England* [Cambridge: Cambridge University Press, 1997], 105).

37. Quoted in the "General Introduction" to *A Critical Edition of Richard Brathwait's Whimzies*, ed. Allen H. Lanner (New York: Garland, 1991), 73. Interestingly, Brathwait's full title reflects the emergent theatrical use of the term: *Whimzies: Or, A New Cast of Characters*.

38. Helen Hackett, " 'Yet Tell Me Some Such Fiction': Lady Mary Wroth's *Urania* and the 'Femininity' of Romance," in *Women, Texts & Histories, 1575–1760*, eds. Clare Brant and Diane Purkiss (New York: Routledge, 1992), 42.

39. This sixth edition of Overbury's collection was, however, the first to be given not the usual quarto format, still shared with romances, plays, and other light reading, but the idiosyncratic and intimate octavo form.

40. Wright, *Middle-class Culture in Elizabethan England* (1935; reprint, Ithaca, NY: Cornell University Press, 1958); Caroline Lucas, *Writing for Women: The Example of Woman as Reader in Elizabethan Romance* (Milton Keynes: Open University Press, 1989).

41. Hackett, " 'Yet Tell Me Some Such Fiction'," 40–41. See also Helen Hackett, *Women and Romance Fiction in the English Renaissance* (Cambridge: Cambridge University Press, 2000); Wendy Wall, *The Imprint of Gender: Authorship and Publication in the English Renaissance* (Ithaca: Cornell University Press, 1993).

42. I say "once more" because critical dismissals of Shakespeare's sources have a long, complex history. (See chapter 3.)

43. Nashe's boundless interest in predicting the uses of scrap paper by food-service workers and housewives, despite its class condescension, always reflects his vivid awareness of the ephemerality of his own "stuff." A lower meaning of "wast-paper" is evident in William Cornwallis's meditation on ballads in "Of the observation, and use of things": "They lie in my privy; and when I come thither . . . I read them (halfe a side at once is my ordinary), which when I have read, I use in the kind that waste paper is most subject too but to a cleanlier profit" (Don Cameron Allen, ed., *Essays by Sir William Cornwallis the Younger* [Baltimore: The Johns Hopkins University Press, 1946], 50).

44. Alexander B. Grosart, ed., *The Works of Gabriel Harvey* (1884; reprint, New York: AMS Press, 1966), 1:190.

45. Certainly the taste for novelty itself offended Harvey. Reflecting on Greene's prolific issue of "new, newer, & newest books," he wrote, "I would, some Buyers had either more Reason to discerne, or lesse Appetite to desire such Novels." Ibid., 187, 190–91. The word "Novel" encoded a struggle between social prejudices and fiction readers' desires that would later name an emergent genre.

46. Cressy reproduces a number of "personal marks" made on documents by illiterate craftsmen in Norwich, 1580–1620. A man who could not write his name might take as his signature an improvised hieroglyph based on a tool of his trade, as did the glover John Shakespeare (*Literacy and the Social Order*, 58–60).

47. Parrot's *The Mastive, Or Young-Whelpe of the Olde-Dogge*, is quoted in Wright, *Middle-class Culture in Elizabethan England*, 95–96.

48. Michael McKeon, *The Origins of the English Novel, 1600–1740* (Baltimore: The Johns Hopkins University Press, 1987), 131–33, 218–37.

49. Quoted in Wright, *Middle-class Culture in Elizabethan England*, 95. This poem, *Ad Bibliopolam*, is multiply invested in the profession of print, since it directly imitates Jonson's epigram, "To My Bookseller." Ironically, it appears that the work of at least one bookseller has been lost here, since Parrot's imitation apparently draws on a lost 1612 edition of Jonson's *Epigrams*. See Ian Donaldson, *Jonson's Magic Houses* (Oxford: Clarendon, 1997), 209–11. Parrot draws on the medium of print to reproduce Jonson's condemnation of print as excessively reproduced.

50. Henry Fitzgeffrey, *Satyres: And Satyricall Epigrams* (1617), quoted in Wright 97.

51. Quoted in E. H. Miller, *The Professional Writer in Elizabethan England* (Cambridge, MA: Harvard University Press, 1959), 49. Niccols was another Oxford graduate with a number of publications, mostly verse. *The Furies* appeared in octavo.

52. In Samuel Rowlands, *Complete Works 1598–1628*, vol. 1 (1880; reprint, New York: Johnson Reprint Corporation, 1966). For discussions of the genre of the gossips' meeting, see Wall 204–5, and Linda Woodbridge, *Women and the English Renaissance* (Urbana: University of Illinois Press, 1986), 224–43. For a brilliant discussion of Rowlands's work as "commodity-pamphlet," see Halasz 171–75.

53. The breeziness of "some" allows for uncertainty about just how many of "Greene's" pamphlets really were his work.

54. Or at least he uses the shop's lack of the complete set for an excuse to back out of this substantial purchase.

55. According to Miller, Chamberlain bought "pedlarie pamflets and threehalfpeny ware," as well as James's *Basilikon Doron*, and sent them to an English friend in France. In January 1599, Chamberlain sent "certain odde epitaphes and epigrammes that go under the name of pasquills" (50).

56. Neither the gentleman nor Chamberlain—nor the apprentice—claims any moral justification for pleasure reading, contradicting Wright's familiar thesis about *Middle-class Culture in Elizabethan England*. I doubt that a "puritanical middle class"

needed a veneer of moralism "to assure them that they were not wasting their time in frivolous and unprofitable amusement" (Wright 405; the claim is applied to Greene on 387). Nor is Wright accurate in imagining a monolithic middle class with tastes distinct from the elite's. Rowlands's obscure gentleman and cocky apprentice span either side of Wright's middle class but understand each other when they speak of Greene. Nashe's buddies, Harvey's friends, and Baltic-bound merchants, although not uniformly middle class, share acquaintance with Greene's books.

57. Despite the epistle's putative address to women, unlike Suzanne W. Hull, *Chaste, Silent and Obedient* (San Marino: Huntington Library, 1982), I cannot believe that it evidences an appeal to female readers. Just as the book slyly offers a peep at male-conceived "women" talking dirty in the alehouse, the opening dialogue invites the reader, already constructed as male, to look at an epistle that addresses women as men imagine them, comparing gentlewomen to their lapdogs: *"some of you keepe prettie Curs for sport,/Yet you your selves become no currish creatures"* (9). The link back to Lyly seals the familiar associations between books and lapdogs, between pleasure reading and women's leisure and desire. The opposition between frame and dedication may evince resistance to women entering bookshops during this period; I have found no direct references to their book shopping.

58. Annabel Patterson, *Censorship and Interpretation* (Madison: University of Wisconsin Press, 1984), 159–202.

59. Richard Helgerson, *Self-Crowned Laureates* (Berkeley: University of California Press, 1983), 124–30.

60. Ben Jonson, *Every Man Out of his Humour*, 2.3.224–28. In *Ben Jonson*, eds. C. H. Herford and Percy and Evelyn Simpson (Oxford: Clarendon, 1927), vol. 3. The word "ordinary" may allude to Greene's famous self-description in the 1592 *Repentance*.

61. See *Every Man Out of his Humour*, 2.3 and 5.10. 34–36.

62. Title pages of first three quartos reproduced in Herford and Simpson, eds., *Jonson*, vol. 3.

63. Nicholas Ling, who published the Third Quarto of *Every Man Out of his Humour*, also published Greene's *Menaphon* in 1599 and 1605, *Ciceronis Amor* in 1601 and 1605, and *Never Too Late* in 1599, 1602, and 1607. John Smethwick, his successor in the *Every Man Out of his Humour* copy at the time of Jonson's 1616 Folio, inherited these Greene copies as well; he reissued each of them in 1610–11, again in 1616, and again in the next decade.

64. John Stephens, *Satyrical Essayes, Characters and Others* (London, 1615), 276. Cited in Martin Garrett, ed., *Sidney: The Critical Heritage* (New York: Routledge, 1996), 22.

65. Lording Barry's *Ram-Alley* was performed by the King's Revels Children at Blackfriars; *Eastward Hoe* (George Chapman, Ben Jonson, John Marston) by the Queen's Revels Children at Blackfriars. In Jonson's *Epicoene* (1609, Queen's Revels Children, Whitefriars), Truewit explains that women's ways (not maids' ways) are learned by spending "a month together upon *Amadis de Gaul*, or *Don Quixote*." Quota-

tions are from Thomas, *Spanish and Portuguese Romances*, 287–92; performance data is from Harbage, *Annals of the English Drama 975–1700*, 3rd ed. (London: Routledge, 1989).

66. *Poems of William Browne of Tavistock*, ed. Gordon Goodwin (London: George Routledge & Sons, 1894), 2:240. Browne published *Britannia's Pastorals* in 1613 and 1615, while a member of the Inner Temple; he then joined the literary circle at Wilton until an advantageous marriage allowed him to live independently (A. H. Bullen, "Introduction," in Goodwin 1:xvi–xxxiv). This epistle comes from an unpublished manuscript dated 1650, containing many poems written throughout his life.

67. Thomas 287–88, 292. Thomas, anxious to assert that the chivalric romances were considered fit reading only for "ignorant and lower classes," not for ladies, explains that these higher-ranking readers are "not healthy-minded" (288).

68. Wye Saltonstall, *Picturae Loquentes. Or Pictures Drawne forth in Characters* (1631; reprint, Oxford: Basil Blackwell, 1946), 47.

69. On the relationship of luxury, femininity, and royalism, see Lois Potter, *Secret Rites and Secret Writing: Royalist Literature 1641–1660* (Cambridge: Cambridge University Press, 1989).

70. On "sexual arousal" and Caroline women's reading of the New Arcadia, see Mary Ellen Lamb, *Gender and Authorship in the Sidney Circle* (Madison: University of Wisconsin Press, 1990), 112–14. Quarles's frontispiece depicts a curtain, and the accompanying verse promises "unshowne" pleasures behind this "silken Frontispiece" (sic); "To the Reader" echoes this image (not to mention Lyly) by telling "Ladies" that "in your silken laps I know this book will choose to lie" (Francis Quarles, *Argalus and Parthenia*, ed. David Freeman [Washington, D.C.: Folger Books, 1986], 44–45, 50). Also see Garrett 22, 259.

71. *Pandosto* had been gradually shrinking to an atavism. In the editions of 1614 and 1619, the largest typeface is given to the subtitle, *The Triumph of Time*.

72. These changes seem too late to be directly inspired by the appearance of the word "shepheardesse" in the First Folio text of *The Winter's Tale*, fascinating as it would be for stationers to have linked the two texts. The use of the word *"bergère"* in Puget de la Serre's play of 1631 supports a link between gender-inflected terms and Continental pastoral.

73. It is unlikely but possible that this woodcut originated in Faulkner's previous edition, dated to "1640?"; one issue has an unillustrated title page, while another exists only in a copy lacking a title page.

74. The composition was originated by Daniel Mytens (c. 1630–32), reworked by Anthony van Dyck (1634), and copied in paintings apparently commissioned by courtiers; for reproductions of the most authoritative versions and discussion of their attribution, see Roy Strong, *Charles I on Horseback* (London: Allen Lane The Penguin Press, 1972), 72–73; Oliver Millar, *The Tudor, Stuart, and Early Georgian Pictures in the Collection of Her Majesty the Queen* (London: Phaidon Press, 1963), 1:97; Erik Larsen, ed., *The Paintings of Anthony van Dyck* (Freren: Luca Verlag, 1988), 2:318–19; and John

Peacock, "The Visual Image of Charles I," in *The Royal Image: Representations of Charles I*, ed. Thomas N. Corns (Cambridge: Cambridge University Press, 1999), 176–239. A related medal by Nicolas Briot (1635) provides the most immediate precedent for the *Dorastus and Fawnia* woodcut, since it eliminates the laurel wreath and "has the royal couple clasping hands" (Peacock 226, 239*n*145). The engraving and medal were mass-produced but still relatively expensive, so the woodcut may have drawn on them through other, cheaper printed portraits of king and queen. Charles wears court dress in the paintings and engravings, but armor and a beaver hat in the woodcut, both of which were iconographically associated with him. The armor is constructed much like that in the heroic van Dyck canvas *Charles I on Horseback* (see Strong), and beaver hats appear in popular engravings of Charles from around 1640 (see Peacock).

The woodcut's Royalist associations may be confirmed by its use to illustrate a black-letter broadside, "Love in the Blossome," in 1673. Published by ballad partner William Thackeray, this first-person account of a lonely voyeur who follows an amorous pair through "the Park" to "th' Court" seems a product of Interregnum fantasy despite the later date of this copy. Its author "J.P." has been identified (perhaps wishfully) as John Playford (1623–1686?), the Royalist musician, by J. Woodfall Ebsworth, ed., *The Roxburghe Ballads* (Hertford: The Ballad Society, 1886), 6:108–12. The tune, "Amarillis told her swain," is by Henry Lawes.

75. In addition to Frederick E. Pierce, ed., *The Winter's Tale. The Yale Shakespeare* (New Haven: Yale University Press, 1918), 128–30 and Horace Howard Furness, ed. *The Winter's Tale. By William Shakespeare* (1898; New York: Dover, 1964), 321–24, see also Geoffrey Bullough, ed., *Narrative and Dramatic Sources of Shakespeare*, 8 vols. (London: Routledge Kegan Paul, 1975), 8:118–24; Kenneth Muir, *Shakespeare's Sources I: Comedies and Tragedies* (London: Methuen, 1957), 240–47; and J.H.P. Pafford, "Introduction" to *The Winter's Tale*, The Arden Edition (London: Methuen, 1963), xxvii–xxxiii. Inga-Stina Ewbank gives a nuanced reading of the play's "combination of affirmation and denial of its source" in "From Narrative to Dramatic Language: *The Winter's Tale* and Its Source," in *Shakespeare and the Sense of Performance*, eds. Marvin and Ruth Thompson (Newark: University of Delaware Press, 1989), 33. Other thoughtful accounts include Leah Scraggs, *Shakespeare's Mouldy Tales* (London: Longman, 1992), and Pauline Kiernan, *Shakespeare's Theory of Drama* (Cambridge: Cambridge University Press, 1996).

76. P. G. Thomas, in the introduction to his edition of *Greene's 'Pandosto' or 'Dorastus and Fawnia' Being the Original of Shakespeare's 'Winter's Tale'*, comments: "It is interesting, in view of the close relationship between the two books, to find in the speech of the second gentleman what seems like Shakespeare's direct reference to his original" (xv).

77. Important critical readings of Autolycus appear in Michael Bristol, *Big-Time Shakespeare* (New York: Routledge, 1996) and William C. Carroll, *Fat King, Lean Beggar: Representations of Poverty in the Age of Shakespeare* (Ithaca, NY: Cornell University Press, 1996). My argument is especially consonant with Barbara Mowat, "Rogues,

Shepherds, and the Counterfeit Distressed: Texts and Infracontexts of *The Winter's Tale* 4.3," *Shakespeare Studies* 22 (1994): 58–76.

78. Stanley Cavell, *Disowning Knowledge* (New York: Cambridge University Press, 1987), 199.

79. Both expressions figure storytelling as a acceptable pastime only because labor is no longer an option: to the old wives because they are past laboring years, to their fireside listeners because it is too dark to do anything useful. On the orality of "old tales," John Aubrey's comment is evocative if unreliable: "Before Printing, Old-wives Tales were ingeniose, and since Printing came in fashion, till a little before the Civill-warres, the ordinary sort of People were not taught to reade. Now-a-days Books are common, and most of the poor people understand letters; and the many good Bookes, and variety of Turnes of Affaires, have putt all the old Fables out of doors: and the divine art of Printing and Gunpowder have frighted away Robin-goodfellow and the Fayries" (quoted in Oliver Lawson Dick, "The Life and Times of John Aubrey," in *Aubrey's Brief Lives* [Harmondsworth, Eng.: Penguin, 1972], 17). Also see Mary Ellen Lamb, "Engendering the Narrative Act: Old Wives' Tales in *The Winter's Tale*, *Macbeth*, and *The Tempest*," *Criticism* 40 (1998): 529–54.

80. Pafford notes that his name, Rogero, also denoted a ballad tune ("Introduction" 147).

81. D. Jenkinson, *The Triumph of Faith* (London: 1613), D4v; quoted in Pafford, "Introduction," liiii.

82. On Mamillius's nursing, see Gail Kern Paster, *The Body Embarrassed: Drama and the Disciplines of Shame in Early Modern England* (Ithaca, NY: Cornell University Press), 215–80.

83. See *The Republic of Plato*, trans. Allan Bloom (New York: Basic, 1968), and excerpts from *The Republic* in Hazard Adams, ed., *Critical Theory Since Plato* (New York: Harcourt Brace Jovanovich, 1971), 19–46. Book 3 separates poetry into the unacceptable histrionic forms that Socrates called mimesis and the more dispassionate forms he called narrative. These terms were inadequate to the proliferation of vernacular genres that produced Renaissance epic and lyric poetry, prose and verse drama, and prose and verse narrative.

84. Chartier briefly discusses "Neoplatonic hostility to the seductions of illusion," citing B. W. Ife, *Reading and Fiction in Golden-Age Spain: A Platonist Critique and Some Picaresque Replies* (Cambridge: Cambridge University Press, 1985), in his "Reading Matter and 'Popular' Reading," in *A History of Reading in the West*, eds. Gugliemo Cavallo and Roger Chartier, trans. Lydia G. Cochrane (Amherst: University of Massachusetts Press, 1999), 277–78.

85. Jonas Barish, *The Antitheatrical Prejudice* (Berkeley: University of California Press, 1970).

86. These are the same lower-ranking groups as the "children" and "masses" targeted in Book 3 as the most eager consumers of damaging mimetic, poetry. See Adams, 30.

87. For a sophisticated analysis of antimaterialist bias in theater that complicates these relationships among Plato, Marx, and Bourdieu, see Scott Shershow, *Puppets and "Popular" Culture* (Ithaca: Cornell University Press, 1995).

88. Samuel Butler, *Characters*, ed. Charles W. Daves (Cleveland: The Press of Case Western Reserve University, 1970), 169–70. Butler composed these characters between 1667 and 1669 but did not publish them.

89. *An Apology for Poetry*, ed. Forrest G. Robinson (Indianapolis: Bobbs-Merrill, 1970), 57–58.

90. Thanks to Zachary Fisher for vigorously arguing this point in an unpublished undergraduate paper.

91. Surprisingly, the identification is rare even among those who claim that *The Winter's Tale* retaliated against Greene's *Johannes fac totum* slur in *Groatsworth of Wit* (Grosart, *The Works of Gabriel Harvey*, 12:144). Yet Harvey described Greene by listing various epithets for worthless trades: "An artificer, a botcher . . . an omnigatherum, a gay nothing" (quoted in Pruvost 101*n*11). Many textual scholars now regard *Groatsworth* as the work of Henry Chettle, perhaps incorporating fragments by Greene or perhaps simply imitating his style. As John Jowett points out, that mixed textual attribution does not exonerate Robert Greene from holding or expressing a grudge against Shakespeare. Fascinatingly, however, Jowett reads "factotum" as Chettle's word choice; unlike Greene, Chettle, as a bookseller, would know the term's definition as a versatile but hollow typographical element that turns an ordinary capital into a grand initial. See "Johannes Factotum: Henry Chettle and *Greene's Groatsworth of Wit*," *Publications of the Bibliographical Society of America* 87 (1993): 482. For other Shakespeare characters who have been identified (unconvincingly) with Greene, see Crupi 155*n*78. Two key studies of Renaissance imitation begin with Greene's jibe: Max Bluestone, *From Story to Stage: The Dramatic Adaptation of Prose Fiction in the Period of Shakespeare and his Contemporaries* (The Hague: Mouton, 1974), 7; and Linda Woodbridge, "Patchwork: Piecing the Early Modern Mind in England's First Century of Print Culture," *English Literary Renaissance* 23 (1993): 5–45.

92. Harvey is quoted in Pruvost, 551*n*19; Nashe in McKerrow, *Nashe*, 1:287.

93. These are reprinted but not discussed in detail in Bullough. One of Greene's audience of gulls "falls upon the ballade singer, and beating him with his fists well favouredly says, if he had not listened his singing, he had not lost his purse" (8:218), a response that suggests the reaction of Bartholomew Cokes in the scene that Jonson wrote in response to Shakespeare's.

94. Achinstein suggests that the social distinction here created between play and ballad is ironized by Shakespeare's "gibe" that his audience, too, has paid for a "swindle" ("Audiences and Authors," 315).

95. On-stage books and references to the book trade are surveyed in Frederick Kiefer, *Writing on the Renaissance Stage: Written Words, Printed Pages, Metaphoric Books* (Newark: University of Delaware Press, 1996), 275–80. Also see Eve Rachele Sanders,

Gender and Literacy on Stage in Early Modern England (Cambridge: Cambridge University Press, 1998).

96. Seeing a good thing, Jonson built a corresponding scene into *Bartholomew Fair* (1614).

97. See, for example, *The Pack of Autolycus*, ed. Hyder Edward Rollins (Cambridge, MA: Harvard University Press, 1927), xi. Tessa Watt also invokes the line as evidence of reading practices, although she sees Mopsa as speaking to the power of print, not the authority of the ballad genre ("Publisher, Pedlar, Pot-Poet" 37).

98. See Cavell, *Disowning Knowledge, passim*, and the discussion by David M. Bergeron in "Reading and Writing in Shakespeare's Romances," *Criticism* 33 (1991): 104.

3. *Material Alteration: Re-commodifying* Dorastus and Fawnia *and* The Winter's Tale, 1623–1843

1. Jean Genest, *Some Account of the English Stage, From the Restoration in 1660 to 1830*. 10 vols. (Bath: H. E. Carrington for Thomas Rodd, 1832), 4:447.

2. J. J. Jusserand, *The English Novel in the Time of Shakespeare* (1890; reprint, New York: AMS Press, 1965), 179.

3. For critics who claim *The Winter's Tale* gives life to *Pandosto* as well as the statue, see, for example, Howard Felperin, *Shakespearean Romance* (Princeton: Princeton University Press, 1972), 244; and B. J. Sokol, *Art and Illusion in* The Winter's Tale (Manchester: Manchester University Press, 1995), 6. Critics who call the statue scene "miraculous" range from John Payne Collier, in "Mr. Collier's Introduction," *Shakespeare's Library* [ed. H. C. Hazlitt], 6 vols. (1843; reprint, London: Reeves and Turner, 1875), 4:11, to Robert Miola, *Shakespeare's Reading* (Oxford: Oxford University Press, 2000), 132. Miola usefully points out in his introduction that most critics now understand Shakespeare's "habits of appropriation" as synthesizing "creative imitation" of specific texts with "creative use" of broader literary traditions (2, 15).

4. By specifying "entertainments" I exclude Holinshed and Plutarch, histories that would still have been read by many of the educated, and that may have fed into cheaper printed stories of famous kings and heroes. Those complex historical traditions are outside the scope of this book. Most of the other romance sources, many of them English translations from Italian, were not in print after the Elizabethan period, and certainly not as popular classics. The *Arcadia* was not recognized as possibly contributing the Gloucester plot for *King Lear* until much later.

5. Jean Marsden, *The Re-Imagined Text: Shakespeare, Adaptation, and Eighteenth-Century Literary Theory* (Lexington: University Press of Kentucky, 1995).

6. According to Kenneth Muir, "There are more verbal echoes from *Pandosto* than from any other novel used by Shakespeare as a source" (*Shakespeare's Sources I: Comedies and Tragedies* [London: Methuen, 1957], 247). Eighteenth-century readers were less aware of verbal echoes than of the unusually close conformity between the plots of the two works.

7. Stephen Greenblatt, *Shakespearean Negotiations: The Circulation of Social Energy in Early Modern England* (Berkeley: University of California Press, 1988), 95. Greenblatt's essay "Shakespeare and the Exorcists" has been an influential argument for intertextual readings, but does not dismantle the assumptions of source study. By reading Harsnett's *Declaration of Popish Impostures* as a response to early modern theatricality, the essay questions the assigning of historical primacy to source material. However, as a hymn to theatricality, it continues to elevate Shakespearean drama above other forms of writing. The first uses of the term "source" that I have found are in the *New Variorum Shakespeare*, edited by H. H. Furness in the 1890s. These editions routinely include a section on "the Sources of the Plot." Referring to the sources of the *play* apparently comes later.

8. The problem of defining the work precedes the transition from copy to copyright that made authorship central. Until 1710, it was apparently content, title, and genre that determined when a competing bookseller could claim right to copy in a work that re-commodified one assigned to another bookseller. On the shift from rights in copy to copyright, see Mark Rose, *Authors and Owners: The Invention of Copyright* (Cambridge: Harvard University Press, 1993). Among the appropriation studies, Paulina Kewes, *Authorship and Appropriation: Writing for the Stage in England, 1660–1710* (Oxford: Clarendon, 1998) is distinctive in setting the Restoration adaptation of Shakespeare's plays in a larger theatrical context of "appropriative licence." This informal principle fostered the adaptation of romances into dramas and suspiciously monitored the adaptation of older dramas into new ones. While Kewes focuses on attitudes that grounded the articulation of authorial rights in copy, she provides a suggestive new model for tracing changing attitudes about plays' relationships to their sources.

9. Michael Dobson, *The Making of the National Poet: Shakespeare, Adaptation, and Authorship, 1660–1769* (Oxford: Clarendon Press, 1992), 5. On the inevitability of adaptation, see the essay in *Adaptations: From Text to Screen, Screen to Text*, eds. Deborah Cartmell and Imelda Whelehan (New York: Routledge, 1999). As Will Brooker says in "Batman: One Life, Many Faces," "Like the work of Austen and Shakespeare, Conan Doyle and Fleming, it is through being adapted that Batman has survived" (197).

10. J. H. P. Pafford, "Introduction," *The Winter's Tale. The Arden Shakespeare* (New York: Routledge, 1963), xxiii, xxiv; John Munro, ed., *The Shakespere Allusion-Book*, 2 vols. (New York: Duffield & Company, 1909), 1:241, 321.

11. In 1602, when John Manningham noticed that *Twelfth Night* followed Continental analogues, he did not bother to identify the form in which those analogues circulated (*Twelfth Night. The Oxford Shakespeare*, eds. Roger Warren and Stanley Wells [New York: Oxford University Press, 1995], 3). The closest to a comment on playwrights as re-commodifiers is probably the complaint by Stephen Gosson (who knew from guilty experience) that "the Palace of Pleasure, the Golden Asse, the Ethiopian historie, Amadis of Fraunce, the Rounde table, baudie Comedies in Latin, French, Italian, and Spanish, have been throughly ransackt to furnish the Playe houses in London"

(quoted in Diana E. Henderson and James Siemon, "Reading Vernacular Literature," in *A Companion to Shakespeare*, ed. David Scott Kastan [Oxford: Blackwell, 1999], 206).

12. Inga-Stina Ewbank, "From Narrative to Dramatic Language: *The Winter's Tale* and Its Source," in *Shakespeare and the Sense of Performance*, eds. Marvin and Ruth Thompson (Newark: University of Delaware Press, 1989), 42; Dennis Bartholomeusz, *The Winter's Tale in Performance in England and America 1611–1976* (Cambridge: Cambridge University Press, 1982), 27.

13. Forman's concern was to re-commodify the play for himself, recording in his commonplace book a few useful episodes to "Observe" and "Remember" for his own life and astrological practice (Pafford, "Introduction," xxi–xxii).

14. W. W. Greg, *The Shakespeare First Folio: Its Bibliographical and Textual History* (Oxford: Clarendon, 1955), 436–39.

15. Joseph Hunter's *New Illustrations of the Life, Studies, and Writing of Shakespeare*, 2 vols. (London, 1845), comments ruefully: "It seems as if we had been in some danger of losing this play." Indeed, his own "copy of the first folio actually wants the *Winter's Tale*" (1:417).

16. Alfred W. Pollard connected the two missing texts in *Shakespeare Folios and Quartos* (1909; reprint, New York: Cooper Square Publishers, 1970), 135–36. W. W. Greg demurred in *Shakespeare First Folio*, 436–39. In 1963, J.H.P. Pafford concluded that the Revels record "has no bearing at all on the apparent delay in printing" the play (xvi–xvii).

17. Had the 1619 edition really taken ten years to sell off, Francis Faulkner probably would not have reissued the work at three-year intervals for the next twenty years. Most editions of *Pandosto* before 1640 have left only one copy extant out of the probable run of 1,500. With such a low survival rate, the complete loss of an edition is quite likely.

18. Ben Jonson, *Bartolmew Fair*, ed. G. R. Hibbard (London: Ernest Benn Ltd., 1977), induction, line 125.

19. See "Black Letter as Social Discriminant in the Seventeenth Century," *Publications of the Modern Language Association* 98 (1953): 627–30. Mish argues that since drama appeared almost invariably in roman type in quartos after 1600, while many chivalric and Elizabethan romances (including *Pandosto*) appeared in black letter right up until 1700, drama had a more educated and fashion-conscious audience and romances were by 1600 already consigned to those in a lower stratum of literacy. For a more recent account, see Peter W. M. Blayney, "The Publication of Playbooks," in *A New History of Early English Drama*, eds. John D. Cox and David Scott Kastan (New York: Columbia University Press, 1997), 414–15. *The Painfull Adventures of Pericles* complicates that theory: it appears in black letter as the play appeared in roman type, but appeals to the currency of the play with its title and a reference to the King's Men in the subtitle. The use of black letter for this romance claims the antiquity of the tale in a way that a current stage play cannot. This suggestion of antiquity would long

remain important as a generic signal for romance, consistent with the generic label of "histories" under which they were sold.

20. See the examples given by Heidi Brayman Hackel in "The 'Great Variety' of Readers and Early Modern Reading Practices" in *A Companion to Shakespeare*, ed. David Scott Kastan (Oxford: Blackwell, 1999), 146–47. Shakespeare would have had reason for greater consciousness that his plays were publishable toward the end of his writing career, given the growing frequency of quarto publication, including those attributed to him by name, as well as the publication of the sonnets and the "False Folio" forgeries of 1609.

21. *The Tempest* alone does not rest on a recognizable romance plot, although it does rely on the *Aeneid* and obviously is concerned with "books," not identified as manuscript or print. Barbara Mowat has recently proposed that the late plays' self-consciousness about their physical medium reflects aspirations to a literary worth then associated with nondramatic, printed genres ("The Theater and Literary Culture" in Cox and Kastan, eds., *A New History of Early English Drama*, 213–30). She links the bookish quality of *Pericles* to its vexed textual history, in which the quarto play texts are inextricably bound up with the black-letter prose version published simultaneously as George Wilkins's *Painfull Adventures of Pericles Prince of Tyre. Being the true History of the Play of Pericles* (not to mention Lawrence Twine's version). The Pericles story circulated "fluidly and recursively among the forms of print, script, and performance" (Mowat 219). The point that I take back from *Pericles* and *The Painfull Adventures* to *Pandosto* and *The Winter's Tale* is not that there was an absolute boundary between literary print and nonliterary performance, but that such boundaries were variably recognized, by readers, by stationers, and by increasingly print-conscious playwrights.

22. David McPherson, "Ben Jonson's Library and Marginalia: An Annotated Catalogue," *Studies in Philology* 71(5) (Dec. 1974): 50.

23. Paul Salzman, *An Anthology of Elizabethan Prose Fiction* (Oxford: Oxford University Press, 1987), 204.

24. "Upon Master William Shakespeare, the Deceased Authour, and his Poems," in Brian Vickers, ed., *Shakespeare: The Critical Heritage*, 6 vols. (London: Routledge and Kegan Paul, 1974), 1:27. Digges also contributed a well-known poem to the First Folio.

25. From Margaret Cavendish, *Sociable Letters*, in *Women Reading Shakespeare 1660–1900*, eds. Ann Thompson and Sasha Roberts (Manchester and New York: Manchester University Press, 1997), 13.

26. For instance, William Cavendish drafted an episodic play while in exile called "A Pleasante & merrye Humor off a Roge," which featured a shape-shifting rogue, drawing on Jonson's Nightingale, and therefore also on Shakespeare's Autolycus. Astonishingly, by the end of the play, the rogue is also figured as Lear and even Christ. See *Dramatic Works of William Cavendish* (Oxford: Malone Society Reprints, Vol. 158, 1996). This play came to the stage in the Restoration, adapted by Thomas Shadwell as *The Triumphant Widow*. William and Margaret Cavendish's contributions to drama,

usually treated separately, are integrated in Dale B. J. Randall, *Winter Fruit: English Drama 1642–1660* (Lexington: University Press of Kentucky, 1995), 313–36.

27. On the strange blend of royalism and populism in Interregnum ephemera, see Lois Potter, *Secret Rites and Secret Writing* (Cambridge: Cambridge University Press, 1989), esp. 26–28.

28. Martin Butler, *Theatre and Crisis, 1632–1642* (Cambridge: Cambridge University Press, 1984), 132. Butler goes on to discuss a circle of writers who crossed this popular/elite divide, including Jordan (185).

29. On Jordan's stage career, see G. E. Bentley, *The Jacobean and Caroline Stage*, 7 vols. (Oxford: Clarendon Press, 1941–46), 1:487–90.

30. Susan Wiseman sets some of the other poems in the volume in the context of the reopening stage in 1659–60, but the items I discuss are in another signature and may have been written or even printed later (*Drama and Politics in the English Civil War* [Cambridge: Cambridge University Press, 1998], 198).

31. John Payne Collier, *A Bibliographical and Critical Account of the Rarest Books in the English Language*, 2 vols. (London: Joseph Lilly, 1865), 2:186–88. Further references will be cited parenthetically as Collier, *Bibliographical*.

32. *Shakespeare's Comedies, Histories, Tragedies, and Poems*, ed. John Payne Collier, 6 vols. (London, 1858), 3:8. Further references will be cited as Collier, *Shakespeare's*.

33. Stanley Wells, *"Perymedes the Blacksmith" and "Pandosto" by Robert Greene. A Critical Edition* (1961; reprint, New York: Garland, 1988), 182.

34. From *The Royal Arbor of Loyal Poesie* in *Illustrations of Old English Literature*, ed. John Payne Collier (1866; reprint, New York: Benjamin Blom, 1966), 3:125. Further references will be cited parenthetically as Collier, *Illustrations*.

35. Nancy Klein Maguire, "The 'Whole Truth' of Restoration Tragicomedy," in *Renaissance Tragicomedy*, ed. Nancy Klein Maguire (New York: AMS Press, 1987), 220.

36. Lois Potter, " 'True Tragicomedies' of the Civil War and Commonwealth," in Maguire, ed., *Renaissance Tragicomedy*, 214.

37. *The Winter's Tale* was among the 108 early plays to which Thomas Killigrew was granted rights by the King in 1669, but no record of a performance survives. It was mounted by James Ashbury at the Smock-Alley Theatre in Dublin in 1663–64. See Beverly E. Schneller, "No 'Brave Irishman' Need Apply: Thomas Sheridan, Shakespeare and the Smock-Alley Theatre," in *Shakespeare and Ireland*, eds. Mark Thornton Burnett and Ramona Wray (New York: St. Martin's, 1997), 177, 191*n*4.

38. Sheppard's last confirmed work appeared in 1655, which has led some scholars to question the earlier attribution of *Fortunes Tennis-Ball* to him, given that it survives only in editions of 1672 and 1688. Hyder E. Rollins suggested Samuel Smithson as its author ("Samuel Sheppard and his Praise of Poets," *Studies in Philology* 24 [1927]: 537). However, many features of the adaptation point to Sheppard, including the disparity between its learned generic markers and its doggerel rhymes. A previously unidentified fragment of the "Most excellent history" in the National Library of Scotland restores the possibility that *Fortunes Tennis-Ball* was written by Sheppard and published

in the mid-1650s. It lacks a title page, but the overall typography and at least one substantive variant lead me to believe that this copy is earlier than the other two extant editions. The distinctive form of *Fortunes Tennis-Ball*, three "Cantos" of several eight-line stanzas each, connects the work to Sheppard's known oeuvre, in particular his unfinished and unpublished epic, *The Faerie King*, in six books, each of six cantos in *ottava rima* (Potter, " 'True Tragicomedies,' " 122–30).

39. Gunnar Sorelius, "An Unknown Shakespearian Commonplace Book," *The Library* 28 (1973): 296.

40. Cited in R. C. Bald, "Francis Kirkman, Bookseller and Author," *Modern Philology* 41 (1943): 23.

41. Kirkman may also have employed street hawkers for his books, according to the rivals' complaint quoted in ibid., 25.

42. W. W. Greg, *Bibliography of the English Printed Drama to The Restoration*, 4 vols. (Oxford: Oxford University Press, 1939), 3:1353.

43. "Youth" in early modern England included older children and unmarried adults well into their twenties. See Ilana Kraus Ben-Amos, *Adolescence and Youth in Early Modern England* (New Haven: Yale University Press, 1994), 23–28. Expanding on Margaret Spufford, *Small Books and Pleasant Histories: Popular Fiction and Its Readership in Seventeenth-Century England* (Athens: University of Georgia Press, 1982) (cited parenthetically hereafter as *Small Books*), Anthony Fletcher has claimed chapbook romance as a subcultural favorite for young males, pointing to evidence of its readership among apprentices; see *Gender, Sex and Subordination in England 1500–1800* (New Haven: Yale University Press, 1995), 88–89. I do not believe this evidence precludes a female readership for chapbook romances.

44. Salzman points out that this claim is spurious (*English Prose Fiction, 1558–1700* [Oxford: Clarendon Press, 1985], 269). Further references will be cited as Salzman, *English*.

45. According to Bald, *The Unlucky Citizen* was "written in something of the same spirit as Robert Greene's later pamphlets had been, with the same desire to exact some profit from personal misfortune" ("Francis Kirkman," 29).

46. Henry B. Wheatley surveys the history of the book collections in *Samuel Pepys and the World He Lived In* (London: Swan Sonnenschein and Co., 1907), 77–99. The epigraph to the chapter on Pepys's collections is "a snapper-up of unconsidered trifles."

47. On similar lines, Michael Denning argues that early twentieth-century nostalgia for the dime novel was possible only once "the immediate menace of cheap sensational fiction to genteel culture was repressed," both on the social scene and in the memories of gentle observers (*Mechanic Accents: Dime Novels and Working Class Culture in America* [London: Verso, 1987], 9–10). R. A. Houston implies such a gap when he notes that "the 'romantic revival' of the late eighteenth century stressed peasant values and made the reading of *Volksliteratur* chic" (*Literacy in Early Modern Europe* [London: Longman, 1988], 195).

48. The nonelite origins of Selden and Pepys should be noted. Pepys began collecting his penny merriments in the 1660s and was particularly systematic in the

1680s; his ballad collection included 1,671 items by 1703. Anthony à Wood collected chapbooks and a huge number of ballads during the late eighteenth century (Spufford, *Small Books*, xix–xx; Alan Bold, *The Ballad* [London: Methuen & Co., 1979], 67–68). The first collection of ballads to be published appeared in 1723 (Sybil Rosenfeld, *The Theatre of the London Fairs in the 18th Century* [Cambridge: Cambridge University Press, 1960], 138). By this time, interest was also developing in "literary" production by low-born authors: the works of various "literary domestics" were published toward the middle of the eighteenth century, mostly in periodicals (J. Jean Hecht, *The Domestic Servant Class in Eighteenth-Century England* [London: Routledge Kegan Paul, 1956], 191).

49. Quoted in Victor E. Neuburg, *Popular Literature: A History and Guide* (Harmondsworth, Eng.: Penguin, 1977), 61.

50. Gerard Langbaine, *Lives and Characters of the English Dramatick Poets*, continued by Charles Gildon (1699; reprint, New York: AMS Press, 1976), 67.

51. Edward Arber, *Term Catalogues 1668–1709 A.D.*, 3 vols. (London, 1906), 2:180. This title was a grander version of a jestbook, sold bound for a shilling. Its author, "R.B.," was simply a pseudonym for its printer, the productive Nathaniel Crouch, who would later sell such titles in Ireland under the name "Richard Burton."

52. See Arundell Esdaile, *A List of English Tales and Prose Romances Printed Before 1740* (London: Bibligraphical Society, 1912), 70, 145–46.

53. Some of the signatures are partially covered by the engraved bookplate of Charles, Lord Maynard.

54. Blare's stock has been linked to that of Woodgate and Brookes, the dominant late eighteenth-century chapbook publishers based in Aldermary Churchyard. Neuburg says that a later apprentice at Blare's shop (the Looking-glasse) moved to the Golden Ball in Paternoster Row, and became an affiliate of Henry Woodgate (*The Penny Histories* [London: Oxford University Press, 1968], 23). I have seen one of their chapbooks of *Dorastus and Fawnia*, which does not include this woodcut.

55. It helped, too, that these publishers worked on different routes out of the city, and thus tended to offer their wares to separate sets of chapmen. But even among neighbors, partnerships were common. Matthew Wootton of Fleet Street, due west of Conyers's shop, advertised *Dorastus and Fawnia* in the back of a sermon he published in 1702. No *Dorastus and Fawnia* copy bears a Wootton imprint. He may have bought a share in one of Conyers's notably frequent reissues of this period, or an edition may be lost. The two published many works together.

56. In the back of the book is advertised another Conyers title, *The Way to Get Wealth*; it appeals to a broad audience, with sections on math for "Traders, especially those that are not good Arithmeticians"; on "the Duty of Servants, and comportment for masters, mistresses, and upper servants"; and on serving everything from "Cyder" to fashionable "Coffee, Tea, Chocolate."

57. However, a different, roughly medievalized couple appears in the one surviving Newcastle imprint of the romance, dated sometime between 1730 and 1760, and now in the Bodleian's Harding collection. This woodcut seems to have been used reg-

ularly in *Fortunatus*; see Roger E. Thompson, ed., *Samuel Pepys'* [sic] *Penny Merriments* (New York: Columbia University Press, 1977), 69.

58. William Dodd, *800 Decorative Woodcuts for Artists and Craftspeople* (New York: Dover, 1999), 26.

59. Gerard Langbaine, *Momus Triumphans* (1688; reprint, New York: AMS Press, 1970), 22.

60. Gerard Langbaine, *An Account of the English Dramatick Poets* (1691; reprint, Los Angeles: William Andrews Clark Memorial Library, 1971), 466.

61. D. F. McKenzie, *Stationers' Company Apprentices, 1641–1700* (Oxford: Oxford Bibliographical Society, 1974), 151.

62. Wood is quoted in the entry in the *DNB*. The publication history of *The English Rogue* does not lend credence to Wood's report, although it is far from certain. Part II was published in 1668 and authored by Kirkman. Parts III and IV were published in 1671 and were allegedly written by Richard Head and Kirkman, although Head later denied that involvement. See Salzman, *English*, 221–23. Given the dates, Langbaine could only have been commissioned to write Parts III and IV—or a nonexistent Part V. If Langbaine is simply being confused with Kirkman in this story, that in itself points to their close association.

63. Anthony à Wood, *Fasti Oxonienses*, ed. Philip Bliss (1815; reprint, New York: Burt Franklin, 1967), 1:245–46. "Trifles," in the proximity of "ballad-mongers," recalls Autolycus.

64. Quoted in Munro 1:274, as published from the Hawthornden manuscript in *Archaeologia Scotica*, 1831–32 (not as it appeared in the 1711 *Works* of Drummond).

65. *The Works of Shakespeare: in Seven Volumes Collated with the Oldest Copies, and Corrected, with Notes Explanatory, and Critical, By Mr. Theobald*, 7 vols. (London, 1733), 3:99.

66. As quoted in Charlotte Lennox, *Shakspear Illustrated*, 2 vols. (1753–54; reprint, New York: AMS Press, 1973), 2:87.

67. On Bell, see Stanley Morison, *John Bell, 1745–1831: Bookseller, Printer, Publisher, Typefounder, Journalist, &c.* (Cambridge: Cambridge University Press, 1930); the introduction to Kalman A. Burnim and Philip H. Highfill Jr., *John Bell, Patron of British Theatrical Portraiture: A Catalog of the Theatrical Portraits in His Editions of Bell's Shakespeare and Bell's British Theatre* (Carbondale and Edwardsville: Southern Illinois University Press, 1998); and an interesting discussion in Margaret Ezell, *Social Authorship and the Advent of Print* (Baltimore: The Johns Hopkins University Press, 1999), 131–36. On the relationship between Bell's editions and the Scottish bookseller Alexander Donaldson's challenge to copyright law, see Andrew Murphy's *Shakespeare in Print: A History and Chronology of Shakespeare Publishing, 1590–2000* (Cambridge: Cambridge University Press, forthcoming).

68. All information is drawn from the Chadwyck-Healey database, *Editions and Adaptations of Shakespeare* (London: Chadwyck-Healey, 1995).

69. Gamini Salgado, ed., *Eyewitnesses of Shakespeare* (New York: Barnes & Noble, 1975), 343–44, 344–45.

70. William Brough, *Perdita or the royal milkmaid: being the legend upon which Shakespeare is supposed to have founded his Winter's Tale: a new and original burlesque* (In Lacy's acting edition of plays, dramas, farces, extravaganzas, etc. etc. as performed at the various theatres. Volume 28.) (London: Thomas Hailes Lacy, 1856), [3]. See *Nineteenth-Century Shakespeare Burlesques*, ed. Stanley Wells, 5 vols. (London: Diploma Press Ltd., 1977), 3:xiv–xix.

71. Collier, *Bibliographical*, 2:88.

72. However, the history of *Hero and Leander* qualifies Stanhope's originality and indicates that despite appearances, this omnibus edition is a product of the chapbook market. The myth of Hero and Leander circulated in multiple forms in the English Renaissance: Christopher Marlowe's uncompleted poem (publ. 1598), Chapman's continuation (1616), Henry Petowe's more modest verse version (1598), James Smith's "mock poem" (1651), William Wycherley's burlesque (1669), and Humphrey Crouch's "excellent sonnet" (ballad) (1674, 1755). The puppet version proposed in *Bartholomew Fair* may respond to actual productions. John Blare published a short prose adaptation called *The Famous and Renowned History of the Two Unfortunate, though Noble Lovers, Hero and Leander* in 1680. At twenty-six pages, it is a close counterpart and contemporary to the Dennisson *Dorastus and Fawnia* first redaction. The preface, signed "J.S.," promises the story is being published "that our English Nation may not be left in Ignorance"—a phrase repeated exactly in Stanhope's preface. Stanhope was clearly following this adaptation closely in the main text as well, and it, perhaps together with Blare's 1700 redaction of *Dorastus and Fawnia*, must have provided the precedent for his moralized rewriting of *Dorastus and Fawnia*. Thanks to Kim Woosley for her work on the tale.

73. In Midwinter's edition, the title page to *The Fortunate Lovers* reads "Written in the Year MDCCXXVII," although the omnibus title page is undated.

74. His apprentice Thomas Gent describes going to a new employer who is surprised by the fine compositorial skills that Gent has learned in a "ballad house" (*The Life of Mr. Thomas Gent, Printer of York, Writ by Himself* [London, 1832], 74). Gent went on to marry a relative of John White of Newcastle.

75. Henry Robert Plomer, *A Dictionary of the Printers and Booksellers . . . in England . . . from 1668 to 1725* (London: Bibliographical Society, 1922), 34.

76. Pat Rogers, "Classics and Chapbooks," in *Books and Readers in Eighteenth-Century England*, ed. Isabel Rivers (New York: St. Martin's Press, 1982), 32.

77. Just how unsuccessful is demonstrated by the fact that he died in 1735 while acting on stage (*DNB*). Johnson maligned Bond's contributions to the *Plain-Dealer*, the periodical that he coedited with Aaron Hill (itself possibly printed by Samuel Richardson). Robert P. Mayo holds that the *Plain-Dealer*'s engaging frame anticipated narrative aspects of the novel (*The English Novel in the Magazines, 1740–1815* [Evanston: Northwestern University Press, 1962], 47).

78. Midwinter advertises a "novel" that would also have a long life, "Cynthia: A Tragical Account of the Unfortunate Lovers of Almerin and Desdemona," as well as *The*

Whole Duty of a Woman. The volumes briefly described in the Bettesworth, et al. edition include the new sensationalized "*Histories*—one *Tragical*, one *most Entertaining*, and the *Secret Histories* of Mrs. Eliza Haywood."

79. That label is a later coinage for a particular subgenre, but imperiled female virtue is a growing concern of Restoration and eighteenth-century drama. Susan Staves gives a rich treatment of the variety and political significance of the theme in *Players' Scepters: Fictions of Authority in the Restoration* (Lincoln: University of Nebraska Press, 1979).

80. Keith Thomas, "Literacy in Early Modern England," in *The Written Word: Literacy in Transition*, ed. Gerd Baumann (Oxford: Clarendon, 1986), 121.

81. Lennox, *Shakespear Illustrated*, 2:32. See also Stanhope, *The Fortunate and Unfortunate Lovers* (London: E. Midwinter, 1733), 27–28, who added "acknowledge," "submission," "vanity," and "groveling" to Greene's original.

82. Jonathan Brody Kramnick, *Making the English Canon: Print-Capitalism and the Cultural Past, 1700–1770* (Cambridge: Cambridge University Press, 1998), 120. While I find this reading acute, I do not believe that it shuts out the possibility of reading her loyalty to prose fiction as a gendered commitment. Kramnick is very dismissive of the feminist analyses of *Shakespear Illustrated* in Margaret Anne Doody's "Shakespeare's Novels: Charlotte Lennox Illustrated," *Studies in the Novel* 19 (1987): 296–310, and her "Introduction" to *The Female Quixote*, ed. Margaret Dalziel (Oxford: Oxford University Press, 1989).

83. See Eithne Henson, *"The Fictions of Romantick Chivalry": Samuel Johnson and Romance* (Rutherford, NJ: Fairleigh Dickinson University Press, 1992); and *Boswell's Life of Johnson*, ed. George Birkbeck Hill, rev. L. F. Powell, 6 vols. (Oxford: Clarendon, 1934), 1:49.

84. Important recent efforts to break down barriers between legitimate and informal dramatic performances include Terry Castle, *Masquerade and Civilization: The Carnivalesque in Eighteenth-Century Culture and Fiction* (Stanford: Stanford University Press, 1986); and Kristina Straub, *Sexual Suspects: Eighteenth-Century Players and Sexual Ideology* (Princeton: Princeton University Press, 1992).

85. Rosenfeld 16, 33, 119–20.

86. George Winchester Stone Jr., ed., *The London Stage 1660–1800*, Part 4: *1747–1776*, 2 vols. (Carbondale: Southern Illinois University Press, 1962), 1:119. Rosenfeld remarks that its 1749 appearance proves "the conservatism of the fair offerings" at mid-century (120).

87. Information on Shakespeare adaptations is compiled in Charles Beecher Hogan, ed., *Shakespeare in the Theatre 1701–1800*, 2 vols. (Oxford: Clarendon, 1952).

88. See Marsden, *The Re-Imagined Text*, 76, and Dobson 146–61. Also see Emmett L. Avery, "The Shakespeare Ladies Club," *Shakespeare Quarterly* 7 (1956): 153–58.

89. Wells, *"Perymedes,"* 188. Also see Stanley Wells, "A Shakespearean Droll?" in *Theatre Notebook* 14(4) (1961): 116–17.

90. See Wells, *"Perymedes,"* 187; Hogan, ed., *Shakespeare in the Theatre 1701–1800*, 1:457, 471.

91. The theater was advertised as "Mrs Martin's, Nag's Head, James Street." Unfortunately, no other record survives of this female devotee of Greene. See George Speaight, *The History of the English Puppet Theatre* (London: George G. Harrap, 1955; new ed., 1990), 317. Wells also reported this performance play (*"Perymedes,"* 189).

92. Among the puppeteers with Shakespeare in the repertoire were Charlotte Charke, Colley Cibber's cross-dressing youngest daughter, who offered in 1738 *Richard III, Henry IV*, and a program combining *King Henry VIII* with the same pastoral piece her father had raised simultaneously at Drury Lane. In 1779, the proprietor of the Patagonian Theatre offered a puppet masque based on *The Tempest* (Speaight 103–4, 120). These puppet Shakespeares circumvented the restrictions of the Licensing Act and the high costs of production. Scott Cutler Shershow has argued that puppet performances, which required narration by a showmanlike "interpreter," interrogated the very notions of authorship and textual authority that might ground literary distinctions. See " 'The Mouth of 'hem All': Ben Jonson, Authorship, and the Performing Object," *Theatre Journal* 46 (1994): 187–212.

93. This visit was in 1668; in 1667, Pepys reports, "my Lady Castlemayne" saw another chapbook story, Patient Griselda's, performed by puppets (Speaight 77).

94. Irene Dash, "A Penchant for Perdita on the Eighteenth-Century English Stage," in *The Woman's Part: Feminist Criticism of Shakespeare*, eds. Carolyn Ruth Swift Lenz, Gayle Greene, and Carol Thomas Neely (Urbana: University of Illinois Press, 1980), 271–84.

95. These cuts were followed closely by George Colman the elder in his 1777 adaptation, and more generally in Thomas Hull's adaptation of 1773 (printed in a Bell's acting edition).

96. See Dobson 194; and *Perdita: The Memoirs of Mary Robinson*, ed. M. J. Levy (London and Chester Springs, PA: Peter Owen, 1994). The autobiography denies a sexual involvement, claiming that prince and actress met only in "midnight perambulations" through Kew Gardens in greatcoats—Elizabethan pastoral disguise replaced by a distinctly eighteenth-century masquerade (111). After she was cast off by "Florizel," Robinson reinvented herself as a radical journalist, poet, and novelist.

97. *The sheep-shearing: or, Florizel and Perdita. A Pastoral comedy Taken from Shakespear. The songs by Mr. Arne* (London: J. Truman [etc.], 1762), lines 137–40 (cited from *Editions and Adaptations of Shakespeare*).

98. *Florizel and Perdita. A Dramatic Pastoral, in Three Acts. Alter'd from The Winter's Tale of Shakespear. By David Garrick. As it is performed at the Theatre Royal in Drury-Lane.* (London: J. and R. Tonson, 1758), lines 542–43.

99. *Boswell's Life of Johnson*, ed. Hill, rev. Powell, 2:79. Genest, quoting this passage, continues: "Boswell has not quoted the line accurately—neither he nor Mrs. Thrale, nor Dr. Johnson, suspected that Garrick had borrowed the song—and Garrick would not own that he had not written the line" (*Some Account of the English Stage* 5:449–50). Genest thinks this song is in Morgan's *Sheep-shearing*, but I have not found it, only the analogous lines quoted above. In any case, the confusion of authorship that

Genest imagines pervades the history of the *Winter's Tale* adaptations, and the free quotations of Mrs. Thrale and of Johnson only further the point.

100. James Orchard Halliwell in *Notices of Fugitive Tracts: A Catalogue of Chap-books, Garlands, and Popular Histories* (London, 1849), 45, 46.

101. John Payne Collier, "An Old Ballad upon the *Winter's Tale,*" *Notes and Queries* 62 (Jan. 4, 1851): 1–3.

102. Their mass production proved a fine capitalist undertaking: the founders' grandson bought a country house; his son graduated from Cambridge in 1811 and became a Midlands railway magnate (Neuburg 23, 27–29). *Pandosto's* plot may have been wish fulfillment, but its profits helped make provincial booksellers into metropolitan gentlemen.

103. The only significant textual change is in the last words, where the young couple "reign . . . many years happily over Bohemia" (24). All the Aldermary versions have them reign over "Bohemia and Sicilia." Since there is room for both countries to be listed on this page, the omission looks deliberate—a rejection of long-distance rule in a newly self-governing nation?

104. The paper is dull blue and patterned with a fine stripe alternating with a strip of stylized flowers. It is not the gilt "Dutch-paper" used to bind more expensive children's books.

105. Gary Taylor, *Reinventing Shakespeare: A Cultural History from the Restoration to the Present* (New York: Oxford University Press, 1989), 129–30.

106. Victor Neuburg, "Chapbooks in America: Reconstructing the Popular Reading of Early America," in *Reading in America*, ed. Cathy N. Davidson (Baltimore: The Johns Hopkins University Press, 1989), 81–113. Magee is known to have published an Irish edition of Bell's *Hamlet* in 1776; it is pleasant to imagine copies of *Hamlet* bound for America in that year.

107. One of the Dublin imprints reads "London: For the booksellers" as in Dicey productions, but is believed to be an Irish production from around 1800. It is at Trinity College, Dublin.

108. J.R.R. Adams, *The Printed Word and the Common Man: Popular Culture in Ulster 1700–1900* (Belfast: Institute of Irish Studies, Queen's University of Belfast, 1987), 137.

109. Robert Irwin, *The Arabian Nights: A Companion* (London: Allen Lane, 1994), 16, 22; see C. Knipp, "The 'Arabian Nights' in England," *Journal of Arabic Literature* 5 (1964): 44–74.

110. The "German Princess" subtitle appears only in Scottish editions from the 1790s and beyond. It does not seem to draw on the earlier notoriety of Mary Carleton, the self-styled German Princess who was the subject of numerous pamphlets, some allegedly autobiographical. One flurry of publications surrounded her first arrest in 1663, and another (including Kirkman's *Counterfeit Lady Unveiled*) surrounded her execution in 1672. There is no particular reason for her story to be current in Scotland over a century later. Conceivably the emphasis on Germany points to an analogy between

Pandosto's jealousy and the Hanoverian King George III's madness, first evident in 1788. But after the first page of *The Royal Shepherdess*, I see little support for that reading.

111. David D. Hall postulates several overlapping "popular cultures" in early America, imagining the nonexclusive coexistence of "readers of devotional literature . . . ; readers of 'fashionable' books, especially fiction; and readers of traditional prophecies, fairy tales, and romances" (Hall, *Cultures of Print: Essays in the History of the Book* [Amherst: University of Massachusetts Press, 1996], 50). Books oriented toward children, as they emerged, would have overlapped with all of these.

112. Margaret Spufford, "First Steps in Literacy: The Reading and Writing Experiences of the Humblest Seventeenth-Century Spiritual Autobiographers," *Social History* 4 (1979): 407–35.

113. Indeed, as Jan Fergus has shown by consulting the records of bookshops patronized by Rugby schoolboys, these boys were among the primary consumers of cheap print fiction by the late seventeenth century. See "Women Readers of Fiction and the Marketplace in the Midlands, 1746–1800," (unpublished paper), 59. Also see "Eighteenth-Century Readers in Provincial England: The Customers of Samuel Clay's Circulating Library and Bookshop in Warwick, 1770–72," *Publications of the Bibliographical Society of America* 78(2) (1984): 155–213.

4. *The Romance of Service: The Readers of* Dorastus and Fawnia, 1615–1762

1. J. H. P. Pafford, ed., *The Winter's Tale*. The Arden Edition (London: Methuen, 1963).

2. David Cressy, *Literacy and the Social Order: Reading and Writing in Tudor and Stuart England* (Cambridge: Cambridge University Press, 1980), 129, 4. Because literacy grew most rapidly among those whose occupations permitted or required writing skills, domestic servants would have been much more likely to read than servants in husbandry (124, 130). On the "cultural nexus," see J. Jean Hecht, *The Domestic Servant Class in Eighteenth-Century England* (London: Routledge Kegan Paul, 1956), 200. Literate maids were often expected to read aloud to their mistresses. While this practice was primarily devotional, at least one Jacobean drama mentions a servant reading *Amadis de Gaul* to her mistress (Henry Thomas, *Spanish and Portuguese Romances of Chivalry* [Cambridge: Cambridge University Press, 1920], 291). Margaret, in Deloney's *Thomas of Reading*, is the only literate servant I have found in a romance of service. Her literacy attracts attention at a hiring fair and encourages Mistress Gray to love her "as dearly as any child that ever she bore of her own body." Only when Margaret is found to be daughter to a banished earl, however, does the clothier's wife want her as a daughter-in-law (in Merritt Lawlis, ed., *Elizabethan Prose Fiction* [New York: Odyssey Press, 1967], 614).

3. Criticism on the novel has increasingly recognized that anxiety about consumption haunts the novel's self-definition. See, for example, Terry Lovell, *Consuming Fiction* (London: Verso, 1987), and Anita Levy, *Reproductive Urges: Popular Novel-Reading, Sex-*

uality, and the English Nation (Philadelphia: University of Pennsylvania Press, 1998). Patrick Brantlinger argues that although such anxieties sometimes were projected onto romances, novels themselves often internalized critiques of novels' poisonous potential. See *The Reading Lesson: The Threat of Mass Literacy in Nineteenth-Century British Fiction* (Bloomington: Indiana University Press, 1998). That such concerns stretch back before the eighteenth century is seldom acknowledged in novel criticism. An exception is William B. Warner's *Licensing Entertainment: The Elevation of Novel Reading in Britain, 1684–1750* (Berkeley: University of California Press, 1998), which argues that the debate over leisure reading, ultimately working to raise the novel, is representative of the challenges presented by any new cultural medium. My reading of scenes of romance consumption converges closely with his account of the stereotype of female novel readers (141).

4. Carolyn Kay Steedman, *Landscape for a Good Woman* (New Brunswick, NJ: Rutgers University Press, 1987), 11.

5. Charles Mish, "Best Sellers in Seventeenth-Century Fiction," *Publications of the Bibliographical Society of America* 47 (1953): 360.

6. Servants figure interestingly in many major statements on the history of the novel, including Erich Auerbach, *Mimesis: The Representation of Reality in Western Literature*, trans. Willard R. Trask (1946; reprint, Princeton: Princeton University Press, 1953); Ian Watt, *The Rise of the Novel* (Berkeley: University of California Press, 1957); J. Paul Hunter, *Before Novels: The Cultural Contexts of Eighteenth-Century Fiction* (New York: Norton, 1988); and Bruce Robbins, *The Servant's Hand: English Fiction from Below* (Durham: Duke University Press, 1993). However, the reading of servants in fiction that I respond to here is specific to Michael McKeon, *The Origins of the English Novel 1600–1740* (Baltimore: Johns Hopkins University Press, 1987).

7. Ibid., 240, 191. On the revealed-parentage motif, McKeon (457*n*3) cites Christopher Hill's claim that

> the most marked physical differences in pre-industrial England were probably those between the ruling class and the mass of the population. . . . This no doubt confirmed the ruling class's belief in its own innate superiority. In seventeenth-century plays, and in the fairy stories, any beautiful peasant girl who shows sensitivity turns out to be a princess in disguise. . . . This inheritance of physical class distinctions, still dinned into most of us in the fairy tales on which we are brought up, still seemed to be justified in our period by the physical differentiation which the undernourishment of the lower classes produced. (*Reformation to Industrial Revolution, 1530–1780*, Pelican Economic History of England, vol. 2 [Harmondsworth: Penguin Books, 1971], 59)

Such theories are not sufficient to identify revealed parentage as an ideology relevant only to aristocratic interests and feudal society.

8. McKeon's genre categories, like his ideological categories, leave no room for the ways that fiction narratives could be variously reappropriated. Although Hunter simi-

larly refuses to see the usefulness of romances to readers "while they were waiting for the novel to rise," his reconstructions of audience needs have influenced my argument here (*Before Novels*, 67, 87, 91; also Hunter, " 'The Young, the Ignorant, and the Idle': Some Notes on Readers and the Beginnings of the English Novel," in *Anticipations of the Enlightenment in England, France, and Germany*, eds. Alan Kors and Paul J. Korshin [Philadelphia: University of Pennsylvania Press, 1987], 259–82).

9. McKeon 19. He does not imply, of course, that romances or romance ideology disappeared once the novel began promulgating progressive ideologies, but he stops examining them once he glimpses novels on the horizon. The complaint that popular romances were politically conservative is common. Keith Thomas remarks that "most of the literature aimed at the lower classes was politically anodyne," especially the "romances of a trivializing, escapist, and often highly traditional kind" ("Literacy in Early Modern Europe," in *The Written Word: Literacy in Transition*, ed. Gerd Baumann [Oxford: Clarendon, 1986], 121).

10. Margaret Spufford, *Small Books and Pleasant Histories: Popular Fiction and Its Readership in Seventeenth-Century England* (Athens: University of Georgia, 1982), 249.

11. On medieval and early modern service as a life-cycle category, as opposed to a status group, see Keith Wrightson, *English Society, 1580–1680* (New Brunswick: Rutgers University Press, 1982), 42–43; Philippe Ariès, *Centuries of Childhood: A Social History of Family Life*, trans. Robert Baldick (New York: Vintage, 1962), 367; Christopher Dyer, *Standards of Living in the Later Middle Ages* (Cambridge: Cambridge University Press, 1989), 212.

12. I quote the modern-spelling edition of *Pandosto* (1588) from Paul Salzman, *An Anthology of Elizabethan Fiction* (Oxford: Oxford University Press, 1987), 184, 190, 198; further references will be cited parenthetically as *Elizabethan*. See Catherine Bates, *The Rhetoric of Courtship* (Cambridge: Cambridge University Press, 1992). Louis Montrose and Annabel Patterson, among others, have shown that in pastoral poetry, service gave the Elizabethan elite a metaphor for the relationships between granters and seekers, rulers and ruled. See Montrose, "Of Gentlemen and Shepherds: The Politics of Elizabethan Pastoral Form," *ELH* 50(3) (1983): 415–60; and Patterson, *Pastoral and Ideology* (Berkeley: University of California Press, 1987), 106–92. I wish to articulate the poetics of service for a less privileged group of early modern readers.

13. For a trenchant analysis of this debate and its centrality to *The Winter's Tale*, see Richard Strier, "Faithful Servants: Shakespeare's Praise of Disobedience," in *The Historical Renaissance: New Essays on Tudor and Stuart Literature and Culture*, Heather Dubrow and Richard Strier, eds. (Chicago: University of Chicago Press, 1988), 104–33.

14. Salzman, *Elizabethan*, 176. On the other hand, Caroline Lucas (among others) holds that the submissiveness of Greene's idealized females served a strongly "prescriptive" purpose for female readers (*Writing for Women: The Example of Woman as Reader in Elizabethan Romance* [Milton Keynes: Open University Press], 78).

15. My reading of *Dorastus and Fawnia* as a tale of youth service is structurally similar to Gail Kern Paster's interpretation of Perdita's fate in *The Winter's Tale* as "a ver-

sion, romantically heightened, of what happened soon after birth to countless babies in the wet-nursing culture" (*The Body Embarrassed: Drama and the Disciplines of Shame in Early Modern England* [Ithaca: Cornell University Press, 1993], 273). I attend to the cultural contexts of Fawnia's work and maturation, not her infancy, both because the former is central in Greene's original (as it is not in Shakespeare's dramatization) and because youth service, not the more exclusive practice of wet-nursing, would have been the most familiar imaginative correlative to Fawnia's life for *Pandosto*'s countless nonelite readers.

16. Keith Wrightson has described the mobility of early modern youth as "startling" (41). Ann Kussmaul, in *Servants in Husbandry in Early Modern England* (Cambridge: Cambridge University Press, 1981), sums up the mobility implicit in service:

> The mobility of farm servants set them apart from all others, both literally (because mobility broke those social bonds that depended on contiguity) and conceptually (because no other group shared this characteristic movement). . . . Servants were mobile over time, in moving frequently; they were mobile over space, in moving some significant distance; and they were mobile socially, in changing their status when entering and eventually leaving service. (49)

Typically, an Elizabethan man or woman's exit from service "comprised mobility in status, from dependent servant to married householder or wife, and mobility in occupation, from farm servant to labourer or farmer" (84).

17. Ilana Krausman Ben-Amos, *Adolescence and Youth in Early Modern England* (New Haven: Yale University Press, 1994), 22.

18. The fullest historical treatment to date of servants as a youth formation is in Paul Griffiths, *Youth and Authority: Formative Experiences in England, 1560–1640* (Oxford: Clarendon, 1996).

19. Lawrence Stone memorably describes service as part of "a mass exchange of adolescent children" (*The Family, Sex and Marriage in England 1500–1800*, abr. ed. [New York: Harper Torchbooks, 1979], 84). According to Susan Dwyer Amussen, the practice was common but "on the wane" among "the upper reaches of the gentry and aristocracy" in the sixteenth century, but continued "among lesser gentry, tradesmen and yeomen—as well as their poorer neighbors—at least through the seventeenth century" (*An Ordered Society: Gender and Class in Early Modern England* [Oxford: Basil Blackwell, 1988], 68). Kussmaul estimates that about 60 percent of youths in early modern England (1574–1821) were servants (the remainder included apprentices, whose parents paid for their training). Youth service has been variously explained as: "*ex post facto* family planning," "family-balancer to small farmers, and labour force to larger farmers," a means to delay marriage until property could be amassed, and a safeguard against masterlessness (26–33); a form of protection against youth unrest and incestuous desires (Stone 84); and "the family economy's Youth Training Scheme" (Bridget Hill, *Women and Work in Eighteenth-century England* [Oxford: Basil Blackwell, 1989], 77.

20. This argument complements Mark Thornton Burnett's path-breaking *Masters and Servants in English Renaissance Drama and Culture*, which reads representations of

service in drama, popular pamphlets, and conduct manuals as interrogating systems of authority and obedience (New York: St. Martin's Press, 1997). Constance C. Relihan has argued that the socioeconomic instability experienced by many Elizabethan romance heroines must have matched a similar sense of "uncertainty" in readers' own experiences (*Fashioning Authority: The Development of Elizabethan Novelistic Discourse* [Kent, OH: Kent State University Press, 1994], 98).

21. Kussmaul 83. Contributory causes included enclosure and other agricultural changes; a shift from labor shortage to labor surplus; a decline in real wages; and the gender division of labor that moved women from field to domestic work.

22. At the other extreme, McKeon dismisses such remarks unilaterally:

> If the more subjective apprehensions of contemporaries are any guide, women and servants of both sexes were devoting much of their time in the early eighteenth century to reading "novels" and "romances." But if there is good evidence that the opportunity for such leisure activity existed, there is little to confirm that it was actually used for that purpose.

McKeon feels that these "subjective apprehensions" are "evidence less of the rise of the reading public than of the persistence of anxiety about women" (52). Instead of belittling the reading of women and servants, this response implies that they were too idle to read at all.

23. On the ambivalence of servant status, see Kussmaul 8. See Stone 50–51 for marital endogamy. According to Dyer, servants "often were related to their employer. . . . The links between families and servants who were not relations were close enough for servants to marry the son or daughter of the house, or to receive bequests of goods, cash, or land on their employer's death" (212). Such practices faded as employment became depersonalized. The most common pattern of status crossing occurred when the children of laborers joined the households of prominent landowners. Reciprocal crossings could also occur, although youth service naturally disappeared most quickly among the landowning classes. For very approximate class breakdowns of the incidence of service, see Stone 84.

24. Sigmund Freud, "Family Romances," in *The Complete Psychological Works of Sigmund Freud*, eds. James Strachey with Anna Freud (London: The Hogarth Press), 9:239. More famous is the next stage, in which, Freud says, the child imagines his mother an adulterer. But the earlier stage offers the intriguing possibility that a primary drive to narrative might arise from a child's dawning awareness of her social as well as her sexual subject position.

25. The phrase "temporary shepherdess" comes from Mary Patchell, *The Palmerin Romances in Elizabethan Prose Fiction* (1947; reprint, New York: AMS Press, 1966), 114.

26. Salzman, *Elizabethan*, 188. As discussed in chapter 2, only in later editions were references to Fawnia as a "shepherd" changed to the more gender-marked and romanticized "shepherdess."

27. Ibid., 173; also 202. The *OED* lists Greene's later *Menaphon* as the first use of "mercenary" to describe a hired laborer.

28. *The Winter's Tale* defuses the shepherd's rise with humor: he lacks even a first name but is declared "a gentleman born" (5.2.120–137). See the discussion of the economics of the play in Michael Bristol, *Big-Time Shakespeare* (New York: Routledge, 1996), 147–74.

29. According to Paylor, this later set of Characters, first seen in a variant of the sixth impression of 1615, may be by John Webster; it is probably not by the late Overbury. The author seems to have deliberately linked his Characters to the earlier editions' (Paylor xvii–xxiv).

30. Suspicions that serving maids hid pregnancy by going to London rose as increasing numbers of rural women went into urban domestic service.

31. See Kussmaul 3–5. One 1598 tract argued: "the Yeomans Sonne leaving his dayly labour . . . and taking upon him the degree of a Serving-man, breedeth as many inconveniences in the Common wealth, as want of exercise begetteth diseases in a corpulent body." The author bewailed the decline of the service fraternity from its medieval glory days: "the estate, degree, callyng, and profession, of every poore Servingman, in these latter dayes" was, he felt, "more waveryng and unconstant, then Winters weather, Womens thoughtes, or Fortunes wheele" (*A Health to the Gentlemanly Profession of Servingmen: or, The Servingmans Comfort* in W. C. Hazlitt, ed., *Inedited Tracts: Illustrating the Manners, Opinions, and Occupations of Englishmen . . .* [1868; reprint, New York: Burt Franklin, n.d.], 137, 166).

32. The classic account of this process is Alice Clark's *The Working Lives of Women in the Seventeenth Century* (1919; reprint, New York: A. M. Kelley, 1968); some responses to its thesis are synthesized in Susan Cahn, *Industry of Devotion: The Transformation of Woman's Work in England 1500–1660* (New York: Columbia University Press, 1987), and in Merry E. Wiesner, *Women and Gender in Early Modern Europe* (Cambridge: Cambridge University Press, 1997). Bridget Hill addresses this problem in *Women and Work*, incorporating Kussmaul's work on service (*Servants in Husbandry*).

33. Servants' decreasing prospects are reflected in the cheap chapbook manuals of courtship published for rural buyers during the late seventeenth century: they seem to assume that only careful financing would enable servants to marry, much less prosper. See Spufford, *Small Books and Pleasant Histories*, 59–60, 165; Tessa Watt, *Cheap Print and Popular Piety, 1550–1640* (Cambridge: Cambridge University Press, 1991).

34. Hugh Stanhope, *The Fortunate Lovers* (London: E. Midwinter, 1735?), A4–A4v, A5v. Stanhope's account of Porrus's decision to adopt the baby also provides moral judgments of lower-class behavior, attributing the adoption almost entirely to greed. While Greene's shepherd was "perplexed with a doubtful dilemma" upon finding the purse with the babe, Stanhope's shepherd instantaneously decides to "keep the Money for his own Use" (Salzman, *Elizabethan*, 174; Stanhope 16).

35. On calls for servant humility, see B. Hill, *Women and Work*, 83; also J. Jean Hecht 71–92, 179; and Kussmaul 44–48.

36. On the "myth of social betterment" said to attract young women to service, see B. Hill, *Women and Work*, 144–45. On the fineness of servant dress, see Hecht 119, 209–11; Bridget Hill, *Eighteenth-Century Women* (London: George Allen & Unwin,

1984), 238–39. The skills of good housewifery learned in service lost their exchange value on the marriage market, since the wife's responsibility for domestic production was decreasing markedly and in inverse relation to social status (Cahn 170–71).

37. On marital self-advertisement, see Amussen 159. On exploitation, see Stone 381; Ben-Amos 202; and Wiesner. Orest Ranum comments that Samuel Pepys's success in fondling maids must imply that "behavior of this sort was part of the role of . . . chamber-maids"; note that he comments on *their* behavior, not Pepys's ("The Refuges of Intimacy," in *Passions of the Renaissance*, vol. 3, *A History of Private Life*, ed. Roger Chartier, trans. Arthur Goldhammer [Cambridge, MA: Belknap, 1989], 255).

38. Griffiths presents numerous examples of Jacobean women servants who protested the abuses of their masters and discusses illegitimacy rates that might point to master-servant involvement (whether abusive or consensual); see *Youth and Authority*, 269ff. For a 1601 parliamentary debate about servants pregnant by their masters, see Anthony Fletcher, *Gender, Sex and Subordination in England, 1500–1800* (New Haven: Yale University Press, 1995), 219–20. Thomas Creede, who would print the 1614 edition of *Pandosto*, was the subject of a paternity suit in 1608. Suzan More was a twenty-five-year-old servant to Creede's friend, the bookseller Hugh Jackson. Her case was not brought in the bawdy courts, but prosecuted by John Scales, described as a "friend" from her hometown of Cambridge. Her master and mistress both had assisted her effort to obtain financial recourse from Creede and deposed against him. See Laura Gowing, *Women's Worlds in Seventeenth-Century England* (New York: Routledge, 2000), 142–45. The case shows that in this period, a servant could seek and find support within the existing power structures of gender and rank—if, that is, she had strong alliances with her superiors. She did not need to get information from books (indeed, More may have been illiterate; she assisted her mistress in making points, rather than in the bookshop). By the eighteenth century, few servants could hope for such backing from their social superiors, making the guidance of fiction all the more important.

39. Stanhope 47. Of course, readers know that Fawnia's royal birth ironizes this claim, but Fawnia herself does not.

40. See, for example, Terry Eagleton, *The Rape of Clarissa* (Minneapolis: University of Minnesota Press, 1982); Frances Ferguson, "Rape and the Rise of the Novel," *Representations* 20 (1987): 88–112; Nancy Armstrong, *Desire and Domestic Fiction* (Oxford: Oxford University Press, 1989); Terry Castle, *Clarissa's Ciphers: Meaning and Disruption in Richardson's "Clarissa"* (Ithaca: Cornell University Press, 1982); and William B. Warner, *Reading* Clarissa: *The Struggles of Interpretation* (New Haven: Yale University Press, 1979). Anna Clark has argued that pro-working class fictions exploited the female body as a symbol of the abused working class and blamed aristocratic men in a "melodramatic evasion of the realities of working-class sexual violence"; see "The Politics of Seduction in English Popular Culture, 1748–1848," in *The Progress of Romance: The Politics of Popular Fiction*, ed. Jean Radford (London: Routledge & Kegan Paul, 1986), 58.

41. Stanhope's Fawnia is "call[ing] upon the elite to take its own rhetoric seriously," as James C. Scott puts it (*Domination and the Arts of Resistance* [New Haven: Yale Univer-

sity Press, 1990], 106). While, as Scott shows, such resistant appropriations of ideologies are especially rife in oral culture, this instance would be through *print* culture.

42. The other striking pattern of emendations made by Stanhope *increases* Fawnia's submission to Dorastus in the courtship scenes. In both versions, Fawnia consents to be Dorastus's "handmaid" (Salzman, *Elizabethan*, 188; Stanhope 32), but in Stanhope her banter is softened by such meek phrases as "with submission," and "give me leave to say, (and I speak it not out of Vanity)" (27, 28). These phrases establish the submissive norm that her speeches to Pandosto can appropriately violate.

43. There is a very large body of work on the social importance of eighteenth-century consumption. Two central volumes are *Consumption and the World of Goods*, eds. John Brewer and Roy Porter (New York: Routledge, 1995), and *The Consumption of Culture, 1600–1800: Image, Object, Text*, eds. Ann Bermingham and John Brewer (New York, Routledge, 1995).

44. The first phrase comes from B. Hill, *Women and Work*, 47; the second quotation from Cahn 4. On the primacy of consumption, see B. Hill 48; Cahn 7–8, 62–63. For one view of the literary role of consumption, see Colin Campbell, *The Romantic Ethic and the Spirit of Modern Consumerism* (Oxford: Basil Blackwell, 1987). The remark about consumption, dated 1767, is quoted in Hecht 178; also see 16.

45. The phrase "mimetic venture" comes from ibid., 219; "country-Joan" is quoted in B. Hill, *Eighteenth-Century Women*, 238. *A Serious Advice and Warning to Servants* (1746) counsels against "that foolish affectation of imitating your betters" and advises servants to "Avoid idleness": "when you have any leisure time, employ it by reading good books" and in prayer (quoted in B. Hill, *Eighteenth-Century Women*, 235–36). On the market forces that gave servants and farm workers access to fashionable goods, see Neil McKendrick, John Brewer, and J. H. Plumb, *The Birth of a Consumer Society: The Commercialization of Eighteenth-Century England* (Bloomington: Indiana University Press, 1982), 57–62. As Lorna Weatherill has warned, we should suspect the elite's "theory of emulation" as a description of the social and material relationships to which these complaints responded. Emulation is hardly the only reason anyone, of any class, desires consumer goods; the theory disregards the diverse needs of various groups, addressing only elite interests (*Consumer Behavior and Material Culture in Britain 1660–1760* [London: Routledge, 1988], 194–95). The elite, when pressed, admitted their preference for gentility in their servants but still blamed the poverty of ex-servants on their inflated tastes (Hecht 213, 223). Judith Rollins shows that the contemporary practice in which an employer gives useless used consumer goods to her domestic servant benefits the employer's self-image by re-producing her servant's exclusion from privileged systems of taste (*Between Women: Domestics and Their Employers* [Philadelphia: Temple University Press, 1985], 193).

46. Elite codifications of "superior" fiction had become sophisticated enough to give English criticism its first fiction genre theory, designed to privilege novellas like Congreve's *Incognita*. The romance was pressed into service as whipping girl for the elements deemed unacceptable in this newly classicized form—violations of the unities, fantasy, and improbability.

47. Samuel Richardson, *Clarissa, or The History of a Young Lady*, abr. and ed. George Sherburn (Boston: Houghton Mifflin, 1962), xxi.

48. Quoted in Robert Folkenflik, "*Pamela*, Domestic Servitude, Marriage and the Novel," *Eighteenth-Century Fiction* 5 (1993): 261.

49. Richardson, *Clarissa*, 44. Compare "simple" to Langbaine's "delectable history," which sounds like something of a joke. The first edition does not capitalize "history" or use the italics characteristic of a title. Later editions corrected by Richardson italicize only the proper names by eighteenth-century convention, not the phrase "pleasant history." All editions, but especially the first, thus blur the boundaries of the title, separating the story from literary convention and implying its lifelike immediacy to the maid. Later editions read "the pleasant history of *Dorastus and Fawnia*." On Richardson's deliberate and expressive use of italics, see Joe Bray, " 'Attending to the Minute': Richardson's Revisions of Italics in *Pamela*," in *Ma(r)king the Text: The Presentation of Meaning on the Literary Page*, eds. Joe Bray, Miriam Handley, and Anne C. Henry (Burlington, VT: Ashgate, 2000), 105–19.

50. Jonathan Swift, *Gulliver's Travels and Other Writings*, ed. Louis A. Landa (Boston: Houghton Mifflin, 1960), 44. The rescue liberates Gulliver from his previous, "too servile," manual labors. Yet, while Gulliver congratulates himself for his "presence of mind" in the rescue, the corporeality of his service provokes the "abhorrence" of the ungrateful Empress (45). Richardson's Clarissa, on the other hand, is justified in abhorring Lovelace's "generous care" for her body (262). For the record, the similarity between Richardson's careless servant and Swift's does not seem justified as social realism. Even Swift's satiric set of *Directions to Servants* does not include reading by candlelight among its many recipes for disaster. In her 1743 *Present for a Servant-Maid*, Eliza Haywood alludes to the very real danger of domestic fire caused by candles but does not blame the problem on servants' reading (on which her tract, after all, depends) (1743; New York: Garland, 1985), 18–19.

51. Richardson, *Clarissa*, 261. Clarissa uses the same word, highly significant in this metafictional context, writing that Lovelace "formed a *plot* to fire the house, to frighten me, almost naked, into his arms" (278; emphasis added). Those commentators on Greene who have noted this late reference to the romance, including René Pruvost and Caroline Lucas, have missed its ironies (Pruvost, *Robert Greene et ses romans* [Paris: Publications de la Faculté des Lettres D'Alger, 1938], 284; Lucas 51).

52. See T. C. Duncan Eaves and Ben D. Kimpel, "Richardson's Revisions of *Pamela*," *Studies in Bibliography* 20 (1967): 61–88.

53. D. C. Muecke, "Beauty and Mr. B.," *Studies in English Literature* 7 (1967): 467. Also see the discussion of "Horrid Romancing" in Carol Houlihan Flynn, *Samuel Richardson: A Man of Letters* (Princeton: Princeton University Press, 1982), 145–95.

54. T. C. Duncan Eaves and Ben D. Kimpel, *Samuel Richardson: A Biography* (Oxford: Clarendon, 1971), 11. Further references will be cited parenthetically as Eaves and Kimpel, *Richardson*.

55. Margaret Anne Doody, *A Natural Passion: A Study of the Novels of Samuel Richardson* (Oxford: Clarendon, 1974), 33–34.

56. The detail of a stride of "two yards" for Colbrand seems to derive specifically from the verse version of *Guy* published by Samuel Rowlands in 1607.

57. Henry Fielding, Joseph Andrews, *with* Shamela *and Related Writings*, ed. Homer Goldberg (New York: Norton, 1987), 15.

58. See Jennifer Brady, "Readers in Richardson's *Pamela*," in *English Studies in Canada* 9 (1983): 164–76.

59. Samuel Richardson, *Pamela*, eds. T. C. Duncan Eaves and Ben D. Kimpel (New York: Houghton Mifflin, 1971), 26. Further parenthetical references to *Pamela* cite this edition.

60. William M. Sale, Jr., *Samuel Richardson, Master Printer* (Ithaca: Cornell University Press, 1950), 107. For the work of Haywood and Richardson as author/publishers, see Catherine Ingrassia, *Authorship, Commerce, and Gender in Early Eighteenth-Century England* (Cambridge: Cambridge University Press, 1998).

61. T. C. Duncan Eaves and Ben D. Kimpel, "The Publisher of *Pamela* and its First Audience," in *New York Public Library Bulletin* 64 (1960): 143–46.

62. Isaac Bickerstaff, *Love in a Village; a Comic Opera* (1763). In *The Plays of Isaac Bickerstaff*, ed. Peter A. Tasch (New York: Garland, 1981), I:4.

63. In Bickerstaff's underacknowledged source, Charles Johnson's *The Village Opera* (1729), the analogous character alludes to "Reason and Honour." See Peter A. Tasch, *The Dramatic Cobbler: The Life and Works of Isaac Bickerstaff* (Lewisburg, PA: Bucknell University Press, 1971), 48.

64. Presumably the main buyers of the ballad of Rossetta and "Thomas" would be the villagers, represented to the opera's audience mainly as the young working women whom Woodcock and Hawthorne had "chuck[ed] . . . under the chin" at the statute (hiring fair for servants and laborers) (Bickerstaff, *Love in a Village*, 21).

65. Arthur H. Scouten, *The London Stage, 1660–1800, Part 3: 1729–1747* (Carbondale: Southern Illinois University Press, 1962), I:cxxxi.

66. Stanley Wells, ed., *"Perymedes the Blacksmith" and "Pandosto" by Robert Greene: A Critical Edition* (1961; reprint, New York: Garland, 1988), 187.

67. Similarly, "Chamber-Dam'sels neat" were said to attend performances in 1717 (Sybil Rosenfeld, *The Theatre of the London Fairs in the Eighteenth Century* [Cambridge: Cambridge University Press, 1960], 46, 22–23). The free admittance of theatergoers' servants to the upper galleries was a fiercely defended privilege in the mid-eighteenth century (Hecht 136–39).

68. Stone I:clv.

69. Jan Fergus, "Provincial servants' reading in the late eighteenth century," in *The Practice and Representation of Reading in England*, eds. James Raven, Helen Small, and Naomi Tadmor (Cambridge: Cambridge University Press), 221.

Epilogue

1. Margaret Spufford's collection of chapbook reminiscences quotes an 1872 manuscript by William Morris on his memories of the "ghost stories read long ago in queer little penny garlands with woodcuts" (*Small Books and Pleasant Histories: Popular Fiction*

and Its Readership in Seventeenth-Century England [Athens: University of Georgia Press, 1982], 75). Julius Lloyd's biography of Sidney mentions "Argalus and Parthenia" chapbooks being sold by hawkers in the 1860s (see chapter 2). Henry Thomas, in *Spanish and Portuguese Romances of Chivalry* (1920; reprint, New York: Kraus Reprints, 1969), gives a number of references to chivalric titles from John Keats and Sir Walter Scott, but it is unclear whether these writers are working from contemporary or antique editions (297–99).

2. Patrick John Dowling, (London: Longmans, 1935), 79–80 (list excerpted). Also see Mary Castelyn, *A History of Literacy and Libraries in Ireland* (Aldershot, England: Gower, 1984).

3. E. M. Forster commented that this was still available in Ireland in 1919, sold under the counter by provincial grocers (J. R. R. Adams, *The Printed Word and the Common Man: Popular Culture in Ulster 1700–1900* [Belfast: The Institute of Irish Studies, Queen's University of Belfast, 1987], 172).

4. First Report to the Commissioners on Education in Ireland (House of Commons 1825) (400), XII. Appendix no. 221, 553–60; reprinted in Dowling, *The Hedge Schools of Ireland*, 154–61.

5. Adams 176–80, 198, 202.

6. Niall Ó Ciosáin, *Print and Popular Culture in Ireland, 1750–1850* (New York: St. Martin's Press, 1997). Ó Ciosáin's study, drawing on tremendous archival research, concludes that chapbooks, particularly chivalric romances, were both educationally and ideologically valuable to Irish readers. I regret not finding this fascinating study until after writing this epilogue.

7. Paul Salzman, *English Prose Fiction 1550–1700* (Oxford: Oxford University Press, 1985), 268.

8. Elite resistance to nonstandardized literacy often betrays the ideological agenda of literacy efforts. On their hegemonic force, see Harvey Graff, *The Labyrinths of Literacy: Reflections on Literacy Past and Present* (Pittsburgh: University of Pittsburgh Press, 1995).

9. M. Pollard, *Dublin's Trade in Books 1550–1800* (Oxford: Clarendon, 1989).

10. Declan Kiberd, *Inventing Ireland: The Literature of the Modern Nation* (Cambridge: Harvard University Press, 1995), 10. Also see Michael Cronin, "Rug-headed kerns speaking tongues: Shakespeare, Translation and the Irish Language," in *Shakespeare and Ireland*, eds. Mark Thornton Burnett and Ramona Wray (New York: St. Martin's, 1997), 195.

11. On the Jacobean turn toward treating Ireland as a colonial marketplace rather than as a full partner in the United Kingdom, see David J. Baker, "Where is Ireland in *The Tempest?*" in Burnett and Wray, eds., *Shakespeare and Ireland*.

12. This letter is from the son of the fifth Earl of Bothwell (Pollard 221).

13. William Jaggard, *Shakespeare Bibliography* (Stratford-on-Avon: Shakespeare Press, 1911), 498. Later sets of Shakespeare's works, generally derived from English editions, appeared in 1739, 1747, 1766, 1771, 1791, and 1794. Many cheap editions of single plays were issued, including Magee's 1776 edition of *Hamlet*. I am grateful to

Andrew Murphy for kindly sharing excerpts of his forthcoming *Shakespeare in Print: A History and Chronology of Shakespeare Publishing, 1590–2000* (Cambridge: Cambridge University Press).

14. See Richard Cargill Cole, *Irish Booksellers and English Writers* (London: Mansell, 1986).

15. That innovation in re-commodification would continue through the nineteenth century: Adams holds that it was Irish publishers who originated the landmarks of cheap paperback reprints in serial publication, as Simms and M'Intyre's Parlour Library was imitated by Routledge's Railway Library, pointing toward a true mass readership (162).

16. For patterns of literacy after 1750, see Ó Ciosáin, especially 25–51 and 154–69.

17. For the English precedent, see Susan Pederson, "Hannah More Meets Simple Simon: Tracts, chapbooks, and popular culture in late eighteenth century England" (*Journal of British Studies* 25 [1986]: 84–113). Pederson argues that More's tracts not only met chapbooks on their commercial ground, but by integrating genteel values with chapbook appeals, sought to reintegrate divergent popular and elite cultures.

18. Ibid., 141. These titles do appear in the 1825 *First Report of the Commissioners*, which integrates data from both northern and southern counties.

19. But a blue-paper cover for "DORASTUS AND FAWNIA, WITH Hero & Leander," bound into the 1843 edition but dated "1833," invites poor readers to identify with the illustrated lovers, presumably Dorastus and Fawnia (figure 1). Fawnia, simply dressed and barefoot, leans against a stile in the arms of equally plain Dorastus; they seem to illustrate the rural adolescents who might have read *Dorastus and Fawnia* in the hedge schools. We have no Irish reader from the period who reports reading *Dorastus and Fawnia*. But Henry Cooke, a Presbyterian minister from County Tyrone who had been educated in hedge schools to the age of fourteen, testified to a commission in 1825, "I recollect reading *Hero and Leander*, *Gesta Romanorum*, and *The Seven Wise Masters* . . . *Don Belianis of Greece*," and other "extravagant tale[s]" (Ó Ciosáin 50).

20. Dowling explains that these are named "Burton Books," in reference to the pen name sometimes used by English popular author Nathaniel Crouch (81*n*12).

21. Sir James Prior, *Memoir of the Life and Character of the Right Hon. Edmund Burke* (2nd ed., 1826), 1:15. Quoted in Thomas 296–97.

22. On panicked reactions to the reading of the English poor, see Patrick Brantlinger, *The Reading Lesson: The Threat of Mass Literacy in Nineteenth-Century British Fiction* (Bloomington: Indiana University Press, 1998).

INDEX

❧

Achinstein, Sharon, 93, 281n3, 292n4
Adams, Hazard, 291n83
Adams, J. R. R., 249, 256, 304n108, 315n3
Adams, Robert P., 282n6
adaptation(s): modernizing, 10, 173–79, 224, 227; necessary, 17–18, 135; redaction, 183; *see also* chapbooks; *Pandosto*, abridgments; Shakespeare; *Winter's Tale*
advertisements, 101, 150, 161–62, 196, 237, 242–43, 248–49, 253, 256; *see also* sequel(s)
Allestree, Richard, *Whole Duty of Man*, 235, 252, 255
Altick, Richard, 267n4
Alwes, Derek, 47, 277n32
Amadis de Gaul(e), 109, 305n2
Amussen, Susan, 223, 308n19
anecdotes, 6–7, 81, 105
Angus, Archibald Douglas, 8th Earl of, 40
antimimeticism, 119–27, 220, 251; and antitheatricality, 120, 126–29

appropriation, 14–15, 134–35; *see also* re-commodification
appropriative license, 141, 294n8
Arabian tales, 137, 196, 256, 259, 260
Argalus and Parthenia, 31, 111, 235, 253, 315n1; *see also* Quarles, Francis
Ariès, Philippe, 307n11
Aristotle's Masterpiece, 248, 253
Armstrong, Nancy, 311n40
Ascham, Roger, 106, 121, 282n6
Aubrey, John, 291n79
audiences, popular: growth of, 1, 8, 77–78; mixed social class of, 7, 10, 10, 31, 104, 213, 243–45; not passive, 7, 16, 175–77, 204–5, 245, 256–60; regional preferences of, 188, 199, 204, 256; threateningly heterogeneous, 10, 80; *see also* readers; literacy
Auerbach, Eric, 306n6
authors: aspirant, 8, 10, 79, 92, 101, 127, 151, 233; classical, 44, 70, 94, 255, 293n4; coterie, 33, 40, 45, 93, 100; rights of, 175, 294n8;

servants (*continued*)
220, 229, 285*n*31; marital freedom,
222–26; serving men, 46, 97–100,
244; sexual vulnerability of, 159,
175–77, 178, 225–26, 241, 311*n*37,
311*n*38
service: life-cycle, 214, 219; shifting
from status to class, 214, 216, 223;
women in, 90: eighteenth-century,
210, 219–20, 223; Jacobean,
217–19, 220–23; marginalized
from husbandry, 112, 114, 118,
224, 229 (*see also* shepherdess[es])
Seven Champions of Christendom, The, 235,
248, 256, 259
Seven Wise Masters, The, 152, 154,
196–98
Shadwell, Thomas, 296*n*26
Shakespeare, John, 287*n*46
Shakespeare Ladies' Club, 181
Shakespeare, William: *Hamlet*,
304*n*106, 316*n*13; *Henry IV*,
303*n*92; *King Lear*, 239*n*4, 296*n*26;
Love's Labour's Lost, 87; *Midsummer
Night's Dream*, 87; *Pericles*, 39, 140,
145, 296*n*21; *Richard III*, 303*n*92;
Romeo and Juliet, 87; *Taming of the
Shrew*, 183; *Tempest*, 123, 139,
296*n*21, 303*n*92; scholarship, 6,
136, 139, 173, 206; source study,
5–6, 13–14, 17–18, 117, 131–33,
136, 166–73, 177–80; stage adaptations, 132–33, 180–85 (*see also*
imitation); *see also Winter's Tale*
shepherd(s), 116, 146, 157, 186–87,
199; *see also individual characters*
shepherdess(es), 185–86, 215, 222; *see
also individual works*; *Pandosto*, alternate titles
Sheppard, Samuel, 143, 145–46, 165
Shershow, Scott C., 272*n*30, 272*n*31,
292*n*87, 303*n*92

she-tragedy, 175, 301*n*78
Shrewsbury, bookshops in, 56–57
Shrewsbury School, 32, 56–57
Shuter, Ned, 243, 244
Sidney, Sir Philip, 15, 16–17; death,
24, 30, 32–33; education, 32; **individual works:** *Arcadia*, 16–17, 21,
50, 123, 293*n*4: "Greene's," 31, 64
(*see also* Greene, individual works,
Menaphon); "Old," 38, 39, 40, 41,
52, 65; "New," 41, 47, 65; 1590
Countess of Pembroke's, 38–39, 54,
66–67, 68; title, 39, 53; 1593,
1598 composite, 39, 67, 68, 69;
reception of, 30, 52, 110, 148, 153;
reception of vs. *Pandosto's*, 94,
105–10; shares generic web with
Pandosto, 30, 63–64; *Astrophil and
Stella*, 67–68, 70; *Defence of Poetry*,
52, 63, 68, 72; on mimesis, 122; De
Mornay, translation attributed, 59,
66; Du Bartas, translation, 66; letter to Queen Elizabeth, 52; as literary author, 25, 36–37, 75; and
manuscript publication, 33, 39–40,
52, 63–65; name, 32, 48–54, 70;
and patronage, 53; position and disposition, 29–33, 36, 39–40; and
print, 33, 52, 64; reputation produced, 23, 30, 64; "toys," 37;
works, 69
Simons, John, 271*n*24
Smith, Barbara Herrnstein, 273*n*33
social mobility, 7–8, 80, 88, 100, 104,
175, 186, 215–16, 224–27, 238,
304*n*102; *see also* ideology; status
inconsistency
Sorelius, Gunnar, 148
Speaight, George, 303*n*91
Spufford, Margaret: on Ballad Partners,
163, 165; on cheap print, 9, 268*n*8,
298*n*43, 310*n*33, 315*n*1; on fiction,